Also published by Enigma Books

Hitler's Table Talk: 1941–1944
In Stalin's Secret Service
Hitler and Mussolini: The Secret Meetings
The Jews in Fascist Italy: A History
The Man Behind the Rosenbergs
Roosevelt and Hopkins: An Intimate History
Diary 1937–1943 (Galeazzo Ciano)
Secret Affairs: FDR, Cordell Hull, and Sumner Welles
Hitler and His Generals: Military Conferences 1942–1945
Stalin and the Jews: The Red Book
The Secret Front: Nazi Political Espionage
Fighting the Nazis: French Intelligence and Counterintelligence
A Death in Washington: Walter G. Krivitsky and the Stalin Terror
The Battle of the Casbah: Terrorism and Counterterrorism in Algeria 1955–1957
Hitler's Second Book: The Unpublished Sequel to *Mein Kampf*
At Napoleon's Side in Russia: The Classic Eyewitness Account
The Atlantic Wall: Hitler's Defenses for D-Day
Double Lives: Stalin, Willi Münzenberg and the Seduction of the Intellectuals
France and the Nazi Threat: The Collapse of French Diplomacy 1932–1939
Mussolini: The Secrets of His Death
Mortal Crimes: Soviet Penetration of the Manhattan Project
Top Nazi: Karl Wolff—The Man Between Hitler and Himmler
Empire on the Adriatic: Mussolini's Conquest of Yugoslavia
The Origins of the War of 1914 (3-volume set)
Hitler's Foreign Policy: 1933–1939—The Road to World War II
The Origins of Fascist Ideology 1918–1925
Max Corvo: OSS Italy 1942–1945
Hitler's Contract: The Secret History of the Italian Edition of *Mein Kampf*
Secret Intelligence and the Holocaust
Israel at High Noon
Balkan Inferno: Betrayal, War, and Intervention, 1990–2005
Calculated Risk: World War II Memoirs of General Mark Clark
The Murder of Maxim Gorky
The Kravchenko Case: One Man's War On Stalin
Operation Neptune
Paris Weekend
Shattered Sky
Hitler's Gift to France
The Mafia and the Allies
The Nazi Party, 1919-1945: A Complete History
Encyclopedia of Cold War Espionage, Spies, and Secret Operations
The Cicero Spy Affair
A Crate of Vodka
NOC
The First Iraq War: Britain's Mesopotamian Campaign, 1914-1918
Becoming Winston Churchill
Hitler's Intelligence Chief: Walter Schellenberg
Salazar: A Political Biography
The Italian Brothers

Nazi Palestine
Code Name: Kalistrat
Pax Romana
The De Valera Deception
Lenin and His Comrades
Working with Napoleon
The Decision to Drop the Atomic Bomb
Target Hitler
Truman, MacArthur and the Korean War
Working with Napoleon
The Parsifal Pursuit
The Eichmann Trial Diary
American Police: A History
Cold Angel
Alphabet of Masks
The Gemini Agenda
Stalin's Man in Canada
Hunting Down the Jews
Mussolini Warlord
Election Year 1968
American Police: A History, Vol. 2
Spy Lost
Deadly Sleep

Jochen von Lang

Top Nazi

SS General Karl Wolff

The Man Between Hitler and Himmler

Enigma Books

Published in the United States by
Enigma Books, New York
www.enigmabooks.com

Translated by
MaryBeth Friedrich

Original German title:
Der Adjutant
Karl Wolff: Der Mann zwischen Hitler und Himmler

ISBN 978-1-936274-52-9 (paperback)
ISBN 978-1-936274-53-6 (e-Book)

Printed in the United States of America

Library of Congress Cataloging-in-Publication Data

Lang, Jochen von.
[Adjutant.]
Top Nazi : the man between Hitler and Himmler / Jochen von Lang.

p. : ill. ; cm.
Includes bibliographical references and index.
ISBN: 978-1-936274-52-9 [pbk]
ISBN: 978-1-936274-53-6 (eBook)
"Translated by MaryBeth Friedrich"—T.p. verso.

1. Wolff, Karl, 1900-1984. 2. Nazis—Biography. 3. Germany—Politics and government—1933-1945. 4. World War, 1939-1945—Germany. I. Friedrich, MaryBeth. II. Title. III. Title: Adjutant.

DD247.W59 L36 2005
943.086/092 B

Table of Contents

Foreword

THE DECEASED didn't want it any other way: a black pillow covered with medals and mementoes from an inglorious age. According to the obituary, retired General Karl Wolff was buried in Prien am Chiemsee in the middle of July 1984. The usual comment regarding the specific branch of the service was missing after his name. Was this because it would have touched on the most sensitive chapter of his life? The advertising agent and retired lieutenant was in the NSDAP (the Nazi party) and joined the SS in the fall of 1931. He was part of the Black Guard of German Fascism and within a decade rose to the rank of lieutenant. Then general of the SS and general of the Waffen SS, finally becoming Heinrich Himmler's right-hand man and a close confidante of Adolf Hitler. Although there are absolutely no supporting documents, people believe his statement that on April 20, 1945, shortly before the collapse of the Third Reich, he even reached the rank of general and senior general of the Waffen SS. He could not rise any higher.

From early youth, he consistently wanted to go above and beyond, and once he succeeded he credited it to the virtues the Germans had always claimed: diligence, honesty, obedience, and loyalty. Beyond that, he possessed innumerable tactical skills, the talent to persuade people, and sharp elbows. He certainly would have made his way in business, but with his love of the military, he was cut out for pseudomilitary party management. At the time of his death, many newspapers wrote that at the end, Karl Wolff was the highest ranking among Hitler's surviving followers, not counting the life prisoners at Spandau Prison, the Führer's former deputy, Rudolf Hess.

Had he been alive, Wolff would have been flattered. In truth, he was one of the unknown giants of Hitler's Reich who worked in the shadows. Only the top five hundred in the party and state knew his name and his functions. Of course, he too wanted to be in the limelight, but there were other higher-ranking "state actors" nudging and shoving. He wore a uniform well decorated with tinsel, but that was common at that time. He was not an actor in public; he worked through conversations, orders and written material. Granted, he was the representative of his city in the Reichstag, but in that make-believe parliament only one player was allowed to shine. Wolff's job was to cheer him on, vote "Yes," as ordered, and sing when the national anthem was played. After events the newspapers sometimes mentioned his name on the special list of honored guests as a constant escort of the Reichsführer SS, but he was only one of many.

At the beginning of the war, Wolff worked as Himmler's eyes and ears at the Führer's headquarters. What he did there would not make him popular. He either performed decorative service or was busy with secret information, which Germans only found out about after the war. When he occasionally allowed himself to stray from the party line by helping those in distress, he desperately needed to remain hidden. Only on one occasion did General Wolff take the opportunity to make himself known in public to the whole world, when he and the last intact German army surrendered to the Allied forces in Italy shortly before the end of the war, thereby shortening the Second World War in the south by several days. Whatever moved him to this action shall be assessed by history. The Germans hardly noticed it, as they were busy surviving in the Reich, which at that time was almost entirely occupied by the enemy.

The surrender in the south has already been described and critically evaluated in many books. Therefore, it may no longer illustrate the life and work of General Karl Wolff. Even his death at 84 was at best an occasion for obituaries in the press. On the day of his death, this biography had already been written, except for the final chapter. With its many details, it can serve as a contribution to contemporary history. Wolff was often a witness to historical events. He discussed fragments of these stories in unpublished manuscripts or on tape, preferring scenes where he could portray himself as the center of attention. If one compares his presentations to the relevant documents the latter often prove to be embellished. Rather than making contributions to German history, he provided anecdotes. Himmler is one of the few National Socialists whom Wolff described with conflicting emotions. Hitler seems agreeable, understanding and sometimes statesmanlike and strict. Wolff himself is, and remains, the idealist in this environment, someone who always wants what's good. Since he portrays himself as someone who never thought or planned any misdeeds, he remained unscathed by the monumental crimes that were committed by those around him. If someone were to prove to him that he could not have missed knowing about these crimes and that he even played a part in them, he explained with carefully measured words why he could, and even had to, view what was happening as legal. The blue-eyed Parsifal fell very early for the sirens of power in Hitler's magic garden.

Even if he never wanted to admit it, he was also affected by the amorality of the Nazi system. His middle-class respectability disintegrated due to the sick complex whose symptoms of moral and spiritual depravity can be summed up as the Nazi Syndrome. To counter this particular illness, one must study its extreme symptoms as they appear in General Wolff. From the beginning, he was one of those in whom Hitler had placed his hopes, just as, on the other hand, the mass charmer in the brown shirt provided a message of salvation, which could only make the high school graduate, former lieutenant, bank employee, and small business entrepreneur a true believer. When the Führer promised he would free Germany from disgrace and want, Wolff, a member of the upper middle class, saw in Hitler the savior from the threatening problem of doing away with classes. When Hitler announced that the soldier at the front as well as the officer would once again receive special honors, Wolff saw his opportunity for personal advancement. When Germany became rich and powerful once again, Wolff would also be allotted more power and wealth. Hitler's promise that in his Reich only those with "German blood" should receive honors, jobs, and dignity, and that the leadership would be filled with Germans of the Nordic-Germanic race, he strengthened the blond warrior in his certainty of belonging to the nation's elite.

His curriculum vitae shows how strong the temptation was, especially for him, to march in the "Brown Battalion" singing the Horst-Wessel. It is clear why so few of those marching found the strength to turn around. It also explains why so many closed their eyes when terrible things were happening and why they eased their consciences by saying, "Things get dirty when work is being done."

General Wolff received the biography he wanted so much only posthumously and it turned out differently from the way he had wanted for thirty years to write it. Had he been able to do so, it would tell the German people what he had done for them and what he had to put up with for them. Instead, they now learn that he was typical of his generation, a man who always considered himself a patriot cannot therefore deny this service to his country, even after his death.

Jochen von Lang

Chapter 1

Where Did You Serve?

In September 1964 a jury in Munich sentenced Karl Wolff, the former general of the SS and general of the Waffen SS, to fifteen years in prison. He was found guilty of having participated in the murder of 300,000 Jews by arranging for railway transport cars in which the victims were taken from the Warsaw ghetto to the gas chambers at the extermination camps. Five years after the sentence, Wolff was released because the court-appointed doctors declared him unfit to remain in prison due to his poor health. From then on he lived in Darmstadt, Munich, or Prien am Chiemsee when he wasn't traveling. His travels took him as far as South America. He never stopped protesting that he had been sentenced unfairly because he had only found out shortly before the end of the war that the Jews had been killed. The court did not believe him. For almost a decade he had been one of the closest confidantes of Heinrich Himmler, the Reichsführer SS, Hitler's highest ranking police officer and master of all the concentration camps. Himmler called him "Wolffie." At the very least, however, he must have discovered what was really happening to the Jews during his service for Hitler and Himmler at the Führer's headquarters between 1939 and 1943.

On the other hand, as the highest commander of the SS and police in Italy, and also as the authorized representative general of the German Armed Forces in Italy, SS General Karl Wolff played a considerable part in the capitulation of Army Group South of the German Armed Forces to American and British forces on May 2, 1945. Thanks to this action, the war on the German southern front ended six days prior to the general ceasefire in Europe. Under Hitler's state law (still operative at the time), capitulation was treason, punishable only by death. In some towns of the southern Tyrol Wolff enjoyed being celebrated from time to time for saving that region from war and destruction. By ending the war early, Wolff further asserted that he had spared German and Allied soldiers six full days and nights of fighting and, therefore, many casualties.

As with several of Wolff's contemporaries, even his own feelings fluctuated, torn between approval and hatred of the Nazi party. He contributed to this himself. Whenever the responsibility for the crimes of the Third Reich was raised, he professed not to know, not being involved, or at the very least as a powerless opponent.

Anyone seeking the answer to the question of why the Germans fell under the spell of the crafty agitator Adolf Hitler and his mesmerizing swastika over half a century ago, and why they remained true to him to the bitter end, will find the equally vivid and universal explanation of this phenomenon concentrated in the person, and the rise and fall, of SS officer Karl Wolff. He would have loved to have been, like the vast majority of people, an excellent German, but his career came to a forced ending in the general catastrophe. And so he turned into a metaphor of an era in German history, an example of his generation, although not by choice.

His career began on October 7, 1931. On that day, Karl Wolff left his seven-room house at Am Priel 10, in Bogenhausen, Munich's upper-class neighborhood, to go into the city; and its no less distinguished Briennerstrasse. There, in a much larger building, was where the Reich's NSDAP leadership was now operating. Among Party comrades, and the people at large, Hitler's residence was called "the Brown House," not only because of the color of the paint, but also because the uniforms of the Party and its units—something new, incidentally, in the political landscape of the Weimar Republic—also used that color. The advertising agent Karl Wolff wanted to join Hitler's ambitious party only there, at headquarters, and not anonymously in an ordinary cigar store or in some right-wing bookstore.

In Berlin in those days Chancellor Heinrich Brüning, head of the Catholic Center Party, was attempting to govern the country. More than four million Germans were already unemployed and the number was increasing daily. Three months before, in mid-July 1931, one of the country's four major banks had collapsed. As a result, all money-lending institutions had to remain closed for several days because too many of their customers wanted to withdraw their funds. In a wave of bankruptcies, old established companies disappeared, world-renowned breweries failed, insurance agencies closed their branch offices and worse still, the smaller businesses of tradesmen and craftsmen were wiped out. The majority of Germans had lost faith in the government and many considered the parliamentary system incapable of handling the crisis. For this reason, the National Socialists had become the second strongest party at the Reichstag elections more than a year before. But the Communists also gained a considerable number of seats. Many believed that Germany had to decide between these two extremes because all the other parties had been unable to provide solutions to fight the awful misery.

Because Karl Wolff wanted to save his Fatherland, and naturally himself as well, from both misery and Communism, he "joined the ranks of the brown battalions," according to the official party slogan. In those days he was only one of many new recruits. His party card was number 695131. To veterans of the Nazi party that number labeled him as an opportunist and a "September recruit" because it was only after the sensational growth of the Party at the elections in September 1930 that he decided to join. Once he reached a high-level position, he felt he had to apologize for this shortcoming. He would customarily say that in 1922 he and his new wife moved to Munich because even then he expected to see Germany's revival coming from that city and Adolf Hitler. Only his promise to remain politically inactive during his first year of marriage for the sake of blissful togetherness kept him from taking part in the now historic beer hall putsch of November 9, 1923, and therefore in the march on the Hall of Generals. For love, he sacrificed the Medal of Blood that party veterans were allowed to wear.

This was the reason why his career did not begin until October 1931. Besides signing his application for membership in the Nazi party, he actually signed another form at the same time: two pages in the standard A4 format, which was an "SS Acceptance and Commitment Certificate." Young, strapping youths who were acting as both guards and porters at the same time had placed this paper in front of him in the foyer of the "Brown House." They were wearing brown shirts, black breeches and black boots, a black leather belt and shoulder straps, a black tie and a high black cap that had a miniature skull shining martially above the visor.

In the space indicating: "2. Occupation:" of the form, Wolff wrote, "retired lieutenant, businessman." The reverse word order would have been closer to the truth because as the owner, along with a few employees, he earned his living from the "Karl Wolff-von Römheld Advertising Company." The small company was going through hard times and had been dragged into the economic crisis when many clients whose advertisements were already published could no longer pay and the newspapers passed the bills along to the agency. Wolff's house served as both the family's residence and the company office. The business was, in spite of everything, more apt to secure income than the carefully laundered peacetime uniform of a lieutenant of the guards in the Kaiser's army that was neatly hanging in the closet.

Even as a schoolboy, after he had seen an infantry regiment on maneuvers in the Hessian town of Butzbach where his father was district court judge, Karl Wolff had wanted to lead brave soldiers into battle as an officer riding a steed. Alas, this wish was never granted. He did reach the rank of lieutenant in the First World War, the springboard for a military career and he even ended his career in 1945 as a general, but the romantic, heroic pose was to remain a dream. Understandably, when he was filling out the form, he let his precarious middle-class lifestyle take a back seat to the retired officer.

After the routine questions 3–7 (birthday, address and such), he gladly filled in the next space of the form. In number "8. In the field from ___ until ___ " he could write that he was with the fighting troops at the front from September 5, 1917, to the end. Before that he had gone through four months of basic training in Darmstadt, his birthplace. He began training the day after his high school graduation, and he was not quite seventeen years old when he got into uniform. Due to his bravery and ambition, wartime volunteer and officer cadet Wolff was noticed so many times that he was promoted unbelievably quickly. Before the war had ended, he was wearing the uniform of a lieutenant and was decorated with the Iron Cross First and Second Class on account of his bravery.

Who knows how far he would have gone back then, if the top army leadership had not requested an immediate ceasefire in the face of an impending collapse of the western front, and if the supreme war commander, Kaiser Wilhelm II, had not left for neutral Holland on November 9, fearing a mutiny by the front line soldiers.

The next question on the form "with which unit" he had fought, Wolff answered in the glorious words filled with tradition: "Bodyguard Infantry Regiment 115 of the Grand Duke of Hesse." Those lucky enough to serve in this unit could feel particularly chosen. For the ranks and for the non-commissioned officers' corps, only the healthiest farmers' sons of Hesse were good enough, and to be chosen as an officer basically meant that one came from a noble family. The regiment was so exclusive that the Social Democrats in the Reichstag under the Kaiser were outraged because there were no middle-class soldiers in the entire officer corps.

The commander of this regiment was His Highness, the Grand Duke of Hesse-Darmstadt himself. Like the Kaiser, he was a grandson of Queen Victoria. The military, however, was not necessarily a priority for Grand Duke Ernst Ludwig, as it was with his cousin the Kaiser in Berlin, who was nine years older. He was instead the proud sponsor of seventeen scientific and musical societies in Darmstadt and founder of the artists' colony in Darmstadt which, because of the internationally famous exhibits, is thought to be the predecessor of the "Bauhaus." The Ernst Ludwig Press exists thanks to his initiative. Among experts, their book-lover's prints are still sought-after rarities in the art of book printing. The duke was a patron of painters, sculptors, and architects, an all-around aesthete, with the ambition of making Darmstadt the Weimar of the twentieth century, a spiritual center of the "other Germany" for poets and thinkers. His family relations also placed Darmstadt closer to the big world: an uncle and cousin (at a later time) were kings of England, a sister was the tsarina of Russia, a sister-in-law was the queen of Romania, another cousin was the crown princess of Greece.

The flags of almost all the European dynasties flew at different times above the castle in Darmstadt and its people enjoyed basking in this light.

Next to the castle and the Grand Ducal Theater stood the barracks of the Bodyguard Infantry Regiment, whose officer corps considered themselves not only of equal birth to the Prussian Guard but secretly felt they were more universal, more worldly and, as an elite, more aristocratic. And even if Karl Wolff served the regiment only in battle dress, enough of the Grand Duke of Hesse's self-awareness rubbed off for him to convey the sense of his elite exclusive status, without ostentation and as modestly as humanly possible, but impressively nonetheless.

The high school graduate was only admitted as an officer cadet thanks to special recommendations: a laudatory report from the "National Youth Brigade," for whom the grammar school boy brilliantly proved himself during the two-year volunteer pre-military training, and a guarantor and supporter in the person of his brother-in-law, who was a real count. His family's reputation also played a role. Wolff's father, who died very early, was a regional director of the court; and, therefore, the family belonged to the dignitaries of Darmstadt. Lastly, a great uncle on his father's side had served many years before in the same regiment, and had been promoted to the rank of general.

In such an illustrious unit Lieutenant Karl Wolff marched back to his homeland after the armistice in November 1918. In the barracks he had left less than a year before as a private, the lieutenant now hoped to continue wearing the uniform in peacetime. But the victorious Allies, as they were to do once more twenty-five years later, put an end to his profession and career. The Treaty of Versailles reduced the army to 100,000 men. For a time, Wolff was able to sneak into a unit called the "Hessian Independent Corps," which attempted to by-pass the dictates of the Allies, but there was neither a purpose nor a legal explanation for their continued existence. In May 1920, at just 20 years of age, he was forced to wear civilian clothes. The demobilization hit him first as the youngest officer of the regiment. Later, when he was older, he would be glad to have earned the right to a modest pension through the officer's commission, but, more importantly for his future, he had acquired the perfect manners and the appearance of an active officer while serving in that feudal regiment.

From then on, he was convinced that he belonged to the elite. Hadn't he always been drawn to higher and greater things? He had been educated in the most distinguished gymnasium in the royal seat of Darmstadt, he was close friends with a classmate from the house of Countess Dohna, and he took dancing lessons with a former ballet soloist of the Grand Ducal Royal Theater, together with the young people of the cream of Darmstadt society. Among them was the daughter of a baron, with whom he shared the joys of young love. Was this not evidence enough that this young man was destined to a brilliant future?

This elitist feeling made the businessman and retired lieutenant easy prey for the trained SS recruiters (who were on the lookout for new comrades to form what was to become the Guard of the Party) at the "Brown House" on that October day in 1931. Soldiers with experience at the front, even better those from a Bodyguard Regiment, were especially welcome to foster military virtues. It was incumbent upon the bodyguard of the National Socialist movement to physically protect the leadership, and especially Adolf Hitler, at meetings and marches. They were also called to gather the Germanic-Nordic men as the elite of the nation and the "new nobility of blood and soil" to influence the people and its fortunes. Wolff, with his appearance and six-foot frame, blond hair, blue eyes, light skin complexion, was the perfect specimen of a man, and his soldierly achievements showed that his character also placed him among the national elite.

Enchanted with the prospects of such a task and its ideals, he signed the forms. This time he even had to provide references. Again he first named his brother-in-law, now a retired lieutenant as well. Second, he listed a former comrade from the Bodyguard Regiment, Captain Julius von Bernuth, an officer of the German army and member of the Military Academy in Munich, who was already prepared to march on Berlin with the revolutionary Hitler in November 1923. At that time, von Bernuth was serving in a branch of the ministry of the German army and had, therefore, reached one of his goals.

What Karl Wolff had gotten himself into became clear on the second sheet of the form, in the paragraph under the heading "Commitment," which he had to sign again separately. There it was stated, "I commit myself to support Adolf Hitler's ideas, to observe the strictest party discipline, and to conscientiously carry out the orders of the Reich SS leader and those of the leaders of the Party. I am German, of Aryan descent, I do not belong to any Masonic Lodge or secret societies, and I promise to promote the movement with all my strength."

We can see from the stamps and annotations on the form that it had traveled the official channels, from a Sturmführer to a Standartenführer, to an Oberführer, and a Brigadeführer and all the way up to the Reichsführer SS, Heinrich Himmler. No one viewed this progression as being anything special. In any case, within three weeks he went from being an SS candidate to a full, low-ranking SS private.

Wolff felt that he had been admitted below his true level. Later he complained, "As in 1917 with the army, they had me start from the very bottom a second time!" He referred to his comrade, Reinhard Heydrich, who, upon joining the SS, received three stars for his collar patch, allowing him to be inducted as a Sturmführer with the rank of officer.

However, the SS private Karl Wolff was not treated all that badly. The SS muster roll recorded his first promotion to company leader two months after joining the "Black Corps," passing ahead of many others who had been serving for a longer period. After another five weeks, a second star on his collar patch made him squad leader. At the same time he was named Sturmführer of a group of one hundred SS because no leader of higher rank was available. As a result he was already in line for another promotion, but because it involved a third star that was tied to admission to the Officer Corps, it required a ritual that the National Socialists had lifted from military tradition.

On January 20, the Führer of Company 1, Heinrich Hoeflich, wrote a "Service Report on SS Troop Leader Wolff, Karl," who had only been promoted to that rank the previous day. This task was performed with a great deal of effort because Hoeflich was much more eloquent with his fists than with a pen. Wolff's personal characteristics were confirmed as "mature in appearance, very well versed in social situations, and well liked by his subordinates." His performance in service was praised as "very satisfactory to date," while "no exact information" could be gathered about his political education and "overall knowledge" as he "has only been with the SS for a short time." Regarding his military discipline, "his unit is very good." His promotion was approved.

Once again, just as when he joined, Wolff had to hand in a résumé, only this time it had to be somewhat more detailed. But it was not until two months after Hoeflich wrote his evaluation that the recommendation for him to stand for promotion was presented to the corps leadership. Since "nothing can be held against his promotion," all twenty present signed the document. This took place on March 22, 1932. The entire case then lay on Heinrich Hoeflich's desk for three months. It wasn't until the end of June that it was sent on to the Führer of the SS Group South, also located in Munich. Hoeflich's accompanying letter stated: "Membership Book [i.e., the Party Book] can not be presented, since Wolff has only a membership card."

That sentence could possibly be the reason for the delay, because anyone who joined the Nazi party in those years received only a red card for identification and a space to paste in his dues markers. Only after one year, and if the newly admitted member was not marked negatively, would the card be traded in for the little red book stamped with the Swastika-Eagle. A further explanation could be that Standartenführer Hoeflich and his staff had more important things to do in those days. From mid-February to mid-April 1932, the rank and file were kept very busy with two election campaigns for president of Germany, in which Hitler ran twice unsuccessfully against Hindenburg. A few days after the 84-year-old field marshal was reelected, Chancellor Brüning obtained his approval for the "Emergency Order for the Security of State Authority," outlawing the SA and SS anywhere within the boundaries of Germany. The ban was lifted only on July 14, 1932, when the rightist Center Party politician Franz von Papen replaced Brüning in office. Maybe the influence of a "system government" (as Hitler liked to call it) delayed Wolff's promotion. Nevertheless, the promotion was dated back to February 18 in his personnel files.

On that February 18, a Thursday, the future SS Sturmführer spent the day in an empty factory building in Theresienwiese in Munich. The building was being used for something quite different than its original purpose; it housed the Reichsführer School of the SA. The chief of staff, Ernst Röhm, was a former Reichswehr captain who had risen, in the meantime, to the rank of lieutenant colonel in the Bolivian army, but was still above Heinrich Himmler and in command of the SS. Up to that point, the factory had been used only to train SA leaders in ideology; now the school was available to the SS for the first time. Some one hundred members who could prove worthy of a career had three weeks of SS training pounded into their heads. They slept on cots on the ground floor, were fed on the second floor in a manner reminiscent of a field kitchen, and on the third floor they received propaganda training for the imminent final battle for power in Germany. Prominent members of the party spoke to them almost every day. Xaver Schwarz, the treasurer of the Nazi party, naturally withheld information concerning the debts of the Party as well as the names of its patrons from heavy industry. Retired General von Epp, leader of the military-political office of the Nazi party, was there to make the Party look respectable. Walther Darré, leader of the agrarian-political office of the Nazi party, praised the farmers as a source of power within the nation and expected the salvation of the world to come from people of the Nordic race. A young unknown Sturmbannführer gave a lecture looking for volunteers for the intelligence service that Himmler had ordered him to organize. Some people in attendance whispered that he had been with the SS for less than nine months. That was the first time Reinhard Heydrich and Wolff met; within a few years they were to become the closest confidants of Heinrich Himmler.

Naturally, Himmler also spoke to the course participants about the underground activities of the Freemasons, the supranational powers of the Catholic church, some of the false teachings of the Christian faith, and the craziness of the Jews, as they were depicted in the Old Testament. In 1939, as Himmler was being celebrated by his closest colleagues on the tenth anniversary of his being appointed by Hitler to the head of the SS, Wolff summarized a nostalgic look back in which he, full of sacred fervor for the speeches by Himmler at this training course, remembered: "The worldly seeds that were then sown in our believing, open hearts later blossomed in a wonderful way and bore fruit." Enraptured, Wolff described in his account how Himmler paced in front of the course participants and, "with his strangely clear eyes, gazed down into the bottom of our souls. From that moment on, the bond was sealed... casting an overwhelming spell on each one of us." The experience was "especially unexpected and deepened as our foremost SS leader sat down with us during our evenings of camaraderie and spared no effort in getting to know each of us in his uncommonly natural and winning manner."

A moving anecdote ended the manuscript. On the last evening together, the wives of the course participants, who lived in Munich, were allowed to take part. As Himmler gave the sign, well after midnight, that the evening was over, the last streetcar from Theresienweg had long since left. Wolff, his wife, and Standartenführer Hoeflich, who was a guest participant, had a seven-kilometer walk in front of them on a cold February night. According to Wolff, none of them would ever have suggested calling a taxi because they "probably would not have scraped five marks together between the three of them." But Himmler helped out. He had a car available and "would not think of not bringing us home before he drove back to his house in Waldrudering."

Hitler spoke to the participants many times. As he walked up and down the rows of assembled SS officers, he stopped in front of Wolff. Seeing the Iron Cross First Class he asked, "Where did you serve?" It was a standard question, but it made Wolff happy and proud. Years later, he maintained that Hitler remembered this first meeting. For his part, Wolff remembered that on the last day of their training, the SS were taken to the "Brown House," to the so-called Senator's room. There never was a Party Senate meeting held in this room, though, because Hitler never wanted such a committee. It was there that Hitler promised he would take power legally and never try to overthrow the government again. Furthermore, he solemnly announced, "I will never give you an order that goes against your conscience!" With that, Wolff felt that he could assume all the way to the end of the Second World War that no order from the Führer could violate humanity or civil rights.

For eight months, until the end of September 1932, Wolff marched at the head of Sturm 2 of the Second Sturmbann of SS Standarte 1. It was during the undeclared civil war when national socialists and communists, militants of the democratic Reich Banner units and German National Steel Helmet fighters died in the streets, at meetings, in barroom brawls, and from treacherous "accidents." "Beat the Fascists wherever you find them," was the slogan of the leftists. "Beat the Red Front to a pulp!" sang the Brown warriors. Two Reichstag elections, both for the office of German president, and eight state parliament elections in the course of 1932, caused incredible tension, leading to uninterrupted violence. Hitler attacked the "system" relentlessly; he did not want any relaxation of the tension because the fanaticism of the propaganda coming from the extremist parties was demoralizing to his middle-class opponents. He celebrated those in his Party who died as martyrs: "They died so that Germany may live…"

Members of "Assault unit 2-11-1" only removed their jackboots to sleep from time to time. The Party flooded the city and countryside with rallies, and at least one uniformed assault soldier with a flag had to march at every event to show the colors and the armed units. Rumors of plans for a coup were heard everywhere. To be ready if their own people revolted or to be on call in case their opponents attacked, a storm trooper unit was occasionally camped out at Wolff's house. Almost every Sunday morning and on some weekday evenings, he would climb up into the cab of a truck, with his men singing and waving the flag on the flatbed, and travel around the Bavarian countryside. In the small cities and towns they would link up with other units, often accompanied by drums and pipes, kettledrums and trumpets, beating out the rhythm for propaganda on the march. He exemplified order, discipline, and a strong hand that promised to set the lurching ship back on the right course.

The regular meeting place, called the Sturmlokal, was at the Zum Goldenen Hirschen Inn on Tuerkenstrasse in Munich. The owner of the inn certainly could not get rich on those guests. Many were unemployed or students without any income. Even the Sturmführer could not foot any large tab. The fact that he already had to walk to the celebration at the close of the Führer training class and had less than five marks in his pocket did not exactly speak for a flourishing business.

On the other hand, the Wolff couple owned and lived in a house with seven rooms, many of which served as offices for the "Karl Wolff-von Römheld Advertising Company." Although the husband was the sole owner of the business, his wife brought nobility to the company shingle. Her father, His Excellency von Römheld, was the head of the cabinet of the last Grand Duke of Hesse and was awarded the hereditary nobility title for his services. He owned shares in a paper factory, among other things, and was therefore more than just wealthy. Wolff's mother received the pension of a civil servant, which for the director of the district court was not negligible. Karl, however, never wanted to take it for granted that a university education would be paid for. The family was certainly not poor. His maternal grandmother came from a rich Frankfurt family. The friends and acquaintances of the Wolff family in Darmstadt were well off. The Wolffs were on friendly terms with the industrial family Merck, whose factory already enjoyed a worldwide reputation for pharmaceutical and chemical products.

Influential relatives and acquaintances also helped the retired lieutenant when he had to decide on a profession and was looking for a job after leaving the Reichswehr in 1920. They managed to secure a suitable position for the twenty-year-old in Frankfurt at the bank owned by the von Bethmann brothers, whose family had belonged to the monied aristocracy of the financial metropolis on the Main for two decades. Even during the two-year training period, the young man attached great importance to living a suitable lifestyle in an elegantly furnished two-room apartment in a well-to-do neighborhood, renting, if possible, from a noble landlord. "Because of the change from *Gardeleutnant*, it was a constant battle to avoid moving downward socially," he remembered many years later. In all of his dealings, therefore, he paid a great deal of attention to reputation; he preferred names coming from the aristocracy, including that of his future wife, Frieda von Römheld. Both liked to dance and danced well; the smart couple even took home prizes at various competitions. They became engaged in July 1922, just as Karl Wolff finished his bank training.

The former Excellency Karl Alexander Konrad Gustav von Römheld had no male heirs. Therefore, he enjoyed having his son-in-law as his successor in his business. Karl Wolff was to gather experience as an industrial manager at Trick-Zellstoff Ltd. in Kehl, the company with which His Excellency had dealings, but less than nine months later he returned to Darmstadt. The couple married in August 1923, just as inflation was racing to impossible heights. At that time rumors were flying around that the republic formed in Weimar four years before would sooner or later be replaced by a better regime. Karl Wolff was drawn to Munich. During those months, the city became the mecca of the nationalists. Most of the right-wing radical revolutionaries were already gathered there, more or less legally, because the authorities closed their eyes even to the most "wanted" subversives. Wolff found work at one of the city branch offices of the Deutsche Bank.

But on November 9, 1923, just three months after Wolff's wedding, Hitler's vociferously advertised march to Berlin, where he attempted to copy Mussolini's march on Rome, ended after just a few kilometers, at the muzzles of the Bavarian police platoon's rifles in front of the Hall of Generals in Munich. Whether or not he was directly involved, as one of Hitler's supporters, Wolff had reason to mourn the failure. Shortly thereafter, however, he encountered bad luck of his own. At the end of the inflationary period, a stable Rentenmark replaced the old mark whose value was reduced to the paper it was printed on. Because of this, the banks were no longer forced to calculate in trillions, the exchange rate of the dollar no longer changed hourly, and the bank's clients once again became stingy with their pfennigs. By the end of June 1924, Karl Wolff was unemployed.

Three days later he became an employee of the Munich branch of the "Walther von Danckelmann Advertising Company," with headquarters in Hamburg. He was chosen out of more than four dozen applicants on the basis of his engaging appearance, and because he had offered to work for the same amount of money he received from the unemployment office until he could prove that his efforts were worth more than that. He learned the fine points of the advertising business so quickly that he was given the management of the branch after just a few months; six months later he was able to quit his job. Then, on July 1, 1925, he opened his own company in the same field. In case the clients of Walther von Danckelmann wanted to take the opportunity to change their agent, they wouldn't even be giving up the title of nobility when they chose the new "Karl Wolff-von Römheld Advertising Company."

By 1932, the company name was in trouble. Even the elegant lifestyle of the boss was threatened. Therefore, he felt comforted that at least with the Party things were moving in the right direction: the comrades admired his military record; he was allowed to sit on the same bench as the hereditary Grand Duke of Mecklenburg at the Führer training on Theresienwiese; and was again picked for a new task. The Sturmbann II needed an adjutant who knew the rituals of the military and could express himself with confidence.

Possessing these qualifications, Wolff was assigned a position that he would hold very successfully for more than a decade, growing in influence and moving up in rank. Martin Bormann, one of the most influential Nazi leaders in the Reich, who eventually rose to become "Secretary to the Führer," often condescendingly referred to the aides as "coat carriers." But Wolff's ambition would never let him be content with such a secondary position. He naturally knew that in such a job one always had to stand in the shadow of someone higher up, but he was confident, and rightfully so, that he had the ability to work his way out of obscurity without having to bear full responsibility. Of course, he also knew that the position of adjutant could only be held for any length of time if he could sense the mood of his superior. But he was successful, thanks to his skill in dealing with very different kinds of people, his ability to organize things on his own, and his tactics in the daily battles with his rivals. In this way, the new adjutant of Sturmbann II of the Elite Unit I was able to achieve general approval. Standarteführer Heinrich Hoeflich certified him in a subsequent Personnel Report and Evaluation, stating that Wolff possesses an "amicable, friendly personality." He also called him a "dedicated National Socialist. Furthermore, he shows an understanding for the needs of the individual SS soldier."

With this evaluation, Wolff was already being proposed for his next promotion: to Hauptsturmführer. The announcement was made on January 30, 1933, a date in the calendar chosen for the higher ranks of the SS to be showered with stars and silver oak leaves every year from that point on. It was the day of the Nazi ascent to power.

As Hitler moved into the German Chancellery in Berlin and a flood of brown uniforms waltzed through the Wilhelmstrasse on that January 30, 1933, there was nothing triumphant going on in Munich. In rather unorganized fashion, groups gathered to cheer and celebrate in the streets and beer halls. There were occasional brawls as the Communists loudly protested those events. In Bavaria, the Catholic clerical party of Prime Minister Dr. Heinrich Held was still holding on, and for the immediate future would continue to remain in power unchallenged. His cabinet in the state parliament, voted in nine months before, still had a sufficient majority.

One success usually leads to others, and even in Bavaria people of all party denominations began to drift to the National Socialists. However, as the state government announced that it would not allow itself to be drawn away from its democratic course by the new government, it could be sure that its people concerned with their Bavarian independence would, for the most part, stand behind it. Dr. Held announced that the state government resist being driven out of its legitimate offices, even by a Reichskomissar dispatched from Berlin. Such a messenger from Prussia would be arrested upon stepping over the state border. According to rumors, the government of the Free State of Bavaria was secretly negotiating with the clerical and authoritarian government of Austrian chancellor Dr. Engelbert Dollfuss about breaking away from Berlin and joining up with Vienna. That news placed the SS and the SA in Bavaria on the alert. Wolff's house once again filled up with a permanent commando of Party men, ready to march.

A renewed war of 1866 between northern and southern Germans did not take place, however. A new parliamentary election on March 5, 1933, the third within eight months, gave the National Socialists, together with the German Nationalists, the absolute majority in the Reichstag. That election also showed how much the democratic parties south of the Main had disintegrated. Those governing in Bavaria felt they were in no position to stop these developments, and were actually just waiting to be legally overthrown. A commissioner did not even need to cross the border to take over; he had already been residing in Munich for quite some time and was popular locally for over a decade as the savior who rescued the state from the tyranny of the leftist intellectuals in 1919. He was General Franz Ritter von Epp, not a Prussian, but rather a fellow Bavarian, and one ennobled by the Wittelsbach King, no less. Besides, von Epp was so pious that his comrades in the Nazi party called him the "Mother of God general."

Historians are still arguing as to whether the takeover of power by the National Socialists could be called a revolution. For the swastika-loving SS guards, with their taste for martial drama, there was no doubt. The fact that the takeover took place practically without any violence only proved that the Weimar "system" was no longer capable of offering resistance and, most importantly, that a spiritual revolution had taken place within the deeper reaches of the German soul. It was also a legal revolution, just as the Führer had once predicted under oath.

A few revolutionary incidents were required, however, and they could not be carried out without the SS. They marched in Munich on March 9, four days after the Reichstag elections, in front of the sovereign center of power. Wolff enjoyed telling time and again among the circles of comrades how those who had been in power were properly thrown out. He and his marching company had orders to occupy the Landtag as a start that day. Only a handful of riot police were protecting the parliamentary building. As a precaution, they did not stir when they saw Wolff's numerous forces step up to the doorway and caught sight of him, in his shining uniform wearing all his medals, entering the building. With a smile on his face and in a very clear voice, he let the police officers know that any resistance made no sense because, legally, even Bavaria had to conform to the Reich's government now. It was his responsibility to make sure that "things ran smoothly," as stated in a report by Hauptsturmführer Karl Wolff.

The official defenders of democracy took this message to their superior who, after a long string of questions and answers, gave the order over the telephone to give in to the threatened violence. Because this victory was achieved without losses, Wolff left an appropriate number of men behind and moved on to the prime minister's chancellery. Here the procedure was repeated, only it took less time because the man in charge was expecting the visit and stayed away from his office. Thanks to Wolff's personal charm, there was no violence in carrying out his orders. In other areas in Munich, however, the old thugs vented their well-honed hatred of many years and ran rampant against their political opponents.

Wolff received a new order from Himmler that same evening: General von Epp, the new ruler in Bavaria, needed an aide from the SS. The 65-year-old general requested a retired officer, if possible, one decorated at the front, still young and tough, with exceptional manners and experience with paperwork. This was almost exactly the personal description of Karl Wolff. Himmler seemed to think that Wolff could certainly free himself from his business for two or three hours a day. The Reichsführer had obtained very little from the division of power so far, and felt it was important that one of his own could see and hear what was going on at the top in political circles.

From the very first day at his new task, it was apparent that it required full-time attention. But Wolff did not complain. He enjoyed the many public appearances where he could be seen just two steps behind the new representative of state power. He listened carefully during the confidential meetings, soon making the acquaintance of this or that party dignitary, and even being allowed to sit in one of the best seats at the celebratory High Mass that the Archbishop of Munich, Cardinal Michael von Faulhaber, offered for the new ruler of Bavaria. The general was so pleased with his black-uniformed aides that he did not want to do without them when he was named governor of Bavaria and had to give up the position of prime minister.

The new prime minister, party comrade Ludwig Siebert, however, was of the opinion that Wolff was one of his perks in office and was to remain available to him. Meantime, Himmler had also come to appreciate Wolff's talent to calm abrasive people and soften reluctance in an obliging tone of voice. He wanted to use Wolff on his own staff. The one obstacle in his path was that the Hauptsturmführer had performed all services up to this point without compensation, as did most of the lower ranks in all National Socialist formations. With this constellation of go-getters, Wolff had even wondered what chances he would have if he got out of his insecure business. Epp offered to have him called up again in the Reichswehr, but he would have had to go back to being a lieutenant, in an officers' corps shut off to Nazi protégés. As a start, this was not a very attractive prospect for a career. So he took Himmler's suggestion and, as the aide to the Reichsführer SS, he became a full-time member of the Black Corps. The SS was just in the process of admitting a flood of new members and setting up new units. Whoever was close to Himmler could be assured of quick advancement.

On May 10, 1933, the Reichsführer SS wrote to "Mr. Secretary of State Röhm" at the Munich state government, "asking most obediently that SS-Sturmhauptführer Wolff, who was made available as an aide to the Reich governor in March, if at all possible, could once again be made available to the SS. [...] The SS has a rather extensive shortage of leaders at this time..." Ernst Röhm, as chief of staff of the SA and at the same time commander of the SS (and of Heinrich Himmler), agreed. On June 15, 1933, Wolff began his new duties. He sold his advertising business to one of his SS comrades. For his services at the beginning he earned 450 marks a month. This was enough at the time for a small family to enjoy a middle-class lifestyle. Wolff could not really ask for more money at first because before the rise to power the Party had requested that in this time of need no German earn more than one thousand marks a month.

The Reich leadership of the SS in 1932 still occupied a small number of rooms on the top floor of the Brown House, and even Himmler had only a modest little office. They had since moved into a large building, and their Reichsführer now sat at the desk of the Munich police president; the office had been temporarily assigned to him in March. Without a doubt, Wolff felt that he was being paid much less than he was worth and for much less than he did. The Party members from the political Führer Corps, who were already disrespectfully and jealously labeled as "big shots" and "administrators" by the marching soldiers, divided the better positions among themselves. They argued that the solution to Germany's problems no longer depended so much on physical strength as on one's brain, and in this regard the corps of political leaders was definitely much better equipped than the units that marched in step.

Chief of Police Himmler could not complain about the lack of work. First of all, he had to guarantee that the "Reds," the Social Democrats, and everything that stood left of that, would completely disappear from the stage. For the sake of simplicity and as a preventive measure, they were mostly arrested and, without any court proceedings or sentencing, held prisoner behind the barbed wire of the former military camp at Dachau.

Some members of the Munich National Socialist circles had collected a number of special enemies over the years. Now in Dachau they were given the opportunity to understand that a new era had begun. Guard shifts had to be set up and procedures enacted. SS soldiers were deputized as policemen in a matter of minutes by wearing an armband. There were only very few National Socialists at police headquarters, and even if the interim Standartenführer Reinhard Heydrich managed to transform the most efficient former opponents into obedient Nazis within a few days, the Reichsführer still had very little time for his SS.

Wolff always said later on that he had been called to the SS building as a sort of right-hand man for the incredibly busy Himmler. The Reichsführer actually did have a chief of staff, the SS Gruppenführer Seidel-Dittmarsch. He was the office chief and ranked above the newly recruited Hauptsturmführer, like a general to a captain. In Wolff's personnel file, it was noted that he had simply been temporarily commandeered to the staff of the Reichsführer as of June 18, 1933, and only from September 1, 1933, was he considered an adjutant. Apparently he was just one of many. In the fall of that year, Hauptsturmführer Suchsland, equal to Wolff in rank, was writing letters for Himmler and signed them in his name.

That was precisely Wolff's task. He checked all later recruitments, separated the wheat from the chaff, answered miscellaneous and routine questions, made suggestions for letters, which Himmler could either sign or alter, and collected documents for any case in which Himmler would have to form an opinion. Furthermore, it was his responsibility to proof any questionnaires that had been filled out by SS applicants. These were certainly huge piles at times because, in those days, many comrades considered it necessary (for whatever reason) to openly affiliate themselves with the National Socialists, and since the Party was now closed to new members, the units drew all the interest. The so-called "better circles" preferred the SS—whether it was because of their "nicer" uniforms, or because they considered themselves an elite unit and several notches above the unrefined, proletarian SA—with the motto, "small but fine."

The proofing of those questionnaires could not have been too difficult, however, as the forms had already passed through the offices of all SS administrators from the Stürmen upwards, and had been stamped accordingly. It is easily understandable that Wolff wanted to be rid of this pointless task in his office duties. But it is not exactly believable that he managed to hand off this paperwork to his highest superior, chief of staff and Gruppenführer Seidel-Dittmarsch.

According to Wolff, the chief of staff was secretly busy in the months following the takeover, alienating the black-uniformed storm troopers from the Reichsführer. Supposedly he wanted Himmler to concentrate on the police, meaning the state sector, so that he, Seidel-Dittmarsch, could one day take over the Party unit. Wolff considered it to his credit that he protected Himmler from such a loss of power.

But any prerequisite for such a change did not exist at that time. Himmler would certainly have liked to have all the police forces of the Reich under his control back then, but there were still too many points of resistance. Everywhere the command of the police had been handed over to Party comrades, and they had no desire to hand over the newly acquired sinecures to the Reichsführer SS governing in Munich. Not until the beginning of 1944 was Himmler allowed to assume command of the political police in most of the German states. In Prussia, however, he still had no say. Hermann Göring governed as Prussian prime minister, and any attempts to steal into the police there only earned him displeasure with Hitler's most powerful Party comrade.

Therefore, it is highly improbable that Gruppenführer Seidel-Dittmarsch's plan was followed at all. Besides Wolff, no one else mentioned that possibility. Wolff was actually warned by Himmler about the secret dealings of the chief of staff. He also took that opportunity to point out that many of the SS newly arrived on the staff were good friends of the underhanded Gruppenführer. The matter, if it existed at all, took care of itself, since Seidel-Dittmarsch became severely ill during the winter of 1933 and died in February 1934.

It can be seen from Wolff's calendar of promotions that he enjoyed the special favor of his Reichsführer beginning in the fall of 1933: on each of the National Socialist commemoration days that quickly followed one another, he was promoted a rank. On November 9, 1933, the anniversary of Hitler's putsch, he became Sturmbannführer; on January 30, 1934, the anniversary of the takeover, he became Obersturmbannführer; on April 20, 1934, Hitler's birthday, he rose to Standartenführer. That amounted to three promotions within seven months, and one can truly see these as a reward for loyal service. For Christmas in 1933, Himmler honored his adjutant Karl Wolff by giving him a large portrait photo with a handwritten dedication, "Very Sincerely."

Wolff explained his uncommonly rapid rise by saying that Himmler needed the advice and help of someone with experience at the front who had been decorated for bravery. The Reichsführer had had the bad luck that World War I ended before military cadet Heinrich Himmler could be transferred from the garrison to the front where he could have experienced his baptism under fire. A man who received his commission while under enemy fire (as did Wolff) was enriched with particular experience in leading men.

The retired lieutenant successfully played up to the glorification of the soldier at the front, which retired lance corporal Adolf Hitler had elevated to a dogma of his Party. It is still rather difficult to explain, however, why an adjutant of Himmler's at that time was required to have had such experiences, since the Black Corps was not made up of soldiers, but rather of political activists. A civil war was no longer expected after the seizure of power had been carried out so harshly. Fights still took place only between Party comrades, but instead of shooting with powder and lead, they savaged each other with rumors and slander.

One salvo in that war was a Prussian law enacted by Göring on November 30, 1933, removing the secret police in Prussia from the state ministry of the interior and placing it directly under his authority as prime minister. This move spoiled Himmler's chances of ever having a unified political police throughout the Reich. So the Reichsführer found the time to concern himself once again with his SS. Imitating his model Hitler, he went out into the streets, in a snappy open Maybach automobile, driving to the locations of all the SS units and giving speeches in front of the assembled troops. On these occasions Wolff, as his constant companion, was to arrange the visitor's program and, together with local leaders, be sure that the Reichsführer was always received with the appropriate ritual. Sometimes these business trips were arranged with the ladies: on the front seat was the Reichsführer with his wife, Marga, a nurse and the daughter of a West Prussian landowner and seven years older than her husband; and Wolff and his wife Frieda. The couples grew even closer socially, outside of their work.

In those days Wolff had to hear Himmler's standard speech everywhere they went: the SS is an order into which one is sworn for his entire life; the SS is the racial elite of the German people; the SS as a guard that practices National Socialism in its purest form; the SS are the toughest fighters against Freemasons, Jews, Marxists, democrats, pacifists, and anyone with foreign beliefs; the SS are protectors of German virtues of loyalty, honesty, cleanliness, humility; the SS is an environment of unconditional obedience. Such statements were the confirmation for Wolff of a belief rooted in his early youth: the Germans are the elite of humanity, the SS is the elite of the German people, and whoever in this corps is called to be a leader, and is logically the elite of the elite.

Wolff felt his anger even more justified upon hearing and seeing how the Sturmabteilung of the SA, a competitive command of retired captain Ernst Röhm, was discrediting the new and better Germany. As he arrived in Breslau with Himmler, the waiters at the best hotel in town told him that the leader of the Silesian SA, the gigantic Obergruppenführer Edmund Heines (a retired lieutenant of a volunteer corps, death squad killer, professional revolutionary, and the main figure in a homosexual ring), made it his habit of holding wild drinking bouts in the hotel, turning off the lights by shooting at them with a pistol. In Röhm's Berlin staff headquarters on Matthäi-Kirch-Strasse, Wolff was able to see for himself how the victory over the "system, namely democracy," was still being celebrated with incredible amounts of French champagne, cognac, and heavy Bordeaux wines. There was no longer a lack of money; Röhm had increased his unit to more than three million members and more or less forcibly integrated them into the SA. This group was originally a monarchist-leaning "steel helmet unit of soldiers from the front." The puritan Himmler was especially incensed at the excesses of alcohol. He told Wolff that the Reich treasurer, Xaver Schwarz, administrator of all Party funds, had already cautioned the SA leadership that they should at least use, in a more economical, nationally conscious manner, German champagne, German brandies, and Rhein wines.

Historians are still debating whether Chief of Staff Röhm, as Hitler later maintained, was actually planning his break from the Führer by the end of June 1934. Because of his position, Wolff could have been expected to add important information shedding light on the matter. This was not the case. Of course, Wolff mentioned events that he viewed as a plot involving high treason, but these are simply the observations of a man who was not directly involved in the mass murder ordered by Hitler on June 30, 1934, but certainly one of those who benefited from the bloodbath. It was even obvious to him that resentment had built up among the SA men of long standing service because they fared worst when it came to dividing the spoils of victory. For many of them the slogan and promise "Work and Bread" remained unfulfilled, despite the fact that the number of unemployed had already been reduced by half. Often people from the old days still occupied those extremely desirable positions at the administrative desks, not out of generosity, but because the new government could not operate without their knowledge. Party administrators now occupied the positions of their political opponents who had been removed from those attractive posts. Following Hitler's seizure of power, the majority of those working in civil service demonstrated amazing flexibility and declared themselves very quickly in favor of the new Germany by donning the uniform of one of the many satellite organizations of the NSDAP. Others found friends and protectors among the higher ranks of the National Socialists. The "Night of the Long Knives" itself should never have happened. This was the night when the brown shirted thugs and sadists expected to be rewarded for their efforts during the so-called period of struggle. Was the SA at all necessary anymore? Many asked themselves this question. The slogan was being spread that the National Socialist revolution still needed to be completed so that Hitler could free himself from the bourgeois constraints of the capitalists and other big shots.

Supported by this emotional dissatisfaction, the head of the SA doubtlessly set his sights on his own goals. He gladly allowed himself to be called the Napoleon of the twentieth century; he considered himself capable, just like the great Corsican, of leading his Fatherland to fame and greatness. A people's militia would step in to take the place of the Reichswehr with its long-serving soldiers. The militia was not to be led by the old fogies of a politically uninvolved officer corps, but rather by young revolutionaries. At first, the SA should carry weapons and be placed alongside the Reichswehr, with the predictable result that its strength in numbers would soon be decisive.

Wolff offered no evidence that these plans had ever gone beyond the stage of alcohol-induced bragging. In the spring of 1934, he began to worry about the speeches that Röhm was making locally and the very rapid succession of SA deployments. A very aggressive tone was used in blaming the "reactionaries" for wanting to hold back the National Socialist revolution and preventing the struggle for work and bread from being more successful. Not without reason, the Reichswehr, as well as the Party organization, became distrustful.

Anyone seeking to understand why Himmler and Karl Wolff, who in the meantime had risen to the position of first adjutant, followed these developments carefully must also be aware of several connections within the National Socialist leadership clique. There was already the previously mentioned insinuation from Himmler regarding the chief of staff of the

SA, Röhm. If he wanted to start a putsch, the SS could be drawn into it. Above Röhm there was only the "Obersten SA Führer," no less than Hitler himself, who trusted none of his paladins, and constantly spoke of *his* SA and SS men.

Only a short time before activist Nazi groups enjoyed a certain independence from the Party. Until August 1930 the "Oberster SA Führer" for the Reich was retired captain Franz Pfeffer von Salomon, who relinquished that honor when Hitler curtailed his independence. Since then, a chief of staff led the SA. Röhm only took the position in January 1931 when Hitler called his putsch comrade back from Bolivia, where he held the top rank as a military advisor.

Up to this point the SS had been deliberately kept small. When Himmler took over the leadership in January 1929, the number of men had shrunk to 280. Following that, the number of members was never allowed to rise above ten percent of the SA troopers at any one location; it was forbidden for years to recruit SA men. If it came down to a disagreement between the SA and Hitler and the Party, the SS would still have the possibility of becoming independent.

For that reason the security force (SD) led by Heydrich, within the SS, observed the course of events in the SA very carefully. At the end of April 1934 Himmler felt it was the right time to warn his friend Röhm—either in the name of the old comradeship from the days of the 1923 putsch in Munich in the anti-republican organization called the "Reich War Flag," or simply as protection in case events took a different turn.

In one of his many interrogations by Allied examiners, by German de-nazification functionaries, and officers of German criminal justice, Wolff described the scene. According to his account, Himmler took his adjutant, whom Röhm regarded very highly, along as a witness to SA staff headquarters in Berlin. Supposedly the Reichsführer SS begged the SA chief of staff to part with such terrible company who, with their dissolute lifestyle, alcoholic orgies, vandalism and homosexual cliques, were just an embarrassment to the entire National Socialist movement. "Chief of Staff, don't force me to order my people to take action against you," Himmler supposedly begged, with tears in his eyes.

Röhm, according to Wolff's description, at first rejected the reproaches indignantly, but then agreed he had to rein in his incorrigible herds who were by now completely out of control. With tears in his eyes as well, he eventually thanked his comrade Heinrich for being so candid.

If one strips away the melodramatic effects with which Wolff often garnished his tales, one may conclude from that meeting that Himmler already knew at that point in time the kind of trouble that was brewing at the Reich Chancellery. On the same day he reported to Hitler with Wolff present. There, Himmler described Röhm's understanding and remorse in detail, but one may suspect that he actually only wanted to spread salt in his Führer's wounds since he was always fearful of betrayal. It was understood from Hitler's answer that he had already decided on his course of action. According to Wolff, he said he was sad because he found it difficult to act against an old fighting comrade, but this had become truly unavoidable. Himmler should keep the police and SS forces prepared to take action in this case, and report future unruliness.

Himmler could risk these games of intrigue because he had just secured his position by forming an alliance with the second most powerful man in Germany. He had been arguing for months with Hermann Göring because he was not willing to place the Prussian police under Himmler's command, as officials at the same level in all other German states of the Reich had already done. However, he had recently shown signs of relenting; even Göring had bones to pick with Röhm and he knew that he would not survive a victorious putsch by the SA.

Göring and Röhm were mercenary types who needed no particular philosophy of life to assemble military troops. In the early days of the Nazi party, at the time of the Munich putsch, Göring, the former aviator captain and commander of the famous "Fighter Squadron Richthofen," had once been the Führer of the SA. He was a role model of a war hero, with a white swastika on a black steel helmet and a "Pour le mérite" medal for bravery around his neck. Eventually the two retired captains had to cross paths in the chaotic workings of the Third Reich, especially now that they were both striving towards the same goal. Göring didn't actually see himself as the great reformer of the armed forces, but he certainly wanted to become their commander or minister of war. (He did manage to become Reich marshal, the highest-ranking German soldier of all time, but he still had retired lance corporal Hitler above him and no troops to back him up.) If he wanted to get rid of Röhm as a competitor, then he not only needed an ally in the party, but also an alliance with a massive organization as counterweight to a possible SA revolt. Who would be better than Himmler and the SS? And if it were to come to a conflict with the SA, it would be better to know that he had the political police on his side. Hitler also shared this opinion.

In mid-April 1934, Göring handed over his secret state police organization (the Gestapa, which the public renamed Gestapo) to Himmler in Berlin. The most important people on his staff, including Wolff of course, were present at that state event. In the days that followed, the greater part of the SS Reich leadership moved to the Spree, with only a contact office for the Reich leadership of the NDSAP remaining at the Karlstrasse on the Isar. Himmler moved into the most impressive office in the former School of Arts and Crafts on the Prinz-Albrecht-Strasse, where Göring's secret police were headquartered. In the adjacent offices to the right and left, he placed his closest colleagues: Reinhard Heydrich and Karl Wolff. The Röhm affair could be splendidly managed from there.

Certainly the three top SS leaders already knew by then how Hitler would act in this situation, even if they did not know the exact manner by which he would seek his revenge. In mid-April, the Reich Chancellor was steaming across the North Sea aboard the battleship *Deutschland*. In addition to the Reich Minister of War, Generaloberst von Blomberg and the Head of the Navy Admiral Raeder, there were many high-ranking Reichswehr officers present. There is evidence that the introduction of conscription was discussed, and in this regard Röhm and his plan to replace the Reichswehr with a militia were also on the agenda. The three SS chiefs in Berlin understood that Hitler could in no way agree to arming the SA would-be revolutionaries, and that an alliance between the SS and the Reichswehr would happen of its own accord.

In his Justification Speech on July 13, 1934, Hitler maintained that he made the decision regarding the murders spontaneously, late at night, when it was reported to him that a general mobilization of the SA storm troopers was imminent and that the now legendary "Night of the Long Knives" was an impending threat. In truth, his actions were prepared well ahead of time. Wolff did not discuss this, although he accepted Hitler's version uncritically. He, at least, had nothing to do with those preparations, or so he claimed. On the other hand, he did admit that he had played what may be called a key role in the bloody purge.

He remembered that during the second half of June Himmler drove to Karinhall, Göring's hunting lodge at Schorfheide, north of Berlin, to make decisions about the Röhm case. Wolff only learned of this meeting because an assassin shot at the Reichsführer SS's car but only managed to shatter the windshield of the Maybach. When some days later Himmler related to Wolff that a unit of "SS Leibstandarte Adolf Hitler," stationed in the former cadet institution at Berlin-Lichterfelde, was moving by train to the Bavarian troop training grounds at Fort Lechfeld, south of Augsburg, and was being provided with trucks from the Reichswehr, Wolff did not consider this at all strange.

A few days before June 30, Generals Keitel and von Reichenau also came to the Prinz-Albrecht-Strasse. Before they were allowed in to see Himmler, they waited a few moments in Wolff's office, but he learned nothing as to the reason for their visit, and Himmler did not have him join in the conversation. Not until later, as Wolff testified, did he hear that it dealt with weapons and equipment that were to be made available to the Leibstandarte.

On the evening of June 29, Hitler was listening to parade music by the Reich labor service outside his quarters at the Rhein Hotel Dreesen in Bad Godesberg. At the same time Ernst Röhm was at the Hotel Hanselbauer in Bad Wiessee with a few SA leaders. Hitler's orders, given to Röhm's adjutant per telephone the day before, were for the entire top echelon SA leadership to be at the Bavarian spa, and the first ones had already arrived. Göring was still in Essen with Hitler on June 28, but he then traveled back to Berlin. Himmler remained in Berlin; he sent alarming reports about an SA conspiracy to Bad Godesberg. Wolff received the order from Himmler on the evening of June 29 to move immediately to Göring's official residence on the Leipziger Platz for a few days, equipped with toothbrush, toiletries, razor, and an additional shirt.

Supposedly he still did not know what services he was expected to perform there. He met up with two other adjutants: a police officer and Göring's adjutant, Colonel Karl Bodenschatz, who later became a general of the Luftwaffe. The three men stayed there together for three days. Until the end, Wolff gave only very sketchy information as to what they were to do. He said they were on the phone constantly with everyone and anyone, but mostly with Heydrich at the Prinz-Albrecht-Strasse, using a direct line they had laid themselves. There were many questions coming in from the outside: What should be done with this or that person arrested? Heydrich had drawn up lists of names, as had Göring. Gestapo agents armed with pistols rounded up prominent individuals, and the SS of the Leibstandarte at the barracks made up the firing squads. Wolff knew about this as well.

For almost every name mentioned by the three adjutants during those seventy-two hours, it was a matter of life and death. Naturally, none of them shot anyone. They were also not authorized to strike a name from, or add a name to, the list. But they could, as Wolff admitted, dispatch commandos and give instructions as to where someone arrested was to be taken. They searched for one man for three days, to no avail. Hitler mentioned him later in his Justification Speech as "Mr. A., well known to you all ... as a thoroughly corrupt swindler." He meant Werner von Alvensleben, who according to Hitler's version had set up the connection between Röhm, the General of the Reichswehr and former chancellor Kurt von Schleicher and the representative of a foreign power. Schleicher was not even arrested; he and his wife were shot on the spot in his apartment. A bullet was also reserved for Alvensleben, but he happened to be at a hunting cabin in Mecklenburg and reappeared only after Hitler had stopped the killings. "He would have been one of the first to be shot," admitted Wolff. But he only remained in prison for a short time.

The number of murders committed using the excuse of the "Röhm Revolt" was never officially published. If one were to count those that Hitler named in his July speech, these would be about seventy. Actually, it ended up being many more. At another point in his speech, Hitler spoke of one hundred "mutineers, conspirators and plotters." It would have been customary for the Gestapo to put together a final report for Himmler with exact numbers, but Wolff was unable to remember. When U.S. Army Colonel H. A. Brundage at the Nuremberg War Criminals Prison interrogated him on September 5, 1945, Wolff said that most of the victims were guilty, and the rest, maybe ten percent, could be dismissed off hand. It seemed normal that among those shot there were also four members of the SS; Himmler obtained their "execution with Hitler's authorization" because they were suspicious elements. Wolff characterized his role so vaguely that absolutely no responsibility for the events could be pinned on him. "I was sort of an assistant. We three in Göring's house had nothing to do with the executions. No SA leaders were brought to us. They went to Lichterfelde to the barracks of the Leibstandarte and were kept there until the orders to shoot them came in." Individual names? With this question, Wolff could only think of those names that had become well known in the meantime, as well as von Alvensleben, one that even Hitler, although in slightly veiled terms, had also mentioned. Wolff: "When one makes over 7,000 telephone calls in 72 hours, one is so exhausted that one cannot remember anything so precisely!" (One hundred calls per hour, day and night, could be considered an exaggeration.) He was, he says, "very sad" to handle this task, which "made us take action against our own comrades with whom at one time we had marched shoulder to shoulder." He wrote to his wife in Munich on July

2, "We still have an immense amount of work due to the Röhm mutiny, until 3 or 4 in the morning, and after that phone calls every ten minutes. We are exhausted, but, despite that, relieved from enormous pressure."

Wolff's statements, on different occasions, provide further evidence that the murders had been planned for a long time. The Führer, according to Wolff, made it clear to Göring and Himmler in the middle of April that the entire police force must be under one command if "we want to get rid of Röhm." This was the only reason Göring was willing to give up an authority that he had strongly and sometimes even brutally defended until then. His position was slightly weakened, however, insofar as he had chosen a number of police chiefs from the leadership corps of the SA to annoy Himmler, and now the way these men would behave in an action against Röhm was an open question.

In his Justification Speech Hitler heaped the greatest praise on himself; the German people had him to thank in the first place that in the future they would no longer be terrorized by drunken, violent homosexuals living the high life. Some praise was also directed at Göring, who from Berlin destroyed the band of conspirators in the north of Germany, while Hitler himself ordered the murders in the south. Himmler was mentioned only in passing, namely that he and Röhm's successor, former SA Obergruppenführer Viktor Lutze, were rejected by the would-be revolutionaries "because of their fundamental respectability." Of the SS, Hitler (speaking Wolff's opinion as well) said that "they fulfilled their highest obligation during the last few days with an inner sorrow" and his trust in the SS "never swayed." Hitler's thanks to Himmler were hardly noticed by the public. On July 20, 1934, the status of the SS was raised to that of an independent subdivision of the NSDAP; Himmler was no longer under the chief of staff of the SA. Wolff was already promoted from Standartenführer to Oberführer by July 4, two days after Hitler ordered an end to the murders. He had held his previous rank for two and a half months. He must have indeed proven himself worthy on his Berlin telephone line.

But he was not completely satisfied. He had, he later admitted, earned the Reichsführer's special confidence in those days, but the camaraderie of "Du"* that Leibstandarten commander Sepp Dietrich, the Berlin SS Führer Kurt Daluege, the Reich Minister of Nutrition and SS Obergruppenführer Richard Walther Darré, and many others shared with Himmler was

* Informal manner of addressing someone as "you," as opposed to the formal "Sie."

not offered to him. He was addressed as "Wölffchen" when spoken to and in writing, which also sounds very informal.

Hitler's warm praise for Himmler and the new chief of staff Lutze did not necessarily mean there was friendship between the two. The new equal status of the SA and the SS was only one more reason to strengthen the already existing rivalry. When arguments developed now and again, Wolff was often given the task of keeping the peace. With his polished officers' club manners, his jovial and calming remarks in the Hessian dialect, his studied charm and eloquence of the professional salesman, he apparently had the ability to dilute all conflicts. Those talents filled him with self-admiration.

Himmler's problems with the humiliated SA began shortly after the bloody purge. The highest SA leadership, in this case Lutze, had comrades and other participants questioned about how much those murdered could have been guilty of treason and conspiracy. SS Gruppenführer Böckenhauer, a declared opponent of the SA, led the investigation and SA Oberführer Reimann from Hamburg threatened an SS Führer who was present: "one day... the SA will surely be vindicated and others will regret what they had done to the SA."

In August 1935 it came down to a conflict, typical of the permanent tension that existed and was in no way isolated, between the Brown and Black uniformed comrades. After an inspection at a Pomeranian SA Brigade, Chief of Staff Lutze returned to the Stettiner Hotel and, as usual, filled up on hard liquor. A report about the evening, written by the Hamburg SS Standartenführer and Gestapo official Robert Schulz, landed on Wolff's desk. The contents prompted him to stamp the seven pages "Secret" and send them immediately to Himmler, who for his part only wrote the word "Führer" on the first page. The opportunity to inform Hitler did not arise until two months later because the Chancellor and Führer of the German people was traveling once again, as was customary in more tranquil political times, throughout the Reich, being cheered by the masses at the Nuremberg Party rally and at the Thanksgiving festival in Bückeberg in Weserbergland.

SA Chief Lutze had always accompanied Hitler during the days of the Röhm affair, first from Godesberg to Munich and then to Wiessee, but he apparently never made an attempt to slow Hitler's desire for murder. Now, during an evening of heavy drinking in Stettin with a small circle of high-ranking party members, one of whom was a Gauleiter, he named several men who were shot simply "to take it out on someone or to seek personal revenge..." Those guilty would some day "come to a bitter end." SS Standartenführer Schulz did not want to accept this without contradicting it. In his report, he wrote that in Lutze's presence he regretted that "unfortunately everything hadn't been eradicated root and branch and things had been handled far too delicately."

Lutze said, "Orders from Röhm did not exist." By making such a statement he was indirectly calling Hitler's own statement, that the SA were getting ready for a putsch, a lie. He insinuated, without naming names, that no one had flattered Chief of Staff Röhm more than Himmler, that no one had thrown more wasteful parties than the SS. He maintained that even Himmler had kept a homosexual in a leadership position for years—Gruppenführer Kurt Wittje, sometimes head of the SS main office, who disappeared from his position only a few months before, although everyone knew that he had been discharged as an officer of the Reichswehr because of his male friendships. He would always keep on repeating all of this, boasted Viktor Lutze in Stettin, even if he were to be discharged and sent off to a concentration camp. And as always at a late hour and in a drunken stupor, he placed his glass eye on the table to punctuate his words.

Whether or not Hitler ever read that report is unknown; but no action was taken about it. Lutze's attack was mainly aimed at Himmler and mirrored the tactics practiced by the Party chief for ages; he fanned feuds among his henchmen so that their ambition was never directed against him and, most importantly, so that he could show his power of mediation as often as possible. So, the grousing continued unabated. For example, SS Obergruppenführer Fritz Weitzel from Düsseldorf reported in April 1938 "an outrageously impudent statement made by Chief of Staff Lutze at the Leaders' Conference of the Westphalian SA" in Dortmund. In front of 12,000 of his leadership in the Westphalian Hall, the chief of staff announced that the SA "was still as flawless and pure as it used to be." And with the sentence, "We want to be carriers of ideas, not of rapiers," he openly stated, and without hesitation kicked the Reichsführer in the shins, because Himmler not only gave the officers of the Leibstandarte a sable to wear with their parade uniforms, but he also presented the leaders of the General SS, who had earned it, including Wolff, a so-called "Rapier of Honor."

Under such conditions, it is understandable that Wolff recorded with satisfaction an incident in which Lutze, obviously drunk once again, came to blows with a secretary of the Swiss embassy at the Königin-Bar on the Kurfürstendamm in Berlin at four o'clock in the morning. Supposedly the

Swiss citizen had eavesdropped on the chief of staff's conversation, which was surely not difficult considering the loud voice in which the drunken Lutze usually spoke. The chief of staff then, with much yelling and screaming, confiscated the Swiss's diplomat's passport and called the police, who in turn reported the case to the personal staff adjutant of the Reichsführer SS, Wolff. In fact Wolff had no responsibility in the matter at all, but he made sure that the faux pas by the competition circulated within the better Nazi circles by sending the report on to Göring's adjutant Bodenschatz, whom he addressed as "Du" since their joint work at the time of the Röhm murders. In his letter, he asked that the police report be personally brought to the Field Marshal (Göring's former title). Wolff knew that "the fat man" (Reich minister, Commander of the Luftwaffe, Prussian prime minister, Reich Hunting Minister, Commissioner of the Four-Year plan, Reich Forest Minister, Reichstag President and much more, all in one person) collected the indiscretions of prominent party comrades like other people collected stamps.

One year later, on November 1, 1939, with the Polish campaign already victoriously concluded, Wolff got the opportunity on the other side to repair some of the damage to the chief of staff. A report from an SS Führer landed on his desk stating that there was "a complaint in the strongest language that even now Chief of Staff Lutze rides every morning through the forest with his entire family while horses have actually been removed from the officers of the High Command of the Wehrmacht." Himmler decided and wrote in his own hand, "Report to Bormann!" Reichsleiter Martin Bormann already had his office directly next to Hitler at that time. He was the official head of staff for Rudolf Hess, the deputy to the Führer, but his influence on Hitler was far stronger than that of his superior. Wolff reported Lutze's problem with the horses with the comment: "Personal! Confidential! Secret!" and left it to Bormann's discretion "to decide what further measures should be taken."

The fact that Lutze had to justify himself to Bormann ("The horses must be exercised!") did not improve the climate between the former fighting comrades. The snide remarks continued. Wolff had risen so high at this point that he could ignore the running battle with a comrade of lesser rank. In March 1940 SS Hauptsturmführer Dr. Rudolf Brandt, a colleague on the Reichsführer's personal staff, was working on a report from Brigadeführer Gottlob Berger, Chief of the Reserves Office of the Waffen SS, that Lutze is "slowly becoming a danger to the SS, if not to the entire Party," because he used the comrades' evenings that he holds for the SA officers serving in the Wehrmacht to "criticize other parts of the movement, but directed especially against the SS." Lutze also "created an awful morale atmosphere against the Reichsführer in a most outrageous manner" among sergeants at Officers' Training in Döberitz, although he was "in a drunken state" at the time. Berger was advised, "to watch Lutze and at the next opportunity, nail him down." This would not be difficult, since Lutze "is too stupid and conceited to notice a trap."

The SS hit back whenever the opportunity arose. It was reported to Himmlerin February 1943 that Lutze arrived at the Polish spa at Krynica for a several weeks' holiday with an adjutant, although that particular area was closed to Reich Germans and reserved only for wounded soldiers from Stalingrad and children from areas threatened with bombing. Another letter was sent to Reichsleiter Bormann, who in the meantime had been promoted to "Secretary to the Führer" and to "Chief of the Party Chancellery," becoming one of the most powerful men in Hitler's Reich. Himmler suggested that "it be arranged that Lutze rest his doubtlessly weakened state of health at one of the Reich's German seaside resorts."

Three months later, Viktor Lutze ended all arguments. Officially it was announced that the chief of staff of the SA, while on a business trip, was killed in a crash with the party car. Bormann ordered all Reich leaders, Gau leaders, and unit leaders by telex, with the obligation to attend the state occasion, in this case a Party funeral, at the new Reich Chancellery. "In the name of the Führer," he clearly reminded everyone, "all conversations are forbidden at the funeral service and at the funeral procession to follow." The notice was especially fitting this time because there would certainly have been gossip circulating that a) Viktor Lutze had this accident not only with very strictly rationed gasoline but also under the influence of too much alcohol, b) his trip could not have been on official business, since his sons and daughter were in the car with him, and c) the chief of staff died of a crime against food management because a huge number of broken eggs garnished the car wreck, the street, and the corpses.

The Party funeral took place on May 7, 1943. Four days later, SA Gruppenführer Hacker, who was responsible for the SA in the newly created Gau Wartheland, had just returned to Posen from the funeral in Berlin. During a discussion with SS bosses there he said that Himmler should additionally take on the leadership of the SA; the reasoning being that "under the circumstances, a suitable successor for Lutze would not be found among the ranks of the SA... All SA Gruppenführer and Obergruppenführer share the same opinion."

There is no indication that this suggestion ever made it to Hitler. Wolff asserted, however, that the Party chief made the suggestion to the Reichsführer SS directly after Röhm's murder that he take over the command of the SA. Himmler refused, however, because he did not want to create the impression that he had killed to inherit. But contradicting that version, Röhm's successor had been manipulated before June 30; Viktor Lutze was one of Hitler's regular companions during those critical days.

There is another reason why the offer to Himmler sounds improbable. Everyone knew that Hitler avoided such accumulation of power within the leadership of the Third Reich. Lutze's successor would be the colorless Obergruppenführer Wilhelm Schepmann from Saxony. He and his SA were only entrusted with target practice for the Volkssturm during the last phase of the war in the fall of 1944, far under Himmler, as the last contingent, along with many other competent commanders of the reserve army.

Chapter 2

GOT: The Source of Life

On July 2, 1934, at four o'clock in the morning, an order from the Führer put a stop to the hunt for "the Röhm loyalists." Wolff could now catch up on missed sleep. As he arrived at the office the next day, he found an invitation for lunch. Göring called those entrusted with the action and other confidantes to a meal at the Prussian prime minister's residence. The approximately thirty guests were offered a glass of champagne in the foyer. Wolff saw the commander in chief of the army, Generaloberst Werner Freiherr von Fritsch, but his attempt at saying something obliging to the high-ranking new ally remained unsuccessful; Fritsch was not approachable. His face twitched nervously and his glass of champagne at the reception was shaking in his trembling hand.

Wolff was surprised at the absence of a victorious mood. But the general knew more about the mass murder than the SS wanted him to. He knew in what an underhanded manner General Kurt von Schleicher and Major General Ferdinand von Bredow were killed. He was also convinced that the supposedly planned "Röhm putsch" was just made up. Several days before June 30, Army District Commander of Silesia General Ewald von Kleist came to him and reported that he had spoken to the Silesian SA Obergruppenführer Edmund Heines (considered to be one of the most radical mutineers and also shot) because of the rumors about an imminent SA putsch. Heines answered honestly and ensured him quite credibly that not one word of these rumors was true. After this discussion with Kleist, Frisch called Major General Walter von Reichenau, director of the ministerial office at the Reichswehr ministry and well known for his direct line to the Nazi party, requesting that he make a statement. As Fritsch voiced his suspicion that the Reichswehr and SA were only to be turned against one another in some sort of intrigue, Reichenau commented, "That could be true, but it's too late now."

This would explain why Fritsch became so upset at the sight of the black uniforms. Wolff found it amusing, however, that just three days after the bloodbath the disturbed general was just looking very much beside himself. For Wolff, going to receptions, celebrations, and reviews increasingly became a part of his duties, either as his master's constant and decorative companion or as his no less impressive personal representative. With his new office he rented a conveniently located apartment, a seven-room house, in the fashionable neighborhood of Dahlem, despite his low monthly salary, which was the norm for the Party. If his family was to come to the capital of the Reich, he did not want them to feel hemmed in. The house in Bogenhausen was sold and with that money Wolff bought a piece of property in Rottach-Egern on Lake Tegern, now called, for some reason, the "Lago di Bonzo" because more and more prominent Nazis were settling there. Even Heinrich Himmler had given up his modest estate in Waldtrudering for a more suitable home. Wolff proclaimed that he would build the family's ancestral seat on the lake property. Moreover, the house was also necessary since Hitler resided on the Obersalzberg during most of the vacation months.

Himmler now had the rank of Reichsleiter within the Party. Regarding his police duties, the Reich minister of the interior, Dr. Wilhelm Frick, was still above him, but he hardly had to worry about his opinions. During an interrogation in Nuremberg after the war, Wolff said, "As a jurist the minister did not incur the Führer's favor; to him he was just a bureaucrat. Frick never got into any arguments with Himmler because he knew that Hitler would always say that the Reichsführer was right."

In the leadership of the SS, Himmler could just about do as he pleased. Hitler usually only clipped the wings of his birds of paradise if they got in his way. It didn't bother him that everyone had different views of what National Socialist Germany was supposed to be and that the Party and its satellite organizations were anything but a monolithic block. Himmler had even thrown together a rather abstruse program from various kinds of sources: racial delusions, arbitrary interpretations of history, theories by would-be scientists, rules of secret societies and monastic religious orders, heroic cults, the occult, natural medicine, and anti-Christian religious musings.

As first adjutant (April 4, 1934), and even more upon becoming the top adjutant (November 9, 1935), Wolff zealously served that program like a convinced disciple. Typical of this attitude was his relationship to Christianity. As a child he had been baptized in the Protestant church, where religious belief was an integral part of bourgeois respectability. As an officer in the Kaiser's army, he was brought up in the traditional alliance of throne and altar. Like so many middle-class Germans during the Weimar Republic, he saw in the Christian churches a bulwark of defense against godless Marxism and a factor of order in society. He and his family went to church services regularly in their community of Munich-Bogenhausen; sometimes he even attended wearing his SS uniform. He had his daughters Irene (born in 1930) and Helga (born in 1934) baptized. "The fact that he made himself available to the parish council in the church community was further evidence of his upstanding and consciously devout attitude," as retired pastor Ernst Veit was to state later on. This was certainly a de-nazification certificate used by the former SS Führer to whitewash his reputation in 1945 when he was accused of being a militant Nazi during Hitler's reign.

The religious Christian Wolff became a new pagan "Saul" in September 1936. He left the Protestant church and took his children with him. The fact that Himmler viewed Christianity as foreign and that he encouraged a kind of religious belief that Protestants and Catholics alike described as regressing to Germanic paganism, makes it very probable that Wolff turned his back on his family's religion to advance his career. But this change of mind should not be interpreted as simply as that. It must be taken into consideration that shortly after 1933 the "church fight" began among the Protestants. The faction known as the "German Christians" made Jesus of Nazareth into a hero of the Nordic race while the followers of the "German Confessional Church" were opposed to the Aryanization of their beliefs and did not reject the Old Testament in the Bible, for example, as being Jewish. At the same time the National Socialist government tried to undermine the reputation of the Catholic church by uncovering sexual offences in the convents, which, at the behest of the ministry of propaganda, were to be fully exploited, as were the trials that followed. The foundation of Christian beliefs, as well as its organizations, became very suspicious in those days. Leaving the church out of conviction was increasingly taking place.

The National Socialists did not want to get rid of God altogether; they had inveighed against the philosophical materialism of Karl Marx too loud and for too long. So, the SS and its prophets wound up with GOT, apparently an Old German word. They imagined a heavenly, superhuman, superior authority, both monotheistic as a higher being settled somewhere and nowhere at the same time, an omniscient and pantheistic spirit. They went back to the mystics of the Middle Ages, to Goethe, Schopenhauer and any critic of the Jewish origins of Christian beliefs. If the conversation between Himmler and his adjutant turned to anything of a divine nature, they spoke of "Age Old One," as the Teutons addressed their God.

When Wolff's first son (after two daughters) was born in January 1936, the father was already an enthusiastic follower of Himmler's homegrown religion. Because astrology also had a place in this religion, the birth announcement was decorated with a jumping ibex, the accepted sign of the zodiac for the time of birth. A family coat of arms, a "Wolfsangel," that represented a rune from the time of the Teutons, appears for the first time on this card. Wolff's son was named Thorisman, and therefore commended to the most argumentative and aggressive of the Teutonic deities. The additional names were given by the "name gods" or Goden, an Old German expression for godparents: Heinrich (for Himmler), Karl (for SS coat of arms creator Professor Diebitsch), and Reinhard (for Gruppenführer Heydrich, at the time chief of the SD security service and of the Gestapo). Another godfather was SS Brigadeführer Weisthor, a rather diminutive Teuton, but nevertheless knowledgeable about the religion, customs, and runes of the ancestors. He had developed the ritual for naming in the SS and thus assumed the role of high priest in the naming of Wolff's son.

The naming ceremony took place on January 4, 1937, when Thorisman was almost one year old. The event was recorded on a typewritten certificate. The content, language, and form are so typical of all that was sectarian in the SS that it should be reproduced here:

Temporarily: Land at Tegernsee
January 4, 1937
DOCUMENT:

Today, on January 4, 1937, in his home at Schorn zu Rottach-Egern at the Tegernsee, SS Brigadeführer Karl Wolff, in the presence of his Reichsführer SS, made the following announcement:

"Reichsführer SS: I hereby announce the birth of our third child, born of my wife Frieda, née von Römheld, as the first son born on January 14, 1936, at the end of the third year of the Third German Reich."

I replied:

"I thank you. I have heard your announcement in the presence of witnesses, the Goden of this child, myself, SS Brigadeführer Weisthor, SS Gruppenführer Heydrich and SS Sturmbannführer Diebitsch. Your child will be entered in the Birth Register of the SS and a note will be made for the Family Book of the SS."

Brigf. Wolff then gave the child to his mother, who accepted him.

I then appointed SS Brigadeführer Weisthor to carry out the naming ceremony.

SS Brigadeführer Weisthor wrapped the child in the blue ribbon as he spoke the conventional words:

"The blue ribbon of loyalty may stretch throughout your entire life.

"He who is German and feels he is German must be loyal!

"Birth and marriage, life and death are bound by this symbol of the blue ribbon.

"And now may your child be the family's own with my innermost wish that he become a proper German boy and an upright German man."

SS Brigadeführer Weisthor took the cup as he spoke the conventional words:

"The source of life is Got!

"Your knowledge, your tasks, your purpose in life and all insights to life come from Got.

"Every drink from this cup may bear witness that you are bound to Got."

He gave the cup to the father of the child.

SS Brigadeführer Weisthor then took the spoon as he spoke the conventional words:

"This spoon may nourish you until you reach the maturity of youth. May your mother herewith attest her love to you with it and punish you by not nourishing you with it as an offense against Got's laws.

He gave the spoon to the mother of the child.

SS Brigadeführer Weisthor then took the ring as he spoke the conventional words:

"This ring, the SS family ring of the house of Wolff, shall you wear one day when you have proven yourself worthy of the SS and your lineage.

"And now, according to the wishes of your parents and on behalf of the SS, I give you the name Thorisman, Heinrich, Karl, Reinhard.

"It is up to you, parents and godparents to raise this child to be a true, brave, German heart according to the will of Got.

"I wish for you, dear child, that you prove yourself so that when you reach the maturity of youth, you may receive the proud name of Thorisman as your Christian name for your entire life.

"OUR GOT REIGNS!"

I hereby sign this document and have requested the godparents to bear witness by signing their names.

The commander:

The Goden:

1. Gode : Reichsführer SS
2. Gode: SS Brigadeführer
3. Gode: SS Gruppenführer
4. Gode: SS Sturmbannführer

Because it would be some time before the child reached maturity, the son at first was named Karl-Heinz. This combination of "Heinrich" with "Karl" was a favorite name for quite a while, popularized by the sentimental play "Old Heidelberg." The Gode Himmler never missed the opportunity at birthdays or Christmas to send packages to Rottach-Egern to his godchild: a silver plate, a white bear, a game of rollers. Even in January 1945 as Heinrich Himmler was going through great distress, Karl-Heinz was not forgotten. He received from Uncle Heinrich a saw kit and chocolate.

There was a special reason for the naming ritual to be so pompously celebrated in the Wolff household. On November 9, 1936, he was elevated from his position as head adjutant to "Chief of the Personal Staff of the Reichsführer SS." With this new position, he also took over responsibility for the cults of the SS, where Himmler's predilection for abstruse romance always ran amok with new ideas. Wolff also now headed a department of several hundred men, who received the honorary ranks of the SS from Himmler, like the members of the "Ahnenerbe" (ancestral heritage research unit), the "research and teaching community," for which college professors and scientists of completely different disciplines were mainly approached. They gladly came because the uniform of an SS Führer provided them with a National Socialist alibi. As proud of this academic following the graduated chicken breeder and farmer Heinrich Himmler was, he always felt somewhat unsure in their company. But having the cosmopolitan officer's club conversationalist Wolff at his side increased his self-confidence.

Chief of the Personal Staff Wolff also felt his self-importance rise through his frequent contacts with university graduates who were among the first-rate German scientists, and even more so since he was being courted by them. Of course, he did have money at his disposal, for research grants and stipends. He adapted to his new environment and in 1936 information was added to his personal file that he studied law and political economics, even though the diplomas were "not yet" obtained. The question remains open as to where the bank official, officer, advertising expert and SS Führer could have more or less regularly attended lectures. Wolff did not name his universities, but he did state the years of study: "1920–1923 and since 1935." This would mean that, as a bank apprentice in Frankfurt, he attended the university there; during his work as an employee in Kehl, he attended Freiburg University, which was about 80 kilometers away; and then as SS Führer, he attended Berlin University. Given his constant complaint of being overworked, this would be a remarkably energetic commitment.

Due to Himmler's tastes for the bizarre, the "Ahnenerbe" quickly developed into a grocery and general store, where, except for the cultural achievements of the Nordic Indo-Teutonism, one could find a selection of rare items and, finally, even crime. Because Austrian engineer Paul Hörbiger's Cosmic Ice Theory was rejected by serious scientists, but still promoted by the Ahnenerbe, it is, at worst, laughable as an amateurish bad investment. The same held true for the Ura-Linda-Chronik, which was trumpeted for years as a valuable cultural document from pre-Christian Teutonic times, despite the fact that experts in the field had proven to its discoverer and translator, the Dutch scholar Hermann Wirth, that he was dealing with a forgery from the 1900s. There were, however, several cabinets at the Ahnenerbe whose access was restricted (marked "Secret") the content of which was only made public after 1945 through the Nuremberg War Crimes Trials. It shall be discussed further, along with the issue of how much Wolff knew about criminal experiments on humans.

This cultivation of science and art reminded Wolff of the spiritual orders during the Middle Ages. This was the reason why he viewed it as an especially favorable sign of his destiny when, upon visiting the Brown House in October 1931, he was met by the SS, the Guard of the Movement, and not by the mass organization of the SA. That he, as a former officer of the only Hessian Guard Regiment, could begin his second officer's career with the oldest SS Standarte was further evidence that Providence had been assigned to nurture the German elite. To Himmler and to the Führer of his SS, the unit was far more than a simple militant division of the NSDAP; they considered themselves the successors of the German knights who conquered the East for the Germans centuries before. At the same time they admired the Jesuits, who with strict discipline and unlimited obedience fulfilled their tasks. When Himmler referred to them as a "soldierly order," the two images became one in his imagination. The SS should "be bound by discipline and by blood" to the Nordic blood, a family community...people used to say a community of nobility." That feeling of nobility was exactly what Wolff was striving for.

The Ahnenerbe was to develop a type of religion for that aristocratic community. During the first half of 1937 Wolff made an effort to hurry along a plan from his department that would develop the Teutonic heritage." This religion was expected to give the SS "a non-Christian character, the ideological basis for the lifestyle and structure of life as a type of religion and ethics." Himmler revealed what his goals were most succinctly in a speech he held in Berlin in 1942: "We must cope with...this Christianity, the biggest plague that could have befallen us in all of history."

Wolff had already set his sights on the same goal in 1937 with the previously mentioned plan; only he didn't underscore it so crassly. "Overcoming ideological opponents, meaning the unruly Christians of both denominations." This was to be achieved by developing the Teutonic heritage. A collection of examples from the Teutonic past was planned in approximately fifty volumes.

Wolff made every effort to assemble the required committee of respected scientists. The pile of books was to contribute "to the creation of a new type of man, by education and selection...able to master all the great tasks of the future and replace the decadent old aristocracy."

Himmler's historical musings drove him to think that his order also needed a huge, visible focal point. The fat, Reich Chief of Organization of the Nazi party, Dr. Robert Ley, had already stolen the term "Ordensburg" by immediately having three such buildings constructed to train the Party's political leaders but the romantic dreamer who headed the SS had something less mundane in mind, something comparable to Monsalvat, the castle of the Knights of the Grail surrounding their king, Parsifal, or the castle of King Arthur sitting at the Round Table. For him it seemed reasonable to settle into the castle in the Proto-Germanic landscape, so to speak, of North Germany, where Hermann der Cherusker had defeated the Romans. It was here that Widukind, the Duke of Saxony, and his fellow fighters first converted to Christianity, following Charlemagne, which Himmler named Karl the Slaughterer, since he supposedly held mass executions of the pagans of Lower Saxony. The Reichsführer SS, accompanied by his adjutant, Wolff, went in search for a suitable location in November 1933, and visited the neglected and dilapidated Wewelsburg, near Büren, which had offered shelter to the former bishops of Paderborn during times of unrest. When he was told that the county council was looking for a tenant, he considered setting up an SS officers' school at the castle.

It is quite possible that at the time he recalled the old legend, which prophesied that the castle, located on a steep hill in the middle of some flat land, would one day be the last shelter for the German knights before the great hordes of horrible armies from the east. From this castle, or so it was told by people of the region, the knights would begin the fight for liberation, which after many hard battles would also end in their victory. After the First World War, Himmler had belonged to the Artamanen League for several years. The league saw in the farming community the source of the people's energy striving for an agricultural settlement in the east as a bulwark against the Poles trickling into the Reich. He may very well have seen the old legend as a prophecy. He decided to turn the castle into something more than just a training center. After the project was first entrusted to the SS Race and Settlement Main Office, and therefore under Obergruppenführer and Reich Minister of Nutrition, Walther Darré, it was transferred to the Personal Staff of the Reichsführer SS in 1935 because of its expanded duties. That was how Karl Wolff became responsible for the project.

In a few short years, Himmler's plans grew to be gigantic. In 1940, shortly after the victory over France, Himmler and Wolff presented their Führer with a model of the future SS shrine. The new buildings took up so much space that a town that was part of the castle had to be moved almost one whole kilometer into the plains. A fifteen-meter-high wall, 450 meters long, was to surround the castle with a circle on three sides, and parallel to that a road would run in an even larger circle. Hitler, the lover of all things gigantic, authorized the construction.

Because the castle was to be reserved for the Führer's elite circle, no large halls were planned. In the round north tower, the various Gruppenführers and the Obergruppenführers were supposed to assemble, but by the end of 1938 there were only sixty-nine of them. Only the Obergruppenführers were to be allowed into the ground floor—this was a rank, which included forty-three men plus the two superior Obergruppenführers Dietrich and Hausser in 1943. They had therefore reached the highest rank under that of the Reichsführer. The floor of the basement was made of natural rock; there was a circular-shaped seating hollow chiseled in the rock. Visitors today call the room "Valhalla," named after the seat of the Teutonic gods.

Himmler forbade anyone who did not belong to the higher Führercorps of his order from visiting the castle. In 1939, as he once again inspected the construction, he told the commander in charge that it was a particular honor to be invited to the castle. The press was absolutely not to be allowed in, because any publication of the inside of the castle was forbidden. Himmler would not allow this under any circumstances because he feared being ridiculed by the fuss of the SS cult. But even more than that, since he was having the Freemasons persecuted as a secret society, he wanted Wewelsburg to be shrouded as a modern mystery meant to become an object of shy admiration for ordinary people.

SS Brigadeführer Karl Maria Weisthor, who had played such a grotesque role during the naming ceremony of Wolff's son Thorisman, always stimulated the Reichsführer's preference for things mystical. Weisthor was sure to find a willing listener for his fantastic ideas in Heinrich Himmler, the musing self-taught dreamer who despised exact science. The Brigadeführer's real name was Wiligut. He claimed to have come from the family of Hermann der Cherusker, and that almost all of his relatives had been beheaded. The rest of his family roamed through Europe as refugees, founded Vilna, and also found shelter in Swabia. They then wandered into Austria. He was born in Vienna in 1866 and supposedly managed to rise to the rank of captain during the First World War in the K.u.K. (Austro-Hungarian) Army. In Salzburg in 1918 he founded an anti-Semitic group, accusing the Jews, the Freemasons, and the "Rome churchmen" of multiple crimes, and occasionally spent time in a mental institution. Nevertheless, he became part of the personal staff of the Reichsführer SS. Because he supposedly had access to the spirituality of the ancient Teutons through his family traditions and other supernatural inspirations, he was promoted as high as Brigadeführer, a rank comparable to major general in the SS. It wasn't until 1939 that the SS realized that they were dealing with a madman; he was dismissed from the Black Corps by reason of insanity.

Wolff discussed the purpose of Wewelsburg many times, even if it was always in a rather hazy way. In 1947, when testifying at the war crimes trials in Nuremberg, he was asked about the castle. His response was that the SS leadership did not even see it finished. Later he admitted that Himmler's advisor, Weisthor, with his belief in old legends, told everyone that, in fact or in fantasy, the next and final attack by the Huns from the east would break down against this stronghold. As Wolff explained to his interrogator at Nuremberg, "The castle was meant for the highest leadership as a place to gather on special occasions." There is evidence of this in a speech by Himmler on November 9, 1938, in which he announced that the swearing in of the Gruppenführers would take place at Wewelsburg every year. In addition to the many oaths a National Socialist had to swear in the course of his life in the Party, Himmler would still have created several more...

It never got as far as that ritual. The reconstruction of the ruins was never quite finished because the plans were constantly being expanded, and after 1939, with the beginning of World War II, there were hardly any suitable craftsmen available. The SS, however, knew how to get things done and set up a concentration camp in the neighborhood of the castle in which several hundred prisoners were being held as forced laborers at different times. Over 1,200 prisoners died in that camp.

As Wolff was questioned about the financing of the project after the war, he said that 11 million marks had already been spent on the building. It must be taken into consideration that most of the land was leased from the administrative district for one mark per year. The prisoners of the concentration camp, naturally, received no pay. In addition, the mark had a different purchasing power; for 11 million marks, one could build 500 single-family homes at that time. According to the final plans, construction was scheduled for 20 years and the entire costs were expected to reach 250 million marks. The splendid building that became the new Reich Chancellery in Berlin in 1938–39 cost a total of only 80 million marks.

On February 1, 1936, an organization was created specifically for the financing of the project called the "Society for the Promotion and Cultivation of German Cultural Memorials," with headquarters in Munich. In order to fulfill the requirements of a registered organization, rules had to be established and signed by six members. Himmler was the head of the organization; Karl Wolff signed immediately after him; then his closest coworker, Luitpold Schallermeier; SS Führer Dr. Walter Salpeter; Himmler's secretary Dr. Rudolf Brandt; SS coat of arms expert Karl Diebitsch; and Gruppenführer Oswald Pohl, head of the Administration and Economic Office of the SS. That office also took over the business management of the organization. Wolff was responsible for all personnel decisions, plans, promotion, and development of training operations, while the personnel staff handled the crew working on the castle. He did not need to bear any responsibility for the concentration camp, because this camp, as well as all the other camps, was under the supervision of his old friend, Gruppenführer Oswald Pohl. The situation was such that it obviously prevented Wolff from finding out anything about conditions behind the barbed wire fences.

Wolff handled a very sensitive situation during the disorderly festivities at the castle on May 1, 1937, with his usual skill. At the drunken May 1 celebrations, called the "National Day of Work" by the Nazis, an Obersturmführer from the castle detail beat a man from the town of Wewelsburg badly enough that he had to be taken to the hospital. It was not surprising that tensions would eventually lead to a fight because the town was strictly Catholic and the SS did not make it a habit to respect the religious feelings of the townspeople. In June, when the townspeople were celebrating their "Schützenfest," the younger people did not want to let the SS men into the tent. Several SS Führers, however, forced their way in. When one of them demanded to dance on the stage with a girl, a brawl broke out. The captain of the castle at the time feared a farmers' revolt and called in a train of SS reserve troops stationed in Arolsen for help. The soldiers who arrived with steel helmets and rifles found no rebels, but the Gestapo placed five of the townspeople into protective custody the next day anyway.

Wolff was given the task of handling the incident with as little sensation as possible. He was right to view the situation as just another fistfight that can break out anywhere when strangers behave boisterously at a public festival. He made sure that the fight had no consequences for the village people. The captain of the castle, on the other hand, was forced to resign his position. With this decision, Wolff was probably fulfilling the Reichsführer's secret wish, since Chief of the SS Race and Settlement Office, Walter Darré, who, in the meantime, had fallen out of favor, had appointed the ousted dignitary. Even worse, Darré was Himmler's brother-in-law, and the two were not getting along.

Wolff was even allowed to participate in raising funds. Every year Himmler's "circle of friends" deposited their donations with him. The members of this circle of friends were among the most influential men from the world of finance, industry and trade and, because they had all been awarded with honorary ranks and uniforms of the SS, they also had to be formally lined up for the sake of order, as members of the personal staff. If the funds of the Reichsführung SS were running low, the fact was called to Wolff's attention. The SS had particularly strong ties to the "Deutsche Bank," and Wolff took out loans for the Wewelsburg Castle totaling 13 million marks.

The actual use of the castle for the SS was out of proportion to the expenditure. Himmler held only one Gruppenführer conference there in the middle of June 1941, one week before the attack on the Soviet Union. Obergruppenführer von Bach-Zelewski was fighting the partisans in the east during the war. During the Nuremberg trials he stated that at the castle, Himmler announced that the purpose of the campaign about to begin was to kill 30 million Slavs. Wolff, who had organized the meeting, denied this and maintained that Himmler only spoke of millions of people who would be killed during the campaign.

Himmler's intention to hang the coats of arms, carved in wood, of all the Gruppenführers at the Wewelsburg created a lot of work for Wolff. He asked them all to bring in sketches or at least descriptions of their family crests. If Wolff were to write to any top officials of the Party who held high honorary ranks, like Reichsleiter Martin Bormann and Max Amann (responsible for the press and at the same time publisher of all party papers), he signed as "Your very humble ..." Lower ranking officials, like the Gauleiters, had to be content with a simple "Heil Hitler, Your ..." The letters to the active SS Führers reveal how deliberately Wolff selected his friends. He was on the "Du" (personal) level with

Obergruppenführer Kurt Daluege, Chief of the Ordnungspolizei, and senior ranking SS member behind Himmler; along with Sepp Dietrich, Munich's age-old fighter who, thanks to Hitler's favor, was raised from a beer hall rowdy to the rank of commander of the SS Leibstandarte; and with Hitler's adjutant and confidant Julius Schaub, who always had the Führer's ear. Wolff was on a first name basis with Gruppenführer Theo Eicke, Himmler's favorite, although his reputation was not the best. The same was true of Gruppenführer Oswald Pohl, who was in charge of the concentration camps and also had to provide Eicke with the guard detail. Wolff, however, was closest to "dear Reinhard" (Heydrich, Chief of the Security Police, therefore also of the Gestapo and of the SD, and later the supreme leader in charge of Jewish annihilation). Heydrich was allowed to call Wolff "dear Peter"—a nickname that, at the beginning, only Wolff's wife used for her husband.

Aside from the many aristocrats among the Gruppenführers, hardly anyone could produce a coat of arms. Heydrich and Wolff had already had Comrade Weisthor design such family decorations for them. Ernst Kaltenbrunner, later to become Heydrich's successor, could at least produce a family crest, which his ancestors, scythesmiths by trade, had usually stamped onto the steel of the tools they manufactured. The majority of those addressed had, as did Wolff and Heydrich, to turn to the crest, rune and family researchers of the SS for help. The initiative, however, never came to a conclusion. "Another presentation for after the war," Wolff noted in a colored pencil on the final document regarding this activity.

He also busied himself intensely with the interior furnishings of the castle. When he was told in September 1942 that "a mass of antiques (furniture, porcelain, etc.)" was brought up by the personal staff of the Office of Raw Materials—although these were almost certainly the belongings of the deported Jews—he gave the chief architect of Wewelsburg the task of selecting suitable items. Among the purchases were a Queen Anne coin cabinet, a Chippendale mahogany table, and a Flemish carved oak cabinet. All told, the castle at Wewelsburg bought antiques valued at 200,000 marks in this manner. These values were calculated according to the usual standards of thievery.

In a similarly honest manner, Wolff helped the castle secure another treasure. As the rich cloisters along the Danube in Austria were being confiscated by the Nazi party for transparent reasons, Himmler allowed himself to be guided through the Canon Foundation of St. Florian, near

Linz, where he couldn't help but notice a large round rug that would certainly brighten a large, round room at the castle. Himmler demonstrated his desire so blatantly to August Eigruber, the Gauleiter of the Upper Danube, that Eigruber was left no alternative but to offer the rug as a gift to his prominent guest. The Gauleiter was not so quick with the delivery, however. Perhaps he hoped in this way to keep the valuable piece in his own country.

When once again Himmler visited his castle in the middle of July 1942, he noticed that the rug was not there. Wolff, who accompanied him, hurried to the telex machine installed at the castle and dictated an order. The receiver was the supreme SS Führer of Austria in Vienna, the Gruppenführer Ernst Kaltenbrunner: "The Reichsführer SS requests in as friendly and pressing a way that the Gauleiter remember to fulfill his promise and that he supervise the same."

Two weeks later, Kaltenbrunner reported to Wolff that the rug would be shipped "expertly packed to Wewelsburg in the next few days." Eigruber, however, still did not want to part with his valuable piece so quickly. Kaltenbrunner had to warn him yet again, and after another month the Gauleiter wrote in an abrupt manner to Himmler that he had "already handed the rug over to the Linz state police for further delivery." On August 18, 1942, the captain of the castle at Wewelsburg could finally report to Wolff in Berlin "that the round rug...had arrived. After being unpacked, it was cleaned, de-mothed and appropriately placed in the new museum." The sender of this report was Siegfried Taubert, who, according to Wolff's examination procedures, was given the job following his fist-fighting predecessor. Wolff was promised more tolerance of the Catholics in the region by the new commander, a retired major decorated in the First World War. In the SS, he had the rank of Gruppenführer—this showed the importance given to the castle on the part of the SS leadership. However, when he made a request to have a staff division of the Waffen SS, meaning an armed unit at the castle, Wolff had to tighten the reins. At the same time, he forbade him any intervention into conditions at the local concentration camps. When it came to the concentrations camps, Wolff was always in favor of a strict division of responsibilities.

The practice of plundering for the benefit of the castle was pursued in the conquered East. SS Obersturmführer W. Jordan, who belonged to the teaching staff at the castle as its prehistoric researcher, went to the Crimean peninsula in December 1942. From this rich landscape of ancient culture he sent back whatever treasures he could lay his hands on.

From a professor of archeology who lived in Yalta, he obtained ancient Greek gold earrings, coins, Persian miniatures, a golden phallus from the first century A.D.—everything in exchange for a few meager sacks of flour. In the following shipment he sent gems and Russian coins made of precious metals stamped during the period of the tsars.

This became the treasure of the castle that Himmler wanted to stash away for rainy days. After the war, the land around the castle was meticulously dug up, but nothing was found. Rumors maintained that Taubert had prisoners immure the treasure at the end of March 1945, and he supposedly announced that he would have those workers shot once they had finished the job. During criminal proceedings dealing with crimes at the Wewelsburg concentration camp, no evidence could be found to that effect. Himmler was kept informed when American armored forces were approaching the castle, and he dispatched an SS officer with an engineering squad from Army Group Weichsel to go west in the direction of Paderborn with orders to blow up the castle.

At that point Wolff had no longer been responsible for the castle for some time; he had been working in Italy for over one and a half years. On Good Friday, March 30, 1945, the demolition squad reached the castle that the SS had already evacuated. As the officer realized that the explosives would not be powerful enough to completely demolish the castle, he blew up the main areas of the building and set fires in the parts that remained. He and his engineering squad had hardly left the scene when throngs of townspeople descended upon the burning ruins and dragged away what they could lay their hands on, including some 40,000 bottles of wine, champagne and high-proof alcohol from the cellars.

Wolff's work relating to the SS shrine was no mystery. His task fit in with his vision of the SS as an order of knights and guards. Himmler's romantic ideas may have been bothersome at times because they were wildly eccentric, but the illusions these two gentlemen harbored regarding the castle only differed in minor details. The assignment as chief adjutant was a much more difficult task for Wolff, but one he enthusiastically embraced because it fully corresponded to his inclinations and abilities. He was responsible for supervising and guiding a group of people who made up the core of the German economy. This "Reichsführer SS's circle of friends" that we already mentioned included some three dozen of the most influential industrialists and money managers that met occasionally.

Wolff's role within this circle can only be understood in the context of its formation. Long before 1933, the industrialist Wilhelm Keppler joined the NSDAP, becoming Hitler's business consultant. He collected donations to the party among the membership. When Hitler became Chancellor, these donors naturally did not wish to sever those ties, and the Nazi party did not want the clique to drift apart. Now that Keppler had an office in the Reichskanzlei and had to be present from time to time, he appointed his relative Fritz Kranefuss to take over his duties. Although both the Party and the SA had refused to let him join, the SS accepted him, and Himmler even took him on as his protégé. Because of his leading position in industry, Keppler was able to recruit new members into the circle.

The members of the group were invited by Himmler to attend the Nuremberg party rally in 1933, and the Reichsführer SS assigned his adjutants with the best manners to look after them. Wolff did his job so well that later it was claimed that Himmler's guests enjoyed more privileges than those of the Führer. As a result, Wolff kept this position in the future. Together with Kranefuss, he organized meetings at least twice a year, sightseeing tours, trips, and lectures by the Party greats in which the guests had the feeling that they were being taken into preferential confidence regarding Party plans and initiatives. Whoever was not already a member of the Nazi party could, although the Party remained closed to new members for a long time, still join with Himmler acting as guarantor. In due course almost all these members received the rank of "Honorary Führer," giving them the right to wear the black uniform, decorated with braid and trimmings, as members of the "personal staff of the Reichsführer SS."

In the years after the war, when Wolff was questioned regarding the purpose of this circle of friends, he replied that Himmler wanted to do something about the dealings of certain hyenas of the business world by providing respectable entrepreneurs with rank and influence—"insofar as an economist having anything to do with money could ever be honest according to the SS." This limitation is understandable when one remembers that during the streetfighting years the SS and the SA were singing anti-capitalist songs borrowed from the Communists, with the lyrics being only slightly modified. However, contradicting this explanation, the circle of friends also included directors with bad reputations, such as Dr. Friedrich Flick. On the other hand, Himmler and Wolff were barely fazed when an honorary Führer thinly veiled his aversion to the National Socialist system; as, for example, Hans Walz, General Director of the Stuttgart Bosch Group, with whom regime opponents like Carl Goerdeler and Theodor Heuss later consorted. At one examination in Nuremberg on December 14, 1949, Wolff claimed, "A man like Otto Wolff, for example"—who was said to use cutthroat methods in business—"we would never have accepted because proper behavior was our priority." The examiner asked, "Which particular advantages and which type of protection did the members of the circle enjoy?" At first, Wolff played innocent: "It seemed after a while that those gentlemen came occasionally with different requests," and gave as an example that one gentleman, in the middle of the war, received permission as well as money for a stay at a health resort in Switzerland. When Wolff was reminded that Obergruppenführer Pohl was also a member of the circle of friends, and that he could decide how many concentration camp prisoners would be made available to industrial companies, and that possibly Himmler's friends took rather significant advantages from this membership, he evaded the issue. "At the outbreak of the war, I went to the Führer headquarters as a liaison officer... I found out... about matters only coincidentally from conversations."

Most members considered it below their level to become openly involved in politics, but they appreciated having their backs covered, a service which they bought through their tax-free donations. They were Dr. Emil Helfferich, chairman of the board of HAPAG, as well as his Bremen competitor Karl Lindemann of the North German Lloyd. Heavy industry was represented among others by Dr. Albert Vögler from United Steelworks; the banks by Karl Blessing, later president of the Bundesbank; the insurance companies by Dr. Kurt Schmitt from Allianz; the chemical industry by the I. G. Farben member of the board Dr. Heinrich Bütefisch—all in all, some three dozen men, hardly any of whom fit into the Nazi party's written program.

This was the reason why Heydrich never trusted the circle of friends. In February 1937, however, at the request of his friend Wolff, he was willing to show the gentlemen around the offices of the Gestapo in Berlin and explain their various functions. They were even taken on visits of the concentration camps; in 1937 to Dachau and in 1939 to Sachsenhausen, each time led by Himmler and Wolff. They were, however, also compelled to take part in a midnight celebration on July 2, 1936, at the tomb of the Quedlinburg Cathedral in memory of King Heinrich, called "the Vogler," who had supposedly been buried there one thousand years before. That king, the first from Lower Saxony to sit on the German throne, victoriously fended off storming cavalries from the east; Himmler, the pantheistic sectarian who also wanted to Germanize the east, believed that a part of Heinrich's soul had been reincarnated into his body. And so on that night a crowd of dignified men stood rapt and bareheaded in front of a sarcophagus with Himmler in the lead, his right arm stretched out for the Heil greeting, and Karl Wolff behind him, obviously overcome by emotion. It was later made clear that there were no royal remains in the sarcophagus.

Wolff's task was to gather the donations of the wealthy gentlemen and manage those funds. At one examination at Nuremberg regarding the indictment of Flick, Wolff said on December 16, 1946, "Himmler was no businessman and I took care of banking matters for him. I learned the banking business in Frankfurt at the Bethmann Bank." At another point he added, "We always checked from whom the money came. It took a long time for money to be accepted from I. G. Farben, and the yearly donation of 100,000 marks was earmarked personally for Bütefisch. We only took the money because of the character and importance of Bütefisch. We did not regard the entire I. G. Farben group very highly... For example, we never took money from Otto Wolff in Cologne. We only took money from honorable people." Following this method Himmler's treasury grew from 600,000 marks in 1936 to over 8 million marks in 1944. This went into the "R" account at the Dresdner Bank in Berlin, an account to which only Himmler and Wolff had access. Some money came from the Party directly into the SS treasury, but it was never very much because the stingy NSDAP Reich treasurer, Xaver Schwarz, counted every penny. It then became very important for the concentration camps run by the SS to earn forever-higher profits. Some of the prisoners worked in the SS's own businesses, but in increasing numbers they were being lent out as slaves to industrial enterprises for cash payments.

At Nuremberg Wolff testified, "I initiated this, the financing of these things. I took over the management of the money. I always made sure that the Reichsführer did not spend too much and that he always had money available." And regarding the beginning of this operation, he said, "I suggested to Himmler that he to allow me go to Funk, who if I remember correctly was already Reich minister. I said, 'Mr. Minister, these are our concerns, our wishes and ideas. We don't want to glue paper bags in the concentration camps, but rather perform productively. We need money. For you as minister of trade and commerce, it is surely not difficult to find a way for us to receive a personal loan.' I believe that Funk [Dr. Walter Funk, who had originally been a journalist, then Chief of the Press for the Reich government from 1933, after 1938 Reich minister of trade and commerce, later also Reichsbank president; in Nuremberg he was sentenced to life in prison] got this done with Kranefuss. They were, however, my ideas and the result of my initiative."

With the money from the special "R" account, Himmler—according to Wolff—"helped many people," such as old familiar members of the SS and the Party, those who had gotten themselves into difficult business situations because of their involvement with National Socialism. He also helped the widow of Gregor Strasser, who was shot on June 20, 1934, and had been the former Reich Organizational Director of the Nazi party and was for a time the second man in the Party, after Hitler. The organization "Lebensborn," which shall be discussed further ahead, was also financed. The "Ahnenerbe" (ancestral heritage research unit) received funds. An expedition to Tibet received money. Great sums of money were poured into the Wewelsburg castle. A good number of SS Gruppenführers who were all paid according to the Party wage scale set by Xaver Schwarz—which was fairly meager—were given the opportunity to dress with a bit more style because Himmler approved an expense allowance for them. Wolff, also received several hundred marks every month.

He was given a much larger portion as he got himself into dangerous and potentially damaging financial difficulties with the construction of his home in Rottach-Egern on the Tegernsee. In April 1936 he bought the property on the south end of the lake, 5,500 square meters with its own beach for 17,000 marks. This was already remarkably cheap at about 3 marks per square meter, considering the great demand by prominent Nazis who just came into money. Himmler was also in the process of settling down at the north end of the lake in Gmund.

Wolff wanted to have an ancestral seat for his family. He imagined a ten-room house with a kitchen, bathrooms, and powder rooms, including (as Wolff explained) a toilet for the employees. Due to the high ground water level, the house had to be built into a tub of concrete. At the edge of the lake, there was also a boathouse and bathhouse.

The house had been built by a general construction company, the "Association of Social Building Works Ltd.," with headquarters in Berlin. The DAF (German Workers' Front) represented what passed for labor unions during the Third Reich. Their branch office was in Munich, "The Building Hut" (Bauhütte), was in charge of the building site. During the negotiations, Wolff left no doubt that he was not in a position to spend much more than 40,000 marks on the new construction. Wolff's demands could never be met with that amount; he therefore rejected the first draft by an architect. The drafts by a Munich architect met with his desires, but according to the calculations of the Bauhütte, the house would cost 80,000 marks. Work started following these drafts without a contract for costs and services ever having been drawn up. Additional wishes were also included. When the house was finished, the bill came to over 154,000 marks. After tedious negotiations, Wolff finally claimed he was prepared to pay an additional 40,000 marks, and not a penny more. He wanted to borrow the money. At the end of 1936 the family moved into the house by the lake, without having reached an agreement on the price.

Shortly after, following considerable mismanagement the DAF dissolved its construction company. Court proceedings were instituted against the director, in the course of which the judges also stumbled upon files concerning the Wolff family residence. On May 22, 1939, the Supreme Party Court wrote to the Reichsführer SS in a tone of reprimand stating that even "the acceptance of the already extremely reasonable offer, and then tolerating the construction of a house whose value stood in no relation to the means Wolff had available to him, were not compatible with National Socialist views." Wolff, "by refusing the remarkably reasonable offer and every other privilege, should have avoided even the appearance that he was using his position as a higher SS Führer for his own personal advantage."

The judges also did not soften the fact that Wolff, in view of the uncomfortable complications, offered the liquidator of the bankrupt company the property plus the house as reimbursement for any of his own expenses. They were critical of the fact that "Wolff should have come up with these considerations at the very beginning, and not now, one and a half years after the inspection of the house... It is not even difficult for a layman to recognize whether a house costs 40,000 RM or double or even triple those construction costs... In this situation, Wolff demonstrated behavior that was not consistent with the duties of a Party comrade and high-ranking SS Führer... Only taking into consideration the issuance of an amnesty by the Führer on April 27, 1938, does the Party Court refrain from carrying out court proceedings."

Himmler, however, did not abandon his "Wölffchen." On June 15, 1939, he wrote a pompous letter labeled "Secret Reich Matter" (the formula for a state secret) to Supreme Party Judge, Walter Buch in which he protested this court decision. "If I can completely step in for someone and am totally convinced that he honestly...undertakes something, that is Party comrade Wolff. The only accusation that could be made would be that he was not enough involved in the matter...because he had too much work." Himmler announced that he would discuss the letter of the court "point for point" with Buch "on his next stay in Munich." Because Wolff supposedly had even been cheated with the sale of his Munich house to the Building Society of the German Workers' Front, the Reichsführer also wanted to have Reich Treasurer Xaver Schwarz present at this discussion, so that the "unintentional injustice could be repaired."

The paperwork regarding the family residence dragged on into 1941. Wolff, of course, was allowed to keep the house. In a settlement it was determined that Wolff still had to pay 21,500 marks. Of that amount, Himmler gave him 20,000 marks from the donations treasury; the other 1,500 marks, he let Wolff have as a loan from the NSDAP treasury. To Schwarz, who had stepped in as negotiator, the Reichsführer SS wrote an intimate thank-you letter: "You actually helped me with a tremendous favor. I have gotten to know SS Gruppenführer Wolff's honorable and irreproachable character on a daily and hourly basis in the last eight years, and consider him one of my most valuable colleagues and have personally grown very fond of him as a friend." The heading of the letter was sealed with a stamp "Secret Reich Matter." The matter was now one level less secret; the fate of the Reich no longer depended on its outcome, but anyone who talked in public would be sent to prison. Who, then, had a guilty conscience?

The fact that the chief adjutant of the Reichsführer SS (since November 9, 1935) and especially as the chief of the personal staff of the Reichsführer SS (since November 9, 1936) was overworked may seem accurate from the eyes of his direct superior. Subordinates, however, have always been known to create the impression of feverish activity for their superiors. It was also part of Wolff's careerist ambition to constantly be on the lookout for new responsibilities. In that respect, he greatly increased his own workload. Even before becoming chief of staff, he already supervised the departments of Chief Adjutant, Personnel Chancellery, SS Court, and Auditing and Staff Treasury. Under Wolff's leadership, this apparatus was further expanded. There are many surviving files from his conglomerate of offices. The person who knows this information the best is Elisabeth Kinder at the Federal Archives in Koblenz: "Wolff quickly became Himmler's closest confidante, accompanied him on trips, and participated in leadership responsibilities."

Himmler showed his gratitude in an order dated November 9, 1936. He decided that the chief adjutant, "given the expansion, and over the years, the strongly expanding areas of service," would receive the title of "The Personal Staff of the Reichsführer SS." It was not clearly stated that Wolff's position in the service had the rank of an SS full time officer, equally important to that of full time SD officer Gruppenführer Reinhard Heydrich. However, Wolff's skillful tactics and his ambition to get ahead in the service quickly created the de facto situation of his being actually a full time chief officer, and therefore equal in status to Heydrich, although, as Brigadeführer, he was still a rank lower than Heydrich.

When the two met for the first time in February 1932 at the training course on Theresienwiese, he was still an independent businessman, and being a troop leader recently part of the noncommissioned ranks of the SS, whereas Heydrich already wore the four stars of a Sturmbannführer on the collar of his brown shirt. According to the comparative standards of the SS, Heydrich had reached the rank of major. The troop leader sat, practically unnoticed by ranking superiors and lecturers, among the hundreds of listeners. He had to make due with the role of student, although the teacher had been neither a soldier on the front, nor did he have any decorations. Even worse, it was whispered that he had been promoted to the rank of officer as a professional soldier in the Marines, but had been released with a simple discharge, which was the equivalent of being dishonorably discharged. Heydrich only joined the SS three months before Wolff in July 1931, but started off from the first day in the service as a paid functionary, whereas Wolff joined the black guards "on an honorary basis" until June 15, 1933, a point he never failed to emphasize.

Once the National Socialists entered the government in Bavaria, the two encountered one another more often, one as the chief of the political police in Munich under Chief of Police Himmler, the other as adjutant of the Reichsführer SS. Their responsibilities hardly ever crossed, but the militant, affected behavior of their relationship required the lower ranking officer, even if he was four years older, to give a loud boot-clicking greeting, standing at attention with his arm outstretched in the Nazi salute. At that time, Wolff's collar glittered with three stars (Sturmführer) and Heydrich's sparkled with the Oak Leaf (Standartenführer). In recalling that situation, Wolff often complained in retrospect that he, the fighter from the front and decorated guards officer, had to work his way up from the ranks and as an honorary Führer was promoted more slowly than his full-time comrades.

From the day Himmler took over the office of the secret state police from Göring in Berlin (April 19, 1934), the two deputies were forced to cross paths constantly. Both had their offices next to Himmler's suite; Himmler was their direct superior and both of them were avidly seeking promotion. This alone, even without a clash because of their duties, made them rivals. Wolff occasionally indignantly relates how Heydrich and his Munich team searched the offices of their Berlin colleagues at the time they took office, and also had broken open the locked desks of those who were momentarily absent. Wolff could not, however, afford to engage in any public reprimand; in the meantime he had been promoted to Standartenführer, but his competition was a second silver Oak Leaf richer. Besides that, Heydrich, because of his position as chief officer of the SD, managed matters within his area of responsibility independently, while Wolff, as first adjutant, could only derive his authority from Himmlerorders.

At that time, Heydrich tried to show his higher rank and difference in length of service (although slight) over Wolff by treating him as one who took orders. But he had not counted on the adjutant's best weapon: Wolff controlled Himmler's date book as well as his telephone conversations. Whoever wanted to speak to Himmler had to go through Wolff first—and Heydrich often had to wait. It finally came down to a loud argument between the two of them.

It was Wolff who suggested making peace, as was customary for officers. They sat together one evening at a Berlin wine bar and, when their moods were relaxed enough, they moved to a nightclub. There, each of them invited a lady to their table. In this cheerful setting and according to time-honored custom, they agreed that from this point on, they would work separately and only join forces to defeat their enemies. As Himmler's closest advisors, they could influence the goals and methods of the SS to a large degree. The Reichsführer, they decided, should know nothing of the alliance at all.

They occasionally repeated the excursion into the nightlife, as long as they were temporary bachelors in Berlin and their wives still lived in Munich. Separately they enjoyed themselves on business trips to Munich in an apartment that was used by the Gestapo as a conspiratorial hideout to which Wolff was allowed access. The mutual knowledge of those masculine sins strengthened the friendship. Covered by Heydrich's apparatus of power, by the Gestapo and the SD, the security service of the SS, Wolff could venture into certain hazardous business, negotiating independently, for which he could have received Himmler's consent only with difficulty. On the other hand, Heydrich could count on the fact that any mines that were constantly being laid for Himmler by his numerous opponents would be reported to him far in advance for him to disarm them.

How skillfully Wolff used the situation was shown by his efforts to help two of his old schoolmates and friends from his youth in Darmstadt, Dr. Carlo Mierendorff and Dr. Theo Haubach, who had gotten into trouble as political opponents of the National Socialists,. Both were slightly older than Wolff, but they knew each other from the schoolyard of the Ludwig-Georg Gymnasium, which according to Wolff was the "oldest high school in Hesse, attended by the sons of the top families!" They not only knew each other from school, but they also often went swimming and occasionally to the "Dachstube," a loose group of high school students with literary ambitions that grew out of the German Youth Movement. At the outbreak of the war in the summer of 1914, they were all under the spell of the same fervent enthusiasm for the Fatherland, and every one volunteered to join the Kaiser's army as soon as possible. Mierendorff and Haubach both returned as officers decorated with medals of courage.

But then they had a parting of the ways. At the beginning, while Wolff tried to remain in the Reichswehr as a lieutenant, and then for lack of a better offer became a banker's apprentice, the two friends went on to the university and joined up with socialist-leaning academic circles. Mierendorff became part of the leadership cadre of the Social Democratic Party based on a paper of his on the unions, and in 1930 he was the youngest representative to be elected into the Reichstag. Haubach graduated from the university and entered the Prussian ministry of the interior as a consultant, after an interim position as an editor of the Hamburg SPD daily newspaper. The two friends both became active in leadership positions in the "Black-red-gold Reichsbanner," the militant formation of the leftist democrats.

The Nazi regime assumed that such "enemies of the state" had to be "re-educated" in concentration camps and, at the same time, prevented from engaging in any further political activity. As the great wave of arrests in the spring of 1933 seized the leading Social Democrats, Mierendorff was in Switzerland. He returned because, so he says, he would never again be taken seriously as a politician had he emigrated then. He and Haubach were arrested and sent to a concentration camp. At least during the first years of Nazi rule, Wolff viewed the concentration camps as necessary to keep the political opponents "from standing in the way of German happiness." He could certainly not ignore that behind the barbed wire there were often cases of abuse and sometimes even torture and murder. Because it had happened in the past, however, that political opponents had attacked, injured, and even killed National Socialists, he could understand up to a point that some of his comrades wanted revenge. Someone had to do the dirty work. A clean glove often hides a dirty hand.

Therefore, he had no reason to worry about his old schoolmates too soon. It took quite a while before he was told of their plight. But as he went to the Reichstag as the representative from Darmstadt for one of Hitler's ninety-nine percent elections at the end of March 1936, he was asked to help. The cries for help from the dignitaries of his hometown were ringing in his ears, mainly from a woman who lived in Berlin, whom he had met at the Römheld house in 1919 and who was a friend of his wife-to-be.

As in many other instances, he was ready to help. One cannot tell how far the feeling of justice, simple kind-heartedness or the satisfaction of showing his friends and acquaintances the kind of power he actually could wield, actually drove him. Wolff had the friends from his youth brought to his office in 1937, after almost a four-year term in the concentration camp. During a conversation lasting several hours, he convinced them to refrain from any future political activity, so he could vouch for them with the Gestapo. Both were then released to freedom. Wolff got Mierendorff a job that paid 800 marks monthly, not a bad salary according to the standards of the time. It entailed looking after the social and cultural affairs of the employees at the central German Brabag (Brown Coal and Gasoline Corporation), whose business director Fritz Kranefuss was a close acquaintance through connections at the "circle of friends." Haubach was given a position in Leipzig with a friend who was a paper manufacturer.

Wolff undoubtedly found out from his friends what they had to endure during their time in the concentration camp. Mierendorff had been at the Hessian camp Osthofen, which the SA had kept during the first months after the takeover of power, without government authorization, and where the prisoners had been sadistically abused. After that, he worked in the quarries of the Papenburg-Bürgermott camp, then moved to the Torgau camp, and then was released from Buchenwald. Haubach told of the murderous work at the Esterwegen camp. The files of Himmler's personal staff, however, do not have any documents showing that Wolff made any note of these reports of inhumanity, even just for the record. In this situation, he could have easily intervened, as he was a close friend of the supreme commander of the concentration camp guards, SS

Gruppenführer Theodor Eicke, as well as with the supreme chief of administration of all camps, Gruppenführer Oswald Pohl.

On the other hand, Wolff's old friends never actually thought of keeping their promised abstinence from politics. Mierendorff used business trips that took him abroad to establish contacts with those having the same purpose and to exchange news. He was well aware of what he was risking. To one conspirator he said, "From now on it can only get better—to victory or to the gallows." He was wrong. On December 4, 1943, he was killed during an air raid on Leipzig.

Haubach joined in with the "Kreisau Circle," which had established itself around Count Moltke, and kept in contact with the resistance groups around Wilhelm Leuschner and Julius Leber. He was told of the plan to remove Hitler by assassination, and then with the help of the military to bring down the Nazi regime. But as Count Stauffenberg's bombing attempt failed, and the revolt of the officers was nipped in the bud, Haubach was also arrested in the onslaught of mass arrests. In January 1945, he was sentenced to death by the People's Court as one of the conspirators and executed.

The woman who initially sought Wolff's aid was, however, increasingly in danger. According to the Nuremberg Race Laws, she was Jewish. Elisabeth Aron, who was the same age as Wolff, was the daughter of a professor of jurisprudence at the Strassburg Reichs University until 1918. When the French took back Alsace after the First World War, he was expelled to Germany. He went to Darmstadt. There, his daughter befriended Frieda von Römheld and her dancing partner and future husband. When Elisabeth Aron studied in Munich, her friendship to the now married Wolffs continued. She was living in Berlin when Wolff reached the Führer honors in the SS, but letters and visits kept the relationship from drifting apart.

"Despite the fact that the deputy to the Führer had forbidden it, he did not break his friendship with me after the seizure of power," said Elisabeth Aron solemnly after the Second World War, as former SS General Wolff, like all prominent Nazis, was arrested and began searching for witnesses (for his "denazification" according to the regulations of the victorious allies) who would vouch for his good behavior during the Third Reich. That Rudolf Hess, of all people, who was allowed to carry this deputy title although he was never credited with having any particular competence, looked into the offensive behavior of a higher-ranking SS Führer may actually bolster Wolff's claim to fame. Had this been the case, then the chief of the Hess administration, Martin Bormann, would have made sure to see that Wolff was degraded because along with Himmler's favorite, the Reichsführer SS would have been humiliated as well.

Karl Wolff's Jewish friend still certified that he protected her "from serious problems through his personal intervention," and took care that she be allowed to maintain her livelihood in Berlin, although her business competitors had enlisted "Der Stürmer," the fanatical anti-Semitic and its rabble-rousing readership, against her. "In the spring of 1942," it further states in the report, "the attacks against him because of me became so strong that he told me he could no longer help me." Six months later, on September 6, 1942, the Gestapo picked her up when the remaining Jews in Berlin were transported to the east.

About three months before, SS Obergruppenführer Reinhard Heydrich, chief of the RSHA and therefore in charge of all persecutors of the Jews, was assassinated in Prague. Wolff's ally, his support in critical situations, was gone. From now on, if he wanted to protect any Jews, he could only turn to the responsible Gestapo specialist, Adolf Eichmann. Someone like Wolff, it is not hard to imagine, could not deal with the likes of Eichmann. Or he had to seek the assistance of Eichmann's direct superior, the chief of the Gestapo (Amt IV in the RSHA), SS Gruppenführer Heinrich Müller.

"Heini" Müller was a police officer in Bavaria until the Nazi seizure of power—that is until March 1933—as an inspector in the political department of the Munich police precinct and a strict member of the clerical Bavarian People's party. Heydrich kept him in that position when he took office because Müller had advertised himself as a communist hater, immediately praising his new masters, and was ready to serve them with equal eagerness. His industriousness, his experience, his criminal tracking sense and his harsh bureaucratic savvy allowed him to rise quickly in official, and therefore also SS, rank. He had already become Gruppenführer when, on October 19, 1942, he wrote the following letter to Obergruppenführer Karl Wolff, who was one rank above him.

Under the seal "Geheim Reichssache" ("Secret Reich Matter") Wolff read:

> According to a report from the SD Main Branch in Chemnitz dated September 27, 1941, SS Scharführer Dr. of Philosophy Kurt Möckel, a chemist, born on July 19, 1901, in Zwickau, resident there, had told an SS Führer, among others, that he had heard from a Frau Bechstein, Berlin, that SS Gruppenführer Wolff in the Staff of the Reichsführer

> SS was having a relationship with a Jewess and could not, despite warnings, break it off. Möckel, who was questioned about this, admitted to the facts. According to his description, Frau Bechstein, who was friends with his parents, had raised the above-mentioned reproach in the company of the family in 1937 or earlier. In response to Möckel's reply that something had to be done about it, Frau Bechstein answered that everything had been done, but to no avail. But since the situation never led to any unpleasant consequences, and had taken place quite some time before, I saw to it that SS Scharführer Möckel was instructed not to repeat any such rumors in the future. In any such occurrences, he was only to report to the department. In the name of the deceased SS Obergruppenführer Heydrich, I admit to being aware of the facts of the case. Heil Hitler! Yours, Müller.

The letter is quite uncommon in more than one respect. After the address in the officially correct form, the letter is not directed to anyone, as was otherwise normal among SS Führers, even if they did not particularly like one another. The entire text had no personal nuances, aside from the "yours" at the end, the only evidence that the sender and the receiver had known each other almost a decade. In correspondence among the staff, there is hardly any similar trace whereby a high-ranking SS Führer wrote so officially and distantly to a higher-ranking officer.

It is also noticeable that the Gestapo head Müller picked up a case that had been reported to him a year before—eight months prior to Heydrich's death. Perhaps he saw to it that the letter remained where it was, unattended. But why was it pulled from the files now? At any rate, Wolff was accused of "shaming his race" (the term for having sexual relations with a non-Aryan), and, according to the laws of the Third Reich, this was most definitely punishable with a prison sentence, and unavoidably carried the consequences of being kicked out of the Party and the SS. Frau Bechstein, the woman mentioned in the letter, was the wife of the piano manufacturer Carl Bechstein, who liked to call herself a "motherly friend" of Hitler. She also supported the Party with money at the beginning of the 1920s. The Führer and Reichskanzler no longer needed her support, and she was no longer allowed among his closest entourage, but among old Party comrades like Himmler, she was still regarded quite highly.

The final sentences of the letter are also peculiar. Müller says that the matter was already filed away, but he pointed out to Scharführer Möckel that if "the situation came up again, he was to report it." Even more improbable was that Heydrich, who had died five months earlier, had given him the task of writing this letter.

All this leads to one conclusion, that the paper was more than simply informing Wolff of a trifle. One can read between the lines Müller's threat that this claim could always be checked, and even more effectively since the Jewess involved in the case had been in the hands of the Gestapo for a month. During the war years, Wolff was constantly at the Führer headquarters, and there he became one of the courtiers whom Hitler especially valued, possibly even more so than Himmler wanted. The Reichsführer SS watched suspiciously, anyway, that none of his underlings could become dangerous to him. After Heydrich's death, he led the RSHA himself for a short time before he entrusted Obergruppenführer Kaltenbrunner with it. These two could have had an interest in dampening Wolff's ambition. Wolff himself was known to say that during the fall of 1942, he felt Himmler's growing irritation, supposedly only because he wanted to divorce and marry another woman. One would have liked to ask Heini Müller about the purpose of his letter. But he disappeared without a trace after the end of the war, in the ruins of Berlin.

If one believes Wolff, then there was no rivalry between him and Heydrich. That may be true insofar as neither was envious of the other's position. The bloody handiwork of his friend would most certainly have gotten to Wolff's conscience; more importantly, it would have been too vulgar for him to consider. Conversely, Heydrich would not have been able to stand the pressures Wolff was exposed to from different sides. Thus, they competed for influence over Himmler. In this regard, Wolff's judgment of Heydrich was not without animosity. He complained about his looks, which somewhat deviated from the Nordic race, which Wolff believed to embody perfectly himself. He found Heydrich acceptable above the navel, but called the wide hips womanly and un-Germanic. This also encompassed the gray eyes, which coldly peered out of thin slits. Because of this, when Himmler was annoyed with Heydrich's personal ambition, he always laid the blame on several ancestors from the hordes of the Mongolian ruler Genghis Khan.

On his part, Heydrich apparently complained occasionally to his wife about Wolff's intrigues. In her memoirs, *Life with a War Criminal,* Lina Heydrich mentions that Wolff achieved something like a "key position in Himmler's entourage" but not just through his soldierly sincerity. She states rather acerbically that Wolff lacked "every prerequisite for a political career," and was predominantly busy "in the area of human relations"—

sending congratulations, handing out flowers, and receiving petitioners. "In that respect, he became indispensable." One does not exactly hear any particular respect for his intelligence in any of this, but the question is how could Lina Heydrich be responsible for such a judgment?

Karl Wolff, on the other hand, felt very capable of managing tasks of a highly political nature with style. Thus, Himmler opened up to him one day, that in the case of his sudden death, he had suggested to the Führer two men—namely Heydrich and Wolff—from whom he could choose to be his successor. "One of the two," Hitler supposedly replied to Himmler, "will have to do it. Please put both of them in the picture." With this statement he could only have meant that Wolff, as well as Heydrich, was to be instructed by the Reichsführer SS about the issues and orders within his jurisdiction. Himmler thought that the choice would depend on the situation: for difficult times, Heydrich would be better than the contemplative Wolff. Lina Heydrich sees this differently. As she realized, so she tells, that her husband practiced "the most dreadful of all professions" (she does not say whether she means the supreme police officer or the mass murderer), he said, "I have to do it. Any other could misuse the system." To that, his wife answered, "Mr. Wolff would certainly have abused it."

Wolff, who was enraged by this, maintained the opposite. Germany's most supreme police officer was a henpecked husband, and had a difficult time finding much to say to his wife Lina, who was a stubborn Fresian born in the east. Reinhard, a friend who was four years older, complained from time to time to Wolff of his family problems. Since Heydrich had his little affairs here and there, he had to accept that when his wife flirted so conspicuously with one of his commanding officers, Walter Schellenberg, inevitably there was talk among the Nazi circles. According to Wolff, Lina did this only to force her husband to pay more attention to her.

According to Wolff, the upper echelon of the SS leadership complained about their high-ranking comrade. If he could not even make his own wife march in step, it raised doubts as to whether he could master greater leadership tasks. That was an unfortunate error, because Heydrich organized the murder of the Jews with diabolical perfection. However, caught in his officer's club standards, Wolff sent his wife Frieda to warn Lina Heydrich. Was this out of friendship? Or was it rather more like a reconnaissance patrol? Lina Heydrich claims in her recollections of Wolff that intrigue was "not foreign" to him. She was not the only one to make such a statement.

Once Lina Heydrich became a widow, Heinrich Himmler showed more concern for her than she wanted. He did not like the fact that she wanted to continue to play a prominent role, and that she increased her claims regarding benefits because her husband died in the fight for the Führer, the people, and the Fatherland. Hitler saw this differently. At the table in his headquarters, he said to his listeners that a man in the position of Protector of the Reich has to reckon with an assassination attempt, and if he rides through Prague in an unarmored car, one can only describe it as "stupidity or mindlessness."

Since Wolff had not been the chief of Himmler's personal staff for some time and was serving in northern Italy as "Highest SS and Police Chief," he received the order to ensure that Lina Heydrich understood that she was to move away from Nazi society, which was ruled solely by men, and back into private anonymity. This was the reason he invited her to Meran for a rehabilitative vacation in the spring of 1944—far enough away from his headquarters on Lake Garda but still close enough to keep her under control. He found her appropriate accommodations in the marble splendor of the Park Hotel, and, so she would not get bored, she was allowed to bring her son Heider and one of her friends. Heydrich's mother was also in Wolff's care. Himmler warningly pointed out to him that there was considerable tension between her and Lina Heydrich. "Mother Heydrich," noted the Reichsführer SS, "is a good woman; however, she has never in her life been able to keep herself busy." In addition, she is always unfavorably influenced by her son-in-law Heindorf, "a man of little value... The disadvantage is only that in taking care of the mother... Heindorf and his wife, Heydrich's sister, must also be included." A few weeks before the end of the war Wolff visited with Lina Heydrich for the last time. She was living on an estate in Bohemia that had belonged to a Jew who had fled. For a time, she had counted on it becoming her property, but Himmler hesitated in making the transfer, and since the Red Army was approaching, all these plans went up in smoke. One day in 1945, Wolff arrived unannounced at the estate. On a trip to Berlin with the plane made available to him because of his position in Italy, he had made a short stopover at a nearby airfield. He was now quite clear about the outcome of the war, unless it was still possible to split the western Allies from the Soviet Union in the final hours, and march with them to the east. He warned Lina Heydrich that within a short time all the Germans in the protectorate would be in great danger because of the Red Army and even more so with the Czechs clamoring for revenge.

Chapter 3

In the Good Graces of the Führer

That Wolff was allowed to spend the last and (he rightly believed) most significant phase of his career in Italy was not a coincidence. He counted a number of Italians among his many friends. These friendships were made as Himmler once again indulged in his foreign policy ambitions and spun some threads to Rome, only with Italian police officials, so that professional foreign policymakers could not claim that he was getting involved in extraneous responsibilities. At that time, the beginning of 1936, Hitler was well disposed towards such an outsider operation because his admiration for Mussolini and his regime was being less and less reciprocated, as Austrian Nazis were pushing harder to come "home to the Reich." The danger for Italy was that instead of the weak Viennese State at the Brenner Pass—Italy's northern border—the much stronger German Reich could encourage the South Tyrolians' allegiance to the nationality of their forebears on the other side of the fence. This was the reason why in June 1935, General Pietro Badoglio and French General Gamelin signed a secret document in which the armed forces of their two countries agreed to proceed together against Germany were the Reich to force the annexation of Austria.

In the meantime, sympathies between the fascist State and the western democracies had soured once again once Mussolini expanded Italy's African colonial territories by attacking the Kingdom of Abyssinia (today's Ethiopia). It was still too early for a friendly meeting of the two dictators. They met for the first time in the middle of June 1934, and it was a disappointment for both. Hitler was looking for a partner who would support his planned foreign policy adventures, and Mussolini, overestimating his own strength, was too smart for that. Now that Himmler was extending his feelers to Rome, Mussolini needed a new friend. The rest of the world was against him because he had attacked a primitive people with bombs and poison gas while they defended themselves against the invasion with spears and arrows.

For all these reasons, when Himmler had the idea to hold an Italian-German police conference in Berlin, it happened to be just the right moment for both countries. On March 29, 1936, the Italian delegation arrived in the capital of the Reich. It was a Sunday. Three weeks before, Hitler had once again dissolved the Reichstag. Just as the Italians were getting out of their sleeping cars at the Anhalter train station shortly before 9:00 a.m., Germans all over the country were preparing to show their trust in their Führer and Reich Chancellor by putting an X on the election ballot. Candidate Karl Wolff could count on the fact that, as of the coming Monday, he would be a member of the Reichstag, because for the first time he had been found worthy to hold such an office. Flags with the swastika were flying in all the streets, and black and brown uniforms proved to the new arrivals that the German dictator sat no less secure in the saddle than the Duce in Rome.

The key man of the delegation was His Excellency Arturo Bocchini, chief of the Italian police, a high-ranking fascist leader. But as much as he praised the culture of ancient Rome, he indulged himself in the luxuries of life developed during the time of the Caesars. These obese, short-legged Sybarites and cynics, of all people, were the ones the purist Himmler was seeking to be friendly with, and in his footsteps so did Standartenführer and Chief Adjutant Wolff. The visit lasted five days. It ended with a grand evening meal in Berlin's finest hotel. The Reichsführer SS made sure nothing was left out; if his guest still wanted to amuse himself in the late evening after the end of the program, the German Reich then also paid for his intimate entertainment.

Six months later Himmler traveled to Rome with a vast entourage to repay Bocchini's visit. On the occasion of the Day of the Italian Police, they swore to fight communism together. Wolff interpreted this later as the beginning of the alliance, the Pact of Steel and the anti-Comintern Pact. This conference was actually a celebratory business excursion, and whoever took part received medals as decorations from the Italians, from the Reichsführer down to the lowliest coat carrier. For Himmler, the Great Cross of the Order of the Crown of Italy was an appropriate decoration to display at his home. Karl Wolff, Reinhard Heydrich, and Kurt Daluege, chief of the Reich Ordnungspolizei, were served with a lower version of the same medal, earning the title of "Grand Ufficiale."

An expert in the art of living, Bocchini would have passed for a miserable host had he not offered his colleague from the north the very best Italy could give, both on this visit and those that were to follow. Himmler only barely took advantage of this largesse. He only enjoyed eating and drinking moderately because his painfully nervous stomach prevented him, and by midnight at the latest, when the men became lively and, as tradition had it, the wives were sent home, he usually went to bed alone. According to tradition, the Italians took their guests to a plush bordello, for their own entertainment as well, because in such cases, the entire establishment was paid out of tax revenues. Wolff and Heydrich always avoided such free enjoyment. They knew the secret of Berlin's Salon "Kitty," which the chief of the RSHA had set up for visiting dignitaries, and equipped each room with microphones.

At those meetings, the black uniforms from the north always met the black shirts from the south (the fascist uniforms were also entirely black, including the shirts) in the most solemn ceremonies that were the staple of totalitarian systems. When Hitler met with Mussolini for the first time in 1934 in Venice, mistakes made by the protocol section made him feel like a country bumpkin trying to look important in front of his experienced model. In September 1937, as the Duce's return visit to Berlin was being prepared, things had changed considerably for the Führer and Reich Chancellor of the German people. He could boast several successes: the Saar had returned to the Reich in 1935 after a people's plebiscite organized by the League of Nations. To strengthen the Reichswehr, which had been limited by the Treaty of Versailles, compulsory military service was reinstituted in March 1935. The air force, forbidden up to that point, was now being rapidly built up. The navy received new ships, legitimized by a naval agreement with England. Germany and Italy had protested together against a Franco-Soviet alliance. Since the summer of 1936, German and Italian volunteers were fighting in the Spanish Civil War on the nationalist side led by General Francisco Franco against the Republicans. The fascist military did not exactly cover itself with glory during that war.

Hitler was now somebody! He was eager to change the impression he made in Venice. Whatever was necessary for pomp and circumstance between September 25 and 29, 1937, was produced more to dazzle the guest than to honor him. Gruppenführer Wolff, who in the meantime had been named General of the SS Provisional Troops (a preliminary stage of what was to become the Waffen SS), was assigned as the Duce's honorary escort. Why was he was chosen for that particular assignment? He hardly spoke a word of Italian, but he was regarded as one of the most representative figures in the Nazi leadership, and rightly so. Tall, blond, blue-eyed, strong with his military officer's bearing, he embodied the ideal German hero; he had an aura of sophistication and know-how with his officer's club manners, and on official visits to Italy he had always quickly made friends with the local dignitaries.

Wherever the illustrious guest went, from the greeting at the border train station at Kiefersfelden on September 25 to the breathtaking festivities from September 27 to 29, Wolff was always only a few steps behind Mussolini when he was not at his side. Understandably he felt that he was at the center of history. Historians, however, measure the significance of the meeting between the Duce and Hitler more as a decorative exercise than a significant political event. It was a play, staged by the propagandists of politics, meant to persuade the world and themselves of the friendship between two countries and their combined power.

Mussolini's state visit was the occasion that filled SS General Wolff with great pride, earning him lavish praise and respect from both dictators, and opening the door to a rapidly rising career. It occurred on the afternoon of September 25, 1937. During the course of the morning, the Duce was greeted at the Munich train station by a group of a hundred people accompanying his host. After both dictators reviewed several lines of men standing at attention with frozen expressions, and adjourned to Hitler's private apartment where he was appointed by his guest as an Honorary Corporal in the Fascist Military—a rank the Führer already found annoying, since the Germans placed it between private and noncommissioned officer.

Wolff enjoyed being within arm's reach of the Duce at that ceremony as well as at the midday luncheon in the newly constructed Führer building. However, he was not allowed on the balcony from which Hitler and Mussolini observed a parade of party units. This was, it later turned out, his luck and that of the other participants. Line after line paraded in their Prussian goosestep on the concrete underneath the balcony. The high-stepping legs impressed the guest so much that he decided to introduce something similar in the Italian army. Wolff was very pleased that the highpoint of the show would be the march of the "Leibstandarte of Adolf Hitler."

The brass band led the marching units with "The Badenweiler March, Tempo 114 Steps." The drum major was marching out in front. With his baton, he signaled to turn so that the musicians would clear the street for the following companies. But his cutting arm movement was too wide, and because the staff lay only loosely in his right hand, it flew straight up in the air, before it turned over high above and finally landed, smashing back down on the concrete. The first men of the first company, the tall black uniformed high-steppers, would reach that spot in a broad marching line in a few seconds. Inevitably, the staff would make many party soldiers fall. They would end up under the boots of the soldiers following close behind, causing many more of their comrades to stumble. Without a doubt, there would be injuries and maybe even deaths, but even worse for the hosts would be the embarrassment that the elite troops, of all people, had failed.

Wolff reported that everyone escorting the two leaders was frozen on the spot with fear. He was the only one to not lose his nerve; he ran onto the road without a moment's hesitation, disregarding all soldierly regulations and rules of protocol, and snatched the drum major's staff out of the way of the relentless beat of the approaching boots just in time. Wolff: "Although, as lieutenant general (SS Gruppenführer), wearing a steel helmet and dagger, I was not really intended to pick up the staff." The spectators breathed a sigh of relief, the prominent guests as well as the crowded citizens of Munich who were being cordoned back behind the uniformed guards. Wolff claims that his deed was rewarded with applause. When the parade ended, Hitler and Mussolini thanked him for his quick-witted and courageous act with a handshake.

According to Wolff, Hitler said, "Whenever the Reich happens to be in danger, may an SS man step in."

As brave as the deed was, it would not go down in history. It was never mentioned in any newspaper articles nor shown on any news program; mistakes are not allowed at the highest level. But even though kept quiet it was not forgotten. From now on, Wolff could count on a great deal of goodwill. He had (as the former bank employee would say) a rather high personal credit limit, and not only with the two main personalities of the show. Wolff: "Up to that point, I was a second-class man, but by the grace of the Führer, I was moving higher up." Three months later, the Italian ambassador in Berlin placed the medal of the "Holy Mauritius and Lazarus" around his neck, which also gave him the privilege of being addressed as "Commendatore." He found it a bit unfair that Hitler did not also hang some colorful enamel jewelry around his neck. Somewhat indignantly, he remembered that in Hapsburg Austria there had been a Maria Theresa medal awarded for particularly courageous deeds that were performed voluntarily and spontaneously, as long as they did not contravene an order or any custom. Such a reward did not exist with Hitler, but from now on, Wolff was almost always on hand when the supreme Fascist and the highest ranking National Socialists would meet.

It is difficult to ascertain what advantages the Germans got out of the friendship extended between the SS and the fascists. The always-congenial Wolff, however, did meet a number of Italian diplomats with whom he would have to deal more closely many years later. Himmler's friendship with the obese police chief, Bocchini, remained politically one-sided, but did bring certain personal privileges for the otherwise very particular Reichsführer SS. Every year, towards the end of the year, an invitation would come for him and his wife to take a trip south, under the guise of a business trip, allowing it to be stretched into a longer more relaxing vacation. On one of these trips, he even visited the North African coast of Libya as a guest of Italian air marshal Balbo, who was the governor.

A number of further attempts by Himmler and Wolff to reap additional foreign laurels was less successful. Instead of the expected approval from the Reich Chancellor, there were complaints from the foreign office, which did not like others hunting in its territory. Joachim von Ribbentrop, who jealously protected his area of responsibility, protested loudly. The disputes with the Reich foreign minister went back to the time he was still ambassador to London, and did not actually end until the final days of World War II, when for the government in Berlin "foreign" meant beyond the Oder River in the east and the Elbe River in the west.

The idea of creating a link to England was presented to Himmler at the beginning of 1935 by the U.S. citizen W. A. de Sager, a native Swiss who was living in Great Britain. In conversations with Himmler and Wolff, he discussed how he could use his connections in the English upper class to stop the atrocity propaganda in the Anglo-Saxon press, meaning any reports on the concentration camps, the harassment of Jews, the persecution of the critics of the regime—in other words, those who were undermining the German government's reputation. He promised to create a friendlier atmosphere towards Hitler's regime at the U.S. embassy in Berlin. He further planned to write a book in English that would contribute greatly to rehabilitate Germany.

Wolff and Heydrich sent de Sager to see Gruppenführer Theodor Eicke, the commander of the SS Death's Head units that guarded the concentration camps. He was allowed to visit the camp at Dachau, which was being specifically denounced abroad. An apartment in the distinguished Bendlerstrasse in Berlin was made available to him so that he could invite foreign press correspondents and traveling Anglo-Americans, as well as the relatives of foreign ambassadors to social occasions. Every now and then Wolff found his way there. On May 8, 1935, de Sager arranged a meeting in this apartment between Himmler and United States diplomat, Finsterwalde.

If de Sager did not exaggerate matters for Himmler's benefit, then the American with the German name was open to Hitler's ideas and the methods of the SS. The U.S. ambassador, William D. Dodd, was said to be biased, however, because his daughter was the lover of Dr. Rudolf Diels, a high-level official in the state of Prussia whom Göring had placed to head the secret state police in Berlin during the takeover of power. He was then apparently pushed out of office by Himmler and, therefore, did not speak favorably of the SS. However, the ambassador, influenced by an opponent of the regime, was removed one year later, as reported by de Sager, and with the help of Mr. Finsterwalde his successor would therefore be better informed right from the start of his assignment.

By mid-July 1935, Himmler and Wolff were informed in writing by their propagandist de Sager as to which prominent Englishmen he had convinced of the respectability of the SS and the Reichsführer during his eight day visit to London. De Sager gave himself credit that due to his lecture concerning the concentration camps and his observations in Dachau, he was able to prevent a huge debate in the House of Commons, which would inevitably have led the English government to issue a protest to the German government. In this speech, de Sager placed the responsibility for torture and murders exclusively on ousted Gestapo Chief Diels. Himmler and Wolff did not correct that error, although they knew that Diels actually shut down a number of the illegal camps that were tolerated by the Party and run individually by single SA or SS units. These also happened to be the worst torture camps.

De Sager took some Englishmen with him back to Germany. Two of these were former officers representing the British Legion, an association of war veterans, and were even smuggled in for a visit to Dachau. They provided a written statement that "after intensive inspections" they felt, "contrary to news of atrocities widely spread around the world, that it was very wise to keep such racially and politically inferior elements in camps." They were invited to a dinner with Himmler and Wolff. In the brotherly atmosphere of a late hour, they bestowed upon Himmler (who never served at the front) honorary membership in the British front fighter's association, and invited him to make a return visit to London.

When all this was reported by German and foreign newspapers, the German foreign office protested loudly, demanding in writing who at the "communications staff of the NSDAP," a link between the Party and the State, had authorized this person "Herr de Sager or de Sage" to handle German concerns. The office dispatched its chief of protocol, von Bülow-Schwante, and Count Dohna, whom Wolff had been friends with at the Darmstadt high school, to investigate at de Sager's Berlin apartment. Wolff's charm had almost managed to settle the matter with these two gentlemen. However, the German ambassador in London (at that time it was still Joachim von Ribbentrop) felt it necessary to summon this unauthorized foreign policy operative of the SS to his London residence. "I did not receive the slightest encouragement from him," de Sager reported to the Reichsführer SS.

Regardless, de Sager continued to send prominent Englishmen across the North Sea to visit Germany. Among them House of Commons representative T. C. R. Moore, retired Admiral Sir Barry Domvile, and a married couple, the Pinckhards, whose living room was the meeting place where London's elite would congregate. They were all invited one after the other, by Himmler, to his house at the Tegernsee, where, after their inspection of Dachau, Wolff's refined conversation helped make it clear to them that life behind barbed wire could be beneficial to certain people. They all agreed to a reunion in London that, according to the guests, should take place "as soon as you [Himmler] are able to speak perfect English and I am capable of speaking perfect German."

This sudden friendship across borders faded rather quickly. Mrs. Ruby Pinckhard was suspicious that when they continued on their journey to Switzerland, her passport was scrutinized with obvious mistrust. "I heard," she wrote to Himmler, "that officials read the name 'Ruby' aloud and became particularly attentive." This happened in November of 1935, as increasing numbers of Jews were emigrating. Then, in her living room, Himmler's emissary de Sage and an exiled Ukrainian named Korostowetz, who was also a frequent visitor, made vague insinuations, accusing each other of being a paid German agent. Himmler apologized in a letter. He insisted that the strict passport scrutiny was meaningless; and he failed to mention that the name Ruby could possibly sound Jewish to border officials trained in anti-Semitism. He assured Mrs. Pinckhard that the Ukrainian gentleman had no connections to the SS, and that de Sager was simply a friend of the new Germany.

In the end, de Sager exaggerated his demands in London by attempting to convince his pro-German friends to secure an invitation for the Reichsführer SS to speak in the House of Commons. However, the English sympathizers set a few conditions: Himmler must master English sufficiently, must address the treatment of the Jews, the dispute between the NSDAP and the Christian churches, and Hitler's imperialistic goals as described in the National Socialist Bible, *Mein Kampf.*

Himmler was neither willing nor allowed to do anything of the sort. In addition, the ambassador to London, Joachim von Ribbentrop, had by now become so alarmed that he issued a protest to Hitler that foreign policy was none of Himmler's business. Hitler now had von Ribbentrop in mind as the future foreign minister, and therefore the Reichsführer SS was now in danger of being barred from the Reich Chancellery. Ribbentrop suggested that if Himmler felt it necessary to discuss politics with foreigners, then it should at least take place on a one-to-one basis and within the confines of a private conversation. De Sager's activities had to stop, as they were generating nothing more than expenses.

Another attempt at success in the east also ended in dismal failure. Himmler started with the Arabs, who displayed a special dislike of the English as colonial rulers. In March 1938 retired Prussian Lieutenant Ottmar Hubert Baron von Gumppenberg-Pöttmes-Oberpremberg (as his name appeared on his business card), spoke to Himmler's top adjutant at the Four Seasons Hotel in Munich, offering his services to the Reichsführer, should Adolf Hitler be interested in pursuing a policy of friendship with the Islamic nations. The leader of the Pan-Arabic Movement, His Excellency the Emir Shekib Arslan, whose following had grown from 70 million to 120 million during the voluminous correspondence with Wolff and Himmler, was an especially close friend of the baron and intended to visit Germany very soon. If the government of the Reich were interested in a connection to the Pan-Arabic Movement, this was a unique opportunity. Gumppenberg would gladly arrange a meeting.

The long aristocratic title, the military rank of officer, a common aversion to the Jews—all of this pleased Himmler a great deal, and he therefore instructed his staff to take good care of this connection. As the baron then handed in documentation about his military work as well, where he not only served with the Prussians and participated in the First World War, but also fought under the Albanian and Turkish flags as a riding master, the confidence among the SS staff grew to the point that they finally began a promising activity. He even appeared to be useful to foreign intelligence because during the First World War he had stirred up the North African Senussi tribes in Libya into invading British-ruled Egypt.

At the end of May 1938, a few days before the Emir's arrival in Munich, Gumppenberg finally wanted to know how far the SS was willing go in receiving him as a dignitary. He recommended that accommodations be paid for by the Reich for a first-class hotel (an apartment suite with a large living room), two servants or adjutants, and a luxury car with a chauffeur for his personal use. For his part, the emir wished to be received by Hitler, Göring, and Himmler. He wished to take this opportunity to express the congratulations on the part of the Arabs for the annexation of Austria to the Nazi Reich.

When the visit was just about to take place, Wolff advised the Reichsführer that with Heydrich's help he may wish to make a final check by inquiring with the foreign office and with the chief of the Abwehr, Admiral Canaris, about whom they would be dealing with at that meeting. Wolff wanted to be on the safe side. Because the emir had already arrived in Munich, Himmler's secretary, Dr. Rudolf Brandt, had to reassure the baron over the phone on May 30 that "the small attentions given to the emir would certainly signal that he would be received."

But even that was promising too much. On June 2, the Gestapo sent a telegram from Berlin to the Reichsführer SS, who was in Gmund am Tegernsee waiting for a call from Hitler from the nearby Berghof. Afterwards Canaris' Abwehr categorically denied that the emir had any kind of leadership role among the Arabs, while the foreign ministry pointed out that they were dealing with a very old Arab who therefore had little influence. Baron von Gumppenberg should in no way be brought in as negotiator, because he was simply discharged as a lieutenant from the Royal Prussian Army "on suspicion of homosexual activity." For that reason alone, Himmler was compelled to break off any connection with him; since the Röhm affair, all homosexuals belonged in the concentration camps when they were not immediately killed.

Himmler and Wolff could not always afford to stand on the side of morality and virtue. In an attempt to topple a corrupt gauleiter, the Reichsführer almost fell out of favor with Hitler. This outraged Wolff so much that he once again toyed with the thought of ending his career in the SS and moving back to the regular army. The matter concerned the professional party functionary Erich Koch, who had worked in the Ruhr region in the 1920s, at times together with Albert Leo Schlageter, the national martyr who was shot by the French for sabotage. Hitler later sent Koch to East Prussia as gauleiter in 1928 because of constant grumbling among ambitious and aggressive party comrades in that region. There the upper class—the landowners, rich farmers, and the wealthy bourgeoisie—was traditionally nationalistic and therefore also tied to the German National People's Party. They only agreed that the "drummer" Hitler was to play the role of preparing the return of the Hohenzollern monarchy. If Koch had wanted to win followers for the Nazi party at that time, he had to begin with those who felt exploited by the landed gentry and the industrialists. In a province that was then separated from the Reich, "nationalism" was taken for granted (since the neighboring Poles and Lithuanians occasionally rattled their sabers), the workers, the petty bourgeois and the industrial proletariat were receptive to the social components of the National Socialist program.

Koch's propaganda was especially effective with one particular profession: the poorly paid estate managers who had to watch while the money they earned was spent so generously by the squire and his family. As long as they were intelligent and industrious enough, Koch recruited his functionaries and SA Führer from among these people. Some improved their meager income through embezzlement. Whoever was let go for that reason was given the chance by the gauleiter to work for the party full time. He therefore managed to create a devoted guard dependent upon him as well as on the success of the Nazi party. Whoever joined the movement after the seizure of power found all key positions in East Prussia already occupied—with one exception: Koch had always placed the SS at a disadvantage in his Gau, and now that they had the possibility of spreading out, the so-called "better" people felt attracted to a unit that kept its distance from the plebeian SA.

The wealthy in the agrarian economy received strong support from Richard Walther Darré, leader of the German farmers, Reich minister of nutrition, SS Obergruppenführer and chief of the Race and Settlement Office. Those functionaries in the farming community for whom Koch's high-handedness went too far, suspected him of "Bolshevik methods." He reacted by excluding them from the Party and arresting them. Darré, called on to help, proved to be powerless. Much worse, Koch threatened that whoever continued to oppose his policies could sit in "the big Moorbruch" (a concentration camp) and "think about who was right." When Himmler advised him to use moderation, Koch played dumb.

Darré called the Supreme Party Court, but before the bureaucratic machine got moving, Koch made some small concessions. Those agricultural functionaries excluded from the Party were once again allowed to pin the swastika on their collars, but they were to officiate in another Gau. However, during the first investigations by the party judges in Munich it became clear that there were even more suspicious things going on in the East Prussian Gau. Higher Party functionaries had used their positions to enrich themselves privately. Koch was not just tolerating it; he led the way with the worst example. He had gotten the National Socialist Gau newspaper going years before by forcing the Party comrades to subscribe. Now the paper was flourishing and became part of the profits of the "Erich Koch Foundation," whose funds only Gau leaders and a few front men he had picked were allowed to touch. Because the foundation also handled a real estate business and pulled in a lot of money through the so-called Aryanization of the property of Jews who were emigrating, it had already become one of the economic powers in eastern Prussia. Koch had been a follower of the left, the Strasser wing of the NSDAP, while he was in the Ruhr region for a time. Now he cynically announced that his foundation was community property and, therefore, a model of National Socialism.

The Chief of the Supreme Party Court, the puritanical ex-officer and Reich leader Walter Buch, wanted to clean up this swamp. He led legal party proceedings against Koch, seeking to exclude him from the NSDAP. To no avail. His son-in-law, Reichsleiter Martin Bormann, and part of the office of the deputy to the Führer tried to warn him. He enjoyed the special trust of the Führer and knew that Koch was therefore protected at the highest levels. Buch remained stubborn; he persuaded two other Reich leaders, namely Heinrich Himmler and Reich treasurer Xaver Schwarz, to go with him to Königsberg to examine the accused and the witnesses. These three should have known from their many years of experience that Hitler appreciated moral defects within his leadership because it always gave him a reason to oust those who had fallen out of favor. The three should have also known that Koch knew a state secret that would lead to foreign policy complications if it became known to the victorious Allied powers: the Party and the Reichswehr in East Prussia were involved in military training together of the so-called "white generation" who, since the First World War, could no longer become soldiers. Heavily weighing in Koch's favor was that he was the first gauleiter who reported to his Führer that no one in his Gau was without work. As propaganda, this was of extreme importance—after a time (eighteen months before) when over six million people were without work and without income.

Koch had even another ace up his sleeve. As the net closed in around him, he avoided any further comments by seeking protection from Hermann Göring in Berlin. As Prussian prime minister, Göring was his employer, due to the fact that as Gauleiter, Koch was also president of the East Prussian province. Because Göring had difficulty giving up the Prussian police to the SS, he helped Koch by making a recommendation to Hitler, and in doing so became popular with other Gau leaders who viewed the SD as an agency which also kept a close eye on them. As a reward and as thanks, Reich Rifle Master Göring was allowed to shoot a couple of deer at the former imperial hunt at Rominten in East Prussia. The deer could not be more royal anywhere else in Europe.

The three Party leaders who were so set on righteousness were ordered back from Königsberg, including Wolff, who had accompanied Himmler. Party judge Buch was immediately subjected to the Führer's displeasure, so strongly in fact that he took a long vacation afterwards. Himmler referred back to Buch's competence and got off fairly leniently. Wolff felt deeply disappointed. He saw in Koch, in his type, manners, and character, "someone low class who had risen up in the world," and a "major embarrassment" to the Party. Much later, when Himmler and Hitler were long gone and Koch was in a Polish prison, Wolff claimed that he openly requested release from the Party and the SS, and intended to join the army.

This was why he and Himmler had words—Wolff told the story rather often. First energetically and then furiously, the Reichsführer ordered him to keep his position, and since this didn't help, Himmler began pleading. It was then that Himmler promised him that he would receive an honorable discharge within a reasonable time, but secretly had him placed on the list of candidates for the upcoming Reich elections. This way, supposedly without having anything to do with it, he was elected by the Darmstadt constituency to Parliament on March 29, 1936. Propelled into the limelight with publicity of this kind, he had to forego stepping down.

But this explanation does not hold. Parliament had become meaningless because Hitler had been ruling through the Enabling Act since 1933. The only interesting thing at each election was to see how close the results had been pushed to a ninety-nine percent approval rate of Hitler's policies. For the representatives there was nothing left to do in the "talking shop"—as the Nazis had taken to calling the Reichstag at the time; their few sittings as well as their votes were preprogrammed. Because of this, an election was forgotten a few days after it was held in the precincts. The representatives, forgotten as well, were mocked by the people as an expensive men's choir. After every session (they met at the most a couple of times a year), the gentlemen sang national anthems and the Horst-Wessel. Each singer received 7,200 marks as a yearly salary, namely parliamentary allowances, and free traveling on all the trains of the Reichsbahn. All of this surely helped Wolff deal with the fact that he must remain in the SS. Besides that, Himmler assured him that they would now fight more strongly against every type of corruption together, and naturally against Koch and Göring as well.

Instead of a fight, however, it became an alliance. It was directed at the leading circles of the army. They balked at Himmler's plans for the Waffen SS. The leadership of the Waffen SS had accepted the existence of the SS Leibstandarte. The SS Death's Head unit was not recognized by the Wehrmacht leadership because they guarded concentration camps and the soldiers would have nothing to do with them. The military resisted every attempt to set up more armed SS units with a statement by the Führer, according to which the Wehrmacht should be the only armed unit of the nation.

Göring already stood above such basic disputes. Since May 1935 there was an official air force and he was its chief. The army still resisted the Luftwaffe setting up its own anti-aircraft defense and intelligence unit. For that reason, the "fat one"—as the people called Göring because of his growing size—lay in wait for an opportunity to reduce the influence of the generals. This occurred as the minister of the Reichswehr, Werner von Blomberg, who was promoted by Hitler to General of the Army for his accomplishments in establishing the Wehrmacht, married at the age of 60. After many years as a widower, he wed Erna Gruhn, a Berlin woman who was 34 years younger. Within a few days, a scandal broke out that took on the appearance of a state crisis. The conclusion could be anticipated. Neither Göring nor Himmler, who both wanted to use the situation, profited significantly. Only Hitler succeeded in strengthening his absolute dictatorship.

Since Wolff, at headquarters, was in charge of supervising the secret state police on Prinz-Albrecht-Strasse, he felt he was at the center of events. He had held the rank of SS Gruppenführer for a year and was, besides, the first SS Führer to be named lieutenant general of the SS Reserve troops. These troops, with Blomberg's agreement, were allowed to recruit up to 25,000 men alongside the police and the army. Wolff was, however, not allowed to wear the heavy-braided rank insignia of general that was a source of concern to him. He described the events of those days, as he saw them, in a manuscript that he offered to book and newspaper publishers on many occasions.

Wolff reported that the relationship between the Reich minister of war and the young stenographer from Berlin began in a Thüringen hotel to which Blomberg had retired for a short holiday. He wanted to remain unknown and free of worries, but the hotel manager had the impression that his prominent guest felt lonely when he sat alone at his table during meals. And so Blomberg was asked if perhaps a young lady from the group of guests would be welcome. Erna Gruhn pleased the General of the Army so well that the father of three daughters and two sons did not break off the relationship even after his return to Berlin, and soon after he proposed marriage to his companion. Before that, he had requested that Göring, by chance, ask Hitler if the supreme leader had any objections if a noble minister of war were to marry a simple girl. The Führer, as Wolff reported, was very pleased that the people could be shown in such a spectacular manner how far the new open-mindedness of a national community without class barriers had already stretched. The wedding on January 12, 1938, a Friday, took place within a small circle, but because Hitler and Göring came as best men and the propaganda effect was obvious—photos chosen by Hitler himself appeared in all the newspapers. The couple was already on a honeymoon by that time.

As an officer of the Berlin vice squad made his rounds the next day, some "professional" ladies waiting for customers in a pub called his attention to a newspaper article and exclaimed, "That's our *good friend*, Erna!" The officer reported this immediately to his superior, who, after thinking about it, had someone leaf through the files. It came to light that Erna Gruhn had ended up in her mother's massage salon (a high-class brothel), and was temporarily suspected of prostitution, but had never been convicted.

For the officer, the case became so hot that he was afraid he might get blamed for it. He carried his files to the chief of police, Count Helldorf, himself. He also hesitated with his decision; he had the relevant ladies thoroughly interrogated, and since the facts in the case remained unchanged, he took the files to General Wilhelm Keitel, chief of the Wehrmacht office in the war ministry on Bendler Strasse. Keitel was a friend of Blomberg. Helldorf asked him if the photo that lay on the vice squad table indeed was a picture of Frau von Blomberg. The answer being positive, he asked for advice as to how the embarrassing situation should be dealt with. This took place on January 23. Wolff objected strongly because the count had not taken the files immediately to the highest police authority—Heydrich or Himmler. But this didn't happen because Helldorf, as SA Gruppenführer, was still angry at the SS leadership about the Röhm massacre. It is probable that Helldorf would have liked to pass the buck of making a decision to the Wehrmacht. This would not work out because even Keitel was not quite sure who the woman in the photo actually was, and therefore suggested asking Göring, who as a witness at the wedding ceremony had seen her up close.

It would be interesting to find out from an eyewitness how Göring reacted to the news—whether or not he had already known about the matter for quite some time, as a few people suspected. It is easy to imagine, however, what went through his mind as he realized that Blomberg had been the Reich's longest serving war minister. Who would be his successor? The list of candidates was very short. The next candidate was the army chief, and in practical terms the supreme commander of the army, General Werner Baron von Fritsch, a dour personality, a strict Prussian monarchist, and one of the most talented soldiers of the Reich. Next on the list within the Wehrmacht going by rank was General Hermann Göring himself, who had risen from the rank of retired captain to general without a hitch, thanks to Hitler's approval. For him, it was a great temptation to trip up the front-runner, and he could claim that his Party comrades viewed Fritsch as a reactionary.

Göring, forever the intelligent and experienced intriguer, quickly hatched a plan. Along with Fritsch and Blomberg, he had been invited by Hitler to the Reich Chancellery less than three months before, on November 5, 1937. The Führer had announced his intention to wipe Czechoslovakia and Austria from the map in a short time. Fritsch contradicted him, warning this would mean war, probably on two fronts, a war Germany was bound to lose. Blomberg and Reich foreign minister Konstantin von Neurath, who were also present, voiced the same concerns. Since then, there were rumors circulating about Fritsch being sick, and the demands of his office having become too heavy for him. Indeed, the general had been in Egypt for over a month to cure a stubborn bout of bronchitis. There is nothing to substantiate the claim that the Gestapo was watching him, or that he had sexual relations with local men.

The reason for any such surveillance reached back some four years. In November 1933, a small-time 29-year-old gangster named Otto Schmidt observed an elegantly dressed man (wearing a coat with a fur collar, a white scarf, dark hat and monocle) in the Berlin Wannsee station in conversation with a male prostitute, Martin Weingärtner, who was waiting for customers. The two disappeared into a dark corner of the train station, and Schmidt observed them engaging in homosexual practices. After the two had separated, Schmidt stopped the elegant gentleman near the Potsdammer Platz, pretending to be a detective. His victim produced an officer's identification from the Reichswehr, asked for discretion, and was relieved of 2,000 marks in hush-money in the course of the next few weeks.

Two years later, Schmidt ended up in the clutches of the Berlin criminal investigations department (the Kripo), under suspicion of other blackmailing activities. After many denials, he felt he was going to be set free without criminal charges because he involved well-known men in the examination, thereby threatening a scandal. He admitted that he had also extorted money from Reich minister of economics Walter Funk, Potsdam chief of police Count von Wedel, tennis champion Gottfried von Cramm, and from a high ranking military officer by the name of Fritsch.

The examining officer at Kripo no longer felt he could handle a case of such proportions. He transferred Schmidt, along with the relevant files, to the "Reich's Center to Fight Homosexuality," a branch of the Gestapo. The head of that unit was Criminal Inspector Josef Meisinger. When the Nazis took over Heydrich transferred him to the Munich political police after years of spying on the NSDAP, turning him into a zealot by not firing him or even packing him off to a concentration camp. With Schmidt, Meisinger had at last found his great case. He showed Schmidt a photo of the general, with his name in the caption, and quickly secured the desired result, "That's him!" He had read the same name on the officer's identification card, "von Fritsch." The incident went all the way up to Hitler, but remained unread; Himmler therefore had to take the "garbage" back. The army chief at that time was in the process of transforming the Reichswehr into the Wehrmacht, making many changes. Hitler was not about to have him disturbed by something so insignificant.

But now in January 1938, Fritsch stood in the way of Hitler's plans. Himmler and Göring knew this. They both had to prevent him from becoming minister of war instead of the more flexible Blomberg. Wolff did not know which of the two came up with the idea to extract the Schmidt file from the archives. On Hitler's orders, it had been for the most part destroyed, at least the parts having to do with Fritsch. But Meisinger was able to complete the file incredibly quickly. This all happened with such dispatch that just a few days after the Blomberg wedding, a Gestapo official was searching for the house on Ferdinand Strasse in Berlin in which Schmidt had collected his money from the alleged General Fritsch. Such prompt reaction could even support the suspicions, expressed here and there, that the SS top brass and Göring already knew all about Erna Gruhn's life before the marriage and were only waiting for the minister of war to destroy himself and leave his post.

On January 24, 1938, Hitler returned from the Berghof near Berchtesgaden to the Reich Chancellery in Berlin. The following day Göring presented him with the Blomberg and Fritsch files. It is reported that in receiving them, the dictator had a nervous breakdown, but no one can swear to the fact that the great actor was giving a performance worthy of the stage. Blomberg was called back to Berlin immediately. Fritsch had already completed his vacation in Egypt. On January 26, Hitler received the minister of war and made it clear to him that he valued him as much now as before, but that the generals in the High Command were demanding his discharge. He could naturally have the marriage annulled because he had been deceived. Blomberg refused this solution; he loved his wife and especially in the face of such bad luck, would not leave her.

Hitler asked him whom he would recommend as successor. Blomberg named General von Fritsch. Hitler replied: "No, he's leaving, too!" The next name was Göring. "It won't be him!" Hitler decided. Then Blomberg recommended that the Führer and chancellor take over the ministry of war in addition to his other duties; this would absolutely be the best solution. The suggestion was more than convenient to the Führer who could then refer to Blomberg's advice when addressing the generals.

On the same evening Fritsch came to the Reich Chancellery. Hitler had forbidden the accusation from being revealed to the general before that moment. He had prepared a theatrical coup, which was meant to lead to a spontaneous confession. But his Wehrmacht adjutant, Colonel Friedrich Hossbach, had not kept to this scenario and had given Fritsch a rough idea as to the nature of the accusation. As the general entered, only Hitler and Göring were present in the room. The chancellor reproached him, citing the results of a detailed investigation regarding an offense against paragraph 175 of the military code. Fritsch indignantly denied the accusation. From the adjacent room, Schmidt was led in and Hitler asked if he knew this gentleman, pointing to the general.

Schmidt: "Absolutely. That's Herr von Fritsch."

It made no difference that the accused solemnly protested that he had never seen Schmidt. Hitler was determined to follow his plan to demote any of the men who did not support his course of aggression and expansion.

There followed a short but bitter argument among the Wehrmacht, the Gestapo and the ministry of justice as to who would handle and manage the case going forward. Hitler would have preferred special court proceedings, but later agreed that only a military court had jurisdiction. He demanded, however, that the Gestapo conduct the investigation. Fritsch was repeatedly interrogated by the Gestapo and confronted with the blackmailer one more time. He naturally stuck to his statement, because he knew what would happen if he capitulated. The Gestapo questioned many boys who had served under Fritsch during his career as an officer. They arrested the world famous tennis champion Gottfried von Cramm as he returned home from America, and also had him testify.

Two members of the Hitler Youth whom Fritsch regularly had as his lunch guests for a time were also questioned. This was part of program at the NSV [National Socialist Welfare Organization] whereby wealthy Nazis tried to help the children of poor Berlin families by having them as guests, not simply to offer them a hearty meal but also to improve their intellect. Fritsch tried to teach the boys some geography, cartography, and military history. Wolff claimed, and he may have gleaned this from his friends in the Gestapo, that the general was in the habit of hitting his young guests on their bare calves with a ruler if they didn't pay attention during the lessons. With apparent expertise, Wolff called this type of corporal punishment "calf fetishism," considering it as the sexual aberration of an unmarried soldier—or something of the sort. There was some truth to that accusation.

Actually, the proceedings took a completely different course than the one Hitler, Göring, and Himmler had wished. Fritsch's defense attorney, Rüdiger von der Goltz, the Reich court advisor, Colonel Hossbach, and Admiral Canaris went to great lengths, along with other friends of the accused, to refute the statements made by the blackmailer, Schmidt. They found the weak point in the intrigue because the real victim of the Gestapo's man in custody was a retired riding master named von Fritsch, who confirmed everything that Schmidt and the male prostitute Weingärtner told the police.

It was then discovered that the Gestapo had known the truth about the case since at least February 15. On that day, an officer questioned von Fritsch. Members of the military court chosen for the case suggested to Hitler that he order that the proceedings stopped. The Führer demanded that the blackmailer should first withdraw his statement. The hearing was then set for March 10, 1938.

As usual, the accused was asked at the beginning of the main proceedings if he pleaded guilty. Fritsch denied the accusation, but the witness Schmidt confirmed it relentlessly. The hearing was unexpectedly interrupted on that day for what appeared at first to be mysterious reasons. The news quickly filtered through that the Austrian National Socialists in Vienna and other cities were conducting mass demonstrations against Chancellor Kurt von Schuschnigg because he wanted to thwart Hitler's plan to seize power through a popular election. Göring was adamant that Germany needed to take action and, later, during the crucial hours, he actually managed the Anschluss (or annexation) of the Ostmark, as Austria was now called, to the Reich.

As the proceedings against Fritsch resumed—again with Göring presiding—Hitler returned to Berlin. His followers in Austria were still celebrating his and their victory in a sea of swastika flags, parades and proclamations using the motto "One people, one Reich, one Führer." But the situation in the courtroom had not changed; Schmidt kept on accusing Fritsch relentlessly. However, on the next day, March 18, 1938, as the prosecution had nearly exhausted all of its possibilities and began fearing it would have to accept an acquittal duc to a lack of evidence—which would have the effect of a charge of not-guilty—they successfully got their last witness, the blackmailer Schmidt, tangled up in contradictions during questioning

Then Göring, the crafty tactician saw his opportunity. Because the prosecution threatened to fall apart, it became preferable to have the Gestapo take the blame of persecuting an innocent person and thereby secure the good will of the generals. He attacked the already stuttering witness Schmidt by shouting, calling him a complete liar and demanding his confession. Schmidt admitted, "Yes, I lied."

Fritsch was found not guilty, but he never returned to his office. On February 4, he had already received his written discharge from the active Wehrmacht from Hitler, taking into consideration his health and his "repeated requests"—which he had never presented—to be allowed to retire. Blomberg was also discharged on the same day. Göring was promoted to General of the Army, General Keitel was appointed to chief of the supreme command of the Wehrmacht (OKW). Hitler took over as war minister and as supreme commander of the entire Wehrmacht, fourteen generals whom Hitler considered as defeatists were retired, the career diplomat Konstantin Freiherr von Neurath was removed as foreign minister and replaced by former champagne salesman Joachim von Ribbentrop, and the ambassadors in London, Tokyo, Rome, and Vienna were removed from their posts. All of this, as well as the annexation of Austria, had taken place before General Werner von Fritsch was acquitted, and in the wake of such momentous events, the verdict became insignificant news to the public, which did not comprehend that Hitler had now cleared the path for a foreign policy of violent aggression.

Two facts from this entire matter are worth mentioning. Wolff reported that Blomberg's adjutant von Friedeburg, with whom he was friendly, had asked him before the wedding to discretely request a character reference on Erna Gruhn from the police. But before the answer came back, Friedeburg had to report for duty in Kiel at the navy supreme command. Had the police actually checked their files, and SS Gruppenführer Karl Wolff would have found out about this woman's past life before she was married. Naturally Himmler and Heydrich knew the truth. Why didn't they warn Blomberg? Or did they share their knowledge with their Führer in the end? It would have been consistent with Hitler's penchant for deceit to let things take their course for the leadership of the Wehrmacht to be humiliated, like the SA had been.

If the head of the SS actually let Minister Blomberg be destroyed by the scandal, then he would never have any entrée to the military. Several weeks after the affair, Himmler, Wolff and the former minister met unexpectedly at the Four Seasons Hotel in Munich. Wolff recalled that Himmler was asking lamely, "What do we do now?" He suggested that they act as though nothing had happened; and Blomberg was so grateful that they happily shook hands.

Fritsch, on the other hand, remained irreconcilable. He never wanted anything to do with the SS again. For his rehabilitation, Hitler did only what was absolutely necessary. The general was too proud to request anything more. He dropped out of public life completely and reproached the generals for not backing him up more vigorously. Wolff explained this attitude in a different way. It was made clear to the retired general that his "calf fetishism" would lead to criminal charges if he did not remain quiet.

When the Fritsch trial was so unexpectedly interrupted on March 10, 1938, the Austrian emergency also involved SS Gruppenführer Karl Wolff. With Himmler he prepared lists of prominent members of the SS that were to be given the task of handling the change of system in the so-called Ostmark. Wolff was most certainly present and active according to the heading "Medals and Decorations" of his personnel file entitled "Ostmark Medal."

The annexation of Austria to the Reich had been planned for years, and now came somewhat unexpectedly. Since the failed putsch by the Austrian SS in July 1934, when Chancellor Engelbert Dollfuss was killed, a bitter struggle ensued between the Nazis and the governing Fatherland Front that viewed itself as a cross between clericalism and monarchist Fascism. In February 1938, the situation appeared as somewhat less explosive; Hitler and Chancellor Kurt von Schuschnigg had agreed at the Berghof that the National Socialists of Austrian nationality would no longer be persecuted, but would, on the contrary, be part of the government. Hitler even held a conciliatory speech at the Reichstag. But three weeks later, Schuschnigg, following Hitler's pattern, announced during a speech in Innsbruck that just four days later during a referendum his compatriots would confirm that they wanted a free, German, independent, social, Christian and separate Austria. Schuschnigg's opponents, besides the many followers of Hitler, also included Marxists and the anti-clericals, who rightfully suspected that he simply wished to underhandedly increase his authority and tighten his fascist course, locking up those who differed in his version of concentration camps. Many protest demonstrations began in many parts of the country; he decided to have the Austrian army security forces take over. Until then his protector, fascist leader Benito Mussolini, had warned him that this was a bomb that could explode in his hand and destroy him. Indeed the police became unreliable in some areas, stepping in too lamely against the demonstrators and beginning to cross over to the rebels.

In this situation, Hitler decided to support the protesters, with force if necessary. With instructions to the Wehrmacht, codenamed "Operation Otto," he directed, "It is in our own best interest if this whole operation takes place without the use of force by marching in peacefully, and being greeted by the people." However, wherever resistance appeared, it was "to be broken absolutely and ruthlessly by force of arms." This was to prove unnecessary. Wherever the "Reich Germans"—the name the Austrians gave their invaders—appeared, whether soldiers, Party members, or the Führer himself, they were met with jubilation, flags and thick rows of people with arms with outstretched high into the air. Since every important Party leader in Austria was expecting to inherit something, Himmler wanted to step in quickly with an entourage of Reich officials and Party organizations already in place before the competition could start. On the evening of March 11, 1938, just as Schuschnigg, under the pressure in the streets and with the threat coming from the Reich, offered his resignation as head of the government, the Reichsführer's raiding party was ready to leave Berlin. He and Heydrich had donned their new combat uniforms—a new design that from then on became standard among the top SS leaders during Hitler's more aggressive operations.

At midnight on March 11, Hitler and his team boarded two Ju 52 transport planes at Berlin-Tempelhof airport. Besides the Reichsführer SS, Wolff, Heydrich, Obergruppenführer Kurt Daluege, and a cohort of Gestapo officials, armed SS soldiers—mostly SS men fleeing from Austria—were also on board. The three-engine planes were significantly overloaded. Walter Schellenberg, responsible for foreign espionage within the SD, maintains that he possibly saved Himmler's life on this flight. The Reichsführer was leaning on an unlocked door during the flight, and Schellenberg grabbed his coat and pulled him back, fearing the door could fly open.

Both planes landed at the Vienna-Aspern commercial airport on March 12 at 5:00 am. Wolff was surprised that he and his fellow travelers had no opportunity to engage in acts of heroism. Dr. Michael Skubl, the Austrian minister of security himself, gave them a very friendly welcome. Until then, he had dealt rather roughly with the National Socialists, but now he warmly welcomed the guests from Germany. He could even justify the change: since Schuschnigg's resignation he no longer held office. Dr. Arthur Seyss-Inquart, a Nazi, had practically taken over in Vienna by then. Himmler and his three warriors, Wolff, Heydrich, and Daluege (each one of them over six feet tall) were invited to inspect an honor guard before getting into the cars belonging to the State of Austria to be driven into the city. Outfitted with machine guns and appropriate ammunition, they must have appeared somewhat out of place, especially Schellenberg, since he was under orders to immediately place Dr. Skubl under arrest.

Himmler's raiding party was not the first enforcement group to come in from the Reich. The South Germans were closer and therefore arrived earlier. For example, Josef Bürckel the gauleiter in Rhineland-Pfalz, who in the fall of 1935 after the vote in the Saar, took his region back into the

German Reich and had experience in the quiet use of the iron fist method. Even Hitler's economic advisor, Wilhelm Keppler, was already in Vienna with his staff. Rudolf Hess, both as Reich minister and as deputy to the Führer for Party matters and who had no duties to perform, arrived by train. This was why Himmler's entourage spent time securing quarters for the days to come. For Himmler, Wolff and the SS staff commandeered the Hotel Regina while the Gestapo took over the Hotel Metropol. Then Himmler and his inner circle, without having had enough sleep, had to drive to Linz to meet the Führer.

On March 12, at 8 in the morning, soldiers of the Eighth German Army had removed the barriers at various border crossings, supported by cheering Austrian customs officials and police officers. Pressed by enthusiastic crowds, their convoy could only progress very slowly. But the streets were not really blocked until shortly before 4:00 p.m., when Hitler arrived in his birth city of Braunau. Because their motorcade was being constantly interrupted by Wehrmacht convoys and throngs of cheering spectators who could only be held back with difficulty, Himmler and his men met up with Hitler about 15 kilometers west of Linz. It was already dark when they arrived. From the balcony of the Town Hall in Linz, Hitler then gave an uncustomarily short speech to the waiting crowd. He spent the night in the Weinzinger Hotel on the banks of the Danube.

On the following day around noon he visited his parents' graves in Leonding, a few kilometers west of Linz. Himmler and Wolff were allowed to accompany him. The rest of the day continued with the Führer's circle handling state business regarding the issue of whether a Nazi Austria should be allowed some degree of independence or whether, along with annexation and the Gau structure of Germany, the entire program was to be implemented. Not until 10 a.m. the next morning did the caravan get underway to Vienna. As usual, they progressed slowly and arrived in the capital at 5:30 p.m. Hitler and his closest followers, including Eva Braun, moved into the Imperial Hotel. Eva Braun was Hitler's lover and had just arrived from Munich. Hitler had supposedly spent his wretched years before the First World War in Vienna shoveling snow to earn a few pennies, and since then it was his wish to enjoy the luxury of this hotel as a guest one day.

For twelve hours, SD Führer Walter Schellenberg maintained that he was responsible for the security of the Führer in Vienna. Wolff claimed that he had also been temporarily entrusted with Hitler's life and freedom from bodily harm. Since Hitler spent only 24 hours in Vienna—like many

Austrians from the provinces, he did not care much for the capital city—from 5:30 p.m. on March 14 to his flight at 5:00 p.m. on March 15, both gentlemen must have been competing furiously with each other on this occasion. For, despite all that has been reported about that day, neither one ever mentioned the other. Actually that responsibility must have been more symbolic than real, since the usual escort unit, the professional bodyguards, the admirers and favor seekers were naturally always present in Vienna. Accordingly, Wolff could not have done much more than serve as a coat carrier on that afternoon of March 15 following Hitler's triumphant speech, when he was allowed to lead his Führer from the balcony of the Hofburg to Geli Raubal's grave.

Geli was the daughter of Hitler's half-sister Angela Raubal, and nineteen years younger than her uncle Adolf. He had her come from Vienna to Munich before the seizure of power because supposedly he wanted her to be trained as a singer. She had a room in his Munich apartment on Prinzregentplatz and soon became his lover, although it was rumored that she did not take loyalty all that seriously. Apparently niece and uncle had come to a strong disagreement, because on September 18, 1931, she shot herself in her room with one of Hitler's pistols while he was on his way to Nuremberg. His Party comrades informed him, and he drove back immediately. He was a psychological wreck for days. If one believes Wolff's account, the glorious victor of the Anschluss wore a very solemn expression at the grave.

During those turbulent days in Vienna, Himmler and Wolff had time to scrutinize several prominent prisoners of the Gestapo. Quite differently from the opponents of lower rank who vanished into the concentration camps where Schuschnigg had imprisoned the Austrian Nazis up to this point, people of rank and status were held at the Metropol, the new Gestapo headquarters. In these elegant rooms the officials lived, worked, and celebrated. For Schuschnigg and his ministers, the attic was good enough, where the waiters and kitchen help were lodged. The rooms, the furniture, and the sanitary fixtures had been neglected for years.

In one of those rooms, furnished primitively with a table, chair, closet, and an iron bed, the visitors met with Louis Freiherr von Rothschild, head of the bank of the same name, in Vienna, and who was connected to the worldwide company of the banker dynasty through family and business ties. The prisoner was under the constant watch of a detective as the Gestapo wanted to avoid an attempted suicide. For a man used to living in a palace since he was a child, this was a very unusual situation, but he was still better off than the Jews from Vienna's Josefstadt, who were being chased in the streets by the rampaging Nazi rabble and forced with kicks and blows to scrub the concrete with water and a broom.

When Himmler and Wolff stepped into the attic room, they were amazed: Rothschild was not in any way like the picture they had conjured of a "financier Jew." He was thin, of medium height, with reddish-blond hair and, according to Wolff, had "radiantly blue eyes." As he rose from his chair and silently scrutinized his visitors, his expression remained so distantly serene, as if he were receiving two of his employees. The somewhat embarrassed Reichsführer SS foolishly asked, "Do you know who I am?" Rothschild stated his name and rank. Himmler promised that he would gladly fulfill any justifiable wishes, whatever he understood those to be. The prisoner expressed no wishes. When asked about his expectations for the future, he said that it would most likely take a long time before it could be agreed upon what was to be done with him and his property. After Himmler inspected the room for cleanliness in the typical manner of a sergeant, he ordered that the bed, table and chair be exchanged for newer furniture and that the toilet seat and washbasin be replaced.

Baron Rothschild had guessed correctly: he was still a prisoner of the Gestapo a year later. There were no specific accusations against him, but being a very wealthy Jew was enough. According to National Socialist standards, he had to be one of the most powerful members of the "secret Jewish world government." It was to be his luck that there were still Germans who did not take such obscure fantasies seriously. Among them was one of the banker's colleagues, Dr. Kurt Rasche, a member of the board of the Dresdner Bank and a member of Himmler's circle of friends. Frankfurt banker Cornelius Freiherr von Berenberg-Gossler was also part of the group. Wolff had become friendly with his son when he was an apprentice at the bank in Frankfurt in 1920. Both moneymen were asked to help Rothschild by business friends in Paris, and both went to the always-jovial Gruppenführer, Karl Wolff.

Whether or not it was his recommendation alone that brought about Rothschild's release from prison several weeks before the outbreak of the Second World War during the summer of 1939 with permission to travel to France, must remain open. Wolff, however, was to claim this as his achievement later on. At that time, he was having constant arguments with his close friend Heydrich, the head of the RSHA, because he wanted to blackmail Rothschild for millions in ransom money—in foreign currency of course. He wanted use those funds to set up Jews wishing to emigrate, because upon entering their new countries, they had to show large amounts of money per person, thereby certifying that they would not quickly become burdens to the local public welfare systems.

Ten years after the annexation of Austria, when only rubble, death, and crime remained of the glitter of the Third Reich, Wolff was in the prison in Nuremberg for the International Military Tribunal. He had Dr. Karl Rasche, who also was being held there, certify that he, Wolff, had been helpful to a world famous Jew. This piece of paper was called a "Persilschein" ["bleach paper"] back then because it could turn a brown shirt lily-white again.

For prisoner Dr. Kurt von Schuschnigg, Wolff could or would not intercede in the same way in 1938. Indeed on Himmler's orders, his attic room was also made more comfortable and even freshly painted, but his guards from Austria understood that he be made to feel the hatred that had built up in them because of the time their party had been outlawed and they were persecuted. In the end neither Himmler nor Wolff decided what was to happen to him, since the decision belonged to Hitler alone. The former Austrian chancellor was sent to a German concentration camp, but given special status insofar as he was allotted his own apartment in a blocked off area and his wife was allowed to share his imprisonment. He was also not forced to work. Shortly before the end of the war he, along with some fifty other prisoners who were also politically important to the State, was taken on a bus to South Tyrol so the victorious approaching troops of the Western Allies were unable to free him. Wolff met him there one more time.

For the chief of the personal staff of the Reichsführer SS, however, the so-called annexation was not only made up of historic events. The new situation caused all kinds of complications. Zealous Party comrades in Linz decorated the sign on the front door of the medical officer, Dr. Eduard Bloch, with the sticker "Jew." They wanted to catch up with their German comrades in the area of anti-Semitism. In this case they were grasping at straws. There were still many people in Linz who remembered that the widow Klara Hitler, the mother of Führer-to-be Adolf, lived in the suburb of Urfahr. She had consulted Dr. Bloch at the beginning of 1907 because of pains in her chest. He diagnosed cancer. Klara Hitler was then operated on, but it was soon discovered that the illness was no longer curable, no matter how hard the doctor tried. The sick woman died on December 23, 1907. The 18-year-old son was convinced that Dr. Bloch had done everything humanly possible, and felt an obligation to show gratitude ever since.

Many people in Linz were of the opinion that the doctor did not deserve to be put out of work by Hitler's followers. They remembered that the son of an attorney practicing in Linz, namely Dr. Ernst Kaltenbrunner, had become a big man in the SS and had recently been appointed to head the SS in upper Austria. Brigadeführer Kaltenbrunner ordered two SS men to clean up the doctor's sign, and forbid any further sticker operations. He sent a report about it to Wolff, who answered in the usual five-week time frame. The Reichsführer SS "was aware of the situation" and "is absolutely in agreement with the way it was handled."

The dreadfully grotesque aspect of this episode is that several years before Ernst Kaltenbrunner had recruited the son of a German citizen living in Linz named Adolf Eichmann to join the SS. In the meantime, he had become the Jewish consultant for the SD and later for the Gestapo. As Obersturmbannführer he was to transport millions of Jews from many countries in Europe to the extermination camps and, therefore, to the gas chambers. Kaltenbrunner later became Heydrich's successor, as chief of the RSHA and the supreme commander of the mass murders, which is why the International Military Tribunal in Nuremberg sentenced him to death by hanging.

Wolff was still to have many more dealings with Kaltenbrunner. They disliked each other from the beginning, the hulking brilliant lawyer from Linz who had the charm of a Styrian woodcutter, and the officer of the guards who stood out effortlessly in any company. For a long time, Wolff kept up the appearance of good-willed but condescending camaraderie with Kaltenbrunner. Soon after the Anschluss he complained to Himmler that he could not manage on his salary as a full-time SS Führer and leader of upper Austria, after having moved to the expensive city of Vienna. Of course he required some decorum and the Reichsführer promised him financial aid. Wolff received instructions to have contributions from the donations of the circle of friends transferred to Kaltenbrunner. Insufficiently informed, apparently, as to the amount of the donation, Wolff asked Kaltenbrunner in a letter how much had been promised to him. If this was intended to be a test of Kaltenbrunner's honesty, he passed. His information matched Himmler's.

For some time the correspondence between Wolff, the chief of the personal staff, and the Viennese SS leader was characterized by a difference in rank and years of service. Once Kaltenbrunner decided to do the man in Berlin a good turn. In his capacity as Higher SS and Police Chief, he suggested to the gauleiter of Lower Bavaria, Dr. Jury, that in the future he should send the profits from the gambling casinos in Baden near Vienna sent to the SS club "Lebensborn," which Wolff was managing. Only then, he threatened, would the concessions of the casino be renewed. But Jury wanted to channel the profits into the treasury controlled by the Gau leadership. With the help of Reichsleiter Martin Bormann, who based himself on the Führer's decision, whereby Gau leaders could initiate projects through their own income sources, independently of the ministries in Berlin. Wolff therefore replied to Kaltenbrunner that it was definitely not in the Reichsführer's best interest to "place Dr. Jury under pressure and be in such a predicament" of having to deliver the money. In addition, the Gauleiter "needed certain amounts of money to finance the spa areas within his Gau." Kaltenbrunner was instructed to negotiate an agreement, which "took equally into account the wishes of the SS and the Gau leadership."

An apology came promptly from Vienna, of course. A misunderstanding created by one of the subordinates had complicated the case, and from now on they would "naturally proceed in a friendly and tactful" manner. During the new negotiations it was supposedly agreed that Jury would deliver "the largest possible recurring amounts." Unfortunately, however, "the casino business has momentarily fallen off." The reason is made clear by the date on the letter: September 30, 1939—the war in Europe had been going on for one month.

At this time, Wolff's letters were already hand stamped "temporary Führer Headquarters." For the next three years, that was to be his permanent residence—according to Hitler's wishes, as Wolff liked to emphasize. This assignment strengthened his self-confidence even more. While he ended his letters to Kaltenbrunner with a simple signature under the obligatory "Heil Hitler," the attorney did not fail to place a "respectfully yours" above his signature. In the autumn at the beginning of the war he zealously sent the Wolff family at Tegern Lake large quantities of fruit, which by then had become very rare. He no longer felt he had to do this once he became chief of the RSHA. Then, as the Third Reich came to an end, and its dignitaries were obeying the dictum "every man for himself," they became rivals. Kaltenbrunner attempted very quickly to dispatch Wolff to the gallows for being guilty of high treason against his country.

Chapter 4

Kristallnacht: The Night of Broken Glass

The first months following the Anschluss of Austria were not very dramatic, but the careerist functionaries of the SS and SA provided more than enough excitement. Two weeks had barely gone by when Himmler ordered an armed SS reserve unit to be set up in Austria. The assignment was given to the inspector of the SS reserve units, Brigadeführer Paul Hausser, who was responsible for setting up, organizing, and training those units.

Hausser did not, however, have the SS Leibstandarte Adolf Hitler under his control. At the beginning, in 1933, the SS was trained by the old Reichswehr Infantry Regiment 9 and received their pay from the budget of the Prussian State Police. They swore allegiance only to Adolf Hitler, and were led by the old Nazi fighter Sepp Dietrich, a highly decorated sergeant and tank driver in the First World War, who changed his life when he took part in the Nazi Munich beer hall brawls, and, of course, in the attempted putsch of 1923. Hausser retired from the Reichswehr as a lieutenant general because of his age, but he felt too vigorous to just live out a quiet life, and was recruited into Himmler's reserve units, the precursor of the Waffen SS. In Hausser's eyes Sepp Dietrich, belting out his strong Bavarian vocabulary and cursing constantly, was a wild farm boy, able at best to command a company. The commander of the Leibstandarte had little regard for the former general staff officer. Up to that point, the two had simply gone their own ways, but when Hitler ordered the newly organized (Austrian) reserve unit regiment to draw part of its core manpower from the Leibstandarte, the argument became unavoidable. In a written report to Himmler, Hausser complained that Dietrich was refusing to give him the men as well as the weapons. Hausser threatened to resign his rank and commission because this case was "not an exception. These are orders coming from the Reichsführer SS and the inspection shows that the training and change were not carried out."

Himmler knew from his own experience about those kinds of difficulties with Sepp Dietrich. It had already happened that the commander of the Leibstandarte managed to get an order from the Reichsführer reversed by Hitler. Very wisely, he passed the arbitration of the fight to Chief of the Personal Staff Karl Wolff. On that same day, with a rush much too hectic for his usual way of working, Wolff met with Dietrich, who was also stationed in Berlin, and later placed a note in his file summing up the conversation. After that, everything went a bit differently from what Hausser claimed. Dietrich did not refuse anything at all; he provided everything that was asked of him, but added a few conditions that Hausser promptly disregarded. In this case, Dietrich didn't want to lose the 193 Austrians in his Leibstandarte because they had just been picked by his representatives and sent on to Berlin, and "because of their height of over six feet should not be placed in the general SS Reserves, but rather in the Leibstandarte."

These were obvious excuses to cover up his unauthorized behavior, but Wolff didn't dare say anything against a Party veteran who counted many Nazi bigwigs as his friends. He simply suggested that the two fighting roosters get together and iron out their own differences. He could tell Hausser that his adversary really wanted to follow the order, and assured Dietrich that Himmler completely disregarded Hausser's letter of complaint. The letter remains in the file to this day.

Wolff was also unsuccessful in his attempt to end an argument within the Party, whose evergrowing stack of files continued to land on his desk incessantly for two years. The fight began with a complaint by Gruppenführer Reinhard Heydrich about a painter, by now rightfully forgotten, but who at the time was well regarded as an art promoter. His name was Wolf Willrich, and he considered it his mission to propagandize Nazi ideas through drawings and paintings of idealized people visibly of the Nordic race in heavily symbolic situations—men usually portrayed as heroic warriors, women as mothers or pregnant, naturally. According to the trend of the times, Heydrich had Willrich paint a portrait of his wife Lina, a blonde girl from Fehmarn Island. Then bizarre doings began to intrude in March 1937: against his wishes he discovered the picture on the cover of the magazine *Volk und Rasse* (People and Race). Given the assignment by Himmler, Wolff wrote to the office responsible for the magazine, the SS Race and Settlement Main Office, asking that Willrich be barred from any further publications.

Little did he know that this would take him to the heart of the dispute about the direction and goal of German art for years. The matter remained underground since the general public was not very interested in the topic, and rightfully so, because the two main squabblers were actually fighting for Party bigwigs who dared not insult each other directly. Wolf Willrich, the saccharine-sweet guardian of the Aryan race, who after many unsuccessful years with the Nazis had finally reached success, represented one side. His burning desire was to make those who had always been successful, the slimy ones and the bolsheviks of culture, pay for his humiliation. He found those who would share in his struggle at the "League of Defenders of German Culture," sponsored by Reichsleiter Alfred Rosenberg, and in Reich Farmer's leader Richard Walther Darré, he even found a consistent client, paying him a monthly retainer. In his book, *Cleansing the Stamp of Art,* Willrich strongly denounced the painters Emil Nolde, Karl Schmidt-Rottluff, Otto Dix, Ernst Heckel, the sculptor Ernst Barlach, the artist George Grosz, and many other modern artists of the twenties as destroyers of culture. He also influenced the exhibition "Degenerate Art" put together in 1936 at Hitler's request. For this, many works in different styles—or by Jewish artists—were removed from museums. They would prove that the "cultural bolsheviks" had tried to weaken the aesthetic standards and the moral strength of the Germans through the fine arts.

At least during the first years following the seizure of power, there were still opponents, predominantly intellectuals and artists within the Party, to such iconoclasts. Berlin university students spoke out in favor of an exhibit in May 1933 where a great many condemned artists were to show their work as examples of a revolutionary era. One of the supporters of this operation was the Reich Leader of Education of the National Socialist Association of Students—Nazi journalist Dr. Johannes von Leers.

At the time Willrich's book appeared, the discussion regarding German and non-German art had long been decided—given Hitler's provincial taste in art. In 1933, while architect Albert Speer remodeled the building of the Berliner Gau leadership and renovated the rooms, paintings by Emil Nolde on loan were hung on the walls. Dr. Goebbels, as Gauleiter of Berlin, was enthusiastic—until Hitler inspected the rooms and demanded that "these lousy pictures have to go." From that point on, even Dr. Joseph Goebbels saw all art only through the Führer's eyes, and most of the artists whom the Berlin students admired had either emigrated or were no longer allowed to work.

Typically enough, none of the denounced artists defended themselves against the defamation, except for art book publisher Willrich, who had been branded a "cultural bolshevik." He went to court referring to Dr. von Leers' report, to prove that he, Willrich, did support official National Socialist ideas, and had been incited by fanatic outsiders to publish the book. Very soon insults and denunciations were being hurled back and forth. Old Party comrade von Leers, now promoted to SS Obersturmführer, was blamed for organizing a revolt with the Berlin student association in 1933 against the Führer's cultural policies.

Attorneys were hired. The SS Race and Settlement Main Office was asked to make a statement. Darré's Reich farming community threatened to withdraw Willrich's retainer if he refused to drop the issue. Defamatory letters arrived at the school. The president of the Reich's Association of the Fine Arts, Adolf Ziegler—dubbed "Master of German Pubic Hair" because of the precision of his detailed nude paintings—was forced to be the arbitrate. Finally, both adversaries turned to Heinrich Himmler. Leers, his opponents demanded, "should be removed from all key positions that he still holds in the Party. A procedure of expulsion should begin..."

Even Wolff, with his extensive experience at smoothing out differences, could not separate the two sides. Without getting involved he turned over the files to Darré, the leader of the Reich farming community, who allowed Willrich to proceed against Leers in court, but the suit died within the justice system because the war broke out eight months later. Willrich could, however, immediately claim success; Wolff bought two paintings from him for the SS, for a total of 4,000 marks, which was equal to the yearly income of a middle-class employee at the time. They hardly fit in with Wolff's tastes, since he liked figurative art. He had a life-size, oil portrait done of himself by Professor Padua, standing in a self-confident pose, like Lohengrin, in a festive white uniform decorated with medals, the formal dress of high-ranking SS officers.

When it became necessary to handle a problem discreetly at the upper echelon, he was clearly the best suited on Himmler's staff. This was why the Reichsführer SS wrote the large German letters "Wolff" on the upper right-hand corner of the letter dated May 30 to "dear Heini." The sender was Count Leo Du Moulin Eckart and the intimate form of address was a relic from the early years of the NSDAP. The count was at the Wehrkreiskommando in Munich, along with Himmler and Reichswehr Captain Ernst Röhm during Hitler's putsch on November 9, 1923. After the ban on the Party was lifted he returned to his old position and had tried to build up an intelligence service for the Party under SA chief of staff Ernst Röhm.

Then in 1932 Karl Leonhard Count Du Moulin Eckart was involved in an obscure matter when leftist newspapers published Röhm's private letters where his homosexual tendencies became obvious. Apparently the entire clique around the SA chief of staff was to be killed in a plot by purist Party comrades. The matter was never really cleared up, but on June 30, 1934, when Hitler had the SA leadership mowed down in Munich, even the count and SA Brigadeführer—who was not a homosexual—ended up among those arrested. He was taken to Dachau concentration camp where—as his merciless Führer said of him—"he should be glad to still be alive," because he "actually deserved to die due to his constant treachery when there was strife at the *Munich Post*."

Himmler kept this statement by Hitler in a note on file after he had asked his Führer whether the count could not be released. The Reichsführer SS was obviously not completely convinced of his guilt. Shortly after that he managed to get his former comrade-in-arms back to Winklarn Castle, which he owned in the Upper Palatinate. Himmler also made sure that the prisoner returning home was not subjected to any form of harassment from the Party.

Indeed, it happened that an archeologist who was busy with diggings for the SS in the Gau of Schwaben, and who occasionally visited the Du Moulin family, was accused by the Gau leadership in Augsburg and the district leadership in Neu-Ulm of being in contact with an enemy of the State. It was after this incident that the count wrote the previously mentioned letter calling for help to Himmler on May 30, 1938. Two and a half weeks later, Wolff dictated a registered letter to the district leadership in which he certified that the count "follows the appropriate regulations and does nothing without letting the Reichsführer SS know." The district leader from Neu-Ulm thus found out that in principle "the matter of the Count Du Moulin Eckart was being handled according to directives from the Führer." Neither the archeologist nor the count were to be bothered by any of Party authorities in the future.

The count's obsequiousness went so far as to ask for Himmler's approval when his sister Aimé wanted to marry the Austrian Hans Schober. His uncle had been a chancellor of Austria for a time and later chief of police in Vienna. Through the RSHA, Wolff had an evaluation of the groom made at his work place in Vienna. The count found out on September 25, 1938, that Himmler "cannot do anything for your brother-in-law, because he received openly unfavorable information about him." He was being blamed for having contact with those favorable to the Habsburg monarchy and Jewesses, as well as for his unhealthy compulsion to waste.

Countess Aimé protested against such reproaches. Understandably she wanted to find out the source but Himmler refused to talk. He let her know through his adjutant that he would give the information to her brother personally. This took place during his next visit to Munich.

Understandably Himmler had very little time for the countess' marriage plans in those days. The crisis in the Sudetenland reached its peak during the second half of September. It had already begun six months before, even though ordinary people hardly felt any of it at the beginning. The Führer gave instructions for Operation Green, the preparation of the invasion of Czechoslovakia, which was obviously a State Secret, on April 22, 1938. Two days later Konrad Henlein, the leader of the Sudeten-German party, realizing that his attempts to reach an agreement with the government in Prague were unsuccessful, declared that his nation "from now on would take a separate path," which was not seen as a warning.

Up to that point all of Hitler's operations had ended well; everyone could still hear the happy sounds of the Austrians cheering.

At the beginning of May the heavens of the Third Reich were shining in grand style as never before. Hitler visited Mussolini in Italy; their friendship was celebrated for eight days. Himmler and Wolff traveled with an entourage of 500 people. Although the royal family and their followers behaved very coolly toward the Teutonic invaders descending in five special railroad cars, their well-known Italian friends in the secret police celebrated the SS leadership that included Heydrich and Daluege. As Hitler told his hosts that he renounced all the claims by German nationals in the South Tyrol, he was in effect thanking Mussolini for keeping quiet during the annexation of Austria. At the same time he issued an advance request for future support when the Sudeten Germans would be brought back home to the Reich.

It was then, with the increasingly bad news from the Sudetenland, that the German people understood that the next thunderstorm was in the making. Prague called up its reservists and there were demonstrations, disturbances, and shootings in the German-speaking regions. Many of the younger Sudeten-Germans secretly crossed the border into the Reich. Just as refugees from Austria were formed into a legion, there was now a Sudeten-German volunteer corps. Because it was politically expedient, they were incorporated into the SS. Henlein, the self-confident sports instructor from the Bohemian border town of Asch, would have preferred to keep the corps under his control, but because he, with his Sudeten-German party, had competed for a while with the Nazi party within the ethnic group, the Reich Party leaders did not entirely trust him. There was a meeting on July 31, 1938, in Breslau at the German Gymnastics Festival—the last one, by the way, that the organized clubs of the German Gymnastics Association was to arrange. Hitler and Henlein agreed how the 3.5 million Czechoslovakian citizens of German nationality were to be brought home to the Reich. Now Himmler received orders to prepare his armed SS units and the voluntary corps for the invasion in Bohemia, in case—as planned—disturbances should break out in border towns.

Himmler and his top adjutant Wolff could already see their names in the history books as great liberators. At the Nuremberg Party rally at the beginning of September, they marched at the head of the SS units that goose-stepped across the main market past Hitler. Himmler led with his arm outstretched, with Wolff in step behind him. As always, they were fired up by the excitement of the Volksfest, the shattering marching music and the approving screams of "Heil" from the masses of people on the plaza. But stronger than ever before was their confidence that they were the creators of a heroic era. Although just a few days before Hitler gave them a terrible damper during his "cultural" speech—when he railed against the "slipping in of unclear, mystical elements" in "the movement against places of worship and cult–oriented fuss in the Party organizations." But on September 11, the day they marched by, they were convinced by this demonstration of power and strength that great days were ahead of them. This was confirmed the next day in the congress hall; at the end of the Party convention, Hitler announced that he would show no more patience with Prague.

Everything went according to Himmler's wishes. For Wolff there was, of course, a small frustration on the fringe of this heroic day. Margarethe Himmler, several years older than the Reichsführer SS, a trained nurse, and according to Lina Heydrich, someone who "diets down to panty size 50," had invited the wives of the highest-ranking SS leaders to the Party rally. With a compulsory schedule of events, she kept them all under her wing. As Lina Heydrich and Frieda Wolff escaped this situation where they were being told what to do, and decided to enjoy themselves among the crowd of Party comrades, they were admonished in military fashion. Both complained to their husbands, who had already protested in their own right about the attitude of the "female Reichsführer SS"—the result was that the mighty man shrugged his shoulders, looked helpless and sad, as if to say "That's just the way she is!" No one close to him was surprised when he found emotional and sexual solace with his secretary Hedwig Potthast after 1940 and with whom he had two children.

As Hitler met with England's prime minister, Sir Neville Chamberlain, in Bad Godesberg to negotiate the Sudeten crisis, and a few days later when he appeared at a mass rally at the Berlin Sportpalast as the dictator, ready to go to war, the SS leadership waited anxiously to be allowed to cross the border. Instead, peace was saved once again by the Munich Conference on September 29, 1938. It goes without saying that Himmler and Wolff could not miss the conference, but they were not asked for advice. They were, as always, brought in for decorative purposes.

Although Hitler's demands were met, whereby Czechoslovakia was forced to immediately hand over the Bohemian border regions to the Reich, he did not feel like a conqueror. His puzzled chief interpreter, Dr. Paul Schmidt, noted his employer's bad mood. He would have preferred to have a small war. Even Himmler thought so, since he was one of the agitators during the entire critical time and his inseparable adjutant Wolff was looking forward to new military fame.

The Reichsführer SS was already playing a double game behind Hitler's back in those days, which is understandable, but almost impossible to prove. Leading army generals, like General of the Artillery Franz Halder and General Erwin von Witzleben, had sworn that at the outbreak of a war of aggression, they would have soldiers arrest Hitler and remove him from office. If the Gestapo had known this, couldn't Himmler have used the situation to further his own plans? Hitler, liberated by Himmler with the help of the armed SS units, would have had to appoint him as his deputy and successor, and a Hitler killed in the confusion of a putsch could have been replaced by the trusted Heinrich. Several years later Himmler and Wolff were to demonstrate that their loyalty to the Führer was mostly skin deep, and when it really mattered, it would not mean loyalty unto death.

Austria and Sudetenland were both returned to the Reich in 1938. The victorious Hitler crowed that "the reintegration of ten million Germans and approximately 110,000 square kilometers of land to the Reich" made the Germans happy. Anyone close to power in Germany was now zealously intent on reaping the benefits. Himmler and Wolff, still fully immersed with organizational and personnel problems in the new Ostmark (as Austria was now named), went to great lengths to claim their share in the newly created Sudeten Gau. Hitler dissolved the Sudeten-German voluntary corps, created only recently, with a simple four-line proclamation, which stated that its members "from now on will fulfill their duties in the Party's fighting units." It went without saying that the SS chose the blondest and tallest individuals with the brightest blue eyes. Prominent leaders of the now dissolved Sudeten-German party (which had also become redundant) received honorary ranks in the SS and were allowed to wear decorations and medals on their new black uniforms. The top man was Konrad Henlein, raised to the rank of gauleiter, although it was whispered among the SS that he had homosexual tendencies.

All of them flocked to the personal staff of the Reichsführer SS, where Karl Wolff, as always ready to take on any task, took care of each one individually. Wolff was thus able to manage the proper distance, according to social conventions, to the wealthy members of Himmler's circle of friends. This, however, did not stop him from accepting small gifts, for example pleasure cruises from the leaders in the shipping industry. His hunting mate was the ball-bearing manufacturer from Schweinfurt, Dr. Sachs, with whom he became so friendly that he was allowed into his estates anytime he wanted, and was even guaranteed a loan to build his house at a favorable interest rate. After knowing him just a very short time, Wolff was on friendly terms with the former Viennese gauleiter Odilo Globocnik, who had been dismissed from the leadership of the Austrian Nazi party for corruption. He called him "Globus," even after this man tried to rehabilitate himself within the Party through the mass murders of Jews.

One cannot infer from this that Wolff was one of those brutal anti-Semitic killers who, in the drunken wee hours, raucously proclaimed that, "When Jewish blood drips from the knife, then nothing could be better!"

Vulgarity had always repulsed him. Since he believed that those of the Nordic race were the elite representing the culmination of a development that had ended centuries before, and since he realized that, at least outwardly, he could be viewed as the prototype of that race, he became so utterly convinced of his superiority that he could not entertain any general feelings of hatred toward the Jews. Naturally there were many subhuman creatures among them, but these could be isolated in concentration camps. They were indeed easy to recognize. With a shaved head, their criminal physiognomy became very apparent.

A man like Wolff had many acquaintances, and unavoidably these included Jews. He did not deny the fact nor did he feel himself endangered by them. His uniform and his convictions protected him against the suspicion of being beholden to the Jews. On the other hand, he never imagined that things would become as extreme as the regulations of the Nazi party's program suggested.

But in the late fall of 1938 it became clear to him that his anti-Semitism was not strong enough for what the highest authorities had in mind. He, as well as Himmler, Heydrich and even the executioner's assistant, the lowly SS Führer Adolf Eichmann, still believed at that time that they were fulfilling the Führer's wishes if they got as many Jews as they could to emigrate. Their life in Germany was becoming awful enough, anyway. They had been pressured out of most of the academic professions, they had been fired from all civil service positions, and those in private business were being actively boycotted. Since the summer of 1938, they were kept out of the trading markets and stock markets and, in addition, they were being forced to use first names as identifying brands: Israel for men and Sarah for women. Next to many town signs on country roads, on a second post, was a sign that read, "Jews are not welcome." For the Viennese and Berlin Jews, Adolf Eichmann perfected a bureaucratic system that moved citizens who had become annoying across the border, on a conveyor belt of sorts.

For fanatic anti-Semites, this removal undertaken by the SS was too humane, took too long and also, over time, did not fulfill the purpose well enough because the adversaries of the regime forced to emigrate to foreign countries only strengthened the opposition front there. The most raving anti-Semite was the gauleiter from Nuremberg, Julius Streicher, self-anointed as the *Leader of the Franks*, which underscored his dictatorial power. Despite acts of violence, money and sex scandals, he demonstrated that the rule of law did not apply to him. He also found a comrade in the

Reich Propaganda Leader of the NSDAP and gauleiter from Berlin, Dr. Joseph Goebbels. This was surprising because the newly ardent anti-Semite, as a student in Heidelberg, had been the enthusiastic disciple of Friedrich Gundolf, a Jewish professor of literature, and had been deeply in love with a Jewish girlfriend, to whom he even dedicated some of his poems.

That Streicher, an uncouth, uneducated former schoolmaster from Nuremberg, was attempting to get the Jews under his control was easy enough to understand. His weekly newspaper *Der Stürmer* described in every issue how "world enemy #1" had been systematically spoiling every nation, turning them against each other in bloody wars. Readers who had little interest in such pseudo-historical fantasies could amuse themselves with detailed descriptions of how those Jews would ruin other races through tainted Aryan virgins. Such reports may have stimulated the imagination of the repulsive Streicher. In 1937, he received a group of handpicked journalists at his headquarters who were being shown the locations of the Party rallies. His half-hour welcoming speech was dedicated to his "feeling for life," which to him meant his sexual potency.

To the intellectual Joseph Goebbels, the alliance with this beast was certainly a necessary, if distasteful, matter. The propaganda minister had fallen out of grace with Hitler because his love affair with the Czech movie actress Lida Baarova had caused a public scandal. She almost caused him to seek a divorce and therefore damage the Party's reputation, while he was actually crusading for German morality. Therefore on October 21, 1938, at Obersalzberg, Hitler ordered the married couple to reconcile and demanded moral good behavior of his minister. It is very probable that he used this opportunity to insinuate that Goebbels could regain some of the respect he had lost by carrying out acts of violence against the Jews.

The opportunity presented itself soon enough and Heydrich unknowingly created it. At that time, a young 17-year-old Jew of Polish nationality, Herschel Grynszpan, was living in Paris. His parents, residents of Hannover, had sent him to France to live with relatives so that he might have a future. The Grynszpan family, along with many other Jews, had fled Poland in 1918 because of the threatening pogroms. Now the government wanted to prevent any of them returning by stripping them of their citizenship. But Hitler's Reich did not want them at all. Heydrich had them picked up and transported by train to the Polish border, and then in the middle of the night driven into the no-man's-land. Polish border police immediately sent them back westwards, so these people spent days and nights going back and forth between border posts, hungry and constantly threatened with beatings. Herschel Grynszpan's parents were part of this group.

After he had heard of his parents' misery, he went to the German embassy in Paris, intending an assassination in order to call the world's attention to the suffering of his mother and father. Because he could not meet the ambassador, he shot the embassy's first councilor, Ernst Eduard vom Rath, wounding him so severely that he was expected to die.

On the evening of November 8, 1938, the anniversary of Hitler's 1923 putsch at the Munich Bürgerbräukeller, Hitler spoke to the "old fighters" and Party dignitaries. Wolff and Himmler were also present. The Führer did not mention the shooting in Paris, although he knew that his listeners were waiting for his orders. He apparently found it more effective to let their rage simmer. Even on the afternoon of the following day when the Nazi veterans, in memory of the bloody end of the putsch, marched through the streets of Munich to the Feldherrnhalle, there was no mention of the Paris attack. But Hitler's plans for the pogrom were certainly already being worked out, and he had already done his part. As during the extermination of the Jews several years later, in this case there was not the smallest piece of paper bearing an order from the almighty Leader. The two avengers appointed by Hitler, Goebbels and Streicher, were only waiting for the news of vom Rath's death in Paris.

During the afternoon, vom Rath died. The report reached Munich in the evening as the Party leaders gathered for their usual meal at the Munich Rathaus. Hitler normally gave another speech there, but this time he only whispered quickly with Goebbels and then disappeared. His propagandist spoke in his place. This speech was not written down, so the exact wording is not recorded, but it is known that he fanned the feelings of revenge among his listeners and spoke of spontaneous reactions with which the people must retaliate against the murder. Here and there, Goebbels announced, the Jews were already experiencing this retaliation: numerous synagogues were already in flames.

While Hitler quietly waited for further developments in his apartment on Prinzregentenplatz, the gauleiters hastily made their way, one after the other, to the telephones and telegram printers in the Town Hall. Typically, they warned the SA and political leaders almost everywhere, but not the SS. They were to be avoided, not just because the SS might bring the police into the picture too early, but also because the pogrom was not the form of persecution of the Jews that the SS were using. Those now causing havoc in the streets, the vandals, thugs, and arsonists, were all dressed in civilian clothes. Neither the Party nor the State was to be involved in such "spontaneous" actions.

The value of property destroyed was in the millions of marks, innumerable store windows were smashed, Jewish businesses and stores were looted, apartments were demolished and their owners abused—36 Jews were murdered—cultural centers and synagogues were burned to the ground. Among a circle of close friends, Goebbels cynically was quite pleased that the Berlin mob finally had the opportunity to shop so cheaply.

That evening Wolff sat in the Four Seasons Hotel with no idea of what was going on—which seems plausible enough. He was preparing for his appearance in the final scene of the fall Party spectacle. Himmler wanted to swear in his new SS volunteer recruits at midnight in front of the Feldherrnhalle—the place where the State police shot into Hitler's demonstrators 15 years earlier, killing 16 marchers. Wolff's role was to pick up the Führer at his apartment one half hour before the beginning of the ceremony and take him to the inner courtyard of his residence so that Hitler could step through a widely opened gate onto the small plaza in front of the Feldherrnhalle and dramatically climb the stairs as the clock finished striking midnight.

In a luxury hotel on Maximilianstrasse, Heydrich and several of his SS leaders were also celebrating. The glow of flames and noise on the streets drew their attention to the synagogue burning nearby. Then Heinrich Müller, chief of the Gestapo, called from Berlin to report that all Jewish shops had been ransacked and that bands of youths dressed like hooligans destroyed the apartments of Jews. Müller wanted to know how the police were to behave. But even Heydrich had no orders. It was a delicate matter. For that reason, he went a few rooms down the hall and asked Chief of the Personal Staff Wolff whether the pogrom was to be encouraged, tolerated, or stopped. The fact that Himmler's closest colleague was also just beginning to hear about those events left them both dumbfounded. Heydrich therefore demanded to speak with Himmler. Wolff slowed him down; it was not quite that simple, since their superior happened to be at the Führer's apartment at that precise moment. He offered to drive over there immediately and request instructions.

This was an opportunity for Hitler to see him one more time. The housekeeper announced Wolff to Himmler, who was sitting in the living room with the Führer and at first did not appreciate being interrupted earlier than planned. Wolff's report clearly surprised him; he went back into the living room and shortly after that Wolff was also called in. Hitler displayed his outrage, and from his remarks of "Shocking!" or "Absolutely not acceptable!" Wolff became convinced (and truly believed to his death) that the Führer had neither ordered nor even agreed to the pogrom. After all, Hitler told Himmler in closing, "Find out immediately who is responsible for this. I do not wish my SS to be involved in any of these occurrences for any reason." He then ordered that looters should be prosecuted, fires in synagogues need not be extinguished, but that neighboring houses, which were in danger, must be protected.

Wolff, through this recollection, tried to prove that Hitler was innocent of the atrocities of the Kristallnacht. One must examine the purported direct quotations very carefully. They appear in almost every report that Wolff published, in statements and interviews that he gave to journalists and historians, and of course again in the long manuscripts of his rudimentary autobiography that was found.

It is an undisputed fact that even later in life he retained an extraordinary memory. It is clear, however, that everyone he quotes speaks in the stilted German that he acquired as a young man in the guard officers' club and had never lost. It is also noticeable that whenever he repeats himself, not only is a particular statement or response delivered in the same word order, but the descriptions of the surroundings are almost identical every time. It is akin to a recording, which does not make his accounts any more credible. It actually raised the suspicion that, because he had been interrogated and questioned so many times, he had simply memorized the version placing himself in the most favorable light.

It is plausible that he did in fact think that Hitler had no idea of what was happening and was "taken in by Goebbels and Streicher"—according to his description. Wolff had probably never noticed how easily Hitler, with the finesse of an actor, could deceive even those closest to him. The dictator had that particular actor's talent of always completely believing what he was saying and being able to convey anything he said at that moment in the most convincing way. Whenever Hitler lied, it was to him the indisputable truth, which did not prevent the absolute opposite from being "true" a few moments later. In spite of this, Hitler had always rejected the accusation of being dishonest with the indignation of a wronged husband. In his tactical choices he was an uninhibited pragmatic; only when it came to his ultimate goals was he completely determined in his persistence.

There are, however, some tangible clues indicating that he did give the order for the pogrom. Already during the September Party rally he reprimanded the Nuremberg Gauleiter that in this "native German city and the treasure of the German Reich" there were still synagogues. Observers also suspected that he gave Goebbels the cue to begin the action just before he abruptly left the Rathaus. Shortly after that, initial instructions were handed to the Gau propaganda leaders, marked "Secret."

Yet there is evidence that Himmler, Wolff, and the majority of the SS leaders really had no idea of what was going on. Wolff dictated a long memo for the files upon his return to his Berlin office in order to put the responsibility of the propaganda minister on record. Himmler complained in one memo about the "ambition for power" and the "airheadedness" of Dr. Goebbels. Himmler ordered Heydrich to carefully examine the crimes of the Party mobs that were out of control, to request reports of abuse and murders from the local police precincts, and to find out the amount of property damage. Hermann Göring then used this number as the guiding maximum of the four-year plan of economic performance increases to argue against Goebbels and to set himself up to handle the Jewish question. The supreme Party judge Walter Buch also became active, but contrary to his intentions, only few criminal cases were taken to the Party court. Acting on Hitler's instructions, Reichsleiter Martin Bormann slowed down the Party courts as well as criminal justice proceedings. Above all, the rapes of Jewesses by Nazis were punished, not because of the deed but because they had intercourse with a Jewess.

Following this attack on his authority and that of the SS regarding the policies to be carried out for Jews, the Reichsführer SS and Chief of the German Police actually had plenty of reasons to accuse Dr. Goebbels and his supporter Reichsleiter Bormann of damaging Germany's image. Very wisely, he decided not to pursue the matter. Hitler had always frightened him, and now he knew what the leader obviously desired. Immediately following the Munich spectacle, he left on vacation, far away to Italy for five weeks, but because he was afraid that one of his top SS leaders would try to damage his standing with Hitler and expel him from the top ranks, he named no deputy. It was a well-known fact that such fears were not without reason, and that Hitler encouraged such behavior. Albert Speer, as minister of defense, was to experience this kind of situation in the most crass way during the war. Wolff apparently carried out the business of the SS leadership during Himmler's absence, but every area leader could undertake whatever he wanted within his own section. Heydrich used this freedom to promote himself retrospectively through an anti-Semitic initiative. He placed 10,000 wealthy Jews in concentration camps, apparently in retaliation for the death of the diplomat vom Rath. Actually, he wanted to improve upon Eichmann's export methods as practiced in the central emigration offices in Vienna and Berlin. The disadvantage, however, was that then only rich Jews were driven away and the poor ones remained because they could not get "token money" together to satisfy the emigration laws of other countries. Now the wealthy prisoners were told that they could buy their freedom by making donations to the common emigration fund. Many paid.

Even Wolff used Himmler's absence to take action. He heard that the commissioner of the League of Nations in Danzig, Carl J. Burckhardt, a Swiss citizen whose mission it was to secure the independence of the neutral city-state, had attempted without success to have a meeting with the Reich propaganda minister on November 14. Goebbels had canceled. Supposedly he was still so busy defending himself against the attacks about Kristallnacht coming from Göring and other Nazi bigwigs. On that occasion in Himmler's name, Wolff invited Burckhardt to the Prinz-Albrecht-Strasse offices in Berlin. The Swiss scholar, who was always working toward peace, was understandably a bit disappointed, to only be received by Chief of the Personal Staff Wolff on November 23.

What he did hear, however, pleased him. In his book, *My Danzig Mission*, published two decades later, he described the meeting. Wolff told him that the Reichsführer, unfortunately, was sick, and that was due to the events of the preceding weeks. Himmler sharply criticized the pogrom. Burckhardt quoted verbatim: "The domestic situation in this country has become unbearable; something must happen. The man responsible is Herr Goebbels, who exercises an insufferable influence on the Führer. We had hoped to slow him down for the propaganda he was responsible for during the Czech crisis, and we believed that this time we had something definite, but sure enough the Führer saved him again. It can't go on like this; someone will have to do something!" But by that time Goebbels had already been declared the victor.

The real question related to who "someone" actually was. Just one SS Gruppenführer, one out of a few dozen? Or his boss the Reichsführer SS? Himmler did work in some ways against Hitler, but that only emerged from a murky background and never without some quick escape route. Fear was always greater than courage. He would openly rebel only when his heroic appearance could also push ahead a powerless Hitler. But this was not nearly the time for that and Goebbels, whom former banker Wolff still believed to be among the bankrupt, was protected once more for quite some time. Already on November 14 at lunch he received Hitler at his private house in the evening; the two made a show of unity publicly by going together to the theater... This was the reward for Kristallnacht.

Neither Himmler nor Wolff noticed in those days that their Führer had once again shut them out. After being forced to keep the peace at the Munich conference because he was given everything he had requested, he consciously headed for the next crisis in the hope that, as he usually expressed himself, "no pig attacks me from behind again." He had already given secret instructions on October 21, 1938, to the effect that "taking care of the rest of Czechoslovakia" was one of the "was one of the Wehrmacht's future tasks." On November 10 at his headquarters in Munich, he made it clear to the top press representatives that the drivel about peace had to end and that their task was to prepare the German public for the coming war; it was logical that he should begin with the hunt for the Jews.

In this connection, the cause of Hitler's pathological hatred for Jews becomes an insignificant issue. He rationalized his craze for persecution by claiming that they had always attempted to demoralize and subjugate the German nation—politically, morally, culturally, economically—in short, in every area. Once he had suppressed them, deprived them of their rights, looted their homes and branded them for the past five years, within the borders of the Reich, they could no longer be such a great danger because the State and the Party were so radically defined as being anti-Semitic and were practically all-powerful. Why then this additional terror, and why the extermination at the end?

Even though it may sound improbable, Kristallnacht was part of Hitler's war preparations. It made clear to the world that the Jews were hostages he was holding. He threatened often enough that the Jews would pay if anyone refused what he claimed were his justified demands. It is characteristic at the same time that the actions against the Jews apparently began among the people and were said to be a spontaneous retaliation. No written order signed by the Führer exists for either the pogrom on November 9, 1938, or the mass murders by the Einsatzgruppen and inside the concentration camps. The world was to be convinced that it was not a single person, such as the head of state, but rather the entire people who were responsible for the crimes. That was the reason why he elicited frenzied applause when he prophesied the "annihilation of the Jewish race in Europe" in each one of his public speeches from January 30, 1939 to 1942. The collective blame of the Germans was also part of Hitler's program. At the Führer's headquarters during the war, usually in conversations with trusted friends late at night, he repeatedly admitted the reasons for these tactics, when he said that the Germans only had the choice between total victory or total defeat, between ruling the world or utter failure. All bridges to peace or to understanding had been burned. To have "gone with, been caught with, and to hang with" now applied to everyone.

"Someone must do something," Wolff had said to Burckhardt, but he had done almost as little as all other Germans. Or was it that he just didn't take the officially prescribed discrimination against the Jews literally? Obviously he could afford such special behavior without suffering the consequences, since he was allowed to climb the SS career ladder almost to the highest levels of power.

We have already shown how, with the encouragement of German bankers following the occupation of Austria, he helped free the Viennese financier Baron von Rothschild. Shortly after Kristallnacht, however, he also helped another Jewish banker, Fritz Warburg, whose relatives in Hamburg, London, and New York were active in the finance business. As the shop windows were being broken and the synagogues went up in flames, Fritz Warburg was in Stockholm. In the spring of 1939, he wanted to negotiate with German officials regarding the emigration of Jews to Sweden. It never even reached that point. As he and his wife landed at Hamburg airport, their passports were confiscated. They had to stay in Hamburg, even though in comfortable accommodations. According to Wolff the Gestapo took the Warburgs as hostages in case there were new restrictions in foreign countries because of Kristallnacht.

A decade later, at his own denazification in Hamburg, working towards his own acquittal, Wolff mentioned how difficult and dangerous it was in 1939, especially for a higher SS official, to help a world-renowned Jewish banker. It is true that Wolff, at the request of an acquaintance from his apprenticeship at a Frankfurt bank, Baron von Berenberg-Gossler, used his influence to obtain the return of Warburg's passports. It is also true that he initiated discussions where the conditions were negotiated. So on May 10, 1939, the couple was able to return to Sweden, although Wolff was not directly involved in the negotiations. The banker von Berenberg-Gossler had used Gestapo officer K. Lischka, who was later to be a colleague of Eichmann—as his contact. Actually the negotiations ended with Warburg being bled for everything he had; he had to provide the "token money" in foreign currency for several poor Jewish families and leave it in Germany for one hundred Jewish children. This was not simply the method used by Eichmann to encourage the Jews to leave

Germany in Vienna and Berlin; it was also the ransom paid for emigration by wealthy Jews.

Wolff could not always go the straight path in such humanitarian operations. With Paula Stuck, who under her former name Reznicek was a tennis champion who repeatedly gave Germany victories in international tournaments, he artfully used the weaknesses of the bureaucratic hierarchy to avoid her being declared "non-Aryan" for many years. Before she married the racing driver Hans Stuck in 1932, she was divorced from Burkhard von Reznicek. Hans Stuck at the time was very famous, and his son Striezel later followed in the same path. At first hardly anyone would have bothered with her ancestry if she had not also been the author of several books. After all, she was very careful in that she chose a Swiss publishing company, which could not be forced to inquire as to the author's grandparents. Despite this, the Reich Chamber for Literature, the compulsory organization all writers had to belong to, demanded from Paula Stuck von Reznicek proof of her Aryan ancestry. Her answer was that "Herr SS Gruppenführer Wolff (Gestapo) was well aware of her case file in detail." As the Reich Chamber for Literature then inquired with Wolff, one of his adjutants dictated the information that Hans Stuck once provided Gruppenführer Wolff with a present for the Führer, which the Herr Gruppenführer passed along to the Führer. On this occasion, the Führer said something to the effect that the omissions on the part of Stuck regarding his not purely Aryan wife should remain omitted... "Obergruppenführer Brückner (the personal and, therefore, highest ranking adjutant to Hitler, as well as a putsch comrade from 1923), was to have been present during that conversation."

With the "is to have been" and "something like" this was anything but precise information, but the Reich Chamber for Literature accepted it. Hans Hinkel, a professional Nazi and someone always on the lookout for a new opportunity to seek power, did not. He was Wolff's age and a jack-of-all-trades. He was an old Party fighter from the time of the Munich putsch, and because no one would trust him with an important position, he was rewarded with the title of State Council, a seat in the Reichstag and a position as aide at the propaganda ministry. There, or so it was said, he could not inflict much damage because he was only handling cultural matters. It was precisely in this area, however, that he was a particularly zealous Jew hunter. For that reason, at the end of 1938 he wanted to know from Wolff "if he wished that Frau Stuck not be hindered in her further duties." For she was "as far as we know, of half-Jewish heritage."

Since Hinkel received no answer, he sent a reminder in mid-February 1939. When he repeated the reminder in May, a Wolff adjutant informed him that someone in the meantime had sent him an evaluation report regarding the matter. Supposedly no such thing happened because in June Hinkel requested an address, since that letter could not be found. He never got it, although Wolff was again reminded in August and September. On September 21, 1939, Wolff finally addressed the matter himself, using as a return address "temporary Führer Headquarters," his permanent residence since the outbreak of the war. What must have made Hinkel more reticent was that Wolff now had passed the report along to Hitler via Himmler, and that anyone could say that "the comments made by the Führer covered the description I gave of the situation." He was "not personally aware... of Frau Stuck's percentage of Jewish blood...I only know of the Führer's general decision." With smug irony, Wolff commented that he would not be able "to decide whether this statement by the Führer was sufficient to reach a decision in the matter of Frau Stuck...."

The stubborn Hinkel then did what he could to obtain information from Hitler's adjutant Brückner. He let Wolff know, however, and advised that he may want to "get in touch with him." So in the middle of May 1940, Wolff received a further reminder it was certainly time to finally clear up an issue that "has been going on for two years." For this reason, on September 6, 1940, Chief of the Personal Staff Wolff requested that the "ancestry expert" of the SS and chief of the Reich Office for Ancestral Research clear up the ancestry of Paula Stuck in "an appropriately careful manner." Three days later, Wolff had the written results in front of him: her father was the Breslau Commerce Counsel Dr. of Jurisprudence Georg Julius Heimann, of Jewish heritage, and her mother was the daughter of the Christian wholesale business family Molinari, whose Breslau trading house served as the model for Gustav Freytag's novel *Debits and Credits,* set around the mid-nineteenth century.

Pretending he had not yet received those results, Wolff informed the Staatsrat Hinkel in the middle of September that "no other facts were known at the local office... A decision by the Führer must be requested in any case." The most expedient would be "if the Reich Office for Ancestral Research were to step in." Hinkel remained patient until April 1941, before sending his last reminder. On this letter, Wolff wrote by hand: "Delay until after the war." He managed to silence the State Council in the propaganda ministry with the information that Reichsleiter

Martin Bormann advised against informing the Führer just then, since the campaign against the Soviet Union had been going on for a month.

We cannot tell why Wolff used so much energy in allowing Paula Stuck to slip through the threads of the race laws. After all, she and her husband had many connections to the former movers and shakers in Munich, to Hitler's private photographer Heinrich Hoffmann, as well as Hoffman's former store apprentice, Eva Braun. It would certainly have been a mistake to upset those circles. Hans Stuck, who had become unemployed as a racecar driver on account of the war, was also given the secret task from Himmler and Wolff to use his foreign connections acquired through sports for the Reich. He was to sell the bucket version of the Volkswagen to the armies of Switzerland and several Balkan states. He did not succeed because he could never obtain demonstration cars that the German army needed. Paula Stuck slowed down her literary ambition for a while. But two years after the end of the war Luis Trenker, who was famous for his films, wrote to her from the South Tyrol saying that the memoirs by and about the Nazis could be sold for a lot of money. There was great interest in Eva Braun, whose existence was revealed to the public only because of her suicide in the Führer's bunker. Therefore Trenker wrote to "dear Paula," who was of course so well acquainted with prominent Nazis in the past. Could she please assemble even gossip and rumors from those circles about the young woman who had suddenly become a public figure? He would reward her efforts with "a lot of Olio Sasso," or Italian olive oil, which was worth more than money in a postwar Germany plagued by hunger. Trenker received several dozen sheets of typewritten anecdotes, more or less credible, which were only passed along with the author's reservation, since some were most likely only rumors.

No payment was made. But Paula Stuck was able to read in a newly published weekly paper, the first example of the new German tabloid press, the "diary" of Eva Braun in installments based on her manuscript. Trenker maintained that these notations by Hitler's lover were discovered in his South Tyrolean home in Grödnertal in cartons stored among old NSDAP files. Naturally they were not authentic.

Chief of the Personal Staff Wolff once again had to get involved with the consequences of official party anti-Semitism. Oberführer Wilhelm Bittrich was a member of the SS Volunteer Troops, and later of the Waffen SS. As a Standartenführer, in April 1938 he had been transferred to Vienna, where a new unit was being created. An apartment was assigned to him and his wife through the Gestapo. Up until the Anschluss, it had belonged to general director Dr. Benno Schwoner, a Jew who had fled; the only property he took with him was what he was able to carry physically. The SS officer, however, generously refrained from using most of the possessions left behind. He had been married since 1922 and wanted only to borrow the things he had not yet purchased himself: a grand piano, a gramophone cabinet with record player, a vacuum cleaner, a refrigerator (all appliances that at that time were only affordable to the wealthy), lamps, many oil paintings, ten Persian rugs and a silver set of cutlery made up of almost 200 pieces. Measured according to the standards of 1938, this was considerable luxury, but when the Gestapo sent over their certified appraiser, he calculated the total value to be 1,327.98 marks. (Bittrich later: "As far as I can remember, 1,000 marks.")

When Wolff received the list of objects and their related values he became suspicious. The Gestapo used different appraisers, and they reached a value of 4,779 marks. This correction, which was still largely below the true value, did not help the refugee who had been robbed of everything once his entire fortune had fallen into Nazi hands. Bittrich was allowed to use all of this only for a short time. He was not being treated better or worse than many other Nazis who improved their living conditions in the same manner. If they were part of the SS leadership, an order from Himmler forbid them to purchase any of their conquests; no one was to get rich due to the sacred goals of the Party. The property of Jews who had fled went to the Reich finance administration and the Gestapo had to answer to the authorities if anything was sold.

The Viennese state police precinct asked Bittrich shortly before the end of 1940 what would happen to the borrowed property. Having been promoted to Oberführer in the meantime he was understandably in no hurry to answer. Three months later he wrote to Wolff asking that he use his clout with Himmler to allow him to either buy everything at the appraisal value or at least be allowed to continue to keep it as borrowed for purposes of entertainment. The nitpicking Reichsführer SS said no as a matter of principle. On the other hand the Gestapo, under pressure from the Reich Ministry of Finance, demanded a decision from Wolff. Even then Wolff remained true to his time-honored habit despite numerous warnings—namely, that voluminous stacks of files would just take care of themselves if they were kept around long enough. But at the beginning of July 1942 Himmler decided that all the borrowed items were to be removed from Bittrich's apartment and auctioned off.

Bittrich complained to Wolff: "Because the furniture and other objects of the apartment were collected... at this moment, not only my wife, but I too am being exposed to public ridicule, especially in our circle of comrades." And Wolff, who had in the meantime moved up to Obergruppenführer and General of the Waffen SS, actually did manage to soften up Heinrich Himmler's heart. "This entire issue" should be—as Wolff wrote to the Viennese Gestapo—put on ice until the end of the war..." Bittrich, who was now a Brigadeführer, was allowed to keep what he had. So that the Gestapo could close its books, Wolff transferred about 7,000 marks from the treasury of the "Circle of Friends" donations. After the end of the war, Frau Bittrich would be able to buy the things that were, in the meantime, worn down further because she would—her husband assured her—no longer be married to an SS Führer, but rather divorced. He was six years younger than she was and after more than twenty years of marriage, he had had enough of her. The last page in that stack of files read: "The entire procedure is, at the end of the war, to be once again taken to SS Obergruppenführer Wolff..." It was dated March 20, 1943. By then Wolff was only the titular, no longer the functioning, chief of the personal staff of the Reichsführer SS. He was sick, had been removed from his post, and had fallen from grace.

As did most former Nazi party members, Wolff also stated at the end of the war that he was never closely involved with the awful consequences of anti-Semitism. Much remains to be said however about this point. He was right when he reiterated that he had helped many people who were having problems because of the race issue. (It could also be asked why this help was necessary if the Jews were not being threatened.) He helped them of his own accord, without any benefit to himself, and what he did was dangerous at times. One may also assume that the officer of the guards with upper-class ambitions was sincerely disgusted by the blatant inhumanity of the National Socialist system, and the only reason he did not revolt was that he was too deeply involved in the wrongdoing because of his rank and position. Wolff was therefore a white knight within the Black Corps. His acts of assistance prove that he recognized how wrong things were. Otherwise why would he have become involved?

He helped an architect from Göttingen, whom they wanted to forbid building houses because of a grandmother of the wrong ancestry. He managed to have an old woman, who had married into an old noble family, avoid punishment and a concentration camp despite the fact that she, as the descendant of a Jewish family, had defied the prohibition of employing an Aryan girl as a servant. Regarding Jews who had served as officers, doctors, or treasurers in the Reichswehr, for the time being they were simply let go very quietly. But as soon as they were no longer protected by the uniform and fell into the vortex of racial persecution, their former comrades turned to Wolff in seeking help. It was well known in military circles that he was not a radical anti-Semite and that, due to his background, he felt himself bound to the soldiers. With his back covered by his comrade Heydrich, he let some of those being persecuted sneak out of the country ostensibly as SD agents. During one of these kinds of initiatives, Wolff ran into the number one executioner of the Jews, Adolf Eichmann, head of the Jewish unit at the RSHA or Amt IV-B-IV. Wolff had asked the world famous surgeon Ferdinand Sauerbruch, with his military rank of General Doctor of the Reserves, to help two Jewish doctors who had been coworkers of his in the past at the Charité hospital, and were now in danger of being sent to a concentration camp in the east. Wolff could no longer count on Heydrich's help, since the chief of the RSHA had been dead for over a month, killed in a commando attack in Prague. A successor had not yet been named; Himmler had temporarily taken over the office. To ask him for protection for two Jews was completely pointless. The leader of Amt IV, Chief of the Gestapo Heinrich Müller, would have been the next highest authority, but Wolff did not trust him at all. So he turned to the man who was directly in the key position, namely Adolf Eichmann. In a telephone conversation, the Obergruppenführer and General of the Waffen SS Wolff tried to make his wish palatable to the Obersturmbannführer and Gestapo division head. He clearly let his partner at the other end of the line feel, in a very friendly way, that given the difference in rank he should be obedient. But the old bureaucrat, who by then had sent hundreds of thousands of Jews to the gas chambers, would make no exceptions, as long as he was not ordered to do so by a superior. Wolff put on more pressure and finally asked threateningly, "Do you realize with whom you are speaking, Obersturmbannführer?"

"I most assuredly do, Obergruppenführer!" answered Eichmann, still quite correct. "And you are speaking with the head of the Amt IV-B-IV of the Gestapo!" He made it very clear that even such a high SS leader had no say within the police area, if he had no official position there. Wolff then made "mincemeat" of his fractious partner in the conversation, as Eichmann related at his 1962 interrogation by Israeli police "... although I was right, because I ... acted exactly...according to the orders of the Reichsführer...and the exception could in no way be granted...Naturally

I would have liked to grant it, on my part, because when you're dealing with such masses, one individual makes no difference. But I wasn't allowed to...at that time such a decision would have turned into an avalanche of consequences . . . it would have become a pigsty and not one single lousy person would have been able to see through it all."

This Adolf Eichmann was not a wild Jew-hater, but simply a primitive bureaucrat who doggedly completed what the orders and regulations demanded. However, he could have provided the two doctors with an extension if their representative had not been the esteemed Karl Wolff, who was always intent on being honored as it was his due, officially. Eichmann was aware that he and his team were murderers under orders, but he got around his conscience with the argument that someone had to do the "dirty work." So it made him all the more angry—as he told his Israeli interrogator—when "the so-called dandy officers of the SS, who wore white gloves and didn't want to know anything about what's going on," but then talked down to him. "Wolff is a perfect example!"

To pay back the Obergruppenführer for his insolence, Eichmann challenged him to a duel. In principle, this was allowed as part of the SS tradition. Supposedly, however, the Gestapo officer never had any intention of shooting it out with his antagonist, but any challenge had to be approved by Himmler. The Reichsführer SS would in the bureaucratic way, and without anyone being able to call Eichmann an informer, find out how his "Wölffchen" was going down paths that were in contradiction with Party rules. We do not know what Himmler thought about the case. However, he refused Eichmann permission for the duel.

When in the summer of 1964 the accused Karl Wolff stood before the Munich Court, he said he had "never taken the Jewish-related paragraphs of the Party program seriously." But he did agree that the Jewish influence had grown too strong in Germany during the Weimar Republic and should be brought down so that foreign races were proportionate to the rest of the population. The Jews were quietly spreading before 1933, and were pushing the Germans out. Even when he was over 80 years old, Wolff still spoke of the deteriorating ferment of "World Judaism."

Chapter 5

Megalomania as National Illness

As an older man Wolff drafted a timetable to prepare for his autobiography, and wrote, as a memo for "March 1939," "increasing Jewish agitation [by the Jews against Germany] mainly leads to the occupation of Prague and the remainder of Czecho-Slovakia." The same way Goebbels gave the press the written format of the State of Prague using a hyphen to underscore the ethnic division, Wolff also used to the very end the same lies to justify the invasion by German forces on March 15, 1939. As if Hitler, like the fabled wolf and the lamb at the brook, would always find a way to devour what was left of a nation. It had to be liquidated so that he could realize his plans to expand as a world power, if he wanted to be victorious over Poland and conquer Russia all the way to the Urals.

Understandably Wolff still glorified every event of the period because, for the first time, Hitler offered him a role raising him high above the faceless crowd. In retrospect, this role may appear insignificant and may only be decorative, but to the performer this was his first solo appearance on the world stage and also the opportunity to convince the supreme leader of his untapped talent.

In contrast to the invasion of Austria, this time Himmler and Wolff traveled together with Martin Bormann and Hitler in a special train to the

Sudeten Gau. In the Bohemian town of Leipa, the German chief of state got into his armored-tracked Mercedes. He was assured that no resistance would hold him and his armed forces up, after he had already pressed Czech statesmen into capitulation in Berlin. As usual, his Escort Commando was protecting him. They now wore the field gray uniforms. The convoy of cars that included Himmler and Wolff moved slowly through the Sudetenland, because the streets were lined with cheering crowds. On the other side of the Czech border, after 6 p.m., because of darkness and snow flurries in enemy territory, the convoy proceeded with caution. The streets were mostly empty, except for the military columns and small groups of Germans, with their arms outstretched in the Nazi salute, looking rather lonely between the rows of houses in a seemingly empty environment. Even in Prague no one took notice of Hitler's column of cars, as he rode into the castle nestled on the Hradschin at about 8:00 p.m.

Together with Bormann, Himmler, and Wolff, Hitler was led into a room with a window offering a wide view. For a few moments he looked out over the Moldau Arch, the Charles Bridge in the foreground and, behind it, the city on the eastern bank of the river and, most notably, the Josefstadt—the Jewish quarter. The Czechs were cowering that evening; they remained invisible. It was their way of surviving the German dictator. The Jews did not have that opportunity, because the Gestapo commandos were already swarming out to hunt. Wolff saw the Führer standing at the window, his head back, fists clenched, enjoying the view of the conquered city. He heard him say, "Here I stand, and no power in this world will take me away again." Hitler had spoken similar words of power a couple of times, on January 30, 1933, at the window of the Reich Chancellery for example, but Wolff had never been present until now. For that reason, the sentence, "as if uttered at a historic moment," made a lasting impression on him. Hitler immediately delivered a historical addendum: during the Middle Ages Prague was the heart of Europe and it was said back then that whoever rules this city is the ruler of the continent. There was no evidence in history between 800 and 1500 to validate that statement, but it illustrated Hitler's aspirations perfectly.

Just six months had passed when, on the eve of the Munich conference at the Berlin Sportspalast and broadcast to all German radio stations, he thundered away: "We want no Czechs!" No one in his entourage reminded him of this now at the Prague castle. They stood only in thoughtful admiration next to him and felt like participants in the newly acquired power. Hitler, however, could already smell the danger; he harbored no illusions about the feelings of the Czechs. He would not put it past them to attempt an assassination or a coup. In addition, only a few German units so far had reached the capital. He ordered Himmler to secure the castle against all potential threats; therefore SS Gruppenführer and Lieutenant General Karl Wolff would become the castle commander. Hitler did not even stay at the castle for 24 hours, but Wolff with pride fulfilled the assignment, which entrusted him with the life and livelihood of the Führer, even for a short time. Since the SS guards in the entourage were not adequate to secure such a large area, he took over a battalion of motorcycle marksmen—an infantry unit on motorcycles. It was the first time that an army unit was under the command of an SS officer. Wolff enjoyed this even more when he recognized the commander of the battalion as an officer with whom he been in training during the First World War. That officer remained in the army since then; now he was major, far removed from the rank of general.

This assignment ensured that Wolff did not hear much of the political and military conversation taking place at the castle. He was busy through the night looking for weak spots in security within those old walls. Posts had to be set up to block off halls and paths; rooms had to be searched and roofs were secured. The huge cellar vaults with their underground connecting passages, a maze of tunnels, were a big source of worry. Someone could easily stack hundreds of pounds of dynamite beneath the rooms occupied by the Führer. And the overtired guards could easily fall asleep. All this responsibility kept the Castle Commander from getting any sleep at all during the night of March 15–16, 1939.

Before Hitler left Prague that afternoon, Himmler, Heydrich and Wolff were allowed to be present as several hundred German students from Prague University cheered him in the courtyard of the castle. Generals Keitel and von Brauchitsch were also allowed to be there. They could show off their latest medals for the first time: the Party emblem twined with a gold-plated crown. Originally it had been a decoration for older Party comrades with a member number under 100,000. Wolff had no reason to envy the generals, because he had been wearing that decoration since January 30, having rendered outstanding services to the Party.

Six days later, on March 22, 1939, he and Himmler were once again in tow on Hitler's special train. One more piece of land was being added to the collection. There was a German song about an outpost in the northeast: "as far as the Memel…" But since the Treaty of Versailles, the city of Memel, on the river of the same name, and a long strip of the Baltic coast were part of the sovereign territory of the Lithuanian Republic. They had taken over this area and its many German inhabitants through a military coup and kept it until now because no one wanted to risk a war over it. For Hitler, Lithuania was just a small fish compared to his previous conquests, but because he was cleaning up so nicely, he wanted to add 150,000 more people as well. The Lithuanians had hardly resisted his demand that the territory be returned to the Reich.

The special train went from Berlin to the Baltic port of Swinemünde, where they boarded the ships of the German navy, and set an eastward course towards the harbor of Memel. Himmler, with his staff and security commandos, had the assignment to advance from the East Prussian city of Tilsit into the land to be annexed by truck, ahead of the soldiers of the armed forces. Then, in Memel, they were to show the newly appointed mayor and police chief how to receive a Führer.

At the King of Prussia Hotel in the border city of Tilsit, Himmler, Wolff, Heydrich, and Kurt Daluege (the latter two responsible for the police) conferred until midnight. Then, in the first hours of March 23, their column of cars passed across the Queen Louise Bridge over the Memel, led by an East Prussian SS officer who knew the way. But the pilot was in a weaker powered car than Himmler's in his heavy Maybach; the Reichsführer gave the order to pass the "snail."

After a few kilometers, Himmler's driver had to abruptly step on the brakes because the street in front of them was blocked off by a mess of wires. Soldiers in foreign uniforms darted from the right and the left out of the dark forest. They encircled the ten cars in the column, their rifles ready to shoot. No one understood their shouting and they did not respond to German commands. Wolff and Heydrich negotiated with gestures, spread out a map, and discovered under the glow of a flashlight that they were clearly inside Lithuanian territory, having missed a turn.

Before they could come to an understanding whistles sounded out of the forest, and the Lithuanian military disappeared into the night between the tree trunks. The column turned and reached the city of Memel two hours later. There everything went according to plan. Hitler landed at 2:00 p.m., held a very short integration speech from the balcony of the State Theater for those gathered, and awarded the former leader of the Memel-German ethnic group the golden Party emblem. After about two and a half hours, he once again boarded the ship back to Swinemünde. Himmler and Wolff drove around the countryside for a short time and took pictures of the new acquisition. It was not exactly impressive. Border territories are seldom blessed with great riches, especially in the east. If the SS officer had gotten as far as the northernmost corner, they would have reached the new border crossing into Lithuania. They could have taken the town's name to be a prophecy: Nimmersatt (never satiated).

Had Wolff still doubted by then that Hitler wanted to have his war now—which eluded him both at the Munich Conference and again in Prague—the coming weeks would clearly show what the future would bring. On May 13, 1939, Wolff's 39th birthday, the Prague escort was assembled again; it included Himmler, Wolff, Bormann, and Reich Chief Press Officer Dr. Otto Dietrich. The family birthday celebration at Wolff's home had to be cancelled, as the Führer's special train left the Berlin Anhalter station that evening. The destination was the West Wall, a chain of military fortifications of the most different types—cement stubs to block tanks, machine gun bunkers, anti-tank casemates, guns, and howitzers—had been in construction for over two years, employing an army of workers and engineers. The concrete strip between the Belgian border and the bend in the Rhine near Basel required so much iron and cement that these materials were in short supply for private construction. Through weekly newsreels and newspaper articles, the German people were being told that no one could get through! That mistake would surface at the beginning of 1945, when the Allied armies penetrated the Reich from the west.

During the spring of 1939 millions of cubic meters of concrete provided the background of Hitler's appearances. On May 14 he trudged with his satellites and the Wehrmacht general in charge in the area around Aalen and then on the heights of the Eifel. On May 15, they met above the Mosel where a large table was waiting covered with a white tablecloth. The Wehrmacht was inviting the supreme commander to lunch. The sitting arrangements went, as usual, distributed by rank; Himmler and Wolff were to sit in the middle table. Magnanimously neither sat near the Führer; they exchanged their seats with Wehrmacht officers from the side table, because in Berlin they "had already had the honor and privilege to see Hitler during meals so many times." In spite of this, they could see that he enjoyed the classic field meal; that included peas and bacon. The vegetarian Hitler even had seconds.

The inspection tour did not end until May 19 on the upper Rhine near the Swiss border. From there the special train went directly to the drill ground at Munster, where generations of soldiers had been trained. Hitler expected more than the usual simulation of war action with a lot of shooting and noise. On this May 20, the Waffen SS wanted to show him for the first time how far they had progressed in their war preparations. Felix Steiner, a Reichswehr officer who switched over to the SS, was directing the event. After changing positions, he showed how he wished future soldiers to behave in a battalion of the SS regiment *Deutschland* stationed in Ellwangen in Württemberg. In this training, instead of drills in the barracks courtyard, they did high performance athletics. Steiner strove for a "relaxed and elastic type of soldier with an athletic stance, but with above-average marching and fighting ability." Instead of the cumbersome '98 carbine, he preferred using submachine guns as firearms, along with hand grenades and dynamite, which on the whole were less cumbersome for the soldiers in combat. Steiner's soldiers improved their physical condition with tough backpacking marches of over 65 kilometers, in part wearing gas masks.

Was he too hard on his men? His soldiers were volunteers whose status in the National Socialist state had not yet been legally confirmed. They were proud of their performance; they felt they were an elite, and loudly praised the camaraderie, teamwork, and the involvement of the officers. Steiner had left the army because he had made himself unpopular with his suggestions of total reform. Now, there were also generals from the army invited to see this showpiece on May 20 in Munster. What they saw was for them something truly unparalleled. An attack on an infantry position defended by trenches and wire obstacles using real ammunition rather than blank cartridges and where the impact of hand firearms, like machine guns using live ammunition and real hand grenades being thrown, was demonstrated.

For the SS it was a day of triumph over the army, which had always looked down at the Waffen SS. The Supreme Warlord did not spare his praise, although he kept to his opinion that the soldier is best equipped with the conventional rifle because automatic weapons used too much ammunition unnecessarily. The Wehrmacht generals congratulated him and asked whether anyone had been injured. Wolff replied that only a few had been slightly wounded by shrapnel. The machine gun shelling went just above the men's heads, and missed, while hand grenades detonated only where no one could be hurt. Standartenführer Steiner was very much in favor with Himmler and Hitler. Six years later, in April 1945, Hitler was ranting about both men in the underground bunker of the Berlin chancellery. The traitor Himmler negotiated with the enemy and General of the Waffen SS Steiner did not obey the Führer's orders. Steiner was supposed to break open the ring of the Red Army tightened around the German capital with his army group and free Hitler, but he did not wish to lose his weary division for such a futile undertaking at the last moment. The rivalry between the army and the Waffen SS had long been brewing. The officers raised in the idea of remaining politically neutral as stipulated by the Weimar Constitution saw themselves as having a choice: either to take on the swastika themselves or to give up their monopoly as "the defenders of the nation" (according to Hitler). Their distrust was justified. Himmler's troops said that their competition still included reactionary monarchists. There were taunts and arguments that made the climate even worse. In the higher ranks, both camps were intriguing against each other, and sometimes it came down to blows. This was nothing new; similar fistfights took place under the emperor between units or between different classes. Behavioral scientists are not surprised by such herd mentality.

The conciliatory Wolff was often called upon to quiet things down. The former lieutenant of the bodyguard regiment found that officers of the army listened to him because he would tell them that he missed out on his military career due to timing; the Reichswehr had discharged him in 1920 because it had too many men. For that reason in January 1938, when incidents of violence were on the rise, he was brought in to secure an agreement between the SS and the Wehrmacht. He managed to stop the fistfights that simply turned into office feuds. In the summer, the Supreme Command of the Army asked for a new structure that would include all the military units of the Party as well.

Reichsleiter Martin Bormann, who at that time was still the chief of staff to Rudolf Hess, Hitler's deputy for Party matters, was inclined to accept a suggestion by the military where, at first, the highest local Party official and the troop commander would settle any dispute. But Himmler and Wolff demanded an exception for the SS Reserves and the SS Death's Head divisions, which included the concentration camp guards, because otherwise maybe "some dignified member, not quite mature enough to fully comprehend the Wehrmacht's position," (meaning a Party functionary) "could take this onto himself." Finally, it was agreed upon to put the military SS and the Wehrmacht on equal footing if there was any trouble; the respective commanders had to work it out among themselves. In practical terms this meant recognizing the SS as military units, which was precisely what Himmler wanted to accomplish. In December 1938 Wolff imparted instructions to the "SS Court" still reporting to him to pass the agreement down, "so that unit leaders would know that they must get involved in settling these matters."

Wolff knew full well why the SS was reluctant to let the Party settle its clashes with the army—because the comrades in the black uniforms were no angels. They often behaved like nervous young animals compelled to go on a rampage because of the restrained arrogance of the Wehrmacht officers. Oswald Pohl, who was at the time SS Gruppenführer and chief of the SS Economics and Administrative Main Office, complained in July 1938, in a letter to Wolff, about the conceit and arrogance that was being taught in the schools especially set up to improve the bearing of the SS officers and the SS Junkers. As a former navy paymaster, Pohl was setting particularly high standards but, amazingly enough, the young men did not behave that way. They were taught that they were racially, physically, and by their character the best selection the nation could offer. It stood to reason that they, as the crème de la crème among Germans, had special rights. Comrade Pohl received no answer from Wolff, who preferred to handle anything critical in private. He reacted differently when Himmler assigned him to discipline an SS officer. In July 1938 he issued a warning to an Obersturmbannführer and fulltime SS functionary to register his engagement; the girl's parents, whom the defaulting lover had promised marry, had appealed to the Reichsführer. Himmler strongly encouraged marriage because it increased the birthrate.

The Obersturmbannführer at first ignored Wolff's letter. He had to be reminded five times to answer. After seventeen months it finally arrived in December 1939; the author apologized for neglecting his loved one, using the excuse that he had been so taken with political events that it "had not been possible to handle personal matters in what little free time he had with the required energy" he dedicated to the SS service. He did not even set a date for the engagement. Shortly before Easter in 1940, Wolff sent the next reminder, possibly thinking that springtime could encourage love. But this didn't work either. After more letters, all of them unsuccessful, Wolff wrote on the file: "postpone until after the war."

In yet another love story settled within higher SS ranks, the chief of the personal staff could only act as an advisor. An outraged father and retired lieutenant of the Austrian imperial and royal army wrote to Rudolf Hess, who was frequently appealed to when a matter concerned a prominent Party member, that his daughter had been terribly deceived by the "unbelievable conduct of a Party comrade" and horribly offended in her feminine honor. When the Party was outlawed she had "hidden this man and other National Socialists in our house when they were being hunted down." However, when her lover became Gauleiter after Hitler's invasion of Vienna, he had visited less and less frequently. Now he sent a "Dear John" letter offering the bride 10,000 marks as compensation. Could Hess please—so the father asked—see to it that the man honor his promise to marry?

The accusation concerned Party comrade Odilo Globocnik, one of the most brutal Nazis in Austria. Hess passed this on to Bormann and Himmler, since the accused no longer served as gauleiter, but rather as SS Brigadeführer, who was getting ready for his future assignment as mass murderer in the newly conquered Polish district of Lublin. The Reichsführer SS had great plans for him. Therefore, in his talks with the heads of the Party, the soothing Wolff had, at least for a time, to make sure that the affair had no further repercussions. He decided that Gauleiter Friedrich Rainer, who was in Salzburg at the time, be called in as an arbitrator. He did not want to play an active role in this case for several reasons; during his visit to Krumpendorf, he was able to get father and daughter to remain quiet. They were promised that when the time was right, they could present their complaint directly to Himmler. Someone in Wolff's office in April 1940 wrote in the file: "postpone until after the war."

The reason that Wolff's part in this love story was behind the scenes was not simply because, as one of the Führer's many aides at headquarters, he was busy with other assignments. He was also friendly with Odilo Globocnik and therefore wanted to avoid the accusation of not being objective should there be an argument. On top of that, he was himself getting deeply involved in an affair that began as a casual flirt but now threatened to become a serious problem.

It is rather difficult to deal with the love life of the subject of a biography who is meant to be emblematic of an era. How does someone behave under Nazism even in this area? In Wolff's case it is necessary to also deal with family matters, because the general in drafting his self-laudatory autobiography took pains to write a chapter about his women.

A psychoanalyst could better explain how an escapade turned into such a passion (for which Wolff put his rank and position on the line) that ended his marriage with Frieda von Römheld, in order to marry his mistress Inge. In his forties he was one of the most attractive men in Berlin—tall, strong, and athletic. Himmler had in him an SS officer who was thin, blond and blue-eyed, with the confidence of an officer and the cultured manners of a gentleman, a brilliant conversationalist, an excellent dancer, all dressed in a decorative uniform, with a South German accent, easily making friends in the dour Prussian capital of Germany. If he courted a woman, it would be difficult for her to discourage him, especially when so many women clearly signaled that they were attracted to him. Countess Ingeborg Maria von Bernstorff did not conceal her feelings in the summer of 1934, shortly after Wolff moved to the Prinz-Albrecht-Strasse following the Röhm murders. She came to ask for Himmler's support in a charity affair. In retrospect, Wolff called this first meeting "for both of us a feast for the eyes." She saw him as a "charming blond in an adorable light blue suit." She naturally got to see the Reichsführer SS and on that occasion they saw each other again, flirting this time.

She was not quite as blue-blooded as he thought, with his fixation about the aristocracy. She was the daughter of a Hamburg businessman, Ludolph Christensen, and married into the Bernstorff family as a step into the Gotha handbook. Her husband served as head of administration of a local district, which was still at the time the Prussian state of Harbourg, on the southern bank of the Elbe. The couple spent the summer of 1934 there, where even then the rich and the beautiful went on vacation, at Kampen on the North Sea island of Sylt. The star guest that year was Hermann Göring, Reich minister of aviation, Reichstag president and Prussian prime minister, just to mention the most important of his functions and titles of the moment.

As head of the Prussian government, he gave preferential treatment to his officer Bernstorff and his wife. She was young, full of energy and happy; her husband was more than ten years older and in poor health. The Reich minister of aviation had his airplane on the island, which, as a former fighter pilot and a captain in the war (he was decorated with the medal "pour le mérite") he usually flew himself. On the day he left, Göring took the count and the countess to the airport. There, he invited the lady to inspect the cockpit, when suddenly the door closed. In this rather breezy manner, the countess was kidnapped to Berlin. She spent the night at the house of the Reichstag president as guest and was very honorably treated, as Wolff later found out.

This incident of course amused prominent figures of the political scene; they invited the count and countess to many of their private festivities. Wolff learned from Inge Bernstorff later that ministers at these events had surrounded her with the then widowed Army Minister Werner von Blomberg, Rudolf Hess, and a minister without anything specific to do except for ensuring cooperation between the Party and the State. Wolff could not be close to the woman in all her glory at that time because he only had the rank of SS Oberführer and was only allowed to attended society functions as Himmler's shadow.

Both the lady and the gentleman were married at that time, but not with each other; however, she was less happy than he. The count suffered increasingly because of the consequences of his war injuries. Wolff was in the process of having his wife and two small daughters move to Berlin. He had rented a house with a beautiful garden and seven rooms in fashionable Dahlem. This complicated matters considerably. The countess's circumstances, on the other hand, became clearer when her husband died in April 1935. No one expected his widow, a beautiful thirty-one year-old woman, to remain alone and in mourning for too long.

It so happened that Wolff was rewarded with an trip to east Asia aboard the passenger vessel *Potsdam* by a member of Himmler's "circle of friends," the chairman of the board at the North German Lloyd. The countess took the trip in his place. Reinhard Heydrich, whose office was next to Wolff's at the Prinz-Albrecht-Strasse, enjoyed himself by having her watched during the trip and occasionally reporting back to his friend Karl. The Gestapo and SD had already placed their spies on almost every passenger ship. The countess, Wolff found out, let herself be courted by a Wittelsbach prince, who was commonly known in the Vatican to be a priest. She also made friends with an older couple among the passengers, with whom she amused herself now and again when they went ashore; their name was Hecht and they were Jewish. This did not put an end to their love and he was happy when she was pleased.

Wolff's family did not stay in Berlin long. Were they in his way all of a sudden? Whatever the reason for their return to Bavaria may have been, Wolff argued that they had to save money. He had already bought the property at Rottach-Egern on Lake Tegern and had begun the construction of the "my family manor." Much later he would add another reason: the Führer sometimes stayed at Berchtesgaden for months on end, and as the SS officer having special assignments it was more convenient to have a permanent residence nearby. As previously mentioned, the house had caused Wolff a bit of trouble. His sons, born in 1936 and 1938 in Munich, grew up in that house. Another son was born to Wolff three months before his youngest brother. This was no a miracle of nature, since they were half-brothers. The countess came to Bavaria at the end of 1937. Hoping to avoid gossip, he turned to his friend Heydrich, who, given his duties, was experienced in handling secrets and therefore took care of things discretely. He was friendly with a Hungarian colleague and provided the expectant mother with a new name and passport, as well as a bed at the clinic of the most famous gynecologist in Budapest. It was rumored in political circles that one of Hitler's lovers was in the Hungarian capital to have her baby. Because of his presence and rank, her escort, who had just become an SS Gruppenführer, contributed to that legend, did not deny it, and quite enjoyed it.

Wolff's ménage à trois, whatever those involved felt, was kept private, as much as possible. A respectable upper class talented gentleman engulfed in the vortex of National Socialism cannot hide his private life, showing how over the years Nazi ideas and methods intruded into all areas of life. When Wolff was asked in 1978 why he got involved in this situation, he pointed out that his son, Widukind Thorsun, born at the end of 1937 in Budapest, had features found only among the Nordic race. "The children from my first marriage are excellent racially, in character and in performance. Because their father is blond and blue eyed and their mother however has brown hair and brown eyes, their appearance is not markedly Nordic, but rather a mix of both parents." A statement in the spirit and manner of National Socialist thought and training.

What the SS general actually meant was: "I, Karl Wolff, one of the highest SS officers, would have acted irresponsibly towards the nation and state had I wasted my valuable genes in a marriage that could only produce half-breeds. Therefore, I had to procreate other children with a woman of the best Nordic traits. By committing adultery and entering into the second marriage resulting from the affair, I was only serving the Germanic Reich of the German Nation." Whether these arguments were actually part of his innermost beliefs or whether they only served as an alibi to placate his guilty conscience we will never know.

Both in love and in his career things were looking up for Karl Wolff in the spring of 1939, and the German people felt blessed by the gods. A census revealed that they really were a nation of 80 million as Party propagandists, anticipating gain, had boasted of years before. When Hitler came to power the country was still small, but in the meantime it had grown into a giant. The Führer was always reveling in superlatives; and now the Germans were doing the same thing. Megalomania was a national illness.

Wolff's position had grown exponentially since Himmler enlarged it to the SS main office; the chief of the personal staff became independent. He no longer had to get everything approved by Himmler and it became necessary for him to acquire more authority on his own. As

Himmler's right-hand man he felt justified in observing the heads of other main offices. His own main office was divided into seven offices, each headed by upper echelon SS ranks, up to gruppenführer. On the other hand, they directed nine main departments, six departments and one "assigned to canine matters." Himmler created this position on a whim; it was occupied by an SS Standartenführer, equal in rank to a regimental commander; officially he was called "Dog-Müller" because of his family name.

Several positions were essentially copies of those SS main offices headed by Wolff's colleagues. More or less reluctantly they sent him copies of their correspondence for his acknowledgement. Therefore much more paperwork crossed his desk than he could possibly have read. Within his own office, however, he did not like written documents that the recipient could "confidently take home with him." In delicate matters he preferred handling things orally. Although many documents from his office outlasted the war, relatively few documents can be found that he wrote or signed. The signatures of Werner Grothmann, Heinrich Heckenstaller, Willy Suchanek, Otto Ullmann, and Dr. Rudolf Brandt appear more often. This worked to Wolff's advantage after the war. He assured the denazification judges, more or less successfully, that he was basically Himmler's chief of protocol and was only responsible for ceremonial matters.

Correct as that may have been among other things, Wolff's duties did include preparing public appearances by the Reichsführer or taking part personally in any event that Hitler, with his pompous staging effects, turned into the mandatory rituals of the Party and the state. Wolff had plenty of opportunities during those spring and summer weeks of 1939. There was first of all the Führer's fiftieth birthday (he no longer wanted to hear "and Reich Chancellor"). The festivities began the day before April 20, as Hitler, in the 40-meter-long Mosaic Room of the new Reich Chancellery, which had only been completed three months before, was introduced to the young lieutenants—the Untersturmführers of the SS Reserves. They had been through the tough training at the SS Junker School in Braunschweig and were being rewarded with a handshake by the Führer, who walked down the row with Himmler and Wolff. On the following morning, before 11:00 a.m., both were already standing at a grandstand built on the newly created East-West axis. To honor the birthday, soldiers of every kind of unit marched, rolled on wheels or chains, or even flew at low altitude down the avenue for four hours. This was clearly no longer a happy festivity; it was meant to be a threat to anyone opposed to any further aggressive acts. In the late afternoon both SS leaders went to the

Reich Chancellery. All Reich party leaders (including Himmler) were invited to a tea reception.

If Wolff had missed the meaning of the big military parade, then the Reichstag speech eight days later would provide the required commentary. It was very clear to the national representative from Darmstadt that harsher chords would be played in foreign policy from then on. France was told that it depended upon its good conduct as to whether or not Germany would resurrect its claims on Strasbourg and Metz; England found out about the cancellation of the Naval Treaty, which had limited the strength of the German navy; President Franklin D. Roosevelt was strongly attacked for having warned the aggressor Hitler; Poland was clearly told that the revision of its borders was unavoidable and that if Poland did not understand this peacefully, it would take place through war.

In the middle of May retired General Friedrich Count von der Schulenburg died. He had been Chief of the General Staff of an army group in World War I, and had the high rank of Obergruppenführer in the SS, but without much specific influence. Wolff at different times, but always in vain, had suggested him to the Reichsführer for special assignments, seeking through him to strengthen the white glove faction. Naturally the Reichsführer and Wolff drove to the funeral in Potsdam together on the morning of May 23. Hitler had ordered the heads of the Wehrmacht to come to his study that afternoon for "instructions regarding the situation and policy goals." What would be said there was already known ahead of time at the Prinz-Albrecht-Strasse. Hitler announced his "decision to attack Poland at the first suitable opportunity. It's not about Danzig," he said. "For us, it's about expanding our *lebensraum* to the east."

Those who knew what was going on must have smirked when Hitler let it be announced on July 10 that this year's Party rally at Nuremberg would take place at the beginning of September and would be called "The Party Convention for Peace." The SS leadership knew better, and therefore in June, anticipating war, already transferred the III Sturmbann of the Death's Head Division from its garrison in Berlin-Adlershof to Danzig. There the SS Reserves had already been declared the "Home Army," strengthened by local volunteers and equipped with better weapons. Clearly Wolff was informed about these war preparations, as we know from the diary of Major Gerhard Engel, Hitler's army adjutant. At the date of July 4, he noted, "Today I could put one over the SS. From Wolff, who always talks a lot," he found out that Himmler wanted to reorganize the Danzig Reserves and equip them as a brigade. Engel thwarted this plan with an order that he had Hitler sign. Engel triumphed: "... with that the question of the Death's Head division in Danzig is taken care of ..." His joy proved to be short lived; three months later Danzig was "brought back to the Reich," the SS would be as powerful there as in the Reich, and the Wehrmacht would no longer have a whole lot to say in the new Reichsgau. These two opponents would know each other better by then as both were part of Hitler's closest entourage.

Already during the last eight weeks before the outbreak of the war, the tall, smart SS Gruppenführer was often seen near his top commander. So on August 16 at Obersalzberg a really farfetched anniversary was celebrated so that Hitler could show once again how much his soldiers honored him. On August 16, 1914, a 25-year-old artist with Austrian citizenship joined the Bavarian Reserve-Infantry Regiment 16 as a war volunteer in Munich. This became a 25-year military anniversary, with a congratulatory parade, goose-stepping, and marching music.

In the early hours of the evening on August 24, Hitler returned to Berlin, signaling a constant state of alert for top political and military circles. It was no longer a question whether Poland would be attacked any time soon; the only thing not set was the date when the first shots would be fired. Even the procedures were agreed upon, suggesting to the public that the war was an unavoidable defense against mortal dangers. The preparations were already being made for an event that would create the immediate pretext for hostilities, placing all the blame on the enemy. The SD prepared a fake raid by Polish troops to be broadcast on the German radio station at Gleiwitz. It had also already been decided that Hitler would announce the state of war, justifying it during a great speech at the Reichstag. Nazi party leaders throughout the Reich were only waiting for the cue calling a meeting of all representatives to the Kroll Opera House in Berlin.

Chief of the Personal Staff of the Reichsführer SS Wolff worked and lived in the Reich capital. Along with his employer Himmler, he found out the news. They heard that Hitler had already set the start of the war for August 26 at 04.30 (4:30 a.m.). Like many other dignitaries, they made their way to the Reich Chancellery on the morning of August 25; everyone wanting to be present when Hitler gave the cue which would lock in the attack for the following morning. According to army plans, this had to happen by 15.00 (3:00 p.m.) at the latest. And two minutes after the hour those waiting saw the Führer step through his door and heard how he simply announced, "Operation White!" That was the code word for the campaign against Poland.

Wolff assumed he would already be traveling on Hitler's special train due east the following day. As Hitler wished—he always made a point of emphasizing this—Wolff should constantly be nearby. But his assignment was obviously never more specific than that. Later he attached great value at being rated as liaison officer, but at the outbreak of the war the post didn't even exist. Marching against the enemy were the *Leibstandarte*, under their commander, Sepp Dietrich—practically a regiment—along with the regiment *Germania*, the Standarte *Deutschland*, a newly formed artillery regiment and smaller units. All these units were incorporated into the army and on Hitler's orders under the Supreme Commander of the Army. There was therefore no need for an individual representative at the Führer's headquarters, as had the army, the navy, and the air force.

At Wolff's sentencing in Munich in 1964, his role at Hitler's headquarters was described as "Himmler's eyes and ears." In this area he naturally represented the armed SS units according to Himmler's instructions. The most important thing for Himmler was that all of his units be centralized in a closed organization. Wolff's direct connection to the Reserves was, however, rather minimal because they were under the SS High Command, which like the troops repeated that Wolff could never be their man, simply because he had not even served for a single day within their ranks. When despite this he became their first lieutenant general in 1937 he was given the rank and appropriate insignia for obvious decorative reasons. It was all tempered by the fact that his rank insignia were initially narrower and adorned with less tinsel than the Wehrmacht. This changed later on, but to the new Waffen SS he remained a desk general and a political functionary.

For Himmler, Wolff's position at the Führer headquarters was key since the Reichsführer feared that the Führer, surrounded by high-ranking military officers, could distance himself from a Party military unit. The SA, even though stripped of their power in the Röhm affair, was represented in Hitler's entourage by the "personal adjutant of the Führer," Wilhelm Brückner, wearing the uniform of an SA Obergruppenführer, and a trusted comrade since the putsch days in 1923. He was something of an institution, even if his reputation was beginning to wane, as he was getting unmistakably older. Wolff was not as tall, but his intellectual ability was far superior. To fill a precarious position within Hitler's entourage Himmler could find no one better among his men than precisely the one Führer had chosen.

Why Hitler picked Wolff is a matter of conjecture. His appearance may have played a role, along with his smooth officer's manners, an ability to inspire confidence that contradicted the flowery statements like "Jawohl!" and "As you order!" There was also the incident with the drum major's baton during Mussolini's visit in Munich, whereby Wolff showed he could react quickly. Other considerations may have also played a role for those within the SS who were thinking about who might be Himmler's successor should anything happen to him. Would it be Heydrich or Wolff? Hitler always kept the top men in his movement insecure by making it look as if he were setting up a crown prince.

Hitler made sure that neither Wolff nor Himmler had the slightest influence over world events during the final days of August 1939 in Berlin. He didn't even ask for their opinion. They stood around like many others in the upper party echelon at the Reich chancellery, waiting for the decision that was so crucial to their fate. War could increase their respect and power, but defeat could plunge them into ruin. No one can say what Karl Wolff felt in those afternoon hours of August 25, as he believed hostilities would begin the next day. It was said that during the Czech crisis he and Himmler belonged to the hawks but that this time they were among the doves.

Wolff expected to be ordered to attend the Reichstag meeting the next day and get his marching orders to the Führer headquarters. In the course of the evening this proved to be premature. At 7:00 p.m., ten hours before his armies were to start moving, Hitler rescinded his order to attack. He still wanted "to find out if we could get rid of the English interference," he told Göring. But the emergency telegrams to hundreds of Reichstag deputies inside the Reich could not be stopped that evening as they boarded their sleeping cars to Berlin. Not until they arrived in the Reich capital on August 26 and registered in the hotels did they find out that they may not be needed, but should remain available until their taskmaster Martin Bormann gave them further orders.

August 26 was a turbulent day for many Germans. Holiday guests ended their vacations, but the Reichsbahn trains were already not following the normal schedule because military transports had priority. Whoever wanted to travel home by car would find gas stations closed since gasoline stores had been requisitioned by the Wehrmacht. From newspapers that Saturday evening and radio broadcasts Germans found out that they would only be able to obtain groceries, clothing, coal, and other staples in the future by using coupons or tickets. There was no enthusiasm for the war, as Wolff compared it with his recollections of the First World War. People were serious, and many felt depressed by horrible forebodings. Most of them were hoping that the Führer would not let it come to war and, as in the past, the crisis would end in a diplomatic victory at the last minute.

Wolff had already given up hope. He knew that on August 22 Hitler announced to many commanding generals in the Hall at the Berghof, that he would begin this unavoidable war because Germany had the best head start in armaments. In addition, he had the greatest following among the German people than any head of state before, but that he could also "at any time be eliminated by a criminal or an idiot." Due to his agreement with Stalin, the situation for war had become more favorable than it would ever be in the foreseeable future. Wolff was in the know: the date for the attack was postponed, but not cancelled.

This view was confirmed on August 27 at 5:00 p.m. when Himmler, Wolff, and Heydrich met with Goebbels and Bormann at the Reich chancellery. Hitler wanted to give the nervously expectant Reichstag deputies, including the Gau leaders, an explanation to gain some time. They could return home, but he would call them again soon because he was determined "to take care of the question in the east, one way or another." He would then "go to war using the most brutal and inhumane means." What he did not say was that no matter what France and England decided, September 1 at 4:45 a.m. was his final and irrevocable date for the invasion of Poland. Since the British would not negotiate this time, he prophesied—as Colonel Nikolaus von Vormann, liaison officer of the army, noted—"that France and England are only going to act as though they want to go to war," until Poland has been conquered. Many Germans shared that opinion, and Wolff was one of them.

Therefore the Reichstag deputies were alerted by cable for the second time on August 31. When they gathered at the Kroll Opera House on the morning of September 1, Wolff being among them, more than one hundred were missing because they had joined the Wehrmacht. They would not have been allowed to decide anything anyway since their assignment was to celebrate Hitler. On the way from the Reich chancellery to the opera house this time, he had to forego the usual cheering parade. The correspondent for the *Zuricher Zeitung* commented: "a thin row of spectators. Some applause could be heard." The deputies, however, greeted their Führer wildly, as was their duty. He was wearing a field gray uniform, of which he said in his speech, he would "only take it off after victory—or, I will not survive the end." The applause was as long and as loud as usual, because Reichstag President Hermann Göring ensured that the professional cheering crowd would have its normal booming volume, by simply assigning reliable Party comrades to the seats of the men who had been called up by the Wehrmacht.

From this hour on, Wolff awaited his Führer's call. He had to wait, however, until the official declarations of war by England and France reached the Reich chancellery. For two days, Chief of the Personal Staff of the Reichsführer SS Wolff went from his office to the Reich chancellery, always ready to grab his marching gear. Not until September 3 did Hitler decide "to go to the front," as he announced in four proclamations to the people, the soldiers of the eastern armies, the western armies, and the Party comrades.

"To my great and, I openly admit, joyful surprise I was ordered to the innermost Führer headquarters," remembered Karl Wolff in his eighties. "Hitler wanted to have me nearby, because he knew that he could rely on me completely. He had known me for a long time, and rather well." And not without pride, he recalled that even before the war he had often been a welcome guest at the "round table," that Hitler usually offered to his confidants at the Reich chancellery.

Wolff used the privilege during the exciting days before leaving for the front. He certainly didn't benefit from any culinary delicacies, since the vegetarian Hitler, who was anything but a gourmet, suffered from digestive problems and feared that even the slightest sign of a paunch and any hint of high living would reduce his popularity. With all Germans on war rations with grocery tickets, the cooks at the Reich chancellery were to make do with what the average person was eating. This rule was observed until Hitler's final days. His entourage got around this constantly without him even noticing. Arthur Kannenberg, who headed the household, had connections, as did every cook, and Martin Bormann was constantly ordering food supplies from the Party farms (at Obersalzberg and Mecklenburg) for the Führer's table.

When Wolff arrived at the Reich chancellery at midday on September 3, he wore the field gray SS uniform, with the royal eagle holding the swastika on the upper left sleeve. He was given a gas mask, like all soldiers, that members of the Führer headquarters were to always carry in their gray tin cans. He was told that they would not eat until late afternoon and that he was, however, to have his bags ready at headquarters for transport.

In one room there was a large area map of Poland pinned to the wall and stuck with little flags. Happily Wolff realized that the armies had already advanced briskly since the previous day. Czestochowa, a religious shrine, was marked with a "Sepp" flag; that especially pleased the SS officer, because it meant that the Leibstandarte had fought there under its commander, Sepp Dietrich.

That afternoon the company at the table was more numerous than commonly accepted: Party big wigs, ministers, generals—like theater actors who were in Hitler's good graces—all made great efforts to sound confident, even though the second afternoon radio news broadcast stated that now England was also at war with the Reich. A stew was served, and field cooks ladled it from the cauldron for the deployed soldiers as well.

Around 8:00 p.m. the entourage was ordered to take their designated seats in the cars in the courtyard of the Reich chancellery. The stars were shining particularly brightly, because the mandatory darkness throughout Germany also applied there. Not everyone found his car right away. Hitler came out last with his adjutant. The guards presented arms and the convoy took the Wilhelmstrasse to the Stettin train station. All the lights were out in the streets and only from very narrow slits did any light seep through from the houses. The headlights of the cars were covered in black cloth that only let a weak shimmer fall onto the pavement. There were hardly any private cars because the Wehrmacht requisitioned large numbers of them and those remaining had only been allotted very little gasoline. The Head of State slipped out of his capital like a thief in the night. The column left the Reich chancellery at 8:00 p.m. At the Stettin train station, dim blue lights marked the way to the entrance. On a very weakly lit platform the special train was waiting. It was to be the Führer headquarters for the immediate future. Everyone already knew his assigned spot inside. At 9:00 p.m. the train left the station.

It consisted of more than ten cars of the express train type, two locomotives, two flat open freight cars equipped with four antiaircraft guns, one baggage car, and electric power units. Hitler's quarters and the conference room in the next car took up the space of about three express train compartments. Conference sessions took place at a table with eight chairs. Two other compartments consisted of Hitler's bedroom and bathroom. His adjutant and servants lived and slept in the other compartments of that car.

The command center with teletype machines and radio equipment was in the following car, as well as the situation room where the conditions at the front were presented to the Führer at a large card table twice a day. The military had their compartments in the third car: Lieutenant General Wilhelm Keitel (head of the OKW), Brigadier General Alfred Jödl (head of the Operations Office), the liaison officers of the army, navy, and air force. Inside the train there were also the adjutants, General Bodenschatz (Göring's deputy), and SS Gruppenführer Wolff. One of the travelers, Reich chief press officer Dr. Otto Dietrich, published a book right after the end of the Polish campaign where Wolff was not mentioned as part of the military, but rather with legation councilor Walter Hewel, the liaison officer of the minister of foreign affairs, and Heinrich Hoffmann, Hitler's court photographer. Wolff was described as "liaison of the Reichsführer SS." His name was spelled incorrectly with one "f." The two men avoided each other, although Dietrich held a high honorary rank in the SS and both had worked very closely with Hitler during the occupation of Prague.

Chapter 6

"...and tomorrow the entire world!"

On the night of September 4, the train had covered less than 300 km, through Pomerania to Bad Polzin, a little town of 6,000 and more than 10,000 holiday visitors each year. As the vacationers looked out of their windows one morning, they saw a train surrounded by the soldiers of a motorized division. Their commander was Brigadier General Erwin Rommel, decorated with the WWI medal "pour le mérite." The unit guarded both the special train as well as the column of cars in which Hitler rode to the front in Poland with tanks, scout cars, and riflemen on motorcycles. Actually the unit only consisted of seven open Mercedes cars with canopy tops, having three axles, for any kind of terrain and all equipped with strong engines. Wherever those cars appeared, it became the signal that Hitler was nearby. So many prominent figures from the Party and the state in Pomerania and even from Berlin streamed into Bad Polzin. They simply lined up in their cars behind the column.

Wolff was upset in seeing his privilege of being among the very few in Hitler's esçorts devalued, but since Hitler saw this as a show of love by his people no one dared put an end to the growing extension of the column. When it became necessary to drive on unpaved roads through the Tuchel heathlands towards Graudenz and the Weichselbogen on the other side of the Polish border, the cars kicked up enormous clouds of dust. If Hitler got out to see first-hand evidence of the Polish defeat or have one of his division commanders report to him, there were bitter fights about position and rank among his fans. Not until Hitler's third trip to the front that left from Neudorf in Upper Silesia on September 10 were the onlookers ordered to stay back. The group from headquarters flew in three Ju 52 passenger planes deep into Poland and then took the cars that had been sent ahead—a procedure that of course was only possible once the enemy air force had been cut off.

After the campaign, Hitler claimed that he had annihilated the Polish state in eighteen days. Dietrich's book tries to back this up; his timetable ends on September 18, although there was still heavy fighting in Warsaw. September 18 was the day when the Red Army moved into eastern Poland, allocated to Stalin in the secret additional protocol of the German-Soviet Non-Aggression Pact that had been signed shortly before the beginning of the war. Towards the end, Hitler wanted to avoid the impression that Moscow had been instrumental in the victory.

The old Hanseatic city of Danzig provided a splendid background for a victory proclamation. A League of Nations commissioner had administered the city, as well as its surroundings, since the Treaty of Versailles; Danzig freely divided its loyalties between Warsaw and Berlin. Now on September 19 Hitler, arriving from Pomerania, triumphantly entered the city. He drove, as he had in Vienna, the Sudetenland and Memel in an open car through the streets where swastika flags practically covered the buildings, through masses of cheering people celebrating their return to the Reich with loud screams of "Heil!" and often tears of joy. Despite the official end of the campaign, the Führer headquarters were not yet dissolved. Immediately following the cheers, Wolff was reminded that he was not simply one of the Führer's escorts but also continued as chief of the personal staff of the Reichsführer SS. Himmler was also in Danzig. Until then he mainly stayed at his own headquarters, a special train codenamed "Heinrich," which he had to share with Minister Dr. Heinrich Lammers, the chief clerk of the Reich chancellery, and Minister of Foreign Affairs Joachim von Ribbentrop. Until September 25, Hitler held court in the old casino hotel on the Baltic Sea resort of Soppot, where Europe's wealthy came to gamble. Now in this amazing building the winnings were of a different nature, as Hitler distributed new areas of responsibility and power from the spoils of war. Himmler managed to reap a considerable piece, thanks to the observers who kept eyes and ears open for him at headquarters during the past weeks. In accordance to the will of the Führer the conquered land was to be cleaned up and made productive. No one seemed better suited for this than Heinrich Himmler. He had already received a new assignment before the war began; accordingly, there were five work groups of 500 men each, immediately behind the fighting units that spread out into the countryside. Their secret assignment was to exterminate the upper class of the Polish people, making it easier to rule and exploit the masses in the future. They worked so thoroughly that their boss Heydrich could already report on September 25: "There are at the most only three percent remaining of the Polish leadership in the occupied territories."

In Danzig Himmler had to make sure that no competitor outdid him in this business. Albert Forster, the local gauleiter, wanted to lead the spontaneous German guerillas seeking revenge by murdering and plundering the Poles, following years of suppression and the crimes of recent weeks. The organization was called "self defense" but it actually threatened only those Poles living in regions where both nationalities were present. Many German nationals had been mistreated or even killed by agitated Polish mobs, but with a new and apparently better order now in place, those crimes would be turned over to the proper courts.

To stop Forster and at the same time control the "cleansing" of the country, Himmler appointed an SS officer to head local self-defense units. One of them was the SS Oberführer Ludolf von Alvensleben. In the West Prussian county of Bromberg he arbitrarily decided about the life or death of the Poles. He felt justified because in this region in particular German nationals had been harassed and murdered in various heinous ways. As Himmler and Wolff went to inspect the region, Alvensleben was able to provide an attraction: he executed about twenty prisoners handed over by his drumhead court-martial supposedly as murderers who had been sentenced to death. Wolff was convinced as a spectator that the punishment was deserved in every case. He coldly watched the executions without scruples and without pity. On the other hand, the behavior of SS Oberführer von Alvensleben outraged him when he took a pistol and gave the "coup de grace" to many victims who had not been properly shot. Wolff said he rejected "an action contrary to the old principles of Prussian tradition." Even a Hessian knew that.

The crimes of the Einsatzgruppen that Heydrich let loose in Poland caused the SS, including Himmler and Wolff, considerably greater aggravation than an unfortunate "formal mistake." Those crimes were contrary to the old Prussian principles and the Wehrmacht issued a protest. Wolff supposedly had no idea these events were taking place. The Wehrmacht leadership sampled the SS encroachments during the first few days. In a town they had just seized, an SS police unit attached to an attacking tank formation from East Prussia gathered the Jews into a church and murdered them. When this was reported to army commander General Georg von Küchler, he placed the SS formations at the disposal of the OKW because he no longer wanted them within his ranks. An SS court-martial dealt with the crime but the sentence was so mild that General von Küchler refused to acknowledge it.

An Einsatzgruppen that had been sent to Upper Silesia by Himmler "for special purposes" under the SS Obergruppenführer Udo von Woyrsch should have indeed feared being prosecuted. Their assignment was to spread panic and terror in the recently seized region to force the Jews to flee to the east. After that the Fourteenth Army reported to the High Command for the East, Lieutenant General Gerd von Rundstedt, that many arbitrary shootings by the SS had outraged the troops because the Einsatzgruppen was killing defenseless people instead of fighting at the front. Rundstedt demanded that Himmler remove Einsatzgruppen Woyrsch from his area of operations. This actually did take place, but instead of units changing positions, they established fixed RSHA posts throughout the entire region that were less noticeable, but continued to kill just as brutally.

These incidents increased as German armies penetrated deeper into the country. Of course, they were also discussed at Hitler's headquarters among the military. Wolff had to report back to the Reichsführer the disgust and outrage within Wehrmacht circles, and as expected the complaints went as high as Hitler. Lieutenant General von Brauchitsch of the Army High Command was responsible for the accusation. Admittedly he and his colleagues should not have been surprised by the mass murders, because on September 12 Hitler had already given the lieutenant general to understand that he intended to conduct a war of extermination in Poland. If the Wehrmacht wanted to have nothing to do with this, then they had to accept that the SS and the Gestapo would be working alongside them.

Neither Himmler nor Wolff needed to be afraid of falling out of grace with the Führer because of the murders, but at the most because the murders were not secretive enough. On the other hand, the OKH was in no rush to level an accusation, and was seeking more to dampen the outrage among the troops. On September 21, Himmler reminded the commanders "that the police Einsatzgruppen were on assignment by the

Führer and according to instructions from the Führer were to carry out certain ethnic political duties" that "lay outside the purview of the High Command." The following day he discussed the situation with Heydrich, whom he advised—in vain—to use moderation. Heydrich tried to make it clear to him that any moderation was impossible if the SS and the police were to fulfill their duties. What Heydrich concluded from the conversation, he shared with his Einsatzgruppen in memo a week later. He reminded them to carry out "the necessary measures in closest cooperation" with the responsible military commanders, and ordered at the same time to concentrate the Jews in a few areas selected for this purpose as the "first requirement for the final solution." Wolff would have the opportunity to become involved in this situation.

At the same time, Himmler was given another assignment whereby the mass murders that had just begun were to attain a higher meaning in the spirit of National Socialism. A decree by Hitler of October 7, 1939, that was never published in its entirety, named the Reichsführer SS as "Reich Commissioner for the Consolidation of German Tradition." Among his duties there was "the elimination of the damaging influence by foreign elements of the population representing danger to the Reich and the German community." SS Oberführer Ulrich Greifelt, who up to that point was part of the personal staff under Wolff, was appointed as leader of the new SS Main Office, established for this purpose. Naturally the connection to Wolff's main office was not suddenly eliminated; on the contrary, he was the first to be informed as to which regions were to be cleared of Jews and Poles for settlers of German stock and which methods would be used.

Wolff again found time to handle bureaucratic matters in his office. On September 26, he returned to Berlin as part of Hitler's baggage. Officially the Führer headquarters were at the Reich chancellery, but in practice, it dissolved because of the drop in activity and lack of things to do for the large entourage. The war in the west had not even started, the occasional battles between the Maginot Line and West Wall notwithstanding. Hitler also hoped that the great confrontation would not even take place because England and France would have to accept the situation created by the division of Poland between Berlin and Moscow. On October 5, with Himmler and Wolff in tow, he flew once more to the conquered country for a victory parade on Ujazdowski Allee in Warsaw.

On that occasion, however, Danzig gauleiter Forster complained about the military because they interfered too much with his brutal pacification policies in the newly seized country. This was too much for Hitler and the army was taken out of the new Gaus of the Reich. The military lost their authority first in the regions around Danzig and Posen, now absorbed into the Reich, and then in the strips of land that were added to the Gau of East Prussia and Silesia. On October 26, 1939, the other occupied regions were named the General Government and given to former Munich lawyer Dr. Hans Frank to administer. From now on, the Wehrmacht had very little say in the Polish regions; the army was no longer necessary in those areas and the police, the SD and the SS, directed by higher SS and Police commanders appointed by Himmler and reporting to him, would see to it that things were done quietly. Hitler could not be indifferent to the Wehrmacht's reactions to the SS or even what they were saying about them. Hitler still needed the generals and the troops they led—even more so when in the late fall it became very clear that fighting in the west could not be avoided. At the end of November the new commander in the east, Lieutenant General Johannes Blaskowitz, drafted a report in which he protested the crimes of the SS and the police because the danger of disputes—between the army and the SS—was growing, and until then had only been avoided because of the "high demands on the discipline of the troops." Blaskowitz wrote of the troops displeasure "to be identified with the atrocious actions of the security police." They refuse "on their part any cooperation with the Einsatzgruppen that operate almost exclusively as execution commandos."

The report reached von Brauchitsch, who had reservations about presenting it to Hitler. So the army adjutant to the Führer, Major Gerhard Engel, had to pass it along, finally handing it to his commander on November 18. Hitler did not get upset at all about the content, but rather at the author. It was a mistake on the part of the OKH to entrust an army to a man like Blaskowitz. His reproaches indicated his "childish attitude" toward army leadership. However, despite the rebuff, further reports of atrocities were assembled; and the commanders still hoped to move the undecided supreme commander to issue a formal protest to Hitler.

This did not matter much to Himmler. For such an action, files had to be created marked with a SECRET stamp, but that could be read at any time. Wolff, the experienced appeaser, was given the task of calming down the military. After all, one of his assignments at the Führer headquarters had been to further develop the already friendly contacts with high-ranking military officers. His suggestions pleased both sides: Lieutenant General von Brauchitsch as well as the Reichsführer SS were prepared to meet and discuss the matter thoroughly. For this not to look like a clash, the two gentlemen met for tea on January 24, 1940, and agreed to another suggestion from Wolff. The army handed over the entire collection of atrocity reports, and Wolff assigned the SS officer from the Main Office SS Court to examine the accusations. For those already convicted, Himmler promised he would begin criminal proceedings and the sentences would be fair and stringent.

"According to what I can remember there were about forty-six cases of infringements reported," Wolff said many years later, although on other occasions he claimed his memory still functioned so well that he was able to quote his conversations with Hitler and Himmler verbatim. "Upon checking, the justified accusations boiled down to seven or eight cases." Those who were found guilty received harsh punishment. At a second tea between Himmler and Brauchitsch (according to Wolff), "the argument was settled... and played down to the most uncomplicated level possible." The happy reconciliation was to be short-lived for both sides. While this second tea was taking place, General Wilhelm Ulex in southern Poland was drafting a new accusation where he reported the "savagery of the SS Einsatzgruppen": "by their acts, they have tarnished the honor of the entire German nation." When Blaskowitz read that report, he drafted another memorandum containing new material for Brauchitsch. He also made sure that the contents were circulated to other officers on the western front. "The attitude of the troops," wrote Blaskowitz, "towards the SS and the police alternates between repulsion and hate. Every soldier feels sick because of these crimes." Cases of army officers refusing to shake hands when greeting SS officers were increasing. Reichenau was being urgently pressured by the officer corps to step in because another tea session with Himmler was no longer enough to preserve his authority over the army.

On the other hand it was incumbent upon Wolff to restore the peace between the army and Himmler's SS killers. He suggested to Major Radke of the General Staff, representing Reichenau, that the Reichsführer SS personally face up to the army leaders and their criticism. In a talk he would explain the assignment he was given by the Führer. The next day Wolff was already giving assurances to the major by phone that, once the reasons were given, "the Reichsführer SS understood the perception of the High Command" and acknowledged "his wish to hold the talk concerning issues in the east."

The clever negotiator then suggested that Himmler's lecture be scheduled "in the evening, possibly right after dinner" because "the evening creates a more favorable atmosphere for the listeners" and would be more favorable to a possible friendly discussion of an already difficult problem." Himmler preferred a meeting in the west—said Wolff on the telephone—than one in Berlin.

On March 13, 1940, the top army generals gathered—those invited all held no less than the rank of army commander—in Koblenz, at the headquarters of Army Group A. Himmler said that the harshness in Poland was necessary because the subjects had already prepared a general rebellion during the last battles. The guilty parties had been executed according to martial law, and, therefore, the army was spared a terrible partisan war. As far as infringements were concerned, he was having them examined thoroughly. Guilty parties had been punished. This was, however, handled by SS judges because the Black Corps preferred its own jurisdiction.

In summarizing, Himmler admitted: "In front of this committee of the highest ranking officers I can unequivocally state that I do nothing without the Führer's knowledge." He was ready to assume responsibility in front of the world because the Führer himself "must not be connected to this." Later there was some discussion because the generals asked questions, but they did not push the Reichsführer SS too far; as a speaker in front of many groups for more than a decade, he was experienced in avoiding uncomfortable questions. Wolff thought, in any case, that Himmler handled himself well. Besides that, all those gathered secretly believed in Hitler's principle that the crimes of the victors are forgotten and only those who are defeated must pay.

The weeks that followed were to prove this theory. Two months after Himmler's speech the Wehrmacht overran Holland, Belgium, and France, after Denmark and Norway had already been occupied. With so much fame, so many promotions and medals, the atrocities in the east were quickly forgotten, and not only by the generals. Without a doubt it was part of their profession not to be shocked by blood, as long as it was shed for lofty purposes.

Within the SS there circulated two different views regarding the disputes with the army. They came from the two men who at that time were considered Himmler's most important advisors. Wolff delicately maintained, as he was prone to do, that the atrocities took place only because the Reichsführer SS had trusted the Einsatzgruppen and allowed lax supervision. Heydrich, on the other hand, said that the army leadership under Brauchitsch and the leaders of the Security Police neglected to thoroughly inform the commanders of the individual armies of the Einsatzgruppen's assignment. That was the harsh and simple truth.

Hitler and Himmler viewed Blaskowitz's memorandum differently and more seriously than the protests against inhuman treatment. On November 27, 1939, he had warned, "The current situation leads towards a decision making it impossible to exploit that country for a defense economy that would be favorable to the troops." Even the lieutenant general knew that Hitler's Germany in the long run would be inferior to the enemy regarding population, natural resources, and industrial capacity. Military victories could only change something if, in the conquered countries, they could be used towards a German victory. Even the SS knew that those murdered could no longer produce, but they figured that their terror would force the survivors to be obedient and push them to perform even better.

As the Reich Commissioner for the Consolidation of German Tradition, Himmler had to officially consider what to do with millions of Poles. The Einsatzgruppen liquidated the intellectual class—priests, professors, politicians, high-ranking officials—as quickly as possible during the initial weeks after taking over the area. Himmler was worried that this nation with such a high birthrate in due course could again produce capable leaders. In order to prevent this, he drafted a program. His notes for the talk to be held with the generals already contained the nucleus of his plan. "Execution of all potential resistance leaders" was written on one of his memos. On another one he said, "We have to remain hard. One million working slaves and how they should be treated."

Later on, using such keywords, he drafted a detailed instruction manual on ruling Poland entitled: "Some Thoughts on the Treatment of the Foreign Peoples in the East." Stamped REICH TOP SECRET, the document was considered a high-level state secret. Wolff was the first to receive and read it. It also contained instructions that it be discussed with the head of the Political Office for Race of the NSDAP, Dr. Walter Gross, a medical doctor who was part of the office of Deputy Führer Rudolf Hess, where Reichsleiter Martin Bormann reigned supreme. If he first approved the document, it would quickly land with the highest recommendations on the Führer's desk. Because Himmler was always fearful before every meeting with Hitler he wanted to secure his agreement in a roundabout bureaucratic way.

What Wolff read—or so he claimed four decades later—"admittedly, made my hair stand on end. It was the most undisguised, brutal form of tyrannical suppression" whereby those defeated are to be "reduced to a level of pure slavery." Himmler recommended eradicating the strongly developed Polish national consciousness by vigorously promoting the ethnic character of single nationalities—White Russians, Gorals, Ukrainians—so that in the end the former unified people would disintegrate into many splinter groups. All power would then belong to the Germans. The highest office that a non-German could reach would be mayor. The population should be racially selected; whoever could prove himself to be sufficiently Nordic-Germanic would whenever possible be Germanized.

"For the non-Germanic population," Wolff read, "there may be no higher schooling than an elementary school with four grades." Their goal for learning: "Simple arithmetic up to 500 at the most and writing names," being inculcated with orders "to obey the Germans, be honestly industrious and well behaved." Talented children who were "racially faultless" were to be taken from their parents to Germany and remain there for an indefinite period of time. "The population will be available as a leaderless working nation, and because of their own lack of culture, they will be under the stringent, strict, and just leadership of the German people to work on their eternal cultural deeds and monuments."

Wolff says that he told Himmler "with the openness usually existing between us, but naturally politely as well," that this plan "could hardly be suitable for the twentieth century." He asked Himmler "to explain how as Chancellor of the Order of Knights he would later account for such crass points of view." In answer to that, Himmler praised Wolff's "endearingly humane characteristics," but also calling him a hopeless "idealist and optimist," with whom one could "not make policies in a country of defeated enemies."

Wolff melodramatically said: "Something was broken at that point!" He asked himself whether he still belonged in the SS, where he would want to pass on "the more than 300-year-old tradition of my Hessian Guards Regiment." On the other hand, he made no plans to leave the SS or abandon the prominent position he occupied in the front row. Inarguably in certain respects he had performed his "good deeds" against the *conventions* of the SS—he later used that word—as things turned against the Nazis. He saved Jews, helped the persecuted, prevented despotism, got around draconian laws, but never renounced the advantages provided by his office and rank.

Typical of his "resistance" was his attempt to avoid the tattoo that Himmler ordered, whereby all members of the SS had their blood type branded on their left underarm. The reason being that in case a blood transfusion became necessary, the doctors could save themselves the trouble of lengthy laboratory examinations and spend more time saving lives. Wolff could already imagine the disadvantages of this as more SS troops were taken prisoner by the enemy and even more once the Germans left behind were held responsible for the war and its crimes. Wolff did not succeed in talking the Reichsführer out of the idea. He lived under the threat that Himmler would occasionally scrutinize Wolff's underarms when they engaged in sports together. Then one day when an SS doctor, sent by Himmler himself, arrived to tattoo him, Wolff was able to convince him to inject the dye only into the top layer of skin. Inspector Himmler was satisfied with that—and Wolff as well because once the war was over, the marking did not show. This case—according to Wolff—also "damaged our excellent personal and official relationship of many years."

In the large files marked "Personal Staff" there is no trace of any cooling off. Himmler still used the diminutive form "Wölffchen" in writing and in conversation. When they traveled to Finland together (where yet another medal came Wolff's way), the Reichsführer recommended that his adjutant wear long underwear because it was so cold in that country. During the first four years of the war there were, as before, many letters addressed to Himmler with a notation on the left side to pass these on to Wolff for further attention. On the other hand, many letters that Himmler sent out indicated that Wolff had received a copy.

Himmler continued as in the past to pass all delicate cases on to Wolff as well as many personal matters. As, for example, when the 63-year-old Alice Gollwitzer, resident of the county of Rosenheim, widow of the Counsel of the Medical Corps, mother-in-law of a Wehrmacht general, and a friend of Himmler's, came to the Gestapo's attention because she referred to the occupation of the Sudetenland as a crime perpetrated by Hitler, and during the invasion of Poland she declared that the war would be over if someone would murder Hitler. As a Swiss national, she would shoot him if the cowardly Germans couldn't manage to find the courage. With this, she would have signed her own death warrant had she not referred to her friendship of many years with Himmler. The Reichsführer SS confirmed that Frau G. had been an enthusiastic and true supporter of the Führer in the "days of struggle" and had "helped the SS in Augsburg considerably." He slowed the Gestapo down through Heydrich, saying that the old woman was simply "talking nonsense." He ordered Wolff to handle the case quietly and to calm down his old acquaintance.

The lady, however, would not let up and started to argue with anyone and everyone wanting to know if the SS was being used against her enemies. Even Wolff's gentle diplomacy failed in her case. Finally, he could only suggest to Himmler to have the woman placed in a sanitarium, which is what happened.

Contrary to his expectations, Wolff's program for the treatment of foreign nationals, which had been criticized so much, received great praise from the Führer. Two gauleiters wanted to apply it as well: Albert Forster, responsible for Danzig-West Prussia, and Arthur Greiser, who governed in Posen and Warthegau. Both held honorary SS ranks, and accordingly wore the Gruppenführer uniforms, and both competed as to who would be able to report to the Führer that his Gau was "Pole and free of Jews".

They drove masses of Jews and Poles over the Gau borders to the east into the General Government of Dr. Hans Frank, who, however, quickly complained against such an influx. Greiser thought that he could decrease the Polish portion of the population in a Gau by using the Einsatzgruppen, namely through murder. Since many Jews and Poles suffered from tuberculosis, he declared those who were ill to be a public danger, and because they were also unsuitable for hard slave labor, he had no scruples about eliminating additional mouths to feed. Reichsleiter Martin Bormann was asked for advice, who in turn referred him to Reichsleiter Philipp Bouhler, head of an ominous "Office of the Führer," and responsible for dirty tricks. Just then he had some units of experienced mass murderers that were available.

Since the beginning of the war, on Hitler's orders, these people had gone into nursing homes and institutions throughout the Reich; eventually (according to Nazi doctors) several thousand persons, incurable mentally ill patients were killed with poisoned injections or carbon monoxide. Their actions were being called "euthanasia" or "death facilitators for useless life." As to whether it really was not worth living, neither the relatives nor the victims were allowed to decide. The mass murders had been organized by an SS Brigadeführer from Munich, Viktor Brack, a doctor's son. His best executioner was Christian Wirth, an alcoholic police officer who had been promoted to captain, and who was in the habit of loudly ridiculing his victims. The deeds did not remain as secretive as had been planned, and protests, mainly from the church, moved Hitler to stop the euthanasia program temporarily.

Brack took his men to the Warthegau. Because everything was still in a chaotic state of construction, they could begin their macabre activity immediately. Wolff most definitely knew about this, not only on the basis of copies of Himmler's correspondence regarding the issue, but also because he was friendly with Viktor Brack at the beginning of the 1930s. Therefore, Wolff probably also found out that the "Death Helpers" in 1942 were still working for the SS in the east and for the Lublin police chief, Odilo Globocnik ("Globus"), his other good old friend. After the mass murders of the ill, Brack's specialists built the gas chambers in the extermination camps of Belzec, Sobibor, and Treblinka and operated them just as they did the extermination machinery at the concentration camp at Maidanek. But all of this—Wolff says—he only found out after the war.

In the Gau Danzig-West Prussia, Gauleiter Forster came up with yet another trick besides concentration camps and expulsion to reduce the number of Poles. Whoever did not have an absolutely terrible political reputation and was not a determined Polish nationalist, could easily become a German citizen or at least apply for that honor. Himmler and the local SS leadership had a say in the matter. Himmler suspected that in Forster's Gau too much "Polish blood" was seeping into the German nation. Sooner or later, he threatened, he would send his race experts to West Prussia and hold horrible inspections among the new citizens.

Forster's reaction was brutal. He said, "If I looked like Himmler, I wouldn't talk about race!" That vicious talk was attributed to the Higher SS and Police Führer responsible for Danzig, Obergruppenführer Richard Hildebrand. He was quick to call Wolff and report those disparaging remarks. Hildebrand had to rush to the RSHA main office on Prinz-Albrecht-Strasse in Berlin and repeat his story once more, this time to the Reichsführer. The three of them then decided what should be done against the slanderer.

As reserve officers of the First World War, both Wolff and Hildebrand wanted to avenge the insult immediately. If Hitler hadn't forbidden armed duel, only a challenge with pistols, in their opinion, would have been justified. So the next closest thing was a complaint to the Party high court. But Himmler calmed them down; a fight with a gauleiter would create opposition among all the others and possibly even with Martin Bormann, Hitler's confidant and right-hand man. He could not afford, he thought, so many enemies at that time. As a kind of rear-guard battle, he did have several eyewitnesses to the insult questioned, but that was only a threatening gesture. Wolff said, "That he did not defend his honor better was a further disappointment."

Indeed Himmler was not a favorite at the Führer's headquarters at that time. According to Hitler, he and his policemen had failed in a very serious case. They could not prove that British intelligence had created and planted a bomb that exploded on November 8, 1939, in one of the columns of the Munich Bürgerbräukeller during the traditional memorial celebrations of Hitler's 1923 putsch, where he always gave a long speech. But for some incomprehensible reasons the speaker kept it short this time. With his entourage, including Himmler and Wolff, he immediately left for the train station and got into the cars attached especially for him to a regularly scheduled express train.

In Nuremberg the local chief of police had the "Headquarters"—the name used by Hitler and Wolff designating their location during the war—stopped and reported that a number of Party veterans had been buried in the rubble. Eight were found dead. The time bomb exploded ten minutes after Hitler left the room. He was immediately convinced, and remained so, that British intelligence had set a trap.

There was also the good news that SS Oberführer Walter Schellenberg, responsible for foreign intelligence in the SD, was handling two British Secret Service agents, and meeting with them as purported opponents of the Nazis; they were successfully lured to the Dutch border. On Himmler's orders, Schellenberg kidnapped the two Englishmen in Dutch territory and taken across the border. It was quickly determined, though, that they had nothing to do with the attack. The best specialists in the Gestapo were helpless.

In the meantime, the main suspect was sitting in jail shortly after the explosion. He was Georg Elser, a cabinetmaker from Königsbronn, near Heidenheim in Württemberg. He had the bomb from an alarm clock, using an electric battery and dynamite, and in the night had secretly built it into the column of the Bürgerbräukeller. Then he traveled without luggage by train to Lake Constance, looking for a place to hide in Switzerland. He felt that the best chances would be where Constance and Kreuzlingen are so close together that one can hardly be differentiated from the other. In a beer garden, close to the border, a member of the National Socialist Paramilitary Motor Corps, who was at the border as an assistant, apprehended him. Rather than driving around, the officer was waiting for his girlfriend (the waitress) to send the last guests home. Cursing, he did his duty and skipped the tryst, taking the suspect to the police.

Elser was questioned, but no one got anything out of him. They considered whether they should just lock him up in a concentration camp. But then they found out that he had been a Communist at some point, had been in a concentration camp and in addition to that, in his jacket pocket, they found a postcard of the Bürgerbräukeller. The news gave renewed hope to the SS leaders and detectives gathered in Munich where Elser was brought. He confessed, but what he said was not enough for them. For those protecting Hitler's safety, it was a miserable commentary that a single man without help and without an organization behind him almost managed to kill their Führer. "We are not satisfied with one man," criticized Wolff in a letter to an SS leader reporting the results. But there was nothing more to be obtained from Elser, even though Himmler himself had questioned and tortured him. He was sent to a concentration camp, but was treated gently. Possibly the Gestapo hoped they could use him in some way. He was killed only during the last days of the war.

Wolff felt that the Munich assassination attempt prevented a conspiracy of army generals from turning into a coup against the dictator. The military men wanted to take Hitler prisoner and prevent him from continuing the pointless war in the west. They gave up their plan since the apparently miraculous way Hitler's life was saved increased the belief among the people that he was protected by Providence and had been chosen for something great. The generals supposedly did not want to compete with so much popularity and admiration.

Where Wolff obtained information about the subversive plans by the generals remains an open question. Could it be from his friend Reinhard Heydrich? Certainly not from the military, since the "personal credit" of an SS Gruppenführer and confidant of Himmler could not have been that high. It is true, however, that Wolff was making serious efforts at that time to be trusted in officers' circles. To show the Wehrmacht his good will, for example, he would use a letter from Lance Corporal Hermann Weinrich, who in peacetime was an Obersturmbannführer in the General SS, and wrote to Himmler from the western front. Weinrich complained in his letter that he and other members of the SS in the same infantry unit, being non-Christians who believed in God, were repeatedly ordered to go to church, since their regiment was temporarily assigned to a position in a backward little town. When he refused he was threatened with a court-martial for refusing to obey an order. He wanted to know from Himmler if he had to follow such an order and if there were regulations forcing him to go to Christian church services.

This apparently harmless incident involved a troubled area in the relations between the SS and the Wehrmacht. The new heathens were really bothering the military, who still believed in the alliance between the state and the churches and were convinced that victories were a gift from the Almighty. Many officers referred to the godless Marxist Spartakists, whom they blamed for Germany's defeat in the First World War, having stuck a knife in the back of their army "undefeated in the field" by fomenting a revolution at home. In addition, in their circles the principle of "an order is an order" was important. If a column was ordered during a march to get out of line and go to the right and the left of the road to urinate, then every soldier was expected to obey. Those who didn't have to or couldn't go should simply pretended to; the same applied to church services: the pagan did not have to say the Our Father, so long as he simply followed the command: "Helmet off to pray."

Himmler did not want to deal with this delicate matter, and so the Weinrich letter ended up with Wolff on January 6, 1940. He remembered—even though with the long delay that was normal for Wolff—his friend Major Radke when he was planning Himmler's speech to the generals. On April 25 he asked the major in a letter "to examine this matter and then let me know your opinion." He added a P.S.: "Please prevent this unfortunate man from being slaughtered."

By May 1940 Wolff could say, as member of the Führer's headquarters, that he had witnessed almost all key events. On March 18, 1940, he traveled on the Führer's special train for a meeting with Mussolini at the Brenner Pass, not just as a decorative extra, as Hitler usually employed him at meetings with foreign statesmen. Wolff was used as a temporary honorary officer to escort the Duce and develop contacts with allied leaders. Besides that he was attempting to speed up a stalled initiative assigned to Himmler since June 23, 1939.

Back at that time, on Hitler's order, a regional headquarters was set up by the SS for "Immigration and Re-emigration," the job of which was to organize the return of the South Tyroleans into the Reich, after the Führer sacrificed his right to the predominantly German-speaking region to his friend, the Duce, in return for his support of the Anschluss of Austria, the "Ostmark." The regional headquarters in the meantime increased to a much bigger Regional Headquarters of the Reich Commissioner for the Consolidation of German Tradition. But despite all this, little had happened in the South Tyrol. Wolff was responsible because the regional headquarters remained at first connected to the personal staff. By the end of 1939 almost all German-speaking residents of the area, including the Ladiner, had signed up on the resettlement lists. They were tired of almost two decades of harassment to turn them into real Italians. An Italo-German agreement gave them the assurance that they could take their assets and movable property with them and would be compensated for their land. The SS "Ahnenerbe" went to work to record and inspect German art and cultural artifacts. The foundation was attached to Himmler's office, where scientists and those Himmler thought were scientists worked on an array of projects. Because the "Ahnenerbe" was part of the personal staff, Wolff was doubly entitled to handle resettlement issues. This was to be accomplished—as agreed—by December 31, 1942, at the latest.

The operation became a model of true ethnic friendship, but it turned out that the "Rome-Berlin Axis" was not enough to justify the initiative. All those involved were expecting something different from the resettlement. Himmler and Hitler—at least at the beginning—wanted to use the South Tyroleans as settlers for conquered regions or regions yet to be conquered in the east, and at the same time they wanted to have a quiet border at the Brenner. The Italians also expected tranquility, especially in the regions that had been rebellious until then, but they were only willing to allow the most vocal supporters of autonomy cross the border. The others would—or so they hoped—then allow themselves to be reeducated as Italians without opposition. Now they found out that wealthy city dwellers just like the farmers living high up in the alpine pastures wanted to leave their homeland. The valley regions would need to be populated by emigrants from the impoverished Italian south, but they could not create a flourishing economy. There were no applicants for the mountains farms; if they managed to lure an Italian family there, it secretly returned to its former region very quickly. These people suffered from loneliness and the raw climate of the peaks and valleys, and were unable to take the physically harsh and sometimes dangerous work. For that reason Italian authorities did not want to let the South Tyroleans leave.

Wolff's great negotiating skill was useless in this situation. Even the South Tyroleans were not in such a hurry to resettle. They calculated that as citizens of the Reich, they would soon be called to arms. As Italian citizens, they were exempt from military service—at least for the time being, because the Duce was hesitant about going to war, as the "Pact of Steel" treaty stipulated. He first wanted to be sure who was going to win. In addition there was trouble when a commission began arguing about artworks of German heritage that were to be released for export to Germany. When Wolff returned to South Tyrol three years later as High SS and Police Chief in Italy, the experts were still arguing, few people had left the region, and only gullible dreamers still dared discuss their resettlement in the east.

Wolff traveled extensively during the phony war. While the generals at the Führer's headquarters were busy preparing new "victories," decorative figures such as himself could be spared. Around the end of the year he traveled to Poland as part of Himmler's entourage. In the spring, the Reichsführer SS inspected numerous garrisons of Reserve units and the regiments deployed at the West Wall with the ever-present Wolff. He also inspected concentration camps: Buchenwald near Weimar in early April, Flossenbürg in the Upper Palatinate, and Dachau near Munich at the end of the month. Before that, Himmler and Wolff went around the areas annexed to East Prussia, and inspected a newly formed "Death's Head Division" (Totenkopfstandarte), then went to Warsaw. There, Himmler and Wolff stayed at the prime minister's residence—a sign of respect for SS leaders; in the meantime everyone else in their entourage had to stay in hotel rooms.

Wolff was in Berlin for the Führer's birthday on April 20. This time it was only celebrated at the Chancellery where at noon Reichsführer SS and Chief of the Personal Staff Wolff congratulated Hitler. In May, a few days before his own fortieth birthday, Wolff got happy news from the Reich Chancellery. He was promoted to the rank of lieutenant general of the SS Reserves. However, he did not receive any military assignments; he had the insignia of rank, but no troops.

The Reserve troops, to whom he now belonged, had their black sheep, and he knew who they were. When he occasionally took foreigners or even the members of Himmler's "circle of friends" to visit the concentration camps in peacetime, the "Totenköpfler" or "Death's Head," as the future mass murderer Adolf Eichmann called them, were the guard units. On such occasions, the visitors would hardly have witnessed anything terrible. They were shown the "vermin" of humanity being reeducated to civic honesty in an admittedly strict manner, behind high barbed wire fences but with justice and without physical violence. When asked, Wolff even admitted that there were individual excesses and acts of brutality by the guards. But Wolff cautioned that those guilty were severely punished so that a concentration camp prisoner in Germany was safer from poverty and death than any U.S. citizen who went for a walk in a New York park at night.

If at the time he really believed all that, he later had to admit that his view of the Black Corps was not quite right. On May 5, 1940, wearing his general's epaulettes, Wolff visited Himmler's friend "Globus," the former Vienna gauleiter Odilo Globocnik, who now was an SS Gruppenführer in the office of the SS and Police Chief for the area of Lublin in southern Poland. This unscrupulous man was about to build a large concentration camp for Jews and Poles. Besides that, on assignment from the Führer, he had to establish three smaller camps into which one could continuously send in more people, even if none of the prisoners ever left it alive. The "Death's Head"—named that way because of an additional skull on their collars, which the rest of the SS wore as nickel-plated metal on their hatbands—supervised the construction being carried out by the prisoners. During lunch at the officer's mess, it was casually mentioned that a euthanasia team was being transferred there very soon. On that occasion, Wolff met SS Standartenführer Hermann Fegelein, who belonged to an equestrian SS unit, and would later be his successor at Führer headquarters.

On May 6, 1940, Himmler's adjutant Jochen Peiper noted "continuation of the program"—namely a discussion and tour of Lublin, regarding Globocnik's future assignments. Included was the "return flight to Berlin." An event was planned there that Himmler and Wolff could not miss: the offensive in the west. When, how, and where this would take place was still unknown to everyone in Germany. Bormann's forecast came true, however, that the gentlemen at the Führer's headquarters should be prepared to leave in Hitler's special train.

By May 9 the time had come. Once more the departure took place without fanfare and went unnoticed by the public, even though it was shortly after 4:00 p.m. The train was waiting at the small suburban train station of Finkendrug, a weekend excursion near Berlin on the way to Spandau-Nauen. The trip began towards the northwest, in the direction of Hamburg, "to keep up the deception" as Bormann noted in his diary. Indeed many passengers suspected the train was going to Norway. But then after Celle the train turned, continuing west and finally stopping in total darkness at a train station where the signs, in the town's name, had been removed. It was Euskirchen, west of Bonn, where the column of cars that they had used in Poland was waiting. Across the Münstereifel they traveled to the "hideout" in Eifeldorf Rodert, a hill made of concrete bunkers, anti-aircraft gun positions, and barracks converted into a headquarters. The previous evening, Hitler asked for the weather report forecasting clear flying weather. With that piece of news, he ordered the attack to begin at 5:30 a.m.

The men and women (Hitler's secretaries) had hardly gotten into the cars when the heavy artillery on the broad western front began firing. They were far removed from danger and no one needed to be a hero. Most of the participants were busy directing the battle. What Wolff was doing in the "hideout" from May 10 through June 3 will have to be left to the reader's imagination; the military could not and would not use him and SS fighting units in the west were so few that they needed no special representative at headquarters. There were three SS divisions and one regiment, which were never deployed together.

Wearing the broad epaulettes like generals of the Wehrmacht, Wolff no longer felt inferior in the company of titles and ranks. Hermann Göring, who had jumped just as quickly from captain in the First World War to field marshal, asked apparently unsuspectingly about the reason and purpose for the new uniform and decorations. Wolff pointed out that his assignments as liaison to the Waffen SS had "become purely military." For that he needed a "rank insignia that every soldier would recognize." The term "Waffen SS" was then used for the first time. After the war, as we discuss later on, the organization of Waffen SS veterans did not want to recognize its first general as one of their own. Wolff frequently complained at the time (as was normal in his circles) that he was not allowed to take active part in battle, but could only fulfill his duty to the Fatherland from a desk. He also consoled himself in the thought that the Führer knew why it had to be so. He therefore just took care of the mail that was sent to him from his SS Main Office in Berlin, made contacts and regularly attended—or so he claimed—the daily situation reports of the progress of the fighting. On the other hand, however, his name seldom appeared on the attendance lists. He would never have been granted the right to speak by the generals of the army. In the war diary of the senior general, Franz Halder, who was at the time chief of the General Staff, his name appears only once and only casually, on the occasion of his previously mentioned conversation with Major Radke. That Himmler and Wolff were not necessary to Hitler at that time is clear from a report written by Himmler in the manner of a school essay about a car ride through conquered land that they took together. The Reichsführer had stationed his special train "Heinrich" near Altenkirchen in the Westerwald. He, another four SS officers, and the drivers of two cars drove to Aachen on May 17. In the evening, they crossed the border into Holland. They invited a Sturmbannführer of the locally stationed SS Standarte, "Der Führer," to a meal at a town inn. He was from Munich and had been part one of the guards at the Brown House on October 7, 1931, who had recruited Wolff into the SS when he joined the Party.

On May 18 they drove around Holland, ate "unbelievably well and copiously," and decided that it was "a real joy to see men, women, and children." Himmler noted, "These are a benefit for Germany," which implied that he at least was determined never to withdraw from the Netherlands. That night they found only poor accommodations; Wolff and Himmler had to share a hotel room.

After all this stress due to the war, they attempted to reach Brussels, but could approach the city only slowly as the destroyed bridges were continuously forcing them to take detours. In his report Himmler recounts how he and his companions conquered the Flemish city. Apparently no German soldiers had made it that far yet, and the mayor, with the district council and the militia, was waiting at the town hall for someone to whom they could hand over their city. They requested water, electricity, and gas be restored; the Germans found this rather funny. Himmler was even more pleased with Wolff: "He told those good men at the end that I was the head of the Gestapo." The travelers all agreed that Germans behaved in a much more dignified manner in such a situation.

They spent the night in Brussels. On the return trip, they met the "Leibstandarte SS Adolf Hitler Their commander, Obergruppenführer Sepp Dietrich, had picked a castle as his headquarters. The travelers feasted thoroughly with him before returning to the lean stews of Hitler's "Wolf's Lair." That same evening, they reported to the Führer. Apparently on this trip they really became aware of the imminent victory. After they had seen everything, they could confidently cry out that not only Germany and Europe, but also "tomorrow the whole world" would belong to them. They saw many destroyed houses on the trip, drove past queues of frightened refugees, met exhausted and wounded soldiers, and they could not avoid viewing the dead on the side of the road. But the misery of war is not mentioned in the report.

During the journey, they often took pictures. As they got gasoline in a small Belgian town, several soldiers of an army convoy, who were SS members in Germany, recognized Himmler, who posed for a souvenir photo with them. Wolff posed with his head high, almost at attention, his legs slightly spread but his knees together looking like the most important man in the group. Himmler came across looking as common as any of the other soldiers next to him. The picture shows why Wagner-fan Hitler viewed Wolff as the glowing "Siegfried," rather than Himmler with his pince-nez.

From the new headquarters near the Belgian town of Bruly-le-Peche, Wolff had nothing remarkable to report, except for being badly bitten by mosquitoes between June 3 and June 25.

Hitler usually had several guests at dinner; mostly the secretaries and Bormann, but also Wolff, and alternately one officer or another. War and politics were not discussed if Hitler did not mention them; they wanted to spare his nerves.

On June 28, six days after the armistice with France, Hitler visited Paris with a small following. In the woods in Kniebis near Freudenstadt, on the steep slopes of the Black Forest on the Rhine Valley, Hitler met up with his entourage once again. They were staying in an inhospitable bunker system in the West Wall, and when the pounding rain stopped they had a wide view up to the crest of the Vosges Mountains. During two car excursions, Hitler and several of his confidants visited Strasbourg, the Maginot Line, and the city of Mulhouse. Wolff and most of the entourage were bored in the wet concrete caves and were pleased when the Führer's special train pulled into the hall of the Anhalter train station in Berlin on June 6 around 3:00 p.m.

With that, the members of the headquarters were practically on vacation. Hitler went to Obersalzberg. He studied the plan of an invasion army landing in England; and drafted "Directive 16" to the armed forces and chose Ziegenberg near Bad Nauheim as his next headquarters. But he was undecided about the landing, hoping that the English would opt for peace and would allow him to have a free reign over the European continent. But since they refused, he did not go to Ziegenberg, or rather, not immediately. It wasn't until December 1944 that he moved there, long after he had lost his war, and was seeking with a desperate strike to force his enemies in the west to negotiate.

Wolff, who had been placed on vacation from his duties, and Himmler now wanted to see what they (or actually the soldiers) had really conquered. They took a trip in mid-July and inspected Burgundy for three days.

They left Freiburg-im-Breisgau and traveled nearly one thousand kilometers. The summer beauty of this blessed land, hardly touched by the war, made them want more of it. Lothar, one of the heirs of Charlemagne, governed a kingdom from the Rhone to Antwerp. Weren't these sloped vineyards meant for the South Tyroleans? Already the travelers dreamed of an SS city very closely bound to Germany, whose first lord and master would be Heinrich Himmler and whose first chancellor would be Karl Wolff. Filled with such ideas, they flew back to Berlin. Their presence was required as actors in a triumphal production at the Kroll Opera House where Hitler assembled the Reichstag for—as the press wrote—"the most colossal honor in German history."

Throughout his speech he distributed high praise to everyone. The military was showered with promotions. There were eleven new field marshals. Göring became Reich field marshal, a rank that even Prince Eugen never reached. Many top party officials were also praised. Himmler was not among them, but one sentence in Hitler's speech gave Wolff reason for particular pride when he also mentioned "the brave divisions and Standarten of the Waffen SS." It was the first official mention using that name as a unit, a new name that sounded better than the "Reserve troops."

Since Hitler once again retreated to the Obersalzberg, the Himmler-Wolff team could resume its travels. They still needed to visit Alsace and Lorraine in the west at the beginning of September over four days. They began their tour by car near Belfort. In Natzweiler SS Gruppenführer Oswald Pohl, Chief of the Economic and Administrative Office of the SS, guided them through quarries that were superbly suited to become concentration camps. The highlight of their trip, however, was the final destination: the old fortress city of Metz, where the Leibstandarte had set up its quarters with four battalions of motorized infantry, one pioneer battalion, and two artillery divisions. Himmler gave them a new flag in a fort dating back to the Hohenzollern era. The "christening" took place amid a lot of music and national anthems as well as the standard song of the SS. The few Germans there were (hardly any Nazis in Metz) watched in quiet anger as the good-looking boys in their smart-looking uniforms strolled noisily up and down the narrow and winding main street, the Rue Serpenoise, which was already renamed Adolf-Hitler-Strasse.

At this event, the first, and for the time being only, Waffen SS general should have been put on a pedestal, but there is no evidence of this. Perhaps Himmler did not want to see either his Wölffchen or the commander of the Leibstandarte, Sepp Dietrich, stand in the limelight and reap the advantage. Between the troop commander, who had not stopped using rough language since leaving the Munich beer hall environment, and the former guard lieutenant brought up with the good manners of the officer's club, there was not much common ground besides the uniform. Once Dietrich and his warriors earned their laurels in Poland and France, it made the distance seem even greater to both.

Wolff was constantly trying to be a model soldier, but now he feared that role could only be partly believable. He wrote as much to his friend

SS Gruppenführer Richard Hildebrand in the middle of June 1940 as the full extent of victory in the west became apparent. As Higher SS and Police Führer in Danzig, Hildebrand was, like Wolff, a First World War volunteer officer. "As great as the honor is," Wolff wrote to him, "to spend time in the immediate presence of the Führer at the Führer's headquarters, I envy you, commanding a battery. You have a much better chance of breathing the air of the front lines, and you will certainly get a command at the front." Wolff pathetically subdued the glory of war in his letter, playing up his trip through the conquered lands as "the long drive along the front accompanying the Reichsführer SS."

The benefits the Waffen SS front line soldiers received from their representative with Hitler are hard to determine. Wolff was very vague on the subject. He played up the version (as a prosecutor was to say decades later) that he was first and foremost "Himmler's eyes and ears"—certainly someone Hitler liked and who could, within an entertaining conversation, make wishes and suggestions, but Himmler was always the stronger advocate. Nothing for his black-uniformed men was too much for him. In addition, Wolff was not the only high SS officer having responsibility for the soldiers. There was their chief of staff, Gruppenführer Hans Jüttner, Chief of the SS Leadership Main Office, and also the shifty Gruppenführer Gottlob Berger, Chief of the SS Main Office, responsible for the replenishment of the troops at the front, and who, due to the high losses of units, had to constantly enlist new recruits. In many respects, the Economic and Administrative Main Office under Gruppenführer Oswald Pohl was also responsible. The same applied to the SS personnel office, whose head, Gruppenführer Maximilian von Herff, had been a regimental comrade from the Darmstadt regiment of guard lieutenants; Wolff had placed him into the SS. On the other hand, it was more difficult to get along with Gruppenführer August Heissmayer, who was in charge of creating new recruits for the Officer Corps of the Waffen SS from the youth indoctrinated in National Socialism.

There were many cooks in the Waffen SS kitchen, and each was out to protect his turf against his colleagues—at their expense whenever possible. With tactical skill and diplomatic phraseology, Wolff towered over all of them. The variety of offices within the personal staff—a conglomeration of Himmler's crankiness and bureaucracy—allowed Wolff to meddle in almost every matter regarding the SS. This did not make him popular in among his comrades at the head of the SS. Some maintained that he was a schemer, others accused him of fawning, but it was said among all top ranking officers in Hitler's and Himmler's entourage that Wolff was always the most clever and imaginative one in the struggle among Nazi factions.

Berger tried intermittently to place himself at the top of those most decorated through overeager devotion toward Himmler. When he realized, however, that he could not shake the chief of the personal staff from the good graces of the Reichsführer SS, he changed his tactics. Several problems hindered his career; the old Party comrade was one of the longest serving SA leaders in Württemberg, and since the murders of Röhm and his followers, this was viewed as a blemish the SS. Besides that the Party bigwigs in his hometown were his enemies. Lacking any other support he decided to seek Wolff's good will. In a letter to him he swore his allegiance to Himmler's life and health. At the same time, he assured him that if it became necessary, only Wolff was conceivable as the successor to the Reichsführer SS. The naturally cunning Berger probably knew that with this statement he was expressing one of Wolff's secret thoughts.

Wolff began working at headquarters, supposedly as representative of the Waffen SS, consisting of three good but in no way first class divisions and one a regiment, the Leibstandarte, which had until then been mainly trained for parade appearances. Many things had changed in the meantime. The Leibstandarte was in the process of expanding into a brigade. The other regiments were being motorized and were better armed, but this was not because of Wolff's initiative. The same had also taken place with many infantry divisions of the army. Understandably, Himmler and the SS leaders wanted to strengthen the fighting power of their troops and add new units. The army leadership obviously opposed any increase in the SS—viewed as competition. Even Hitler, whose decision it was ultimately, seemed to hesitate in wanting to keep the Waffen SS small, true to his principle of not letting anyone tip the balance and threaten his rule. He also did not want to anger the army generals, whose many divisions had produced victories.

When the Waffen SS wanted to establish a new division, Himmler and Wolff had to obtain permission from headquarters. Hitler had assured the OKH "that units of the Waffen SS in general would not go beyond 5 to 10 percent of the army's peacetime strength." He needed this armed power—as Hitler justified the existence of the SS—as "State Police Troops ... empowered to represent and carry out the authority of the Reich internally in any situation." Not to mention, "the Great German Reich" would "in its final form.... have borders that did not exclusively include people considered favorable to the Reich."

As usual, Hitler failed to honor this agreement as well. By the end of the war the Waffen SS had reached thirty-eight divisions, many of them having less of a headcount, weapons, and equipment than what was described on paper, but the original limit had been greatly exceeded. Berger, who, like most of the Main Office Heads was given the rank of general without having the proper background, guessed that approximately 800,000 men wore the uniform of the Waffen SS. He and not Wolff was the organizer of this increase by constantly discovering new ways to enlist recruits. Wolff most definitely cleared the path for him at Führer headquarters, and certainly successfully negotiated with the Wehrmacht generals for the allotment of weapons, ammunition, and vehicles, but in doing so he was very careful not to overdraw on his often-cited "personal credit."

Himmler also was not about to have Wolff represent the Waffen SS at headquarters by himself. As the Reichsführer SS spoke with the Führer in the Ukraine on September 22, 1942, at the "Werewolf" headquarters, he made a report—as he wrote in his note for the files—"regarding the condition of the Waffen SS." Wolff would find out after the fact that on that occasion, by the Führer's order, the four oldest SS divisions were each increased by an additional armored division and an assault artillery battalion. References of this kind show that Chief of the Personal Staff Wolff was intensely committed to the troops, but there is no trace in the normally voluminous correspondence at the Main Office. It seems, on the other hand, that the SS division commanders were never required to serve as representatives at headquarters.

Gruppenführer Theodor Eicke, commander of the infamous Totenkopf Division, was one exception. The division was at first mainly made up of concentration camp guards; their replacements were also drawn from there. Eicke always wrote to Wolff when he was having problems—which was normal procedure in his case since he never missed an opportunity to argue and thought nothing of placing himself above all regulations. Because of his flaws, the Weimar Republic police refused to hire him, despite the fact that he passed the mandatory tests. The gauleiter of Palatinate, Josef Brückel, had temporarily placed Party comrade Eicke in a lunatic asylum as an unrepentant brawler. During the Röhm affair, his lack of a conscience and robust physique made him capable of murder and when Röhm refused to shoot himself with a pistol in the jail cell, Eicke used his pistol instead.

Eicke usually called Wolff his friend. He poured out his problems to him in a chain of letters during 1940, rebelling against OKW rules. He demanded Wolff's help in securing a number of 15 cm caliber Howitzers that belonged to no one and were just laying around in the Skoda factory in Pilsen. He also implied that he could have them picked up by a raiding party if his division didn't manage to find a unit of heavy artillery any another way. Wolff was also asked to be helpful in getting rifles for the marksmen from the Polish booty. Later, he again asked for Wolff's support against Berger, who was undermining Eicke's reputation with HimmlerOn the other hand, Berger also complained to Wolff about Eicke because he allowed superiors to mistreat the recruits during training. Wolff was also supposed to offer support against Jüttner. Eicke had sent one of his officers, the most talented "organizer" (as it was called by people in the army for those who used tricks and cunning to steal for the unit), to the Dachau camp because he could use some of the supplies there, but the man was arrested as he tried to slip out the gate with a convoy of cars full of stolen goods. Now Wolff had to prevent court-martial proceedings against the officer, since it would reveal that Commander Eicke issued the orders.

During the French campaign, Eicke and his men behaved like pirates. As complaints about him flowed in to Himmler, Eicke wrote to Wolff on October 8, 1940: "Since I left home, some people have been trying in any way they can to undermine the trust the Reichsführer SS has had in me for years."

Again Wolff helped. It seems he was able to prevent some of the accusations against SS units from reaching Himmler. Wolff was not always successful, but when it came to an argument, no one could quiet matters better than he, and no one was more clever at delaying the contentious issues into the future.

Wolff mended the disagreements among comrades during extensive trips in the second half of 1940. Himmler and his constant escort could now leave Berlin without worry; they knew that no earth-shattering news was expected. For operation "Sea Lion" Hitler had indeed pulled together a huge number of barges and landing boats of all kinds along the ports on the coast, but then he dropped preparations for the landing in England. Namely, his plan assumed that, beforehand, the Luftwaffe must practically destroy the RAF—which did not happen. So now the talk was that the last and toughest enemy would be defeated in another way—with submarines, bombs, and kicks in the "soft belly" in Africa and Asia. France and

Spain were to become new allies. With German troops occupying half of their country, the French were dependent on Hitler's good will, and the Spanish owed him thanks because German soldiers of the "Condor Legion" helped Generalissimo Francisco Franco defeat the Republicans. Under the guise of a fall trip to visit the heads of state, Marshal Pétain and Franco, Hitler hoped to win them over to his plans.

This had nothing to do with the responsibilities of the SS, but Himmler really believed that it served his reputation to act like the supreme leader. So he, Wolff, and the usual retinue flew to Paris on October 17 where no one recorded their arrival. The French government was now located at Vichy in the unoccupied part of France, and the military commander in the capital obviously saw no reason to drive to Le Bourget airport to meet the travelers. After a quick lunch the SS team again boarded the plane and shortly before nightfall landed in Bordeaux. There, Wolff had the pleasure of being greeted by his friend Theodor Eicke. His Totenkopf Division was billeted in southern France. They naturally celebrated with a parade for Himmler.

On the following Saturday, the travelers crossed the border into Spain in Irun. Here and for the rest of their trip to San Sebastian, Burgos, Madrid, Toledo, and Barcelona, Spanish hospitality did not miss an opportunity to honor their guests and show them the sights their country had to offer. They saw a bullfight, viewed the magnificent residence at Escorial, the Alcazar that was so viciously fought over during the Civil War, and the paintings in the Prado. Everything took place very quickly over five days. They dined with the minister of the interior, were received by Franco, were awarded medals, but longer conversations could only take place at meals, refraining from politics and commitments.

On the day they flew back to Berlin, their Führer met with Franco in Hendaye on the French border; the SS raiding party was also restrained by the ceremonial perfection of their hosts. Himmler was in a better position than Hitler because he could at least take something with him. The Germanic Western Goths had settled in Segovia, fifteen hundred years before, and now archeologists were in the process of digging up their legacy. By coincidence and as requested by the Spanish minister of the interior a few artifacts were dug up in the presence of their important guest from Germany. The Reichsführer received them as a gift.

Himmler and his clan basked in the glory reserved to victorious warriors, and could even claim that they were slaving away in the service of the Fatherland. They visited and were visited in turn; they went sightseeing and as a return gesture they showed them the sights of the Third Reich. Dutch fascists got to see Dachau concentration camp, a measure of trust among blood comrades, like the Norwegians who were already presenting their newly formed SS units when Himmler and Wolff traveled to Narvik in the far north. Everywhere and at every opportunity, they gave speeches, and at times there were special events. In the meantime the Germans at home had to struggle with the rations they were allotted on their grocery cards, and people in the defeated countries had even less.

The SS officials also had to handle less amusing subjects, for example the quarry near Gross Rosen, forty-five minutes by car from Breslau. It was not marked as a true concentration camp in the travel program because they were reluctant to call embarrassing things by their real names. On March 1, 1941, they toured the concentration camp at Auschwitz where the murder machinery had not yet started. It would be five months later that the Reichsführer SS ordered the camp commander Rudolf Höss to create a vast complex to exterminate people at the neighboring camp of Birkenau. What they saw, therefore, was not serious enough to prevent the happy party atmosphere that followed. It was the birthday of SS Gruppenführer Erich von dem Bach-Zelewski, who was known to take on assignments requiring a man devoid of any scruples.

Chapter 7

The Messiah for the Next Two Thousand Years

The top SS leaders were certainly aware of Hitler's "Directive 16," if not verbatim, then at least the intention to launch "Barbarossa," dated December 16, 1940. It was the order to prepare for the invasion of the Soviet Union. For that reason, it was definitely not a coincidence that Himmler and Wolff inspected a concentration camp that was to become of great importance because of the anticipated events.

Had Himmler and his satellites not known until then what the main emphasis would be for them, then by March 13, 1941, at the latest, they had to know. Hitler decreed in his own wording, which was confusing to outsiders: "In the operational area of the army [during the eastern campaign] the Reichsführer SS will receive special assignments in the preparation of the political administration that will result from the struggle to be held once and for all between two opposing political systems. Within the framework of these tasks, the Reichsführer SS will act independently on his own responsibility."

In those days, the Führer headquarters filled up once again with its familiar players, who had only worked sporadically until then. Hitler had been traveling a lot—to the Berghof, Vienna, and Linz. But when a military putsch in Belgrade toppled the Yugoslav government, which had just signed a pact with Nazi Germany, panic swept through the Reich chancellery. Hitler threatened to crush the Balkan countries in a lightning campaign if they did not agree to join the Axis policies. This became even more urgent since the Duce's armed forces were badly trounced during his attack on Greece. The prestige of the Axis powers was at stake and the defeat threatened to become even more serious because British troops had already landed in Greece to help those under siege and (planned by Winston Churchill) to attack the Germans from the rear.

These issues did not exactly put Hitler in a relaxed mood when the SS once again complained to him, as the trio of Himmler, Heydrich, and Wolff asked for more authority for the SS at the army's expense. They accused Wehrmacht generals in Poland, Holland, and Norway of sabotaging SS "pacification operations" in those countries. They demanded that the commanders of the military administration be filled by SS officers. According to them the submissive population would revolt as soon as they noticed that an army unit disagreed with the police measures. Wehrmacht doctors, for example, were not to treat sick Poles. In Radom a doctor wearing an army uniform even took over the supervision of a Polish hospital—one that was run by Catholic nuns, no less.

Himmler presented his plans whereby all Poles were to be concentrated in several areas within their own country, where they would also be isolated. Krakow would become a purely German city. In Holland and Norway the SS was planning to set up German schools. In the long term, the residents there would once again become closer to their Germanic heritage and united to the German country they originally came from. In Flanders, the SS was working in the same direction, but the resistance of the military administration allied with the Catholic clergy was impairing these efforts. Field Marshal Keitel and Hitler's army adjutant Gerhard Engel were both present when these allegations were made. The latter commented in his notes that the SS were again intriguing against the army. The three presented their accusations "in a straightforward manner" but also maliciously so that, with one "successful shot," they secured Hitler's approval against the army once more.

As Hitler listened to these complaints, parts of the Yugoslav capital, Belgrade, were already in ruins for hours. Without declaring war, German bomber squadrons attacked Belgrade in the early morning hours of April 6, 1941. Four days later Hitler again boarded his special train accompanied by his entourage. After a short stop in Munich on the evening of April 11 they continued into the Austrian province of Styria. A few kilometers from the Yugoslav border, near the railroad station of Mönchkirchen, the train was once more the headquarters, as it had been in Poland. That stretch of tracks was blocked off over a long distance, and during air raids the train would disappear into a tunnel as planned. This was unnecessary; the Yugoslav air force had been destroyed on the ground during the first two days of the campaign. By Hitler's birthday (ten days after the fighting began) the war was actually over, as the rest of the Greek armed forces still fit to fight surrendered to the SS Leibstandarte. Yugoslavia's soldiers had already capitulated several days before. The short campaign left SS Lieutenant General Wolff with almost nothing to do; however, on two state visits, he was allowed to play the role of the decorative extra; King Boris III of Bulgaria and the Hungarian head of state, Admiral Nikolaus von Horthy, paid a visit to the Führer's headquarters. Their armed forces had contributed in a limited way to the war, and now they wanted to pick up their reward.

On April 28, Hitler and his entourage returned to Berlin, but a moment of peace had past. The Balkan campaign messed up the Führer's original timetable for operation "Barbarossa." Now preparations for the eastern campaign became very urgent; the battles of extermination had to be won and Stalin's country crushed before the muddy season at the end of October, and the winter that would paralyze the German motorized divisions.

Only one day after their return to the capital of the Reich, Himmler and Wolff were once again in the spotlight. Candidates for officers in the army, the air force, the marines and the Waffen SS were ordered to the Sportspalast in Berlin so that Hitler, in a great speech, could prepare them for the future. He made them promise that these 9,000 men would "die heroically." After five more days, Wolff, sitting in his Reichstag armchair, experienced how the Führer celebrated victory in the Balkan war.

May and June were rather turbulent times at headquarters. The setting was mostly at the Berghof above Berchtesgaden where Hitler was given the news that his party deputy, Rudolf Hess, flew to Scotland alone in an ME109 fighter Messerschmidt plane because he mistakenly believed he could bring about peace with Great Britain. Admiral Darlan, vice president of the French Council of Ministers, came to the Obersalzberg because a battalion of volunteer fighters from France had been accepted into the Wehrmacht.

In Iraq, a rebellion instigated by the foreign department of the SD broke out against British mandate rule. A few German soldiers were flown to Baghdad, but if at headquarters they had hoped that the entire Arab world would rush into armed revolt, they were mistaken. Already after one week the resistance had been defeated. Several Arab leaders fled and were taken to Berlin by the SD where their main characteristic was to be their incessant hunger for women.

The English suffered yet another setback during the second half of May; Crete was occupied, mainly by German parachute troops, but with huge losses. Besides that, there were still state occasions; Hitler met with Mussolini once more, with Romanian head of state General Antonescu, as did Ante Paveliæ, the dictator of Croatia (established out of the remaining Yugoslavia).

Did Himmler and Wolff already know that three hours after midnight on June 22, 1941, the attack on Stalin's empire along the 1,500-kilometer-long border running from the Baltic to the Black Sea would begin? That the Soviet Union was the intended victim of the next campaign had long been an open secret in their circles, but the exact date was of the utmost secrecy. According to one of Hitler's general orders, each person was only allowed to know what was required to fulfill his assignments, and that person was not allowed to know anything until it became absolutely necessary. Dr. Otto Dietrich, Reich Chief Press Officer, claimed to have noticed that "something monstrous was underway against Russia" because of the hectic bustle in the Reich Chancellery on the day before the attack. Dietrich belonged to the Personal Staff of the Reichsführer SS with the honorary rank of gruppenführer and (what is to be regarded even more highly) was among the leadership of the NSDAP, just as comfortable there as in the ministry of propaganda. On the other hand, however, a German non-commissioned officer, who deserted to the Russians a few days before, revealed the imminent attack and the date—but of course, he was not taken seriously.

In the first few days after June 22, the German people paid little attention to the developments in the eastern campaign. Hitler waited because he wanted to announce a great victory as a prelude, and because the generals did not want to inform the fleeing enemies about the situation at the front. The Reich chancellery remained as headquarters for another thirty-six hours. Not until June 23 at noon did the convoy of cars drive out through the Wilhelmstrasse, this time to the Anhalter train station. The destination of the special train was East Prussia, near the small town of Rastenburg, with its 15,000 residents, some eighty kilometers from the Russian border. Eight kilometers from there, in a thick forest, a more permanent headquarters had been prepared. Hitler named it "Wolfsschanze." Gruppenführer Karl Wolff would make it his permanent home for the next twenty months.

However romantic Wolff may have felt about living in the middle of the forest, in constant physical contact with his Führer, during the initial days after moving to the "Wolfsschanze," the monotonous surroundings, the same faces, and the fixed routine must have affected his disposition. Also the strict security measures had to be bothersome after a while. There were several levels of security. The innermost was number III, surrounding the Führer bunker where only a select few were allowed to enter.

Approximately one kilometer away a fence and a watch station guarded the entrance to Security Level I; the forest warden's lodge, named "Görlitz," checked the identification and the person of anyone seeking to come through the gate. Wolff knew almost all of the SS guards of the watch detail; most of them were from Munich, or he had met them in the course of his duties as Himmler's adjutant. With him, they often disregarded the cumbersome and time-consuming procedures to which every visitor was subjected. One reached the accommodations by a well-paved forest path. They were divided into two complexes to the right and left of the main path, loosely scattered among the trees. There were several different circles of wooden Wehrmacht barracks, but within the security barriers II and III a few were built in concrete, with ceilings and walls up to six feet thick. This massive method of construction was used, of course, only for the protection of the bedrooms. The workrooms in the front part of the accommodations were only safe from fragments.

Wolff's quarters were in Security Level III, only 200 meters away from Hitler's bunker. Nazi party Reichsleiter Martin Bormann, Chief Press Officer Dr. Dietrich, Field Marshal Wilhelm Keitel, and General Alfred Jödl were housed in the immediate proximity. Hitler's adjutants, secretaries, and servants also lived within that level of security. Everyone knew everyone else in the area of about 500 by 250 square meters, but differences in rank mostly prevented people from getting to know each other on a personal level. Inevitably cliques were formed with their members exchanging information and forming alliances. The highest ranks met daily at the officer's mess when Hitler had his meals. Keitel, Jödl, and Bormann constantly sat at regular places at a table near Hitler. In the first few months, his midday meal was taken to the table regularly at 2:00 p.m. The evening meal was at 7:30 p.m. and very often, after the meal, Hitler began his long monologues; if he even got into conversation he hardly allowed anyone to interrupt him. And no one dared contradict him.

Anyone sitting for the first time at one of the twenty oak seats at the massive table made of the same wood was disappointed. Very often vegetable soup was served with bread, sometimes a little bit of soft curd cheese, and even less butter. As in Berlin, the cooks were only allotted what each soldier was actually getting. Every Sunday, for which the Party had planned a stew, the same frugal meal was served. Hitler got used to dragging out the evening get-together until late at night, and in his monologues he constantly repeated himself. Several listeners only listened to their master's voice while half asleep.

Wolff spent the mornings mostly studying the files and mail received by courier from his Main Office. Because he had no designated secretary, he wrote only brief notes on the letters and the office in Berlin composed the answers. They were returned to East Prussia for signature. At noon the official business began with the situation reports, where the military incidents of the preceding twenty hours were presented. In good weather, Wolff would meet people strolling on the streets and footpaths before the meeting. His high military rank allowed him to hold a conversation with most people he met; however, these were usually with Hitler's adjutants, with questions about news items. Because he was not allowed to be present at the situation reports, he had to collect information in this manner. The younger generation soon irreverently called him "General What's New." Also at the afternoon situation reports at 4:00 p.m. the Wehrmacht leadership preferred to be among themselves. They could then be absent most of the time during the evening conversations lasting until well past midnight, where Hitler's voice was practically the only one heard. Wolff was among the Führer's welcome guests—possibly because he remained silent. In the existing record of these conversations, his name is never mentioned.

According to his own description, it was his task to pass along Hitler's orders to Himmler and to present Himmler's wishes to Hitler. Besides that, he negotiated with the Wehrmacht, the Party, and the State in the name of the Reichsführer SS, as long as there was a representative at headquarters. Negotiations like this were necessary because Hitler only gave the blessing of his signature to a suggestion when all institutions involved had agreed. Wolff was kept extremely busy by the unending battle between the Reichsführer SS and Minister of Foreign Affairs von Ribbentrop.

Many people who experienced Hitler closely certified to his winning, even charming, friendliness, which completely contradicts the historical picture of the violent ruler and mass murderer. Wolff, who had known the Führer for years, honored and admired him even more when Hitler occasionally singled out the tall SS Gruppenführer by treating him as a confidant, asking him to accompany him on his short morning walks in the forest of Security Level III. Hitler even agreed to hear contradicting views on such occasions, because no one could witness his authority being placed into question. Also Wolff hit exactly the right tone of voice with his pretentious officer's club phraseology that his Führer valued as the mark of an honest and devoted follower.

It would have been a miracle if Wolff had only met with understanding at headquarters in such a situation. Once everything depends on the will of a potentate, then the people around him are always scheming as to how they can get rid of their competition. With rumors, half-truths, and innuendo friends and enemies come and go, and the climate and scenery did not help in loosening up the tense atmosphere at the center of power. High trees with thick crowns towered above the barracks and bunkers. They served as protection from aircraft, but also blocked out the light. The forest itself was monotonous. On the other side of the last fence there were two lakes with charming banks, but within the camp there were wide patches of marshland that from spring into late fall were breeding grounds for swarms of insects. The concrete bunkers had no windows and the walls were mostly cool and damp. The chief interpreter of the foreign office, Dr. Paul Schmidt, could see that "in Hitler's rooms under the dark shadows of the forest trees, the electric light was often turned on all day." He found the gloomy atmosphere "depressing" and breathed a sigh of relief when he "could leave that dark forest again."

Schmidt pitied all those who "had to live and work like prisoners in the thick forest for weeks or even months." During his examination at the Nuremberg War Crimes Trials, General Alfred Jödl described the headquarters as "midway between a cloister and a concentration camp." Wolff was better off than most other residents: at regular intervals, he could go on leave to Berlin for days on end, return to his office, and visit his lover on the side. The widowed Countess Bernstorff had rented an apartment in Berlin. Just as often, he drove to see Himmler, who stayed at his own headquarters, the special train "Heinrich" stationed about thirty kilometers from the "Wolfsschanze." Every now and then Himmler asked him along on a trip. During those absences, he was not missed at headquarters because his role in those circles, if anything, was more as an observer than an actor. Whoever lived at the "Wolfsschanze" and later wrote about it, either never mentioned Wolff at all or did so only in passing. The reason could be that despite his jovial friendliness, people did not trust him; since he was after all the adjutant of the man who controlled the Gestapo, the SD, and the concentration camps. Furthermore, the hushed conversation about the SS units during the first weeks of the campaign was not conducive to creating trust in the general who represented them.

As early as March 1941, long before the beginning of the campaign, Hitler had announced to the heads of the Wehrmacht, the Party, and the SS that what was about to begin soon in the east was to be "more than just a battle with weapons." This was contained in his so-called "Commissar Order." All Red Army political commissars, "whether captured in battle or after the fighting... must as a rule be eliminated immediately and completely." Special commandos of the SS had been set up with the assignment of identifying and liquidating all active Communist elements among the prisoners of war in concentration camps. The Jews were also to be eradicated as the source of all the misery in the world. As in the Polish campaign, only in greater numbers and even more brutally, the Einsatzgruppen were raging behind the front lines since the beginning of the war. Reinhard Heydrich, chief of the RHSA, sent four Einsatzgruppen of 3,000 men behind the advancing soldiers to prepare for "an assignment of extreme harshness." During the Russian campaign they immediately entered towns with tanks so that no one would have time to flee or hide. Their victims were Communist, state employees, and Jews. Naturally they also fought the partisans who were blowing up train tracks behind the Wehrmacht, attacking transports on the roads, or massacring guard posts and other units. As in the Polish campaign, Wolff's assignment again was to keep the SS's bloodstained image as clean as possible—at least in those instances when officers of the Wehrmacht became incensed.

During the first weeks of the campaign, the Einsatzgruppen in the central section of the eastern front were already very busy. By mid-July, 300,000 soldiers of the Red Army were already behind barbed wire as prisoners of war. According to a directive from Hitler, they were not allowed to be treated as "comrades" and remained enemies, even though they were disarmed, and were meant for extermination. SS Brigadeführer Otto Ohlendorf commanded one of the four Einsatzgruppen in the central section of the front. In 1946 at his examination before the International Military Tribunal in Nuremberg, he described how the commando leaders "before marching out were given oral instructions" that "in Russian territory the Jews were to be liquidated like the Soviet political commissars." Himmler announced that this order was based on Hitler's instructions and that the heads of the Wehrmacht had been informed.

By the end of July 1941, so many protests and accusations against the murder practices of the Einsatzgruppen had reached the Führer headquarters that Himmler decided to take inspection tours. One of his adjutants received the order to prepare those trips. This was how High SS and Police Chief Erich von dem Bach-Zelewski, SS Gruppenführer and lieutenant general of the police, found out by radio: "RFSS [Himmler] plans a two day trip through your territory." Visits to Baranowicze, Minsk, and Orscha were scheduled. Von dem Bach-Zelewski had to take care of accommodations and meals. Wolff was first on the list of participants accompanying Himmler. Also listed was a prominent civilian, whom Hitler greatly admired, "Reich Set Designer" Benno von Arent, who not only decorated the most famous theaters, but was also called when important Party and State functions required a particularly impressive set design.

What the theater expert saw on this trip on August 15–16, 1941, must have disturbed him more than any drama he had ever staged. In Minsk, the head of Einsatzgruppen center, SS Brigadeführer Arthur Nebe, reported on the security situation in his region and von dem Bach-Zelewski described how the killing units captured their victims—during raids in the city and in the country, by combing through prisoner of war camps, with raiding party operations across the land and bigger operations concentrated on towns having a large Jewish population. Where there was simply suspicion of sabotage or of support given to the partisans, they didn't waste time searching for the guilty parties; they immediately shot hostages.

The headquarters of the Einsatzgruppen was a concrete building with many floors in the city center of Minsk. Until recently, it was the office of the NKVD, Stalin's political police operating from the same location. Because the new owners hardly differed from the previous ones, the complex was perfectly suited for the German security police. Here Nebe quietly described to Himmler, the great criminologist, how tough, resilient, and fanatical his opponents were. Among the partisans and saboteurs, there were hardly any Jews, but they were nevertheless dangerous because they had created a closely-knit intelligence network across the country, setting the stage for attacks and sabotage. Himmler's reaction was that Nebe should proceed even more harshly.

On that point Wolff told a journalist in 1961: "Today I consider it possible that [Himmler], during those moments in Minsk, came up with the horrible idea of exterminating the millions of Jews in the east, only a small part of whom were spies." The question remains as to whether or not he meant this seriously. Or did Wolff use this idea to cover up the fact that he had known about the orders for mass murder from the very beginning? If not, then he experienced them very harshly that same day. One of the participants at the meeting, Dr. Otto Bradfisch, SS Obersturmführer and head of Einsatzgruppen 8, admitted after the war that it soon became clear to him that the Jews presented no danger to the fighting troops and that someone simply wanted to get rid of them. Therefore he asked Himmler in Minsk who would take responsibility for those actions. Himmler told Bradfisch that the Führer and he, the Reichsführer SS, would be answerable for all of them.

Years later Wolff provided quite a different picture of what happened in Minsk at the Munich Court as it made great efforts to establish the facts. On the basis of statements from eyewitnesses and documents it was determined that at that time, just four weeks after the start of the eastern campaign, the partisans in the Minsk area were not very active. They began increasing in numbers and therefore became dangerous once the results of the Einsatzgruppen proved that they were doomed if the Germans were to win the war. It was therefore fairly unlikely that Hitler sent the Reichsführer SS on a tour just because of the partisans, saying, "Wolff can accompany you and report back to me later." Wolff replied: "It left me cold!" He wanted to advise against this but never got a chance. "And you go with him," Hitler ordered.

An area of fields and forests outside the city had been prepared for the murders. All participants drove there in cars, the death candidates were in smaller groups. They were not to hear the shots when their fellow victims died. The prisoners had dug two holes, each about eight meters long, two meters deep and two meters wide. That was the normal procedure for a mass grave in the east. Wolff did not have to describe to either the journalist or the court the details of what followed, since the killing methods were always the same. The first prisoners were driven to the hole, pushed off the platform of the truck and into the pit and as soon as they landed on their stomachs on the ground, those standing above them began shooting. The targets were at a distance of about four meters.

Wolff described one particular experience. "After many volleys, I could see that Himmler was trembling. He ran his hand across his face and swayed. 'You could have spared yourself and me this,' I said to him. His face was almost green. And then he said, 'A piece of brain just splattered in my face.' He immediately threw up."

This is a gory tale but what actually happened must have been carried out differently. Even assuming that Himmler was standing on the edge of a pit, the victim's head had to have been more than three meters away from him and five meters from his face. They were shooting with regular 98k carbines and the normal rifle ammunition, at such a short distance, cuts smoothly through the skull. It rips a larger hole at the point of exit and digs a fairly deep hole in the ground. So, if inner pressure builds up caused by hitting the brain, and as a result of the impact parts of the brain are scattered, they most certainly do not fly up almost four meters in the air and across a distance of five meters.

Wolff, by the way, did not dare repeat this nonsense in court. The story he told a journalist differed from the forensic statement, where a "2 to 3 cm piece of brain covered in blood" flew only to hit Himmler's coat.

One possible reason for Himmler's apparent shock, said Wolff, was that his superior (who had not been a frontline soldier like retired Lieutenant Wolff) had never seen a person who had been shot, much less ever seen anyone in the process of being shot. He then mentioned the "trips to the front" that they took together during the Polish campaign, in the West and in the Balkans. They did not advance quite as far as the fighting troops, but drove through battlefields that had not yet been cleared. Besides that, he forgot that he and Himmler had seen how SS Oberführer Ludolf von Alvensleben in Bromberg had a number of Poles shot because they had supposedly killed German nationals.

The Munich court where Wolff went on trial in 1964 ignored those melodramatic descriptions for good reason. Wolff was apparently only carrying out court-martial sentences for espionage and other offenses. From eyewitness statements about the incident, it was ascertained that after the last of the 120 murders, Himmler still found enough vigor to give a grandiloquent speech. He assured the members of the Einsatzgruppen that the highest leaders of state and the Party would recognize their hard work. It was necessary for the nation, the Reich and the Führer so that the German people could live in freedom, security, and peace in the future. This speech and Wolff's presence—it was stated in the courtroom—convinced the officers and their Einsatzgruppen teams that their actions were not only lawful, but even highly commendable.

At the Munich trial, Wolff recalled that following the Minsk murders he had warned the Reichsführer "not to do something like this with me again." Under questioning he was once again able to quote verbatim what he had told Himmler over two decades before: "Reichsführer, since I am not a police official, to follow against my express request the unnecessary order you gave me today undermines our longstanding friendship to the point of tearing it to shreds." This was not just an empty phrase because, in truth, the already strained relationship with Himmler had suffered an "inner break" since the Minsk events. If one were to follow Wolff's autobiographical narrations, this would in no way have been the first time.

Yet the inspection of Einsatzgruppen B was not the first and certainly not the last that the Himmler-Wolff duo undertook in the East in 1941. At the end of July they were in Kovno, Riga, and Dünaburg, in the area of Einsatzgruppen A. The murderers stationed in that area were doing "cleansing work for political security following orders" meaning "the most extensive elimination of Jews," according to Einsatzgruppen commander, SS Brigadeführer Dr. Walter Stahlecker. He kept an exact record of the number of victims. Three months after Himmler's first inspection he could offer a total of 135,000 dead, of which over 120,000 were Jews. Did he speak to the Reichsführer SS and to the chief of his personal staff about this? A further inspection tour by Himmler and Wolff took them to the Baltic during the latter part of September, to Riga, Reval and Dorpat. At the beginning of October they traveled south, and visited Brigadeführer Dr. Otto Rasch in Kiev with his Einsatzgruppen C, responsible for the Ukraine.

They also inspected Einsatzgruppen D deeper in the south under SS Standartenführer Otto Ohlendorf. The purpose of the trip was to bolster wavering morale. Himmler repeated the speech that he had given to encourage the murderers in Minsk. Besides that, the Higher SS and Police Leaders were instructed that they were to continue the work of the Einsatzgruppen as they followed the armies advancing in the east and were to take their operations forward. When the units available to the Higher SS and Police Leaders were no longer sufficient, they were allowed to recruit volunteers from the resident population, give them uniforms and handguns. In the Baltic countries and in the Ukraine, they temporarily found enough murderers, as long as the action was only targeting the Jews.

Accordingly, it can be assumed that everywhere they visited the two highest ranking inspectors had been seriously discussing the issue, which at that time and for them was of the utmost importance. It may be said in Wolff's favor that one may assume that he was not the driving force behind the whole initiative. After the war, he always maintained that he had nothing to do with the crimes against the Jews. That may be true insofar as he only went along with Nazi anti-Semitism to the extent of what seemed necessary to further his career. He mixed with the best society, the aristocracy, business leaders, and famous artists in his circle of acquaintances like other people collect stamps, and only rarely did he lose his composure as a parade ground officer. According to the National Socialist teachings on race, he could consider himself a model of Nordic German aristocracy. For a man like him, the pitiful, Yiddish-speaking, gesticulating, long-bearded and longhaired male Jews of Eastern Europe were something so untouchable and subhuman that he saw no reason to bother with their well being or suffering.

As 1941 drew to a close, the need for the SS leaders to continuously drive the number of those murdered higher by taking part themselves was no longer necessary. The *most clever one* who had in the meantime been promoted to Obergruppenführer, Reinhard Heydrich, had developed a system that bureaucratized and automated the mechanism to murder the Jews. A conference was to be held to present this system by the State and the Party to all the officials involved in the Jewish question, and at the same time introduce it as a general procedure coming down from the highest level. The date for this conference had to be postponed several times, but it took place on January 20, 1942.

The many leading functionaries and officials of institutions involved with the Jews met in Berlin in a luxurious house at 56 Grossen Wannsee. Heydrich was the host and was ordered by Hitler and Himmler orally to prepare the "final solution" of the Jewish question. He had also a written authorization from Hermann Göring, Hitler's designated successor. He was ordered, as stated, "to arrange all the necessary organizational and material preparations regarding the Jewish question." Heydrich was also chairing the meeting.

Since it was a delicate topic, the ministers and Party leaders were all represented without exception. Adolf Eichmann, head of the Jewish department in the Gestapo and the SD Amt-IV-B-IV, kept the minutes and was hardly noticed, sitting in the corner with a stenographer. As an SS Sturmbannführer, he seemed to be no more than an extra in this "Secretaries of State meeting"—as that gathering was referred to in official circles later on. When Israeli police captain Avner W. Less interrogated him in 1960, Eichmann denied that "killing had been discussed" at the conference. They had only spoken of the "Einsatzgruppen in the East." "The naked, brutal words" (Eichmann said) like *murder*, *kill*, *shoot*, *kill off*, and *gas* were avoided there. The entire murder machine developed its own secret codes as a result of this, which allowed all those who knew and the masterminds behind the scenes to suppress the disturbing images. One had to speak in terms of "evacuate, send, resettlement," and "special treatment." Responsibility was constantly being traded, back and forth. Who gave which order to whom? Hitler to Himmler? Himmler to Heydrich? Hitler to Heydrich? Göring to Heydrich? Heydrich to which persons? They were all in it together, so that every one could claim that he was not alone, nor did he have more responsibility. Their tactics made it easier for many Germans to convince themselves that they had never heard of, and certainly not seen any of, these atrocities. Even Wolff resorted to this; he belonged without a doubt to that kind of person who believes what he wants to believe and, instead of facing reality, sees only what he wants to see.

For Karl Wolff's future, *when* he knew about the crimes of the Gestapo and the SD became a significant issue. As an old man he still maintained that he found out the "truth" just a few weeks before the end of the war through contacts with Swiss citizens. His opinion was that one should write that word "truth" in quotation marks because the atrocities had been exaggerated and generalized for many reasons. But this is an argument also frequently used by many Germans to hide their feelings of guilt about the past. Wolff always maintained that Himmler, as well as his friends Heydrich, Pohl, Eicke, and others, kept him from knowing about the atrocities because they did not want to burden his sensitive nature and drive him out of the SS. However, the SS society of men never had that much concern for sensitive souls before; quite the opposite, the men of higher rank were actually quite proud of the fact that they could withstand horrible and dreadful things without showing any noticeable strain. Even if Gruppenführer Karl Wolff, "the most trusted among all the Reichsführer's SS officers" (as his colleague Berger wrote at the end of 1941 in a letter to Himmler), had truly been kept from knowing of the crimes, certain things must have made him suspicious during the course of his constant contacts with those involved, particularly since "General What's New" was such a vigilant observer.

Wolff's friend Erich von dem Bach-Zelewski, who was sentenced to life imprisonment for his participation in mass murders, testified at Wolff's Munich trial that he found it highly improbable that an SS officer of his rank and position would know nothing about the crimes. When the two met in Minsk in the middle of August 1941, the former Reichswehr officer had already left his bloody tracks in eastern Upper Silesia. Both had the same rank and were so friendly that they used "Du" and Bach-Zelewski's letters usually began with a "Dear Wölffchen." Had he not told his friend about his terrible deeds? Von dem Bach-Zelewski became ill after the Minsk meeting. In the SS sanitarium at Hohenlychen, SS physician Dr. Ernst Grawitz diagnosed intestinal colic and a nervous breakdown. He also named the cause: "He is particularly suffering from memories of the shootings of Jews, as well as other difficult experiences in the east." Psychological counseling, therefore, was a "significant factor in the whole healing process."

The patient kept nothing that depressed him secret from the doctor. "I'm at the end," he said to anyone. "Don't you know what's going on in Russia? The entire Jewish population is being exterminated over there." Isn't it likely then that he would tell his close friend Wolff the same thing when, as Himmler's envoy, he visited his bedside? However, the condition of the patient improved only slightly. Besides, he was still somewhat groggy from ether anesthesia. In any case, Himmler was so upset by Wolff's report that he ordered a high-ranking SS officer to stand guard at the bedside of anyone with knowledge of state secrets in the future. The sick man was at that time already an Obergruppenführer, like Wolff, who on January 30 had just had the lapels of Obergruppenführer sewn to his uniform collar.

Should Wolff, however, have returned from Hohenlychen still having no idea, he was now going to get an explanation from the other side. In occupied Serbia there was an SS Gruppenführer State Councilor Dr. Harald Turner working as chief of the military administration. In October 1941, in retaliation for partisan attacks on German soldiers, he had 4,000 Jews and 200 gypsies shot. "It's not a nice job," he wrote to Wolff's friend Richard Hildebrand, an SS Gruppenführer and Higher SS and Police Führer in Danzig, "but this way, the Jewish question gets the fastest solution."

The military did not agree with his crude practices. They tried to get rid of Turner using bureaucratic tricks. Following Hildebrand's advice, he turned to Wolff with the request that he speak to Himmler for him. Once Turner was again secure in his post, he thanked Wolff in a letter on April 11, 1942, "because I am sure that this is all due to your influence."

The letter further states: "After all, I know that you are interested in these things, and the reason why I am calling attention to it now is simply because this issue will become more than acute. Already months ago I had all the Jews within reach in these parts shot, and every one of the Jewish women and children put into a concentration camp. At the same time, with the help of the SD, I got hold of a delousing truck,* which will handle the final clearance of the camp in fourteen days to four weeks… the moment has come when, under the Geneva Conventions, the Jewish officers in the prisoners of war camp, like it or not, are to follow their dead relatives. If those concerned are let go now they will be given their final freedom once they arrive but as with other members of their race, it will not be very long, and the whole issue should be resolved once and for all…"

Once may assume that the addressee read this letter because it was not marked "mail to be read," as Wolff classified all copies that Himmler and others often sent him "for his perusal," where such murderous happenings were sometimes mentioned, but according to Wolff they went unread into the files because as a very busy man he just did not have the time to work through so much paper.

There is one further clue showing that he could not have been that innocent. On July 5, 1942, he informed his personal consultant, Obersturmführer Heinrich Heckenstaller, at the Berlin office by phone to tell Himmler's secretary, Dr. Rudolf Brandt, to notify the Reichsführer SS of an important discussion to be held at the Wehrmacht leadership staff meeting the following day. The SS absolutely had to be represented at that meeting concerned with clearing the captured Crimean peninsula of all residents as ordered by Hitler. The reason was that all South Tyrolean Germans were going to be resettled there. In Heckenstaller's "comment for SS Obersturmbannführer Dr. Rudolf Brandt," written on Wolff's instructions, it stated: "Point of discussion, aside from the installation of assembly camps, resettlement, racial inspection, and the required security forces involved in resettlement, the guarding of the camps, the liquidation by Einsatzgruppen, and the general problems of all issues involved."

Translated into intelligible language, this means: the residents of Crimea will be gathered in concentration camps. The racially useful will be selected and all of the others will be left to the Einsatzgruppen. Wolff would probably have composed the text differently, in better language and more obscure at the same time, but the meaning would have invariably been the same. What could Wolff know or had to have known about the

* A truck (with a boxlike structure on top) into which the victims were pressed closely together and killed by carbon monoxide exhaust fumes.

mass murders? It must have occurred to him that Hitler threatened the Jews with violence or death more during the first half of 1942—in no less than six public speeches and announcements and at least eight times during the "Table Talk" discussions at Führer headquarters.* This accumulation becomes retrospectively clear, because the mass extermination at the death camps was being carried out in full force at this time.

Wolff must have noticed this; he was the ambitious observer and this was precisely his task. So it could not have slipped by him that in closed circles after hours, the Führer was increasingly speaking of the "dirty Jews," "Jewish pigs," "Jewish vermin" and that he only viewed his archenemies as "pests"—perhaps because in this way he could "justify" to himself subconsciously that he was not having humans murdered at all.

Anyone like Wolff, who believed in authority and lived in such a poisoned atmosphere, among generals who made decisions daily about life and death regarding thousands of soldiers, in the end was no longer so disgusted that at any one time a few thousand more Jews or other "inferior" races were processed through Hitler's killing machine. Of course, the man who got the "final solution" going died on June 4, 1942, from an assassination that was not even meant for the murderer of the Jews, but rather for the Reich Protector of Bohemia and Moravia. SS Obergruppenführer Reinhard Heydrich retained his position as chief of the security police when he was sent to Prague to put the fear of God into the Czechs. Hitler ordered a state funeral in Berlin for the victim of the assassination. For this, the highest SS officers formed the honor guard at the coffin in the Mosaic Room at the Reich Chancellery. Wolff was one of those men. Now, the friend, the comrade, and also the rival—as he had thought—for Himmler's succession lay in a casket next to him. The Reichsführer himself even said one day: "If something should ever happen to me, there is only Heydrich or you as my successor; who that will be can only be decided by Hitler."

Wolff saw a different side to Heydrich's death. The Reichsführer too had now been rid of another rival. Himmler supposedly feared Heydrich, whom Hitler characterized as "the man with the iron heart," because the chief of the RSHA had not only created a terrifying apparatus of total surveillance, but also had surpassed his superior in mental keenness, in the ability to make decisions, and in unscrupulousness as well. As Himmler

---

* See *Hitler's Table Talk 1941–1944*, H. R. Trevor-Roper, ed. (New York: Enigma Books, 2000).

and Wolff collected the body in Prague, Heydrich's adjutant handed them sealed envelopes: the farewell words of the dying man. The legacy to Wolff included the request that he always courageously and ruthlessly tell the Reichsführer SS the truth. Heydrich didn't even mention murdering the Jews. In the plane back to Berlin, Wolff let Himmler read his letter, but the expected discussion did not take place. Wolff assumed this because Heydrich discussed his "dirty work" in the letter to Himmler, which the Adjutant was not allowed to read.

Wolff lived up to his description as the SS Parsifal, the pure Thor, one night in a scene said to have taken place at the beginning of July 1942 at Gestapo headquarters at number 8 Prinz-Albrecht-Strasse. He left his offices at about 1:30 a.m., and without announcing himself (something he was allowed to do) went over to Himmler's offices nearby. He found the leader "both psychologically and physically collapsed over his desk." Himmler answered the compassionate question as to whether his faithful paladin could offer him any comfort with woeful smiles, shaking his head. Wolff suspected at that point that the difficulties of love and marriage must have been the cause. He was well aware of the problems Himmler was having. His wife, Marga, was seven years older than her husband; she was a professional nurse when he fell for her motherly care, and since then her large body was all that was still remarkable about her. He was increasingly hesitant about showing her in public. She reacted to this estrangement by quarreling. So, Himmler looked for feminine comfort and found it in his personal secretary Hedwig Potthast. Recently, in February, she bore him a son. Since Wolff in many ways served as the father confessor in this matter, he was now helpful as godfather—a condition that did not particularly point to estrangement or a row between the two men.

It wasn't family worries, said the Reichsführer. "That, dear Wölffchen, I could deal with. But you cannot even imagine all that I must silently take on for the Führer so that he, the Messiah for the next 2,000 years, can remain absolutely free from sin. You know very well, especially now, after Heydrich's death, that if I should pass away or if I am unable to continue in my position, only you could be my successor. It is then better for you and for Germany if you neither have anything to do with nor know about these matters that weigh upon me."

Such lines were not some novelist's or screenwriter's invention. Wolff recited them verbatim from his phenomenal memory, forty-five years after they had been spoken. When he was seventy-seven years old, and set on proving to the world that he did not know about Himmler's crimes and those of the entire SS crowd. One may accept the fact that he remembered these words so well because he could use them as an alibi. "I spent many nights," he wrote further, "brooding about what he could have meant... It wasn't until after the war that I found the answer in my search for the truth: that it concerned the Jewish issue."

Wolff accepted the reasons for Himmler's silence only temporarily. Sometimes he also argued that Himmler feared that the discovery of the abuse of his idealism could have driven the painfully precise guard officer to suicide. Also Himmler may have never said anything about the murders because he would then have placed himself in his rival's hands. This thought immediately assumes that the crimes were being committed behind Hitler's back by an overzealous Reichsführer—a suspicion offered here and there in Wolff's recollections.*

On July 17, 1942, Hitler and his headquarters moved from the "Wolfsschanze" to "Werewolf," a settlement of barracks in the Ukraine, 15 kilometers north of Vinnitza. It was in a small forest near the banks of the Bug River, somewhat far from the southern section of the front, which had advanced successfully in recent days. It was still close enough, however, to feel the proximity to the victories for the greatest military commander of all times (Grössten Feldherrn aller Zeiten—shortened to GRÖFAZ). Wolff also moved with the rest. Himmler was stationed farther north in his special train. He wanted to be closer to the Polish border because he had set himself the goal to "end the resettlement of the entire Jewish population of the general administration by December 31, 1942." Now he had to admit that this would hardly be possible.

There were two reasons for this. Thousands upon thousands of Jews in the former Poland were working for the Wehrmacht. They produced ammunition, uniforms, and cooking utensils. They had been trained and could only be replaced with difficulty. On the other hand, there were not enough train cars to transport the "resettlers" to where they would be so thoroughly exterminated in the gas chambers, crematoria, and incinerators that no trace would be left of them. The death mills for this activity were now ready: Treblinka, Sobibor, Belzec, Auschwitz-Birkenau. In the

* This particular idea—that Hitler did not know what was going on—is used by many Holocaust deniers, and by David Irving in particular. See, among others, two books by Irving: *Hitler's War* (New York: Viking, 1977) and *Goebbels* (London: Focal Point, 1996).

Warsaw ghetto alone there were half a million Jews, but no trains to take them away. The Eastern Railroad, a branch of the Reichsbahn, which was responsible for them, regretted that they could offer no help. The German offensive toward Stalingrad in the Soviet south and the Caucasus was underway. The soldiers needed replacements, and the trains were being used for longer periods of time with the ever-growing distances. The Wehrmacht would not free up any trains for the transport of the Jews.

When Himmler appeared at the "Werewolf" headquarters on July 16, 1942, he probably also spoke with Hitler about his hesitations regarding the extermination of the Jews, but the Führer was too busy with global strategic plans that included a campaign to India. Hitler could by no means involve himself with organizing train transportation. So Himmler went to his local representative with his concerns. With his skillful negotiations Wolff had already achieved some impossible things. He remembered his good contacts with the deputy of the Reich Minister of Transport, Secretary of State, Dr. Albert Ganzenmüller. In a special priority telephone call from headquarters, Berlin assured him that cars and locomotives would be made available and that details would be sent in writing.

Wolff refused to take any blame when he was later accused of having helped transport 300,000 Jews to their death. First, he argued that he only made telephone calls on Himmler's orders. Secondly, he assumed that the Jews were being taken to a sort of reservation, similar to the American Indians, because Himmler told him that they would be concentrated in a few large areas so that the number of guards could be reduced. And thirdly, Himmler had actually wanted to get on the phone himself, but was not authorized for special priority phone calls because he was not a member of headquarters, as far as the telephone exchange was concerned.

Presumably Wolff's contribution to the genocide never would have gone into the files had State Secretary Ganzenmüller not been such a thorough bureaucrat and completed the arrangement in writing. In this manner "Herr Obergruppenführer Wolff, Berlin, SW 11, Prinz Albrecht-Strasse" found out as of the date of 28 July 1942 that, "[w]ith reference to our telephone conversation on July 16, for your information, I am please to send you the following report from my head office at the Eastern Railroad [Gedob] in Krakow: Each day since July 22, a train leaves with 5,000 Jews from Warsaw via Malkinia to Treblinka. A train also leaves twice a week with 5,000 Jews from Przemysl to Belzec. Gedob is in constant contact with security units in Krakow. They agree that the transports from Warsaw via Lublin to Sobibor [near Lublin] must remain there as long as the construction on this stretch of tracks make the transport impossible [approximately October 1942]... Heil Hitler! Respectfully yours, Ganzenmüller."

On August 2, the letter reached the addressee at "Werewolf." The recipient wrote on the envelope by hand: "Many thanks, also in the name of the RF.*" Furthermore, copies were sent to Dr. Brandt [Himmler's secretary], Odilo Globocnik [in charge of murder operations in Lublin], and Obergruppenführer Friedrich-Wilhelm Krüger [who, as Higher SS and Police Führer in the General Government, was responsible for the extermination of the Jews]. They were all well aware of the State Secret of the Great German Reich that had long since been public within the leadership. If anyone could later have told them that Obergruppenführer Karl Wolff was excluded from this knowledge, they would surely have died laughing. This was clearly impossible. Brandt was sentenced to death by the Allied Court in Nuremberg and hanged for crimes against humanity; Globocnik committed suicide during the final days of the war; Krüger disappeared without a trace in the confusion at the end of the war.

In Wolff's Berlin office, one of his colleagues drafted the reply to "Dear Party Comrade Ganzenmüller." At the date of August 13, 1942, it was written, among other things: "With particular pleasure I took note of your report that for fourteen days now a train has been leaving daily for Treblinka with 5,000 members of the chosen people, and that in this manner, we have been able to carry out this population movement at increasing speed. I have been in contact with the offices concerned so that a smooth implementation of all measures is guaranteed. I thank you again for you efforts in this matter and ask you at the same time to continue giving your attention to these things."

Wolff signed that letter at the "Werewolf" barracks. In later years, as he was reproached that the wording of the letter quite obviously came from the Nazi monster vocabulary, and could also be understood that he was in no way as harmlessly, guilelessly, or unsuspectingly involved in the mass murders, he explained that he did not approve the drafting of the letter because he was not an anti-Semite. He only signed the letter because he felt it was a matter of urgency, and he did not want to have to request another draft from Berlin. It also follows that he meant no harm by that letter because he sent it without the secret code, required for all Jewish matters. He regarded the letter simply as a thank-you note and for that

* Reichsführer SS Heinrich Himmler.

reason forgot it so completely and only remembered it again when it was shown to him at the war crimes trials where he was questioned as a witness.

So, on July 22, 1942, the first train ordered by Wolff rolled into Warsaw on a track next to the Jewish hospital. The fifty cars were to be locked, covered, and secured with barbed wire. Early in the morning the Jewish Council, the nominally autonomous administration of the ghettos, was told: "All Jewish people, regardless of age and sex . . . were to be resettled in the east." The Jewish Council made sure that 600 Jews were present at the daily collecting point by the hospital. The one thousand men of the Jewish Service for Order were outfitted with clubs and had to herd the "resettlers" together every day, one hundred into each car. The general administration of the Eastern Railroad in Krakow made sure that deliveries to the gas chambers arrived on time according to "Schedule number 548." They even managed to free up further transport vehicles so that by August 6 another special train could be ready to go to Treblinka every day.

Was it pure coincidence that on July 22, while the first group rolled into the extermination camp, the creators and managers of the camp dictated a long and friendly letter to Karl Wolff from Lublin? Odilo Globocnik, the SS Brigadeführer, was quite pleased with the expected rush. "The Reichsführer was here and gave us enough new work so that all of our most secret dreams will come true. I am so grateful to him for that. He can be sure that these things he wishes will be taken care of very shortly. I also thank you, Obergruppenführer, for I am certain that you also helped with this visit."

What can this good-natured person have meant with "new work" and "our most secret wishes"? What was it that Himmler wished for that would be fulfilled very shortly? Throughout the year, Globocnik reported to the Reichsführer SS that "by October 19, 1943, I will have completed Operation 'Reinhard' [the name of his assignment] and shut down all camps." What remains unclear and ambiguous is why he was thanking Wolff so specifically. Was the general director of the death mills afraid that he would have to close his operations early due to lack of business? And had the unsuspecting Obergruppenführer Wolff freed him from such worries by speaking favorably to Himmler? At this point, we are reminded of a hint that Heydrich gave to the head of the SD Foreign Intelligence Service, Brigadeführer Walter Schellenberg, as he was leaving: "Pay particular attention to Wölffchen. Without Wolff, Himmler seldom does anything; everything is discussed with him first."

In principle, this may be correct, but during the war frequent travel no longer allowed such a close relationship. However, Himmler made great efforts to keep his chief of his personal staff up to date; he was sent copies of almost all the important documents to the Führer's headquarters in Berlin—the previously mentioned "mail to read" that Wolff supposedly never read. He therefore found out (or perhaps did not) about Himmler's order to the Higher SS and Police Officer in the Ukraine, Obergruppenführer Hans Prützmann, that he must "despite existing economic concerns, immediately" clear out and destroy "the Pinks Ghetto" (dated October 27, 1942). Or the "SS order," in force and effect for the entire East, whereby in operations against the partisans, men, women, and children suspected of band activity were to be gathered and transported in groups to the Lublin and Auschwitz camps. What was supposed to happen to the adults once they arrived there was not stated in the order—they were forced to work and die of exhaustion. The children and youths were to be judged according to racial criteria. The worthless ones were to be trainees in the concentration camps and were raised in "unconditional subordination" to their German masters; the racially acceptable ones were to be Germanized in National Socialist reformatories. (Order dated January 6, 1943.)

Five days later, on January 13, Himmler ordered "that all proletarian elements currently suspected of band activity, either male or female, will be arrested and sent to the KL [concentration camps] in Lublin, Auschwitz, and in the Reich on a continuous basis... This operation is to be carried out with the greatest speed. I have asked SS Obergruppenführer Wolff to discuss the issue of ordering trains with State Secretary Ganzenmüller. Any requests or wishes regarding this matter are mainly to be directed to SS Obergruppenführer Wolff." This was taking place during the weeks when all wheels on cars and locomotives were to roll—not, as a propaganda slogan suggested, for the victory, but to keep the disastrous battle of Stalingrad from turning into a catastrophe for the entire eastern front.

The successful arrangement regarding the trains was a possible reason why Himmler took his Wölffchen with him to Warsaw on January 9, 1943. It could also have been that Wolff was experienced in dealing with the Wehrmacht (especially if it concerned the Jews). It had been reported to the Reichsführer that there were still 35,000 Jews living in the Warsaw Ghetto. Actually, including illegal residents, there were many more. Of these, 20,000 were employed in businesses controlled by the Munitions Command of the Wehrmacht. In September 1942, the Armed Forces

Commander of the General Command demanded that the resettlement of these workers and their immediate families be stopped until the orders that were vital for the war effort were completed.

Himmler refused and maintained that the evidence of "purported interest in armaments...in reality only supported the Jews and their businesses." The atmosphere between the SS and the Wehrmacht was once again loaded with tension. Himmler's visit was not announced to the leader of the Warsaw Armaments Command, a Wehrmacht captain; such impoliteness was purposeful. The Reichsführer SS provocatively asked why his order to move the Warsaw operations, along with their workers, to Lublin had not been followed. Everyone in his office knew what would happen to them there. "The Jews there, too," Himmler had written in one of his orders, "would again disappear one day, according to the Führer's wishes." When defendant Wolff was asked about that meeting at his Munich trial, he at first could not "for the life of me" remember. He requested that they prove to him that he had been present. This was done successfully because the war diary of the Warsaw armaments inspection had been submitted to the court with remarks regarding Himmler's entourage. In addition, any of the officers who had kept the diary could have been questioned as witnesses. Wolff then reacted with "a very vague recollection of the visit," but he still had to explain why Himmler would bring the chief of his personal staff with him to Warsaw since he never had anything to do with the Jewish question. Wolff explained the lapses in his otherwise excellent memory by saying that his health had been "very poor" during those days in January 1943. Besides, he had also been psychologically burdened because he had completed the divorce from his wife and the marriage to his lover at that time. According to the statutes of the SS, he needed Himmler's approval to do this. Because it had been denied to him, the estrangement between himself and the Reichsführer had turned into mutual aversion. This too further weighed upon him. So the court wanted to know, at least, how he explained Himmler's comment where he addressed the disappearance of the Jews. He was thinking of Madagascar, Wolff replied. The SD and the Gestapo had both, at times, kept busy with the plan of deporting all Jews in German-controlled areas to that island in the Indian Ocean. But the conference at Wannsee had, in the meantime, proclaimed the much cheaper and efficient "final solution."

After Himmler's visit in January, the second wave of "resettlement" began on January 18, 1943, in Warsaw. For the time being, he ordered the "establishment of a concentration camp inside the Warsaw ghetto" that "is to be moved to Lublin and its surrounding area as quickly as possible"—the three extermination camps under Odilo Globocnik were in the surrounding area. Himmler had copies of all orders regarding these matters also sent to Wolff. But this was none of his business and it can therefore be assumed that the chief of the personal staff simply sent all these copies immediately to the files because he had no time to read them.

When Himmler finally ordered his thugs to clear out the ghetto by force and destroy it, the Jews who were doomed to die decided to revolt. They had nothing more to lose than their lives, if they failed to defend themselves. In the middle of April 1943, the fight began. Only after 28 days could SS Brigadeführer Jürgen Stroop, report to the Reichsführer SS that the Warsaw ghetto no longer existed. Wolff found out about this while he was in the hospital. He was not only incapable of service but also demoted. Himmler had taken over the leadership of his SS Main Office himself.

Wolff repeated again and again: it was not the task of the chief of the personal staff to exterminate Jews. But whoever was in the SS above the common rank and file, at one point or another ended up having to deal with those Nazi crimes. That most certainly applied to Wolff because he had set up his office in such a manner that the range of his influence remained virtually unlimited. If he wanted, he could become involved in every area of National Socialist politics. Sometimes he made use of this to save one person or another, even though it is always difficult to decide in retrospect what would have happened had he not taken action.

On the other hand, there were areas where this intermittent show of humanity was painfully lacking. One of the seven offices within his main office—and not an insignificant one—was called the "Ahnenerbe." Himmler used the renowned Munich university professor, Dr. Walther Wüst, as the leading thinker. His reputation served the purpose of drawing scholars from the most varied fields to the SS, putting them to work to fulfill their own goals. Once they received uniforms and honorary ranks, they were integrated to the personal staff. Wolff then became the director of a wealth of erudition, where quality and trash as well as art and kitsch from the most wide-ranging disciplines were available. And not least because of Himmler's inclination towards the scurrilous and the occult—that field was so far-reaching that no one could coordinate those conflicting efforts. Certainly not Wolff, since his cultural interests did not reach beyond those of a conservative upper-middle-class citizen.

He therefore delegated the internal management to SS officer Wolfram Sievers, a wild careerist from German nationalist circles. Wolff cannot be blamed for such ridiculous mistakes in the "Ahnenerbe," such as the jubilation about the "Ura Linda-Chronicles," that the obscure prehistoric researcher Herman Wirth discovered as proof of early Germanic advanced civilization, and which turned out to be wrong. There were also projects in the "Ahnenerbe" that were just as contemptuous of human life and inhumane as the persecution of the Jews, even if the scope of these actions didn't even come close to the genocide perpetrated in the east. Wolff indisputably knew of these projects, which were part of his main office, and he even collected money for them from the rich men in the "Reichsführer SS circle of friends."

One of these projects began as early as April 1939 when a concert singer from Munich, Karoline Diehl, used her former affair with Heinrich Himmler to recommend her current lover to him. He was an intern, Dr. Sigmund Rascher, who, in addition to his work in a Munich hospital, ran a private cancer research clinic and needed financial aid. One week later, he was already set up in the "Ahnenerbe" and after six more months he was allowed to wear the SS uniform of an Untersturmführer of the Allgemeine SS.

However, at that time he was already wearing the uniform of a Luftwaffe doctor. He had been called up at the beginning of the war. He managed to get himself placed at the Institute for Aeromedicine in Munich. There they tested how pilots remained in control of their senses in the oxygen-poor air at high altitudes, a problem that affected mainly fighter pilots. A pressure chamber was available to the doctors for testing the conditions of the air at different heights through simulations. They only lacked missing people who accepted the health risks involved and would be locked voluntarily in the cabin for tests,. Rascher knew how to solve the problem and in the middle of May 1941 he asked Himmler if he "couldn't hand over two or three professional criminals for this purpose."

The Reichsführer SS was not squeamish when dealing with human lives, and gave his approval. The experiments took place at Dachau concentration camp. Many SS bigwigs watched, Wolff among them, and saw how a healthy person gasped for air, screamed, collapsed and then, depending on Rascher's capriciousness, was either provided with air in time and returned to life, or in an "experiment that was to go through to the end," how this person died a wretched death from an embolism in the brain. By mid-May 1942, approximately 150 of these experiments were carried out; half of them ended in death.

After the war, when Wolff was questioned about these crimes, he maintained that the test subjects had volunteered for the experiments because they could be released from the camp. The thought never crossed his mind that a prisoner working forced labor, vegetating behind barbed wire for an indefinite period of time, was not capable of expressing free will when making such a decision. Two or three of the test subjects died, Wolff said—they had been sentenced to death anyway. He knew that this was not true because in the National Socialist state death sentences were carried out in jails, whereas concentration camp prisoners were locked up without being sentenced. That many more deaths actually took place, he could have read from the reports Rascher sent to Himmler, if he had wanted to. Quite relaxed, he assured, when questioned, that he would have volunteered for these experiments as well, had it been necessary. He claims to have seen prisoners perfectly fit just moments after their rescue from the cabin, and happy to have been able to contribute to victory. A few of the survivors were actually rewarded—if one can call it that, because instead of being released, they were sent to serve in the Wehrmacht, in the Dirlewanger Penal Battalion, a probation unit used for suicide missions.

Had Wolff been gullible or even trusting about Rascher's altitude experiments, that excuse could no longer be applied after August 15, 1942. In a new series of experiments, the doctor was exposed as a sadist who delighted in the suffering and death of human beings. The reason for the new tests was for the pilots who could be downed in cold seawater. Despite life jackets, most of them died of hypothermia. At the Dachau experiments, the test subjects were brutally plunged into a pool of ice-cold water. Not until their body temperature had fallen to under 30 degrees Celsius did they become unconscious and were fished out of the pool. The research centered on how they could be most efficiently warmed up, and brought back to life. One possibility, "the revival by animal warmth" was tried and tested at Himmler's suggestion. For this purpose, former prostitutes were brought from Ravensbrück concentration camp to Dachau, to lay naked under a blanket and warm up the cold men at their sides, and bring them about to have intercourse. With his hypothermia experiments, Rascher abused more than 280 people; one third of them dying.

Wolff later professed having no knowledge of these experiments. But when he was shown a letter that he had written on November 27, 1942, to General Erhard Milch, the Luftwaffe doctor and Rascher's highest superior, the retired Obergruppenführer had to give in. In the letter, he pleaded for the continuation of the hypothermia experiments, even if the Luftwaffe were to cut off its contributions. No one needed to be concerned about the test subjects, as they were only criminals and anti-social people. Rascher was to be removed from the Luftwaffe and placed in the Waffen SS, which was what actually took place. Wolff argued that he neither dictated nor read this letter. He had only signed it because a note from Himmler had ordered it. Only because the dreadful Rascher's case had a grotesquely macabre ending characteristic of the SS does it deserve some further comments. The ambitious couple who craved admiration, Diehl and Rascher, also wanted to profit from Himmler's manic promotion with births. At the end of 1939 Diehl, a widow who was already 46 years old, gave birth to a son in Prague; in truth, she arranged to obtain the child through a midwife. In February 1941, she had another child in a similar manner, a third in November 1942, but with the fourth she had bad luck. She was arrested, and on Himmler's orders taken to Ravensbrück concentration camp without a trial. Shortly before the end of the war she attacked a guard there and was hanged.

Her husband—she married after the second false childbearing—was first kept in an SS barracks in Munich, then taken to Buchenwald concentration camp. It meant a lot to Himmler to keep the case secret, because otherwise he would have been covered with ridicule. When Buchenwald concentration camp was cleaned out at the beginning of April 1945, as the Americans were getting closer, Rascher and a group of prominent prisoners were taken to Dachau. With Wolff's help, the group was eventually freed in South Tyrol, but Rascher was no longer there. On April 26, 1945, on orders from Himmler, he was killed with a bullet in the head at Dachau.

Another doctor received support for his criminal activity by the "Ahnenerbe" as a member of the personal staff. In December 1941 an SS officer and a dangerous race fanatic suggested beginning a collection of Jewish skulls for the purpose of comparative anthropology. Three months later anatomy professor Dr. August Hirt, at the University of Strassburg [Strasbourg], was given the task. At first it was planned to chop off the heads of Jewish soldiers in the Red Army captured during the Eastern Campaign. For various reasons, the plan was not carried out. The professor then occupied himself with the poison "Lost"—already used during the First World War as yellow gas. Prisoners at the Natzweiler-Struthof concentration camp in Alsace were the test subjects. Many died;

the survivors were transported to a camp in the east where they were killed because they had been witnesses.

It is more than likely that Wolff also found out about these crimes, but he was no longer directly involved. The over-zealous business leader of the "Ahnenerbe," Wolfram Sievers, wanted to arrange practically everything by himself. When he couldn't manage on his own, he got help from Himmler's secretary, Dr. Rudolf Brandt, who was more and more intent on eliminating Wolff. In this case, Wolff may not have officially found out about another plan to collect entire skeletons instead of just skulls. When Himmler agreed to this, Wolff was very sick and confined to a hospital. For this "research," on orders from Hirt, "115 people, of which 79 Jews, 2 Poles, 4 Asians and 30 Jewish women" from the masses of prisoners were taken from Auschwitz to Natzweiler. There they were murdered in a gas chamber that had been especiallyset up for them. Their bodies were sent to Hirt at the Strassburg anatomy institute. In order to turn them into skeletons, the "Ahnenerbe" had purchased new machinery.

Chapter 8

"Even the Guard Must Obey"

While he was still in good health Wolff made sure he was not completely excluded from the various medical experiments. Rascher and Hirt had been assigned to the "Institute for Specific Military-Economic Research," a secret department of the "Ahnenerbe," and continued to be part of Wolff's payroll, even though the big money now came from the SS Economic and Administrative Main Office. When he had to make transfers from his "Special Account R," then he may have occasionally asked for what purpose the money was needed.

That Wolff's underlings at the Main Office were always working to dethrone him from his boss's chair should not have come as a surprise. This was part of the Nazi organization's tradition; according to Hitler's Darwinist basic principle that the stronger, and therefore the better, are always right, so it was not in the least frowned upon to use one's elbows to move ahead. Wolff's frequent absence from the Berlin office provided added encouragement to the careerists, as did his sporadic presence at Himmler's field office. Dr. Rudolf Brandt managed that kind of advancement, and Wolff sensed that Obersturmführer Werner Grothmann, in charge of the Main Department "SS Adjutancy," was pushing hard to become his successor. Besides, his many years close to Himmler taught him that he could only conditionally rely on the Reichsführer SS's loyalty (according to the basic principles of the SS "code of honor").

In spite of all this, Chief of the Personal Staff Wolff did not worry too much. The best human specimen at headquarters was sure that the Reichsführer would do him no harm because in a serious situation Hitler would step in to protect him. For that reason, the former bank employee carefully nurtured his "personal credit" with the Führer by regularly participating in the evening chats as a dedicated listener. On the other hand, he did not make a big effort to maintain his credit with Himmler. At the beginning of his autobiography he told in epic terms and with some satisfaction how Hitler once gave him the opportunity to humiliate the Reichsführer SS.

It must have been in November 1942—Wolff does not provide the exact date—after the tiresome, incredibly boring afternoon teas and stressed by the Führer's endless monologues, he got to bed long after midnight. He was awakened by a telephone call and ordered to come to the Führer's bunker immediately. In highly dramatic and, as usual using verbatim quotations, Wolff described in his manuscript how Hitler practically begged him to answer all his questions truthfully and not to cover his boss in any way.

"Wolff," asked the Führer, "do you know where Horia Sima is right now?" Since the Obergruppenführer "could courageously look him in the eye, as always," and "immediately and spontaneously" bellow no, Hitler straightened up (considering the "bad situation . . . he had slumped somewhat") "and said quietly, both aggravated and relieved at the same time, 'Thank god!'"

Horia Sima was a Romanian. In his homeland he was the leader of the fascist organization called the "Iron Guard." In 1940, together with the army, they had engineered a putsch against King Carol, that brought General Ion Antonescu to power. The SS was counting on the Iron Guard because they terrorized Jews and rejected the Francophile Romanian upper class. Hitler, however, felt that it was more effective to support the general. In January 1941 there was a quarrel between the two partners, Antonescu and Horia Sima. The legionnaires were defeated and persecuted, and many of them were killed. With the help of the SD, some 200 of them managed to flee to Germany. Ribbentrop placated Antonescu, his enemies having been locked up in concentration camps; Hitler guaranteed this with his word of honor. He was, however, completely in agreement that the SD hide them in one of its training schools to keep them in reserve and ready should the Romanian head of state suddenly refuse to obey.

Now, however, this valuable political trump card had slipped away and was obviously traveling back to his homeland. Antonescu's Secret Service had found Horia Sima. The general had the German ambassador in Bucharest ask von Ribbentrop to confirm that Hitler did not want to break his promise. Since Ribbentrop and Himmler had a permanent feud, the foreign minister used the opportunity to turn Hitler against the Reichsführer SS.

SS Brigadeführer and Chief of the SD Secret Service Walter Schellenberg reported after the war that Hitler, in his anger, threatened the "Black Plague"; he would eradicate them if they did not obey. It must have been quite turbulent in the Führer's bunker that night because Wolff reported that it was "the only time" that "I had ever seen the Führer throw such a fit—and in this case, he was right." Hitler explained to him why this was so serious just then; Romanian divisions were engaged just outside Stalingrad in heavy defensive fighting, and Germany was as dependent on the oil wells at Ploesti as on the food that this agricultural country was delivering in vast quantities.

Wolff was given the task to immediately call Himmler at his field headquarters just 30 kilometers from there, and ask him what the situation with Horia Sima looked like. He managed this, but only with a delay. At Himmler's location, the SS officer on duty refused to wake up his boss, since this was strictly forbidden. Only when Wolff mentioned that the order came from the Führer, did Himmler's telephone ring.

Himmler admitted shamefacedly: "I respectfully beg the Führer's forgiveness, but Horia Sima actually escaped a week ago." He wanted to report it immediately, but Gestapo chief, Gruppenführer Heinrich Müller, had advised against it. Hitler's nerves were already at a breaking point because of the difficult situation at Stalingrad and Rommel's retreat in North Africa. He could have done without the latest excitement because the escapee would be caught in a matter of days, he commented to Wolff: "I must say that I expected a more resolute statement coming from the Reichsführer."

Hitler was even less pleased with the information. Wolff reported that the Führer paced the small room, shouting for fifteen minutes. His excellent memory did not recall the threat of the "Black Plague," but did remember the praise: the SS was "a wonderful thing," and "I am glad I have them, but even the guard must obey." Wolff had to use the phone again and immediately pass along the following to Himmler: "The Führer expresses his personal displeasure; he does not want to see him at headquarters and will not shake his hand until Horia Sima has been arrested once again. The Führer demands to hear a report twice daily as to what the police are doing."

Wolff took the liberty of suggesting another procedure. He pointed out that a Wehrmacht unit was servicing the telephone exchange. Out of boredom, the soldiers listened in on all the conversations at three o'clock in the morning, although this was forbidden. They would enjoy hearing that the SS were ticked off, and would naturally pass the information along. It was therefore not desirable that Field Marshal Keitel or General Jödl found out about this matter. This was not a matter of malicious intent, but rather of "some lack of attention." He supposedly told Hitler: "I have to say this because I must set things straight." To be more effective Wolff should drive over to see Himmler and give him Hitler's message in person.

The meeting took place in the morning. Himmler became "quite pale" as Wolff was reciting his piece. In his opinion, the Reichsführer had to "reach the obvious conclusions" of Hitler's lack of trust and disfavor. Which ones? Was the Obergruppenführer counting on his superior's resignation? Did he already see himself as his successor? If he did, he was making a mistake. "He answered quite weakly," Wolff recalled. "I quietly set things straight for him, but he never forgave me for that. He thought that the order of things was no longer the same, namely, the Führer at the top as Commander in Chief, then the Reichsführer SS, and only then the liaison General of the Waffen SS at the Führer headquarters. He felt that I was now above him." In the closing days of 1942, Wolff was convinced that nothing could stand in the way of his future career. He believed that he had secured Hitler's favor for good. "The Führer spoke the same language of the front soldiers of the First World War with me while Himmler chattered like a civilian." He wrote this retrospectively and critically as an old man, more than thirty years after the fall of the Third Reich; still seeing himself as the masterful Nordic man in his own mind.

The danger to his career came unexpectedly in an area our hero easily kept very tidy—from his private relationships. According to the strict standards of bourgeois morality, things had become rather messy because for some time he reveled in the joys of a double family life, mindless of any criminal consequences. The situation was well known within the upper levels of the SS, but no one faulted him because of it. Concubines (if this biblical naming of them is even appropriate here) were the norm among top Nazi officers. The wives of those leaders and officers of all types who had risen from humble beginnings did not follow their husbands' flights of fancy, and in time were no longer presentable at State receptions. Since such men were desirable to other women only due to their position, some of the Party men did take on younger and more beautiful women as their mistresses.

The legitimate Wolff family, therefore, lived in Rottach-Egern on the banks of Tegern Lake in a ten-room house, with boats and a bathhouse. His wife, Frieda, born von Römheld, raised their four children there, two girls and two boys. When Hitler resided at Obersalzberg, above Berchtesgaden, Karl Wolff could live with his family. If he was absent, as he was most of the time, his loved ones had to comfort themselves with a life-sized and lifelike oil portrait of their father and husband.

The second family lived in a six-room apartment in Berlin-Charlottenburg. The widowed Countess Ingeborg Bernstorff, born Christensen and originally from Hamburg, lived there with her three children. The youngest, Wolff's son, was now five years old. For the time being, she was Wolff's only companion north of the Main. She received an officer's pension because her dead husband had been a Prussian head of an administrative district. She already had two children when in 1937 she bore Karl Wolff's son. This happened, as already noted, in Budapest, so that very few people rejoiced at the happy occasion and the reason why the infant child with the Germanic first name of Widukind Thorsun and his mother were not allowed to travel back to Berlin immediately. For discrete cases of this kind, there was an office in the main office of the Chief of the Personal Staff of the Reichsführer SS, called "Lebensborn." It had been founded so that the girlfriends of the SS officers and men could bring their children into the world in peace unencumbered by the verdict of their surroundings, and those infants, who were racially perfect, could be given up for adoption to well-deserving SS couples. This was such a case. Wolff's son was put in the "Lebensborn" home in Steinhöring, and cared for there during the first months of his life, and then given back to his biological mother as a foster child.

The fact that Widukind was very blond and blue-eyed pleased his father immensely. However, Wolff also made great efforts to care for the Bernstorff son, who would later become his stepson after his second marriage. That child's uncle, the brother of his late father, was Count Albrecht von Bernstorff, who had become a diplomat, as had many of his ancestors. As councilor to the German ambassador in London, he resigned from state service in 1933; he was opposed to Hitler. Now he was in the banking business. Because he had no direct heirs, and had a fortune, Ingeborg von Bernstorff demanded that her son, the young Count, become his heir through a formal will. When the Count refused—as a witness at the Munich criminal proceedings against Karl Wolff was to testify—he was picked up by the Gestapo and taken to the concentration camp in Dachau. Wolff declared he would only be freed once he signed the last will and testament. After long negotiations, they finally reached that conclusion. But in 1943 the Count was arrested for the second time, and in April 1945 the SS finally shot him to death.

The Munich court was also shown a letter provided by the prosecution that Wolff had written to his wife from Taormina in Sicily in February 1939.

This could be viewed as a symptom of his SS obsession. In the letter, he writes: "...fate made me one of the closest colleagues of a unique man, the Reichsführer SS, whom I not only immensely admire for his quite extraordinary qualities, but in whose historical mission I deeply believe. Our common and my endlessly satisfying work...[is] rooted in thoughts of race. My entire being and effort is for the SS and its future goals. It is, therefore, no surprise that the thought that my sons will not fulfill the SS selection conditions that, according to human expectations, will be valid for the next 15 to 20 years, pains me greatly, especially because I could theoretically give my people children who are racially better qualified. I do not need to discuss with you the absence of children having absolutely complete SS qualities..." Until now Widukind Thorsun was an only child.

It had been his private worry for years: the woman in Rottach-Egern and the four children were healthy, but fate had endowed them with brown hair and brown eyes. If the schoolboy Karl had been more attentive to his biology classes in high school, he could have avoided such bad luck; he would have learned the law of genetics that dark dominates over blond. In the meantime, SS officer Karl Wolff felt guilty of having wasted his Nordic attributes. It was clear to him that he could expect no perfect offspring from his marriage. With Countess Ingeborg this was not the case: her children and especially Wolff's son had turned out perfectly.

How Wolff imagined he would straighten things out in the long run is unimportant. He excelled at sweeping things under the rug quietly, through a barrage of words. He was confident that time, would make certain things become unimportant. As more and more men were dying in the war, the National Socialist bureaucrats calculated how to make up for those losses and deal with the surplus of women. The word "domina" circulated among prominent Party figures. It meant that in the future, every man who had served the Fatherland would receive permission to marry a second wife. The first one was not allowed to be disadvantaged in her rights; for her understanding she would be rewarded with the honorary title of "domina," meaning mistress, but the second wife was not to be any less legitimate and worthy of respect. It was said that following the Thirty Years' War this had become normal practice in Germany. The Führer and the leader of German women, Gertrud Scholtz-Klink, had already been informed of the necessary laws for the period following the war.

Like many other prominent Nazis, in his thoughts Wolff also toyed with this possibility. He felt even more encouraged when even Reichsleiter Martin Bormann, who had now become the Führer's secretary and who knew his plans better than anyone else, supported the project. Peace was of course still far removed, but the interim state of affairs would probably have been just as satisfying for the love commuter from the Spree to Tegern Lake for a long time. But Countess Inge wanted a man for herself, and she was not remotely interested in the role of second wife. She demanded what her lover had promised long ago and many times after that: a divorce, and with that, Wolff's choice between his two women.

Why would she get her way in the end? She was the more energetic of the two women; but it could also be that the picture book German who was so firmly convinced of his own racial qualities also believed he must sacrifice his family that had such a poor appearance on the altar of the Fatherland. Making the people more Nordic was part of the SS program, and it now seemed more necessary than ever before that, given his position, he must lead by giving the good example. If his conscience suffered because of this, the pleasure of the now legal relationship with the younger woman and her attractive appearance would make up for it.

According to SS regulations the divorce and the remarriage had to be approved by Himmler. But he refused both; marriage scandals in the leading circles spoiled the morale of the people, he argued. "Maybe later!" and "Just wait! It is possible for family affairs to disappear in the wake of a great victory!" This went on for months, until it became too much for the Countess, who finally did not want to wait anymore. She barged into Himmler's offices on Prinz-Albrecht Strasse, slammed her fist on his desk and protested so loudly that the Reichsführer promised her that he would no longer stand in the way of her wish. Despite this promise, he continued to hesitate in giving his approval.

Wolff said there were two reasons for the hesitation. First: the Reichsführer was afraid that the resolute woman from Hamburg could cause him trouble within leading SS cliques, while the moderate and properly raised Frieda from the Darmstadt official aristocracy would not do anything like that. Wolff further suspected: "When there were State receptions, the Reichsführer would lead with his wife—white blond hair and blue eyes, but her cheek bones and her hips were anything but Germanic. And then I would come, and if then the perfect specimen had a beautiful Frisian at his side, there would be even more obvious a difference."

After that latest hesitation, Wolff took no further steps to clear up the situation. He waited once again, perhaps for Domina Day. But in February 1943, his growing stomach pains were bothering him. When he told Himmler about it, the Reichsführer recommended the man who had helped him with apparently similar maladies, the masseur Felix Kersten. This practitioner of alternative medicine from Finland, with his kneading hands, had eliminated Himmler's stomach pains, digestive disturbances, intestinal colic and difficulty in breathing. In short, he was a miracle doctor. When Wolff once again took leave from Hitler for a few days in his Berlin office, checking on things and to accept an invitation from SS Gruppenführer Gottlieb Berger to hunt a wild boar in Warthegau, Himmler, in his role as patriarch, scheduled a massage at Kersten's estate called "Harzwalde," located one hundred kilometers north of Berlin, that would replace the hunt.

Wolff's various accounts of his beginning illness differ from one another on several points. In the most aggressive version, Himmler knew that Wolff suffered from pyelitis. The Reichsführer was supposedly even attempting to have Wolff's kidneys seriously damaged by the massage. Whether true or not, Wolff did have blood in his urine after that, and because the famous SS sanatorium at Hohenlychen was near the Kersten estate, Wolff described the symptoms of his suffering over the phone to Dr. Karl Gebhardt, the senior consulting physician there, on February 18, 1943. He told Wolff to come in immediately! A kidney stone, larger than a bean, was discovered as the culprit on the X-ray, and could only be surgically removed. Gebhardt said that the operation would not be simple, and Wolff's general condition was no longer the best. In short, it could lead to a serious situation.

It is understandable that this came as a considerable shock to the patient. Like any unlucky person, he looked for someone to blame. Until recently, he maintained that Himmler ordered him to have the massage to get rid of a dangerous competitor. Gebhardt, who was to be sentenced to death at a war crimes trial, had practically confirmed Wolff's suspicion to the Americans shortly before his execution. However, the SS doctor had been a friend of Himmler's since childhood. The urologist who was called to assist the operation immediately looked puzzled and later told Himmler on the telephone that according to his experience, only one in three patients survived such a difficult operation. According to medical doctors, Wolff's suspicion that the murderous massage ordered by Himmler had ground parts of his kidneys on the sharp-edged stone, causing sepsis, was erroneous because no one could have endured such a painful procedure.

Such dire prospects moved Wolff to put his private matters in order before the operation. He asked Himmler one more time to approve the divorce and the second marriage. And once again he received a stalling answer—with an ulterior motive; as he later discovered, this could be decided when the patient was healthy again. Wolff felt justified in calling on the highest authority. To write to Hitler in the proper way, he stood himself up from his painful position and wore his general's uniform. Luckily he was able to give his petition to a first-class messenger; the Party and SS veteran Julius Schaub, Hitler's most trusted adjutant on the team at Führer headquarters. Schaub was just about to leave Berlin during the first few days of March for "Werewolf" in the Ukraine, the current location of the commander in chief. Besides Wolff's letter, Schaub also took a second divorce petition along with him; by a Party Reichsleiter. Wolff reported with proud vanity that only his petition had been approved. His often vaunted personal credit undoubtedly played a role, but a letter from his wife Frieda that Hitler also had in front of him at the same time was important as well. In this letter, written in very moving words, she agreed to give up the husband she still loved after more than two decades of life together, and supported his petition because she did not want to stand in the way of his happiness.

The divorce became final on March 6. And so finally on March 9, 1943, Wolff's second marriage could be officially registered in Hohenlychen. For Ingeborg, born Christensen, the widowed Countess Bernstorff, this was the third procedure of this kind. Before her marriage to the Count, she had already been married to a middle-class businessman and was divorced from him after a short time.

On March 12, the best team of doctors that Hohenlychen could offer operated on the patient. Two ribs had to be shortened in order to reach the kidney stone. Himmler announced in a circular that the Chief of the Personal Staff was very ill—so ill that no one should visit him, write to him, or even send him gifts. He, Himmler, would temporarily take over the duties of the Main Office. A replacement for him as the representative of the Waffen SS at Führer Headquarters was not even mentioned; not until late autumn did a new man there take over that position, which leads to the assumption that the position did not necessarily have to be filled. The Reichsführer SS never came to visit the patient, who took it rather badly. Once, Himmler dispatched his secretary who was also his lover. She did not reveal that Wolff's return to his former position was not planned and that his future usefulness was left open. As she reproached him that his switch of wives was not morally justifiable, and that he had behaved unfairly to Himmler by writing to Hitler, the Obergruppenführer realized he had fallen out of grace with his superior.

Was he to take this to heart? How many times—as far as one can believe his confessions—in the last few years had he already stated that the Reichsführer had deeply disappointed him? And how often had he asked himself whether he could actually realize his ideals in the SS at all. Despite his objections the corrupt Gauleiter Erich Koch was still in East Prussia, and in the meantime had also become the absolute master of the Ukraine. Himmler's rules for the treatment of the populations in the defeated East had not been revoked and were still in force. The Einsatzgruppen were still operating, just as he had seen in Minsk. And the Gauleiters placed themselves against the SS and Himmler. The mighty Reichsführer SS and Chief of the German Police could not find the guts to take a Party comrade like Danzig Gauleiter Forster to the supreme party court.

Did he already sense the failings of his idol (see the letter from Taormina) as strongly in 1943 as he described them after Germany's defeat? The heavy burdens of the times, the constant balancing act between victory and defeat had turned the totally predictable environment of the past into an objective and sober experience. Their joint shady activities had made them cronies, when there was no further unconditional trust because each one already knew too much about the other. When Wolff saw himself as Himmler's presumed successor after Heydrich's death, then one couldn't blame him for using the opportunity to weaken his rival by removing him from responsibility. It is also understandable that he blamed him for the Horia Sima affair. What superior will accept someone under him making him the target of the dictator's displeasure? That Hitler then approved Wolff's divorce and new marriage on top of that could only lead

Himmler to believe that the Obergruppenführer could expect more favor from the supreme leader than he could himself.

It remains open as to whether the condition of the patient after the operation was as life threatening as he described. He remained at Hohenlychen for two months. On May 15, 1943, he traveled to Karlsbad in the Sudetengau for a spa cure to have his kidneys irrigated. At the end of June he switched to Bad Gastein on the northern face of the Tauern; he hoped to gain new strength at an altitude of one thousand meters. He may have assumed for a long time that he could return to his usual office in Berlin on the Prinz-Albrecht Strasse and to the Führer headquarters. But as several of his colleagues from the Main Office in Berlin were replaced by new employees, and as Dr. Rudolf Brandt took over more and more of the tasks of the former Chief of the Main Office, he began to have doubts.

Wolff did not keep his fears secret from his old comrade Maximilian von Herff, now head of the SS personnel office with an equal rank of Obergruppenführer, during his stay in Bad Gastein in the third week in July. He still did not know where he would be in the middle of August, when his vacation was over. Herff answered him in a letter: "I would consider it very desirable if you were to be used in your former position at least for a few months in order to blunt any such talk, but it must be taken care of appropriately."

As Herff wrote this in August 1943, he still did not know that his comrade had been thrown into a new career by a major political event. On July 25, following a meeting with Italy's King Victor Emmanuel III, Benito Mussolini, the Duce and promoter of the Axis policies in Italy, was arrested and secretly removed from the royal palace in an ambulance. At first no one knew where the prisoner was being held. Most of his political supporters in the Fascist government had melted away. They no longer believed in the victory of the Axis powers since Allied soldiers had landed in Sicily, and feared defeat more than anything. The king appointed Marshal Pietro Badoglio as prime minister to replace the Duce. Both announced that they would remain true to the alliance with Germany and Japan, but they were secretly holding talks towards an armistice and later an alliance with the English and Americans.

The Allied victories were impressive. They had chased Axis soldiers from the Italian colonies in Africa, landed in Sicily, and would predictably soon land in southern Italy. While German troops pulled back toward home, fighting a stalling battle of resistance, Italian units were surrendering one after the other. The situation of German divisions in the south became very precarious. They knew that their strongest ally in Europe would sooner or later switch over to the enemy, but they could do nothing about it. As long as Italian troops were intact the Germans could not risk seeing them strengthening the enemy. So it became politically useful to maintain the disintegrating alliance until Italy's new government decided to break it.

It was possible, however, to prepare for those events. The military requirements were rather clear. What must be avoided was that when the Italians switched fronts, German units in the south were not be cut off from their rear. A new army group was therefore concentrated in Austria, southern Germany and northern Italy under Field Marshal Erwin Rommel, who had been previously victorious in Africa. A German police organization was also to be prepared to secure supplies behind the fighting units and to oversee the economy and the workers as required by Germany, just as in other occupied countries where the task was supervised by the Higher SS and Police leaders. The right man had to be found now for such a task in Italy.

Such a man had to know the country and feel comfortable with the Italians. He must be able to skillfully negotiate because Germany could not treat its former ally the same way they treated Poland. Besides that, the man must also get along with two field marshals who could not stand one another, Rommel in the north and the Commander in Chief of the Southern Front, General Albert Kesselring. Both were rightly considered to have a mind of their own, which was why they could not get along.

Himmler called Wolff on July 27, 1943, in Bad Gastein. He was ordered to immediately, his health notwithstanding, to report to field headquarters near Lötzen not far from Rastenburg. There he found out that he was to get ready for service in Italy. He was appointed to this task because of his excellent knowledge of Italy, but this was really only an excuse. He had traveled to that country numerous times, mostly in the entourage of the Reichsführer SS, and had negotiated with Italians on many occasions in dealing with the resettlement of the South Tyroleans, but he could never manage without an interpreter. He had met a number of men, mostly from the Fascist party whom he called his friends, but he judged them according to German moral principles, always upheld by other Germans compatriots but not always practiced. There were surely many other men in the SS with equally favorable qualifications, but of much lower rank. What was in his favor was that he got along so well with Mussolini, who thought so highly of him since the episode with the baton on the Munich Royal Plaza in 1937. Of course, the Duce must first be found and freed, but Hitler was quite determined to do everything possible to make this happen. He needed Mussolini as a puppet ruler in order to use the country better for his war effort.

Wolff's task was to prepare for the transfer of power in Italy of the civilian sector. He set up an office in Munich that was to be secret at first, knowing that it would not be necessary to always proceed so carefully. Upon hearing the news that the Duce had been arrested, Hitler, in his furious reaction, demanded that Kesselring take the Third Tank Grenadier Division located in reserve near Rome "and without further ado ride into the city...and immediately arrest the whole government, the king and the entire mess." As Himmler instructed his Obergruppenführer of this, he added: "The Signori have a grace period, but to delay does not mean putting it off forever."

It was also well known that Hitler did not trust Italians in general. They were for him, as an Austrian, "Katzlmacher." They had hardly any discipline, only had courage when they could place themselves in a scene, and were all more or less anarchists. Wolff was to outline in a memo how he planned to proceed in that country and its people in the future. He had to present it to Hitler within fourteen days. It cannot be exactly determined on what day this happened. Somewhere between August 19 and the end of the month, Himmler was present at Führer headquarters more often than for six days. Hitler's valet, SS Obersturmführer Heinz Linge, noted these visits in his diary. Wolff's name did not appear in Linge's diary during this time—which agreed with Wolff's statements.

After that, Himmler had the memo delivered to him at field headquarters. He read it, said nothing, and requested that the author accompany him to Führer headquarters. During the trip in his Maybach car—quite an extraordinary automobile—that took about a half hour, he had several points explained further. He did not return the memo. Arriving at the barrier to the "Wolfsschanze," Himmler said: "You can go for a swim, Wolff! I don't need you anymore today!" This meant that he was to get out of the car; the Reichsführer wanted to present the memo himself and this was an intentional affront. Wolff had hoped to get back into Hitler's awareness—Hitler usually eliminated people from his plans if he hadn't seen them even for a short time. Himmler was obviously playing on that possibility. It was also a calculated humiliation to dismiss the Obergruppenführer in such a manner and even nastier in front of the chauffeur. Besides the driver, the other witnesses were an adjutant and a police detective, who always accompanied the Reichsführer as his bodyguard. It had not even been six months since Wolff had privileged status to go through the gate almost daily. The guards knew him and now could see how he was obviously being shut out of the inner circle.

That was why Wolff barely controlled himself when he went to pick up Hitler's decision at Himmler's field headquarters the next day. Upon entering his office, it was already clear to him that he was not being received with favor. In front of the Reichsführer's desk, there was no visitor's chair. Wolff would be handled standing. Wolff justified the following scene by noting that the man who was humiliating an officer decorated for his courage during the war "had never even smelled a shot of powder." Actually Himmler was called up as a volunteer in 1917, just as Wolff, who was the same age. He rose to sergeant, but never made it from the Bavarian garrisons to the front. According to the standards of the party that placed the soldiers at the front above all else, this was a minor mistake. The most recent harassment caused the normally conciliatory Wölfchen to forget all officers' rules. As he tells it he threatened the Reichsführer with a beating and jumped at him with clenched fists. Himmler tried to hide behind his desk; pale and breathing heavily, appeasing Wolff: "For God's sake, don't ruin things for yourself! A physical attack on a superior could cost you your head!"

Did Wolff really reply as he claimed: "After beating you, I will go to the Führer and report to him what I've done. I think that he'll reward me."? There were no witnesses to corroborate this claim. The details of this chapter of Wolff's narration are very subjective impressions; but if true, they could be the mark of glorious resistance to a higher SS officer. In any case, the two contestants decided to get along with each other once again. The formula they used to seal their agreement was "This is about Germany."

The question remains as to why the commander of every conceivable police force, a secret service, and all concentration camps decided so quickly to not take any revenge. Perhaps one issue was stopping Himmler—something both he and Wolff were equally involved in, and therefore he had to fear that some embarrassing information might come to light. For example, Himmler might have been in jeopardy if Wolff had mentioned the names Popitz and Langbehn. Two men who were seeking to overthrow Hitler, deprive the party of power, and end the war. They belonged to a resistance group that included top military men, influential statesmen, former trade unionists, representatives of the church, and a number of influential and prominent figures working together. The connections of Popitz and Langbehn to these groups went back a number of years, but those connections now took on the character of a widespread conspiracy. To them, Wolff was a connection in the SS, and Berlin lawyer Dr. Carl Langbehn was at the other side of that connection.

They became acquainted in 1938. The lawyer represented a former colleague at the time, Dr. Maximilian von Rogister, who was the estate administrator of wealthy families and had emigrated to Holland because he was accused of tax evasion and breach of exchange control regulations. It is very possible, however, that those accusations were just meant to blackmail him. With Rogister's help, Himmler wanted to retrieve pieces of old gothic gold jewelry from the Diergardt Collection, discovered in the Crimea long before and now in German possession, to be placed at the disposal of the SS. It was to be taken out of safekeeping in Cologne and brought to Wewelsburg, the future headquarters of the SS. The pieces were examples of the higher German culture during the period of the great migrations and would go to complete the collection already gathered at the castle. As a relative and financial consultant of the family that owned the jewels, Rogister refused not only because he viewed Himmler's role as protector of Germanic cultural possessions ridiculous, but also because as member of a conservative Berlin gentlemen's club, he deeply despised the crass upstarts of the SS.

Himmler summoned Dr. von Rogister to his office at the Prinz-Albrecht Strasse many times in 1936. After having snubbed Himmler every time, Rogister had to listen to the request once more in 1937, only in much stronger terms this time, with the hint that one of his brothers was already locked up in a concentration camp for speaking out against Hitler. Wolff was a witness to the conversation. He knew the Rogister brothers from school at the Ludwig-Georg-Gymnasium in Darmstadt. Wolff was not a man to forget his aristocratic schoolmates that easily. After the fall of the Third Reich, Wolff swore under oath that he had warned the friends of his youth of Himmler's revenge. Some well-intentioned Party comrades told Rogister that the Gestapo had started to collect his malicious comments. When he fled to Holland in 1937, he gave attorney Dr. Carl Langbehn in Berlin the task of looking after his affairs, saying that Wolff may possibly be expected to help.

By then Himmler knew about Langbehn. His daughter Gudrun was with Wolff's oldest daughter Irene and Langbehn's daughter at a boarding school near Bad Tölz in 1936. The three girls were each about sixteen years old; they became friends and visited each other at home as well. One day the fathers also met, and Langbehn managed to place a good word for his former teacher from the University of Göttingen, Professor of Law Fritz Pringsheim, who was now despised as a Jew and deprived of a teaching position. Wolff and Langbehn were pleased that the professor emigrated and began a new life in London shortly thereafter. All this happened before the war began, at a time when the SD was encouraging the emigration of Jews.

Langbehn could occasionally afford to make such recommendations. He had been a Party member since the spring of 1933 (a "fallen soldier of March," as the old NSDAP fighters condescendingly called them) but he could prove of having sympathized with the Party earlier and was a reserve officer. Once the war began, he was drafted into counter-intelligence, the secret service of the Wehrmacht, because of his knowledge of languages, but he was soon turned over to the civilian service in the armaments industry. This allowed him occasionally to travel to neutral countries during the war. He was not afraid to collect information for the SD at that time, and used that cover to contact Allied intelligence services.

Dr. Johannes Popitz was one of the men who harbored plans for a putsch. In 1933 he was appointed state minister of finance by Hermann Göring, the newly appointed head of the Prussian state, and had also received the golden Party decoration for his service. But he also came to the conclusion that Hitler and his cohorts were leading the people to ruin. He and Langbehn belonged to an opposition group around Dr. Carl Friedrich Goerdeler who, as mayor of Leipzig, had been called by the National Socialists to the office of Reich Commissioner in 1933. He resigned his post in 1937. His resistance group considered him as the future chancellor.

All the resistance groups against the Nazi regime agreed that even at war, despite the mounting casualties, the losses in property because of air raids and the total absence of freedom, a revolt by the people against the current men in power could neither be expected nor even encouraged. The people were also living in great fear of the implacable and ruthless consequences that were reserved to the "enemies of the state," and the still widely held belief that the demi-god Hitlerwould, in the end, save the German people from destruction in a world of enemies. The conspirators had hoped at first that the army would free them from the dictator and his clique, but the operation either did not begin or failed because of unpredictable difficulties. So Goerdeler's group resorted to the idea of enlisting the SS in fomenting a putsch. They had weapons, a tight and rooted organization, and their own information apparatus; they also controlled the police. With Himmler's help—as the plan stipulated—it would be possible to overthrow Hitler. A revolution that started like this would continue and eventually eliminate the SS without difficulty.

Langbehn found out in 1942 in conversation with Wolff, that the leading men in the Party were jealously observing one another and were also concerned about the policies and the leadership of the war. He attempted to find out with Wolff how far the Reichsführer SS could be willing to cooperate and participate in a change in the current power base. In the fall of 1942, the lawyer and the Obergruppenführer met many times. The content of their conversations was, of course, not recorded. It may only be reconstructed from what happened afterwards. Wolff informed the Reichsführer after every meeting; they agreed that the contact should continue. The goal they were both trying to reach remained unclear. One year later, once Langbehn was tightly in the clutches of the Gestapo, Himmler and Wolff maintained that they were only trying to find out how far the conspiracy had spread. There is, however, evidence that the two top SS leaders were prepared to play on both sides and wanted to keep their options open in case Hitler's operations turned into a failure.

It is not possible and not even necessary to describe the wide complexities of the resistance movement where the SS played a secondary role, in fighting the rebels as protectors of the state loyal to Hitler or as allies with the conspirators. What subsequently happened to Langbehn can be tied to the suspicion that the SS played both roles at the same time. At the end of 1942, Langbehn arranged with Wolff to have Himmler speak with Popitz, who was still Prussian prime minister, about the German situation. But they never got to the point of setting the date because Wolff became ill and could not take action from Hohenlychen sanatorium. He did not pick up the thread again until he went to Bad Gastein and had enough energy to engage in this hazardous business.

In agreement with Himmler, Wolff and the lawyer met on August 21, 1943. They agreed that Popitz and Himmler would talk on August 26 at the Reich Ministry of the Interior—one day after the head of the German police was to have relieved his former nominal superior, Dr. Wilhelm Frick, of his duties. When Wolff later gave the Gestapo information about his conversation with Langbehn, he testified that the lawyer argued that the war could no longer be won, and if Germany wanted to avoid a catastrophe, the leadership of the state and the Wehrmacht had to change. The Führer had to accept limitations to his power. The enemy would never negotiate a peace with Hitler, but would agree to do so with the men of the resistance. Popitz had already made contacts in preparation.

The meeting with Himmler took place at the Reich Ministry of the Interior and Wolff had the conversation recorded with a microphone built into his boss's desk. Decades later, he proudly commented, "It worked perfectly well!" While Popitz was trying to convince the new Reich Minister of the Interior that only a thorough change in Germany could prevent the devastating consequences of a catastrophic defeat, Wolff and Langbehn were arguing in the waiting room. It was up to Himmler, said Popitz, to bring the people, the State and the National Socialists to achieve a better future. It was still possible because Great Britain and the United States feared the Bolshevik menace. But the political leadership and that of the Wehrmacht must be handed over to new men and Popitz even named names.

While he laid out the conspirators' plans still relatively carefully, Langbehn told Wolff "very openly and without holding back," per a formulation contained in the indictment by the prosecution against the two conspirators. "Only an open statement would make sense," said Langbehn. "In Germany" there must be "a state under the rule of law set up again by clever, clean, and farsighted men" and "the arbitrariness that has slowly become unbearable" must disappear. Wolff's answer is not in the indictment, and there was no reply from Himmler. The prosecutor as the highest German prosecuting authority merely realized that Wolff only (and with that Himmler as well) "allowed himself to get involved in the conversation for the purpose of finding out in which direction those ambitions were heading." He replied that "the Reichsführer was loyal to the Führer and could not ignore these commitments."

Although the top SS leadership already had its hands on the essential threads of the conspiracy with the statements of August 26, 1943, they did not end the contacts. On the following day, Wolff again met with Langbehn. They agreed to another Himmler-Popitz conversation. They did not set the date yet because Langbehn obviously wanted to let the other conspirators know and on a trip to Switzerland, wanted to find out how the allies would react to Himmler's participation.

All of this took place either just before or after the purported fistfight that had been barely avoided between the Reichsführer SS and his Obergruppenführer. Contradictory to later assertions by Himmler, Hitler at first had no idea of the SS conversations with his archenemies. He found out only when the Gestapo told him—this happened in the first half of September—that they had arrested Dr. Langbehn upon his return from Bern due to contacts with representatives of an enemy intelligence service. With that, he became the first and, temporarily, the only victim of the affair.

In Bern Langbehn spoken with an OSS representative, the German-American Gero von Gaevernitz, and told him that the conspirators were dependent on the participation of the SS; they would initiate the rebellion with the takeover of the Führer headquarters, and the Wehrmacht would then go along. Hitler's fate was still left open in this plan. The Gestapo had found all of this out in a secret radio signal from an allied agent that they had decoded. The Chief of the Gestapo, SS Gruppenführer Heinrich Müller, strangely neglected to tell his boss Himmler about the catch. He reported his success directly to Führer headquarters and, therefore, to the sly Martin Bormann, who at the time was Himmler's opponent and Hitler's closest advisor.

That was clearly the skeleton that Himmler and Wolff had hidden in the SS closet together. It did clear up a few things and was the reason why, for example, Himmler prevented Wolff from presenting the plan for Italy to Hitler himself. Wolff had to be kept away from Hitler because, with his high personal rating, had he mentioned his version of the negotiations with the conspirators, Himmler, who had fallen out of Hitler's graces, would have possibly faced dismissal, and Wolff would have immediately become his successor. The Reichsführer had enough reason to believe that Wolff, after what had taken place in recent months, was capable of such a surprise coup. This would also explain why the violent argument they had at field headquarters had no consequences.

Even after the war, Wolff denied that he had denounced the men of the resistance to the SS. In advance of his trial in Munich, before he had even been accused of any crimes, he told a journalist in 1961 that he had spoken to Popitz and Langbehn "about the Führer," namely "that he was overburdened and perhaps should give up some of his tasks to others. Perhaps even to me." Specifically which job he would have liked to take on he did not reveal. As he told the Gestapo years before, he had only tried to find out "who was actually behind Popitz and Langbehn." In no way did he order Langbehn to "travel to Bern...that would have been extremely dangerous!"

Himmler got himself out of a predicament by moving Langbehn from Gestapo custody to a concentration camp. There the lawyer temporarily enjoyed favorable treatment. At his questioning, he didn't dare even give the impression that either Wolff or Himmler could be involved in the conspiracy plans, knowing that he would then be immediately liquidated as a witness for the prosecution. The prosecuting attorney's indictment was not announced until one year later at the end of September 1944. Together with Popitz, he was sentenced to death by the National Socialist People's Court, at the same time as the trial involving the attempt to kill Hitler on July 20, 1944, the case was buried among the many proceedings. But even then the SS made every effort to cover up any connections they may have had to the resistance. Before the trial began, Ernst Kaltenbrunner, head of the RSHA, wrote to the Reich Minister of Justice: "...regarding the facts in the case, that you are also aware of, namely the conversations between the Reichsführer SS and Popitz, I request that the main trial be carried out before a public committee. Assuming your agreement, I would like to delegate ten of my colleagues for this task. As for a wider audience, I request finally that you allow me the right to check on them." Langbehn was executed shortly after sentencing, on October 12, 1944. Himmler was now in a hurry to close the case. On the other hand, he had plenty of time with Popitz because there were no further witnesses to attest that Himmler had almost agreed to an alliance with the conspirators. There are, however, several clues from the investigations of the would-be assassins from the July 20 conspiracy indicating that Himmler betrayed Hitler. Popitz survived until February 2, 1945, when he was finally hanged.

While Langbehn was organizing the underground movement against Hitler, Wolff was preparing his own invasion of Italy. His task seemed sufficiently clear: he would have executive power in an area from the Brenner Pass in the north to the areas immediately behind the fighting troops. There was one exception in a strip of land along the long coast where the German navy was in control. For civilian affairs, he was to consider himself the Führer's governor, independent of any future Italian government. Of course, the former allies were expected to obey the Führer, not only with threats and terror, but also with promises and diplomacy. This was slightly different than in other occupied territories, but the end result had to be that those who were inferior must obey.

Wolff's special status and position had to at least be credible; therefore, the titles were changed. The usual "Higher SS and Police Führer" became the "Highest," using the highly appreciated superlative favored by the bombastic Nazis. At the same time, Wolff's self-confidence was enhanced. As former head of an SS Main Office, he would stand a head above all of his colleagues in Germany in his new position as well. In the first days of September 1943, it was still not clear when his new position would become official. Before the Italians were to fall under the control of the SS police, the alliance had to be dissolved. It had actually disintegrated some time before; and behind all the assurances of unbreakable friendship there was a growing mistrust. What Mussolini had begun, namely the secret construction of Italian fortifications along the ridge of the Alps, was vigorously pursued by his successors. While Rommel threateningly gathered his divisions on the border, Badoglio consistently and quietly brought troops from the south to the Italian Alps instead of placing them to face the armies of the western Allies.

Whenever Axis military leaders or diplomats met, recriminations, suspicion, and threats followed. After a conversation on August 6 in Tarvisio, Ribbentrop took the German ambassador to Rome, Hans Georg von Mackensen, back to Germany on the spot in his special train. Following this shameful recall, the ambassador was forced to act as an advisor at the "Wolfsschanze." Prince Phillip of Hesse was also forced to stay there; he was married to Italian Princess Mafalda, and therefore always used as a negotiator when things were not going right within the alliance.

All those involved knew that the days of the Axis were numbered, but as much as Hitler mistrusted the new regime, his informers found very little that appeared suspicious to report about. Field Marshal Kesselring, the diplomat Dr. Rudolf Rahn, who was the acting ambassador, the versatile SS Standartenführer Eugen Dollmann, who was functioning as liaison officer, police attaché SS Standartenführer Herbert Kappler, the SD, and the Abwehr all reported that no switch of sides was contemplated. No one discovered the threads that were continuously being woven tighter between the Allies and the Italian leadership.

In the meantime, the situation became increasingly difficult for the German divisions fighting in Sicily and later in the southern end of the Italian boot. The Italian army surrendered one unit after the other, and their forces slowly but surely dissolved, as the soldiers returned home. Fighting a delaying battle, the Germans cleared the country in front of the enemy, who was pushing forward hesitatingly. What would happen—

and this was the great concern—once the king and Badoglio decided to change sides abruptly and form an alliance with the enemy?

Because of such fears an order was issued from Headquarters on September 7 to disarm all Italian units. Many of them were happy to end the war that way. They had no idea that the Germans were going to use them as forced labor. Others, however, mainly the elite units that had been sent north, simply disappeared into the mountains, hid their weapons and prepared for the future resistance to the German occupation. SS General Karl Wolff would have to handle that situation.

Ullstein

SS General Karl Wolff, appointed Highest Police and SS Chief in Italy, September 1943.

SVB Munich

above

Early days in the SS. *Front row, left to right:* Police General Kurt Daluege, Heinrich Himmler, Luftwaffe General Erhard Milch, SA Krüger, SS von Schütz. *Back row, left to right:* Karl Wolff, Captain Bonin, Reinhard Heydrich.

left

Always close to Himmler: Wolff *(third from the left)* listens to the conversation between Himmler *(left)* and Professor Angelini in Rome at a diplomatic reception in 1937.

Ullstein

Prussian Archives

above
SS State visit in Italy, 1937. Mussolini and Heinrich Himmler stand in front. Behind them *(left to right)* are Kurt Daluege, Reinhard Heydrich, and Karl Wolff.

below
In Rome during the 1937 visit. *Front row, left to right:* Arturo Bocchini (head of the Italian police and the OVRA), unidentified Italian official, Himmler, Reinhard Heydrich, Karl Wolff. *Back row, left to right:* Kurt Daluege, German ambassador Ulrich von Hassel.

Prussian Archives

Prussian Archives

left

Himmler *(seated)* and Wolff in the SS offices in Berlin in 1938.

below

At the Führer's headquarters during the French campaign in May 1940: Hitler, holding a magnifying glass, marks a map. Behind him stand General Bodernschatz and Karl Wolff.

Prussian Archives

Prussian Archives

above

The top SS leadership confers at the offices at Prinz-Albrecht-Strasse 8 in Berlin 1938. *Left to right:* Werner Lorenz (head of the Volksdeutche Mittelstelle), Reinhard Heydrich (head of the RSHA), Himmler, and SS Gruppenführer Karl Wolff ("Chief of the Personal Staff of the Reichsführer SS").

right

Wolff *(front, far left)* was present on the morning of June 23, 1940, when Hitler visited Paris.

Prussian Archives

Ullstein

above
During a visit to occupied France and Belgium, Wolff *(center)* always accompanied Himmler *(front, right)*, who is shown in discussion with Hermann Fegelein.

Dollmann Archive

above
In Rome, November 1940, for the funeral of Police Chief Arturo Bocchini. *Left to right:* Wolff, Heydrich, Fascist party secretary Adelchi Serena, Himmler.

right
As soon as the war with Russia began, Wolff spent most of his time at the Wolfsschanze in Rastenberg, East Prussia. He is seen here standing between Hitler and Martin Bormann in 1941.

SVB

Hans Hofmann

Wolff was always present whenever Himmler visited Hitler at Rastenberg, as during this demonstration of a VW military vehicle in 1941. Behind Hitler and Himmler are *(left to right)* Wolff, SS Major General Julius Schaub, SS Major General Hans Jüttner.

MPC Archive

MPC Archive

above left

Odilo Globocnik, the "inventor" of the gas chamber, was a key figure in the extermination policy and in frequent contact with Wolff.

above right

Adolf Eichmann, who never graduated from high school, felt personally slighted by the haughty manners of General Karl Wolff.

MPC Archive

left

During his tour of occupied Russian territories with Himmler, Wolff witnessed the killing actions of the Einsatzgruppen, similar to this infamous photo taken in the Ukraine in 1942.

Ullstein

left

In Russia Wolff accompanied Himmler *(second from right)* to a camp near Minsk in August 1941. Himmler is shown here talking to a young Russian boy.

below

Russian Jews were made to dig their own graves before execution.

MPC Archive

MPC Archive

above

Wolff was held responsible for facilitating the train transport of 300,000 Jews from the Warsaw ghetto to Treblinka in 1942.

below

As head of the SS Ahnenerbe, Wolff was involved in providing financial and other support for a whole range of medical experiments on prisoners (so-called "volunteers"), who were tested for survival limits in icy water or high altitude loss of pressure. The tests generally ended in the death of the prisoner. Here, Luftwaffe Dr. Sigmund Rascher *(right)* experiments with the effects of freezing water.

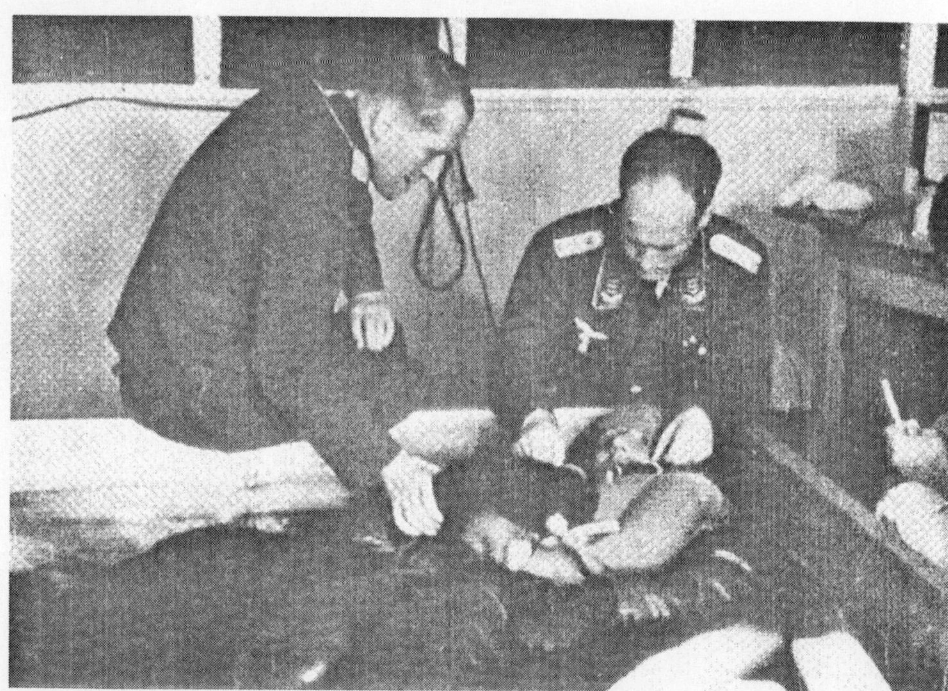
MPC Archive

SVB

Dollmann Archive

above

Wolff as Hitler's personal representative to Mussolini in 1944.

right

Mussolini being briefed by Lt. Col. Zolling, one of Kesselring's staff officers, at Parma in August 1944.

below

Wolff *(right)* at a joint German-Italian conference in 1944. To his right are Fascist party secretary Alessandro Pavolini and Ambassador Rudolf Rahn, and Minister of Education C.A. Biggini.

SG Archives

DS Archive

above

Ernst von Weizsäcker, German ambassador to the Vatican, helped Wolff obtain an audience with Pope Pius XII.

right

SS Colonel Herbert Kappler, police chief in Rome and responsible for the Ardeatine Caves massacre in 1944. He was under Wolff's command.

DS Archive

DS Archive

right

Pope Pius XII. Standing beside him is Monsignor Giovanni Battista Montini, then Vatican secretary of state, who later became Pope Paul VI.

below

The German top brass in Italy. From the left: Ambassador Rudolf Rahn, Field Marshal Albert Kesselring, SS General Karl Wolff, and General Hans Roettiger (closest to camera).

Dollmann Archive

DS Archive

above

Operation Sunrise operatives. *From the left:* Swiss Major Max Waibel, Prof. Max Husmann, and Baron Luigi Parilli, Italian representative for Gen. Wolff.

below

In May 1945 Wolff *(far right)* celebrates the surrender with *(from the left)* General Roettiger, Gero von Gaevernitz (who represented Allen Dulles), and General von Vietinghoff. Behind them stand Major Wenner *(left)* (on Wolff's staff), and Colonel Eugen Dollmann.

Dollmann Archive

U.S. Army Photo

above

On April 29, 1945, at Allied Headquarters in Caserta, near Naples, the surrender of German and Italian Fascist armies is signed by Lt. Col. V. von Schweinitz, with SS Major Max Wenner standing behind him.

right

In 1964 Wolff was in a Munich court to answer for war crimes—specifically for facilitating the train transport of 300,000 Jews to Treblinka concentration camp.

Prussian Archives

above
Karl Wolff in Munich in the 1980s.

right
Allen Dulles in Switzerland in 1945.

Chapter 9

"Take Over the Vatican!"

Wolff was not in Italy during the first few days of September 1943. Himmler and Hitler had ordered him to headquarters. His account of that meeting, partly in conversations with journalists and historians, and among the drafts of his sketchy autobiography, is sensational enough to wonder whether the General's memory was affected by his self-confidence. His stories are all the more difficult to assess because no one else could confirm them, and Wolff could not provide any personal notes from those glorious moments of his career, and had problems identifying the dates of those events. Therefore, one must sometimes fit his version into the sequence of events.

Wolff was present at Hitler's table for lunch at the "Wolfsschanze" on September 6, 1943, from 2:45 p.m. to 4:55 p.m.—according to Linge's diary—together with Himmler, Ribbentrop, and Ambassador Walter Hewel, the foreign minister's liaison at Führer headquarters. The usual frugal meal must not have taken more than ten minutes. Without a doubt, they spent the next two hours talking primarily about Italy and Wolff's mission there. It contained, according to his report, an additional task that was not even discussed at that confidential lunch; Hitler apparently informed only Himmler and his Obergruppenführer.

Himmler had already told him at his field headquarters, says Wolff—he would be ordered to clear out the Vatican. The task was immediately confirmed the by the Reichsführer, who quickly added that this was an opportunity to remove all evidence of German culture. During the Early Middle Ages when missionaries and monks were to Christianize the Germanic peoples, these relics were apparently taken as trophies from the pagan north to the holy city of Rome. "The Führer," Wolff quoted the Reichsführer SS, "is thinking primarily of political ammunition contained in the archives. We, however, as the protectors of the eternal treasures of our race must plan for the future."

During lunch, Hitler announced he would end the "unbearable situation in Italy one way or another" in the next few days. The location of Mussolini's jail had been found and his liberation was being prepared, but had been put on ice because the king, his court, Badoglio, and his generals had to be seized first. The Duce would be returned to power and honor, but the Fascists would from now on be dependant upon German support so that the people did not once again destroy Fascist party offices and burn their flags. The task of Ribbentrop and Rahn was to link a future Fascist government to Axis policies. Himmler and Wolff were to guarantee peace and security. Mussolini must be better protected in the future. To Wolff he said, "You are responsible for the Duce. A specially selected unit of the SS must never let him out of their eyesight." Hitler, Wolff recalled, gave him the secret order, when there were no other witnesses present. He was ordered to occupy the Vatican, clear it out, and take the leading clerics working there, including those close to the Pope, and especially the accredited diplomats and their asylum seekers. "The SD should put together for you a list of the most dangerous persons," Hitler supposedly said. "There will be an uproar throughout the world, but that will soon die down." The political documents of the last decades must be secured. "That will be a harvest, richer than the one from France in 1940!" (Hitler was referring to the files of the French foreign ministry captured from railroad cars.)

The transportation available for the higher clergy and the diplomats must, of course, be commensurate with their high rank. Accommodations for the clerics were to be cloister complexes or even castles. If the Pope so wished, he and his colleagues could later go to the Principality of Lichtenstein, "so that no one could say that we treated His Holiness badly."

When Hitler asked when this operation could take place, Wolff supposedly looked for an excuse and pointed out the difficult and necessary preparations. The Vatican must be taken apart, people must be found who knew every step and every garret, experts had to be recruited who knew how to handle the archives and mastered Latin and Greek. When Wolff set six weeks as the minimum amount of time for those preparations, Hitler was supposedly disappointed, but he then agreed and said: "If one wants a first-class job, it cannot happen overnight." He did ask to receive regular updates regarding the progress of Wolff's preparations.

As we know that operation never took place. Wolff credits himself for this: since he hesitated so long in carrying out those plans, Hitler ended up dropping the idea. In seeking to use this "good deed" to offset the accusations of being a leading Nazi raises the question whether the order was really taken seriously. It seems very plausible that it was serious. Even though Hitler regularly paid his church taxes as a Catholic up until he committed suicide, he always viewed the clergy as a bitter enemy. In 1933, the priests prevented him from obtaining the majority vote in the Catholic areas of Germany by warning voters that the "Catholic Center" would protect practicing Catholics from the actions of the new pagans. The Nazis considered Hitler's concordat with the Catholic Church after his rise to power simply as a temporary cease-fire. He swore revenge when the Bishop of Münster, Monsignor Galen, forced him to stop the "euthanasia" program—the mass murder of the handicapped and mentally retarded in the nursing homes. In bitter fury, he announced many times that as soon as he victoriously ended the war, he would settle the score with the clergy of all denominations.

The conversation at the table on September 6 may very well have turned to the Vatican. The consequences must have also been discussed if Pius XII were to give pastoral instructions if he were under Allied control to Catholics living in Nazi-occupied Europe. Obviously influenced by his long stay in Germany as the nuncio, the Pope had until then avoided a head-on confrontation with the National Socialists, but that could also change.

Wolff, of course, knew these facts, that gave credence to a plan for action against the Vatican appear plausible. Besides that, there were already at least two statements from Hitler that apparently anticipated the order given to Wolff. One statement came at lunch on December 13, 1941, at the "Wolfsschanze" in the presence of three Reich ministers and presumably Wolff as well. In those days German divisions were at the outskirts of Moscow, frozen by winter, defending themselves only with the courage of desperation, against fresh units of Siberian Red Army troops that were just being thrown into the war. Hitler digressed from this, saying:

"The war will be over one day. I shall consider that my life's final task will be to solve the religious problem. ... I don't interfere in matters of belief. Therefore I can't allow churchmen to interfere with temporal affairs ... The final state must be: in St. Peter's Chair, a senile officiant; facing him, a few sinister old women, as gaga and as poor in spirit as anyone could wish. The young and healthy are on our side." And referring to Mussolini's situation: "I'd have entered the Vatican and thrown everybody out—reserving the right to apologize later: 'Excuse me, it was a mistake!' But the result would have been, they'd have been outside!"*

Hitler stated something similar eighteen months later at the situation report on July 26, 1943, when bad news kept coming in from Rome about the collapse of the Fascist system. Back then he threatened: "I'll go into the Vatican immediately. Do you think the Vatican troubles me? It will be seized immediately. First of all, the entire diplomatic corps is in there. I don't care. The rabble is in there. We'll take the entire herd of swine ... What is already... Then we apologize afterward; that doesn't matter to us. We're waging a war there... [...] Yes we will get documents. We will bring out something about the betrayal!"** Was that just an outbreak of blind rage?

It is quite clear that Hitler had certainly considered such action. It remains open whether he actually planned the deed. That he never gave such an order in writing is not unusual; it was Hitler's practice to order crimes orally, just as he avoided documenting the responsibility for the murder of the Jews. It is also conceivable that when the discussion took place, Wolff became convinced that his mission was to realize the Führer's dream. Wolff often expressed the opinion that perhaps Hitler had mentioned murdering the Jews, but that he had never actually ordered it. Himmler and Heydrich may have relieved him of that responsibility of their own accord. There is also the possibility that Wolff fabricated the order hoping to mitigate his own responsibility by the idea that good is just evil that one doesn't perpetrate. At any rate, Wolff only brought up the order about the Vatican long after the war, when he was in serious trouble.

Hitler's plan to have King Victor Emmanuel III, Badoglio, and "the whole gang" in Rome picked up was not carried out either. Kesselring could

---

* *Hitler's Table Talk 1941–1944*, H. R. Trevor-Roper, ed. (New York: Enigma Books, 2000), pp. 142–3, 145.

** *Hitler and His Generals: Military Conferences 1942–1945*, Helmut Heiber and David M. Glantz, eds. (New York: Enigma Books, 2003), p. 216.

have used the armored infantry division stationed around the Italian capital, but that ring was encircled by yet another ring made up of six Italian divisions. Each quarreling ally waited for the next move of the other partner. On September 8 at midday, the king was still giving assurances to German envoy Rudolf Rahn that he would honor his obligations. But a few hours later, Rahn was called by Italian foreign minister Count Guariglia, who informed him what radio stations were broadcasting around the world: Marshal Badoglio, "in the face of the hopeless military situation, was forced ... to ask for a cease-fire." It was an unconditional surrender to the Allies following weeks of secret negotiations.

That evening the code word "Axis" was flashed from Führer headquarters. It triggered the measures that had been planned in the event of a "betrayal." It also warned Wolff and his staff in Munich who left that night crossing the Brenner Pass at exactly 6:00 a.m. the following morning. There were no longer any Italian soldiers or customs officials in sight. The Italian government and high command had prepared orders for such a scenario, but they were abandoned or were simply ignored, because everyone had become weary of the war. A central leadership no longer existed. During the night of September 9, the royal family, Marshal Badoglio, his military staff and his ministers fled Rome in a convoy of luxury limousines, heading south, towards the little port of Pescara on the Adriatic. A small Italian navy vessel was waiting there to take them to the allied lines in southern Italy, at Brindisi.

Fate did not grant Wolff, who was eager for action, the pleasure of becoming involved in the exciting events during those early autumn days. His forces were still too weak; the SS and Police units would follow later on; he had to assemble emergency units on his own. His budget was 70,000 Reichs marks in cash as "an advance towards the newly established position." At that time, Rommel's soldiers were basically driving their former Italian comrades-in-arms into concentration camps. Out of necessity, most of them were then deported to the north as foreign workers, the equivalent of slave labor. The residents of South Tyrol greeted the SS convoys enthusiastically. They took for granted that from now on the German language and their old traditions would be respected, and that they would no longer be forced by law to behave like tried and true Italians as it was under the Fascist regime. It must have been like the weight of the world being lifted from their shoulders that the resettlement, which had often been announced but was never actually enacted, would probably no longer be necessary.

During the following days, the new civilian master of Italy was still unable to actually govern. He was getting organized; in the cities, the positions in the police departments needed to be filled, the existing police stations had to be inspected, and mostly the introductory visits by the new authorities had to take place. Since Wolff's command did not even have the beginning of an organization available, he wisely avoided the clashes that frequently took place between SS commanders and the Wehrmacht generals. Immediately and voluntarily, he placed himself under the authority of Field Marshal Kesselring for all issues involving the military. That move won him a very influential patron. Herbert Kappler, the former police attaché at the embassy, was appointed as the top policeman in Rome, a promotion that the SS Standartenführer would curse for decades as he sat in an Italian prison.

Wolff requested information from Ambassador Rahn about Italy's political reorganization—since he was constantly informed of the activities to free Mussolini, it was clear that Hitler would use him as a nominal leader for appearance's sake. Was he to be the head of state, the prime minister, and party leader all at once? The dictator who enjoyed behaving like an old Roman tribune could still cause a lot of trouble. Could he possibly be placed high enough above as a symbolic figure to cut off from day-to-day politics? Who would run the government in that case?

Rahn suggested an old fascist who had been shunted aside because he was too worried about honesty and his good reputation, the former Minister of Agriculture Renato Tassinari, who was now a wealthy landowner and professor of agriculture at the University of Bologna. In contrast to prominent Fascist figures, he had a very clean slate, was not associated with any violence, and was respected by the people. Together with Dollmann, who had now been appointed as Wolff's liaison officer to Kesselring, Wolff wanted to convince Tassinari to be a candidate as head of the government.

All these issues, including the question of where the government and Wolff would be located, could only be decided if the Duce stepped onto the world stage once again and if Hitler agreed to appoint him to that role. The task of freeing Mussolini was given to Luftwaffe General Kurt Student, who would use his paratroopers. Himmler managed to get it through to Hitler that the SD must also be involved. And so, along with a small number of SS troops, the massive, ambitious and adventurous SS Hauptsturmführer Otto Skorzeny was also assigned to the task. He took part in the paratrooper unit that landed on the Gran Sasso, the highest peak of the Abruzzi Mountains where Mussolini was being held prisoner, in a manner of speaking, at a ski resort hotel. The guards immediately surrendered. Skorzeny was only an auxiliary during the entire operation. But in the photos taken at the scene, he was always standing next to Mussolini, and hailed as the Duce's liberator by Nazi propaganda.

This took place on September 12, 1943, and from that moment on Wolff was expecting a call from the "Wolfsschanze." Hitler had promised him he would be on hand when Mussolini was free. Because the Obergruppenführer had his candidate Tassinari waiting in the wings, he had to speak with the Führer before things were irrevocably set in stone. It was fortunate that Hitler did not wish to see his friend the Duce immediately. Mussolini was flown to Vienna, then to Munich the next day where he was reunited with his family. On September 14 he was finally welcomed at the "Wolfsschanze."

The reason for such a late meeting was that Hitler needed to be clear about his future policies towards Italy first. Now he knew the desolate condition of Mussolini and his family, he knew how the Fascist party had disintegrated, and he understood the complete demoralization of the Italian armed forces. On September 12, he met with Himmler, Bormann, Reich Minister Hans Lammers, Minister of Armaments Albert Speer, and Gauleiters Franz Hofer (Tyrol) and Friedrich Rainer (Kärnten). He certainly did not want the Duce present, while the victors divided up the Italian pie. South Tyrol was practically added to the Gau of Tyrol and governed from Innsbruck. The eastern parts of the Adriatic coast went to the Gau of Kärnten. The new and only temporarily loose areas that had been added to the Reich remained under the jurisdiction of the Highest SS and Police Commander Wolff, but he had to work in harmony with the gauleiters. This was one more example of the confusion of responsibilities and was typical of Hitler's system: he consciously created dissatisfaction so that he could show on occasion that he was the master of the house, and everyone remained dependent upon him.

The call from the Führer headquarters didn't reach Wolff until some time on September 13. He now had his own airplane: a three-engine Ju 52, Lufthansa passenger plane in peacetime, it was reliable but slower than all military planes. In order to avoid enemy planes, he flew to East Prussia overnight with Tassinari. They landed early in the morning at Rastenburg and first visited the Reichsführer SS. The bourgeois conservative Tassinari made a tame impression on him. Himmler advised him to appoint aggressiv old Fascist party functionaries as ministers in a future cabinet—

for example, Alessandro Pavolini, Roberto Farinacci, or even Guido Buffarini-Guidi, whom Himmler particularly liked. He had become friends with the former undersecretary at the ministry of the interior in charge of the police, even though he was a corruptible, cynical hedonist, in some ways the opposite of the purist and moral stickler Himmler.

The next stop that same morning, Wolff was to visit Foreign Minister Ribbentrop. His residence at the time was at the Castle Steinort near Angerburg, the property of Count Lehndorf. Wolff was always well received by Ribbentrop, from the time he gave the minister his support during a conspiracy within the ministry. Wolff had also occasionally reminded Ribbentrop of his close ties to the minister's wife, since the Wolff and von Römheld families were from Darmstadt and had been received as guests at her parents' home (the wine-growing family Henkell) in Wiesbaden. The minister, who was otherwise so arrogant and aloof, had one day even addressed the Obergruppenführer with the familiar "Du." In a good mood, he now looked the professor over and had no reason to oppose his political promotion.

It seemed more difficult to obtain an appointment to introduce Tassarini to Hitler with his, Hitler's, aides at Führer headquarters. His daily schedule was booked up, Wolff was told. But he had not been part of that exclusive men's club for three and a half years for nothing, and had occasionally been helpful to some of those gentlemen during that time. He was even given two appointments, if only for a few minutes. At the first one, before the situation report, he was to report on the situation in Italy. At the second, immediately following the situation report, he was to bring Tassinari.

Wolff described his impressions of that day after the war. He recalled how they were driven by car to the innermost of the blocked circles. From there on, he "had to walk the 150 meters to Hitler's barracks on foot, just like Göring." The bodyguards greeted Wolff "respectfully and very properly"; some of them were former comrades of his even before 1933 in the elite formation of the SS, the "first and oldest SS Standarte 1 in Munich."

Hitler's valet Linge noted the beginning of the conversation with "O'gruf.* Wolff" at 12:25 p.m. Two hours earlier Hitler was still asleep; after rising he would take a fifteen minute walk in the woods, had breakfast and then confer with Reichsleiter Martin Bormann and the chief of staff

* Obergruppenführer.

General Kurt Zietzler. Following Wolff and before the midday situation report, there was still a general on the waiting list. Lunch was to be served once Mussolini had arrived.

Wolff was pleased that Hitler immediately inquired about his health. As he remembered: "It was a nice conversation." Wolff reported his experiences, told of the Italians rioting against the Fascists, said how they viewed the Germans only as unpopular occupying forces that would prolong the war. Therefore, a government must take over the responsibility for cooperation with Germany as soon as possible. Professor Tassinari, whom he had brought and knew as a man of honor, would be ready and could count on the respect of his fellow countrymen.

An hour later Wolff was sitting in Hitler's office, this time together with Ribbentrop and Tassinari. The tall Italian obviously was pleasing; Hitler was charming. But faced with such friendliness, Tassinari forgot the advice he was given, and answered the question about his future ministers, not mentioning a single name from Mussolini's old team. Hitler became impatient: perhaps this or that tried and tested man from the Party leadership deserved a seat in the cabinet, he inquired. It was not expressed as a demand, but Tassinari failed to pick up on that request. He ticked off the Fascist leaders one after the other saying how unreliable this one was, how greedy that one had been, and how malicious the third one had been in the past.

Hitler remained polite. He regretted that he had so little time that day for such an important discussion. In one hour, the Duce would arrive. Tassinari, who knew nothing of this, was ushered out with the request that he provide "very clear suggestions" in writing. To Wolff, Hitler said: "The man had a chance, but he didn't seize it. He is simply not a politician." However, he did not totally eliminate the professor. He gave Wolff the order: "Make sure that Tassinari stays here. Maybe he's just stubborn because he's holding on to a utopian ideal." He could still use him as a potential rival.

A half hour later, on September 14, 1943, a Condor plane from headquarters in Munich landed at Rastenburg airport. As Hitler approached the door of the plane, the Highest SS and Police Führer in Italy, Karl Wolff, was following only two steps behind. The Duce must see his protector and guardian immediately as he got off the plane, both a trusted face and a warning at the same time. As the door opened, Mussolini stood on the steps, older, much thinner, pale, wearing a baggy suit, and an overcoat that was much too big for him. He was no longer the legendary "Man from

Rome," the strongman with a muscular neck and the bronze bust resembling Caesar. He approached Hitler with open arms. Wolff heard how he said in German, "How can I thank you for all you have done for my family and me?" Wolff took part of that gratitude for himself. In Munich, but even more during the last few days he had helped bring the entire Mussolini family, including relatives by marriage, to safety in Germany. The full red carpet treatment, complete with the national anthem, the honor guard and presidential march customary during visits by Mussolini, was not used. Wolff knew why: "It would have meant that we had already recognized him as a head of state, before having even carried out our demands."

The meal began at 3:00 p.m. and lasted two hours. In the evening, the same group sat together once more. In the meantime, at Hitler's request, Wolff had brought the Duce together with Tassinari; the liberated dictator was supposed to notice that no one was dependent on him. The two Italians mistrusted one another and had nothing to say. As Hitler explained at the evening meal, acting completely innocently, he had Tassinari come because Mussolini might possibly want him as minister of agriculture, but the taciturn Duce refused. He said that such a stringent moralist reminiscent of the old Roman Cato would only created unnecessary difficulties for a government, especially in critical times.

It was not like Wolff to break off all ties with someone who could possibly be useful to him, even after a failure. He could still learn quite a few things about the Duce and his sidekicks from Tassinari. Therefore the SS general and the professor met every now and then later on, which was made easier since Tassinari owned a large estate on Lake Garda, very close to Wolff's future office. During the last phase of the war, when private use of automobiles was forbidden (due to the lack of fuel), Wolff managed to get Tassinari permission to drive a small Fiat along with the necessary gasoline. But that favor actually was to be the cause of Tassinari's death. A British fighter pilot shot up the tiny car on the river road along Lake Garda, killing the driver.

After the evening tea at Führer headquarters on September 14, "the Highest SS and Police Chief in Italy" should actually have returned to his viceroy kingdom to take power; however, the Duce was not quite ready for a return to his homeland. Wolff was once again expressly attached to him by "order of the Führer." As of September 10, 1943, he was already appointed as "Special Advisor for Police Matters to the Italian Fascist National Government," which did not exist at that point because Mussolini was still being held prisoner on the Gran Sasso. Even by mid-September, there was not even a trace of such an entity, unless a pale version was identified in the aged and depressed former prime minister of the Kingdom of Italy. He represented the sad shadow of his former imperial splendor, but he was also the only possible source of legitimacy for the German policies unless Italy was declared an enemy. Wolff had to therefore protect the Duce from his many enemies (which without a doubt he had) and to keep watch that he didn't turn away from his friends (who stood up for him).

First, however, Wolff had to find appropriate accommodations for the fallen dictator. On September 19, Mussolini and his wife Rachele moved into Hirschberg castle, in the foothills of the Alps, south of Lake Starnberg. It had been built before the First World War, and therefore offered some added comforts, but the new guests never felt comfortable. The weather was too cool and humid for them, they did not like the furnishings, the food was too German, the table service by SS orderlies too brisk, and the SS guard team was too loud and too obtrusive.

Nearby, in another town on Lake Starnberg, was Count Galeazzo Ciano, the former foreign minister, his wife Edda (Mussolini's daughter), and their family. He had been one of the rebels within the Fascist Grand Council that had toppled his father-in-law, but because the revenge of the anti-Fascists threatened the couple, they had fled to the Reich, with the help of Wolff and the SD. They were much less inclined to accept the German situation than the Duce. Ciano, contrary to his father-in-law, had boarded the plane with a large amount of cash and precious objects. The couple was planning to emigrate to Argentina.

The Germans expected that Mussolini would finally govern—naturally in name only, since Hitler and his governors Wolff and Rahn were to make all key decisions. For a long time they hesitated as to where Mussolini could reside in the future. Rome was not suitable: the enemy was already too near and the people of the great city were hard to control. In the cities of the north, industrial workers were too rebellious. Because Mussolini felt homesick for his family home at Rocca delle Caminate, Wolff picked him up from Hirschberg by car on September 23. From Munich they flew over the Alps together. Mussolini took over the controls on the plane for a time. From the airport at Forlì they drove into the mountains. The family home resembled a fifteenth century fortress, but had actually been built in the 1930s. There was a guard at the gate; Wolff had ordered a unit of the SS Leibstandarte unit garrisoned nearby, which now presented arms, wearing white leather trimmed uniforms.

On the same day Wolff flew hurriedly on to Rome. It became urgent to find a credible minister of defense for the new government. Rahn and Wolff invited Marshal Rodolfo Graziani to the embassy where they successfully appealed to his love of country, saying that with his cooperation, they could prove to Hitler, who was complaining loudly, that true Italians wanted no part of traitors like Badoglio.

In August, while he was still in Munich, Wolff wrote to his ex-wife, telling her how "happily and confidently he had taken on "his first big and independent task. The trust of Hitler and of the Reichsführer SS is a great source of pride for me." In another letter dated September 29, he admitted, "I have never worked as hard as in the last fourteen days...often without sleep, seldom more than three or four hours. But it gives me indescribable pleasure to finally be able to be doing and mastering something independently. Conditions in Italy are actually extremely difficult at the moment and the police force that is available to me is ridiculously small, but that is what makes this especially fun."

In writing this, he had already located what was to be Mussolini's residence: on Lake Garda, in one of the most charming landscapes in Italy, protected from the cold and storms by high mountains on three sides, and where spas function throughout the year. Until then, the confiscated hotels and feudal homes were used for injured and recovering soldiers, and the valley had been declared a hospital area. Now those buildings were being cleared out for Mussolini, his family, his entourage, the ministers and the authorities of the new state, and naturally also for the German officers and guards. All of them would use Red Cross markings; the Allied air force left the region almost undisturbed.

Himmler's disfavor, if it was of the intensity described by Wolff, was long forgotten and he was again friendly and full of goodwill. In a top-secret speech Himmler gave in Posen on October 4, 1943, he boasted long and wide about the murder of the Jews in the extermination camps. The SS had "persevered, when 500 here or 1,000 there... this is a glorious chapter in our history that was never written and never will be written." The entire upper echelon of leadership listened, with the exception of Wolff. He was involved in Italy, but he must have been able to read the text of the speech a few days later at Himmler's field headquarters, because he was mentioned and celebrated by Himmler as one of his closest and oldest colleagues." Furthermore, he was praised for his ability to handle turf disputes; when ugly situations surfaced everyone involved became responsible for their resolution. Himmler was again addressing his letters to Wolff as "dear Wölfchen."

Now that the persecution of the Jews had taken on its most dreadful form, Wolff could not possibly think he could make an exception for Italy. Wolff knew that Himmler had been working on enlisting the Duce to an aggressive form of anti-Semitism. In October 1942 the Reichsführer SS traveled to Rome with Wolff for that specific reason. A report summarized what Himmler and Mussolini had discussed during a confidential conversation. The Jews—as Himmler summarized his arguments—were "responsible for sabotage, espionage . . . as well as the formation of rebel gangs . . . in Russia we had to shoot a number . . . of men and women." Furthermore, Wolff found out from a report from the OKW that since the beginning of December 1942, all the Jews in the Italian-occupied zones of France were to be arrested, but that this agreement with the Italian command had been sabotaged. He also knew that in January 1943 Ribbentrop had pressured the government in Rome "to adapt your procedures against the Jews to ours."

All of these warnings—Wolff also knew this—remained unsuccessful. The current dogmas about race in Germany were incomprehensible to the Italians. Even if Wolff did not want to order any anti-Semitic actions, he could expect that Himmler would quickly find out about any delay in the persecution of the Jews, since he was now in charge of the area. At the beginning of October he found out from Friedrich Moellhausen, the consul at the German embassy in Rome, that SS Obersturmbannführer Herbert Kappler, who was in charge of the German Security Police in Rome, was given the order to "arrest" the 8,000-odd Jews living in the capital "and take them to northern Italy, where they were to be liquidated." The sentence is quoted from a telegram dated October 6 that Moellhausen used to enlist his superior, von Ribbentrop, to counter Himmler's plans. He would have liked to address Wolff, but he was traveling and reporting to Hitler at headquarters late in the afternoon of the following day regarding the situation in Italy.

Moellhausen's attempt at an objection ended in a rebuff from Berlin: "The Herr RAM [Reich Foreign Minister] requests that you inform Ambassador Rahn and Consul Moellhausen that on the grounds of an order from the Führer, the 8,000 Jews living in Rome are to be taken as hostages to Mauthausen. The Herr RAM requests that you instruct Rahn and Moellhausen that they are in no way to interfere in this matter, but are to leave it up to the SS."

This meant: keep your fingers out of things that are none of your business. The mention of Mauthausen was clearly a lie; everyone in the know within the Nazi leadership was fully aware that such transports ended straight into the gas chambers and crematoriums, and that Mauthausen was a concentration camp used for the purpose of murder, not an extermination camp. Particularly offensive in Berlin was the fact that Moellhausen had used the word "liquidated" in his telegram. Not even Himmler managed to be so direct in his correspondence.

However, Moellhausen knew since September 26 the kind of threat hanging over the Jews of Rome. On that day, he found out that Hauptsturmführer Theodor Dannecker, a representative of SS Obersturmbannführer Adolf Eichmann, arrived in Rome, and was well aware of the kind of work this SS officer from the Jewish affairs office of the Gestapo and the SD specialized in. Wolff was still in Italy at the end of September, so he must have known about Dannecker's arrival. According to regulations every SS officer had to report to the appropriate Higher SS and Police Chief if he wanted to work in his jurisdiction.

Did the mass murderer Dannecker somehow not report to Wolff? Or did Wolff not know at that time what kind of work Eichmann and his men were doing? Or did Wolff leave on a business trip because he did not want to know what was going to happen to the Jews in Rome? Eichmann would have said, in such a case, that Wolff once again put on his white gloves.

Already on October 14, a group of one hundred SS ransacked the synagogues and their offices in the Jewish quarter. Two days later, on the Sabbath, the quarter was being combed by patrols. Kappler led the operation, calling "to action all available forces of the security and order police." In his report to Berlin, he immediately added that "the participation of the Italian police was impossible ...due to its unreliability in this area." The population was also said to have practiced "passive resistance," "which in many individual instances became active help" (for those persecuted). Instead of 8,000 Jews, less than 1,000 ended up in the clutches of the SS. Two days later, on the morning of October 18, they were loaded into railroad freight cars and taken away to Auschwitz. During Wolff's reign as "Viceroy," a total of about 7,000 Italian Jews were deported, with most of them ending up being murdered.

During the Munich criminal proceedings, Wolff denied responsibility for the operations against the Italian Jews and correctly pointed out that the orders came from the RSHA Main Office and were sent directly to the commander of the SD. This was the normal procedure for deportations. It was of course also the usual manner by which the responsible Highest SS and Police Chief was informed of planned operations; he could, if necessary, "become involved and alter routine measures."

We have found no document showing that Wolff was told about the deportation of the Jews on October 16, since he was either at Himmler's field headquarters or in the neighboring Führer headquarters when it took place. From there, he cabled instructions to his Italian office to pass along several orders to Obersturmbannführer Kappler. The contents of the orders are unknown; the files only show a confirmation dated October 18, that these "instructions were passed on according to instructions." At the same time Wolff received Kappler's telegraphed report about the raid in Rome along with the notice "Urgent! Secret! Present immediately!" The contents, Wolff said after the war, deeply disturbed him but he learned of the operation so late that he could have done nothing to prevent it.

Why was that not possible? The raid was on October 16 and he was informed on October 18—the day the train loaded, with its victims, left Rome going north. The railroad network was so busy at that time that transports of this type rolled along for days before they reached their destinations. Most probably and theoretically the train could have been stopped before it reached the extermination camp Auschwitz-Birkenau. But that would have required a heroic decision.

During the Munich court proceedings, Wolff considered himself exonerated by the cable with Kappler's report; it proved that he was not present during the events. The prosecutor reached other conclusions, namely, that Wolff had it sent to him with extreme urgency because on the following day, October 19, he was invited, together with Himmler, to have lunch with Hitler and wanted to use that opportunity to show how energetically he was following orders. The meal offered plenty of time; it lasted two hours.

Understandably, after the end of the war, he did not like to speak about the persecution of the Jews, or if necessary, only very casually. During the war crimes trials at Nuremberg, Karl Wolff was also questioned as a witness on that issue to describe what had been going on in Italy. He said: "I vaguely remember that—I believe in the summer of 1943, September, or it could have been October—at the very beginning, when I was sent to Italy and not quite fully trained—an order came from Berlin, as a reminder from Himmler, that Jews in Italy were to be arrested and deported to the Reich. As I remember, at that time in total, there were approximately 1,050

Jews in all of Italy, so that means it was quite clearly not a very high percentage...that was handed over to the Reich." One must therefore assume that during the months of captivity, probably because of deprivations, the witness' great memory, so often praised, was at least temporarily damaged.

In the days preceding the persecution of the Jews, Wolff was unavailable to Consul Moellhausen in Rome; the Highest SS and Police Chief was busy looking for a suitable residence for Mussolini's republic. However, he did not decide this alone: Rommel, whose headquarters were located at the northern end of Lake Garda, and Ambassador Rahn—in fact, everyone claims to have been with Wolff in choosing the seat of the new Fascist government. Only Mussolini was not pleased with the location. He needed many people around him, an audience that he could excite with his speeches. The narrow strip of land on the banks of Lake Garda was barely wide enough to accommodate all the functionaries, soldiers, German and Italian police officers, and servants. Besides that, Mussolini accused the Germans of having put him in a sack on Lake Garda. It is true that a single road along the lake connected the valley to the rest of the world, and that single traffic route could be blocked from the north and the south very easily. However, Mussolini no longer had enough energy to get his way with his rescuers, protectors, and guards. On October 8, 1943, as he got into his car at the Rocca delle Caminate, he did not even know exactly where the trip would end. He had only been told that Lake Garda was the destination.

Wolff was waiting for him in Verona and invited him to take a seat in his car. Followed by a small convoy of other cars full of SS officers and a few fascists, they reached the southern tip of the lake after one half hour. Turning north and following the bank of the lake, they reached Salò, the town that would soon give the new state its unofficial name and its somewhat disparaging title of "Republic of Salò." Wolff had placed himself and his staff in the neighboring town of Fasano. He had prepared the residence of the head of state at Gargnano, less than a dozen kilometers further north, where he ordered one of the most luxurious houses cleared out. It belonged to the rich Feltrinelli business family from Milan, had more than thirty rooms, and was decorated with furniture considered particularly beautiful, in "Liberty" turn-of-the-century style.

The driveway was narrow and full of curves. The mountain rose up steep and jagged behind the villa that remained hidden by very tall trees. Wolff's security measures were perfect. A branch of the SD constantly checked everyone living at the house, the servants and any visitors. All telephone conversations were tapped. Posts and patrols made up of SS troops and Italian militia guarded the park and the entrances. For one month, the head of state lived practically alone in the huge building. A blonde German woman, who was both nurse and housekeeper named Irma, took care of him, and it was being whispered that she had a relationship with her employer. In November Rachele Mussolini was ready to move in.

Mussolini's feeling of being a prisoner was justified, even if Wolff made every effort to let him feel that way only on occasion. One could not deny that the road going north, high above the lake through the tunnel in the rocks, reached the temporary border of the Republic only after a few kilometers. There began the "Operational Zone Foothills of the Alps" that Rommel had set up, and anyone seeking to travel to Trent and Bolzano needed a permit. Rommel did not like the Italians. He blamed them for his defeat in North Africa—due to their aversion to dying a hero's death and their leadership's protective attitude toward their fleet, rather than providing more supplies for the Africa Korps. Rommel offered his opinion quite often with Swabian directness. Mussolini got wind of it, and held it against him. It also bothered the Duce that in the First World War, former Captain Erwin Rommel beat the Italians in the Alps at Caporetto, earning the medal "Pour le merite" in doing so.

The two would not have to deal with each other very much longer. Hitler had already been planning for quite some time to place all German forces in Italy under a single supreme command, and in doing so, Rommel was also to take over Kesselring's southern front. Back on October 18 Keitel, as Chief of the OKW, had presented Hitler with a draft of an order. However, it was never signed and Wolff believed he could explain the reason for that change of mind.

At Fasano, just after he began operating—as he recalled—"a high officer from Rommel's staff, a man generally regarded as irreproachable," came to see him. He requested that the SS general on his honor as an officer agree to never name his informant, if he were to trust him with a secret that must absolutely be shared with the Führer—"in the interest of Germany." After this dramatic introduction, the visitor provided him with the information that his commander General Rommel "after the military disappointments of the last twelve months no longer believed in a German victory at the end of the war." The Führer must know this before he "entrusted Rommel with a new command that was decisive for the war."

On October 19 and 20, Wolff was again at the "Wolfsschanze." Apparently, he gave Hitler the information at that time. However, a problem came up in the conversation when Hitler wanted to know where the SS general got his information. But his word of honor stopped Wolff from saying anything. The Führer did not believe this was at all valid given the situation; he demanded that Wolff "get over the barrier of your word of honor complex and in the interest of Germany entrust me with the name of this officer." As this appeal also remained without effect, Hitler pressured him further and "after a short pause he said 'Now I have it. I relieve you as your Supreme Commander from your officer's word of honor!" That was Wolff's description. Apparently the Führer, who in the course of his life had given and broken his word of honor so many times, did not comprehend the invalidity of such an assurance. He couldn't know better, since Wolff—he obviously was not thinking about it at that moment—only rose to the rank of corporal during the war and had never been an officer. Hitler only stopped pressuring him when Wolff explained that breaking an officer's word of honor would force him to shoot himself.

If one were to follow the tale further, Field Marshal Keitel was called in with the signed orders appointing Rommel as commander of most German forces in Italy. Taking his pen Hitlercrossed out Rommel's name and wrote "Kesselring" above it. Whether it happened like that, with Wolff as the grey eminence, can no longer be confirmed.

David Irving has offended many people with his odious positions but no one can deny that he is a thorough researcher. In his opinion, the change of mind came in mid-October at the "Wolffschanze" when Rommel himself made pessimistic statements in discussing the supreme command in Italy. We must assume that Irving had questioned Wolff thoroughly because the scene regarding the changed certificate was repeated to him. However Irving didn't use it; and obviously doubted its authenticity.

Despite Irving's opinion, a biography of Wolff cannot simply ignore the incident because it is typical not only of the rumors pervading the Nazi leadership, but also of the importance that Wolff attributed to himself until the end. On the other hand, it is quite believable that he did what he could to get rid of Rommel in Italy. Wolff got along with the sophisticated Franconian Kesselring much better than with the unpolished Swabian Rommel, who also occasionally let it be known that his respect for the SS general was tempered because Wolff did not have to learn the profession by working his way up, and had been promoted directly from lieutenant to lieutenant general. Rommel was anything but a diplomat and that was exactly the kind of talent required to work with Mussolini and his entourage.

One of his tasks—said Wolff—was to turn an ageing and sick man who had become lethargic into an energetic Duce ready for action.

However, the conditions in which the head of the new state was placed were not exactly apt to strengthen his lust for life. Attempts to rebuild his army progressed slowly, due to the already weak enthusiasm of the people dampened by the use of German instructors. The economy had to be adjusted accordingly to fulfill German demands; Production and Armaments Minister Albert Speer created an organization of authorized representatives throughout the country who decided what was to be produced and in what time frame. In the areas threatened by the allied advance, factories were dismantled and the machinery was transported to Germany. Because of a shortage of workers, Italian soldiers who were prisoners of war because of the Badoglio government's "treason" became interned civilians, locked in camps, and transported to work. Gauleiter Fritz Sauckel, who was responsible for creating the work force, failed in his attempt to recruit volunteers in Italy. Now he resorted to having pedestrians on the street checked for identification; anyone out of work was taken north as slave labor. In so far as the financial administration worked, its main and most urgent task was to cover the rising cost of the occupation. With their German Reich military banknotes, the field-gray soldiers emptied out the stores that were already only half stocked—which increased and spread the black market.

Wolff had to console his charge about these and other adversities. In order to succeed, he remembered a method that worked for hundreds of years if a potentate needed cheering up or to get his mind off things. Clara Petacci had to be brought over. The daughter of a medical doctor in Rome, she had been Mussolini's lover for years. The relationship was kept secret for a long time. The couple met mostly in the offices of the prime minister, in the Palazzo Venezia, where Mussolini and his Claretta kept a small, furnished apartment. Most Italians, and even Rachele Mussolini, only found out about the affair the day after the fall of the Duce, when the yellow press no longer feared censorship, and Badoglio allowed open criticism of his predecessor.

Claretta was, along with her family, arrested and kept in prison until the SS freed them, at the same time as her lover. She went to Merano and wrote to Mussolini that she was yearning to see him. Her liberators, the officers of the Leibstandarte, took the letter to Lake Garda. Because the Duce was also eagerly waiting, it was not difficult for Wolff to arrange for them to be reunited. At the beginning of November, Claretta moved into a small and fairly modest house at Gardone that Wolff had requisitioned.

In mid-November Donna Rachele (Mussolini's wife) also arrived at Gardone with her family from the Rocca delle Caminate. They filled the residence of the head of state. For that reason, he had Wolff prepare a second building in the center of town to handle government business. The building even had a balcony, where his loyal followers and those who were curious could occasionally cheer him. The separation between the apartment and the office allowed him to meet his lover every now and then. But a small world becomes much smaller for a man everyone knows, especially in a town that had gone years before from a fishing village to vacation and retirement paradise, and now was unexpectedly a royal seat. For a woman to live in secret in such a town when her picture had been in the headlines for weeks was even more unlikely. Wolff had of course briefed Clara Petacci that she was not to leave the house during the day, but, naturally, she did not follow that advice. As Wolff was visiting the Mussolini family home one day, Donna Rachele used the opportunity to lecture him. The situation cannot go on like this, she scolded. Wolff had brought the two together and now he must make sure that they were separated again. She was no longer angry at her husband's affairs, which were were now being politically manipulated, giving Wolff, as the security advisor appointed by Hitler, food for thought. Since Wolff did not react to that, a few days later she clearly demanded that Petacci be removed from the "Government quarter."

It was as simple as the stroke of a pen for the Highest SS and Police Führer and he had decided to fulfill that request. But he took his time. Perhaps he did not want to lose his informant, who occasionally provided him with internal news on the leadership team of the Italian Social Republic that she obtained from Minister of the Interior Buffarini-Guidi, whom she then supported with her Benito.

Drawing pleasure from the scandal, Wolff repeatedly told the story of how Donna Rachele lost her patience in the end—however, he only knew this second hand. She went to Buffarini-Guidi and forced him to accompany her to Petacci's house. When the cast iron gate remained locked despite her impatient ringing, she rampaged around on the street for almost an hour and then finally tried to climb over the gate. Only then was it opened. In the house, she attacked the weeping Claretta vociferously and in the end drew a gun from her purse but Buffarini-Guidi took it away from her.

Following that scene, the situation became too dangerous for Wolff. Petacci was moved to a house high up on the mountain above the lake, where years before the poet Gabriele D'Annunzio had built a huge victory memorial. But even that solution could not last since relatives of the Mussolinis had rented a house nearby and if they noticed anything suspicious, Donna Rachele was immediately informed. The solution was that two or three times a week an SS car went up to Claretta's house and after a short stop would go back down to the valley. Rachele never found out that Wolff was driving and that her husband would get out and then be picked up by the same chauffeur the next day. In the family home, Mussolini was not missed; he slept at the government offices on the banks of the lake most of the time anyway.

Claretta therefore continued to depend on Wolff's assistance. The SS general who very much appreciated feminine charms was pleased to have secured her good will with these favors. In return she reported to him occasionally what her Benito thought about the case of Count Ciano—a matter politically extremely explosive. The son-in-law of the Duce and former foreign minister was always considered as one of the most eager proponents of the Axis; that he had been, at the same time, spreading cynical comments about the alliance between National Socialists and Fascists was well known and joked about in Berlin. But with time, the Germans became suspicious and, finally, Hitler became convinced that the Italian foreign minister was thwarting his war plans. Count Ciano had informed the British at the end of August 1939 that Italy would not join the war if Hitler attacked Poland. This would allow Great Britain to reduce its navy in the Mediterranean, and gave a guarantee to Poland when it declared war on Germany. Therefore no one cried when Mussolini took over the foreign office himself, and his son-in-law Count Ciano became ambassador to the Vatican. It did not surprise anyone to see Ciano join the rebellion against the Duce. He fled to Germany only when the Badoglio government failed to accept his switching sides, and he therefore had to expect reprisals.

In Germany the Cianos were free but kept under observation. Over time, they could feel that they were not well-regarded and very much under surveillance. When they asked to travel to Spain and then go on to emigrate to Argentina, the trip was not approved. Now they were hoping that their plans would be more successful in Italy; Mussolini would hardly refuse his beloved daughter's request, nor that of her husband, whom at times he had loved as much as his own sons.

If Mussolini had forgiven the Count, Hitler most certainly had not. He pushed his Italian friend to secretly seek revenge, but on the surface the withered friendship seemed to be flourishing once more. When on a trip to see her father in Italy, Edda had to go to a sanitarium for a nervous breakdown, her husband also requested to return home. In October Wolff informed the SD guards at the Ciano residence on Lake Starnberger that the Count could fly to Verona, as he wished. When he got off the plane, he was arrested by Italian police officers who were being watched by the SD. In the middle of November Mussolini decreed that the traitors who had toppled him on July 25 were to be tried by a special court. There were only six rebels being held, since most of the others had fled. At the end of September after a conversation with Hitler, Minister of Propaganda Dr. Joseph Goebbels had already noted in his diary what the prisoners were to expect. The Führer was extremely disappointed with the Duce's behavior, criminal court proceedings were imperative, and the son-in-law would "have to be the first to believe it."

With wild energy Mussolini's daughter Edda now fought for her husband's life. She thought she held a trump in her hands with Ciano's diaries from his days as foreign minister and believed the contents were so compromising for Hitler, Ribbentrop, and others that the Germans would trade them for Count's freedom. She managed to flee to Switzerland, and place the diaries in a bank safety deposit box. However, her gamble failed. Hitler's reputation in the world was already so tattered that further incrimination would not upset anyone; besides, the German people would not find out about it anyway.

On January 8, 1944, the court proceedings against Count Galeazzo Ciano and five other accused began in Verona. On January 10, the death sentence was pronounced for Ciano and four others. Wolff had been in Munich the day before. On January 11, shortly after midnight, General Harster of the police called him from Verona. A letter from Edda Ciano, addressed to her father, had been seized. Wolff made sure that the letter was brought to her father's residence by courier. She had written to him several days before, but the letter got lost somewhere. Edda was asking for her husband's freedom. She threatened to use "everything that I have in writing without mercy if Galeazzo is not in Switzerland within three days."

Without a doubt a telephone order coming from Mussolini could prevent or at least postpone the execution set for 6:00 a.m. that morning. Why did this not occur? Was he not allowed to? Did he not want to? The decision was difficult because it involved his son-in-law. If he showed mercy, could he have a deserter from his new army punished with the death penalty? Was mercy in this case not nepotism? Could a head of state agree to be blackmailed, especially by his own daughter? And how would Hitler react? Would this pardon not confirm to the Führer what he generally accused the Italians of, namely, that they were all traitors?

Chapter 10

The Pope and the Anti-Christ

At five o'clock in the morning Mussolini called "comrade" Wolff. The former SS general recounted the conversation verbatim in various reports. The basic thrust was always the same, to find out what Mussolini wanted and Wolff's reply. He basically evaded the Ciano issue, saying that it was solely an Italian matter; as an SS commander, he was not allowed to take a position. But the Duce begged him further; personally and confidentially the general certainly could give him an answer. "What would you do in my position?" was the question. The answer: "Remain firm!" Wolff also confirmed that it would harm Mussolini's reputation with the Führer if he did not carry out the sentence.

With a delay, at nine o'clock instead of at six, the condemned men were taken from their cells and driven by car to the shooting range at the Verona Rifle Club where they were tied to chairs. Perhaps a few placating words from Wolff to the leader of the Italian Social Republic would have convinced him to disregard Hitler's expectations. He did not find these words, although the five men who were shot that morning had only attempted to do what Wolff would do one year later—namely, to get out of a hopeless war, against the will of the head of state. Wolff also ran the temporary risk of facing a firing squad, but he was luckier (or more skillful) than the renegades of Fascism.

If the Highest SS and Police Führer in Italy had been forced to objectively evaluate his own situation, he would have had to admit that he was already in the process of betraying his supreme Führer and Commander in Chief—at least in his mind. Up to that point, he had always interpreted Party dogma his own way, and only followed it if it did not interfere with his own inclinations. As he saw it there had never been a philosophically well-formulated National Socialist ideology. Anyone who believed only in the swastika and the principle that the Führer was always right, and could make no mistakes. Yet SS Obergruppenführer Wolff increasingly doubted the validity of that statement, because he could see that a coming twilight of the gods would not spare him either. As long as there were peacetime successes and the victories at war showed that the so-called Providence would lead to greatness and honor the German people through Adolf Hitler, Wolff had never doubted that principle. However, the military defeats and the political slip-ups led him to doubt Hitler and the system allowing just one man to make every decision alone: less power to the Führer and more authority to his advisors. Popitz and Langbehn wanted to win the SS over to their revolt against dictatorship with that formula and now Wolff and Himmler were pursuing their ideas.

The two guardians of the Führer's unlimited power still used the alibi of being in enemy territory during their conversations with the "enemies of the state." Wolff's attempts to venture into uncharted waters while he was "viceroy of Italy" could hardly be justified by this line of reasoning anymore. Badoglio had collaborated with the enemy on a military level, Ciano in the political arena; Wolff could not achieve anything in either of those areas at present, and so he ventured onto the thin ice of ideological heresy. He looked for contacts and allies in the clergy where, according to orthodox SS teaching, there lurked the archenemies of the Germanic soul.

He went about this through Ernst Freiherr von Weiszäcker, German ambassador to the Holy See. The ambassador was a traditionalist of the Protestant faith and a fundamentally tolerant Swabian liberal. That was the main reason Ribbentrop, whom he had served as secretary of state, had appointed him to what appeared to be a meaningless position. But in the meantime, the embassy became important, because in the Vatican, separated only by a white line from the city of Rome, the diplomats of the warring countries met in close quarters. Therefore, Wolff's question whether anyone among the politicians on the enemy side was willing to discuss a peace agreement, was dealing with the right person in Weiszäcker, who could easily hold such discussions. Both men agreed that Germany could neither win the war nor dictate the peace. That was the kind of thinking keeping the Gestapo and the special courts busy at that time.

With this kind of trust, Wolff said during one of their conversations that he would like to discuss the world situation with the highest dignitary in the Vatican. The ambassador was glad to help, and with the hesitation customary among diplomats, he told Wolff to come and meet the rector of the German theological college at the Vatican, Dr. Ivo Zeiger, a Jesuit priest, at the embassy at the beginning of December 1943. The priest was surprised—he later admitted—that such a high ranking SS officer, who in addition to that had been Himmler's right-hand man until recently, would get together with a Jesuit, of all people, since the order of the Society of Jesus was "on the black list of the authorities of the Third Reich." (It must be remembered that Heinrich Himmler as well as Wolff had always secretly admired the rules and discipline of the Society of Jesus and copied some of the regulations of the Jesuit order when establishing the General SS.)

Wolff did not come to the meeting alone and brought the shrewd SS Standartenführer Eugen Dollmann as a witness. Wolff hoped that the Vatican would support him in his search for a bridge to the western Allies. The man who had left a Christian church to become one of Himmler's SS generals had a powerful motto; in their fight against the godless Marxists, Leninists, and Stalinists, the Germans are in the final analysis also defending the Catholic Church, therefore Hitler and the Pope should actually, in principle, be allies. But up to now the Vatican Curia had not endorsed the struggle undertaken by Germany.

The priest did not list the things that separated their positions. He barely mentioned the "horrible measures" that "were taken by German officials behind the frontline." He mentioned in particular that the clergy in Poland was being persecuted and that awful things were taking place in the concentration camps. At that time, the priest possibly did not know about the systematic murder of the Jews. But those hints were enough for Wolff to avoid arguing with him. Father Zeiger noted Wolff's answer: "Yes, these things are very sad. I thank fate—or if you will, the Lord God—that I had nothing to do with those ugly things." The words—Zeiger noted—"stuck in his memory even more" because Wolff "made some sharp critical comments..." in the presence of Standartenführer Dollmann and the ambassador, "which according to the way the system worked at the time...could have been dangerous."

As Wolff assured the Jesuit priest that "as the German Police Chief in Italy with the top responsibility" it was his "firm intention to avoid all unnecessary difficulties for the Holy See, the Church, and other institutions." Zeiger took Wolff to task and said that "in a fight with partisans on the Slovenian border an older leader of the Carthusian religious order whom I know well was taken prisoner by the Germans. I know that he certainly did nothing wrong politically."

Father Zeiger's request did not fall on deaf ears. Several days later Josip Edgar Leopold—the Carthusian father superior—was released from jail in Laibach on condition that in the future he move to a South Tyrolean cloister of his order. By the way, he had been arrested for a reason, and had been found guilty in a criminal trial for offering support to the partisans, and, for that, had been sentenced to death. With his release, Wolff passed the first test of being well regarded by the Church. "The Vatican wants to find out . . . who this General Wolff really is," Leopold later recalled.

Shortly after that Wolff was tested a second time. Donna Virginia Agnelli, the wife of one of the owners of the Fiat automobile companies, also lived in Rome at the time—where she was at the center of the most influential social circles—she was also by birth a Princess Bourbon del Monte. The Fiat companies made handsome profits during the war, but the Princess nevertheless thought the Germans were even worse barbarians than the Fascists. She didn't even attempt to hide her thoughts when she spoke to friends and acquaintances on the telephone, but because she knew that her conversations were tapped, she spoke in English, never even considering, however, that someone in the SD understood the language. In short, the Italian police arrested the Princess.

Since the top clergy, and even a cardinal, often visited her drawing room, many in the Vatican were concerned about the Princess' accommodations. They also remembered having occasionally met SS Colonel Eugen Dollmann, a sensitive art connoisseur and brilliant conversationalist, in the Agnelli drawing room. Dollmann was now wearing his black SS uniform thickly decorated with a great deal of tinsel. Someone spoke to him; he went to Wolff and obtained orders to free Virginia Agnelli from prison. The Highest SS and Police Führer also helped her travel to Switzerland and his reward was the promise that the Pope would see him in a secret private audience.

The meeting took place in the afternoon of May 10, 1944. It was the first and certainly the only time that Pius XII met with a leading SS officer. Wolff, wearing a civilian suit, came to the cloister of the Salvatorian

Order, near the Vatican, where the prior, Dr. Pankratius Pfeiffer, would escort him to the Pope's private library. On this occasion also, Dr. Dollmann was used as go-between and escort, to request the release of a prisoner almost as a way of gaining entry into the Vatican. The son of a Roman lawyer was in prison for his Communist activities. Wolff promised he would try. But the case only progressed slowly. The prisoner remained in custody almost a month; he was released only a few hours before the Germans pulled out of Rome on June 5, 1944.

Wolff, who spoke no Italian, could converse with the Pope in German. What they discussed and whether the Highest SS and Police Chief agreed to anything with the Pontifex Maximus of the Catholic Church is still kept secret. They agreed to maintain confidentiality and there were no witnesses present. The Vatican had given no notice of this meeting; they had not even recorded it on the visitor's list. Understandably, the SS general was also careful not to publicize the meeting at first. It would be revealed only many years after the war. During the one-hour conversation, he probably argued once more that the enemies of atheism had to fight the Bolsheviks together.

Wolff often wrote about that event, but in many pages he managed to say almost nothing. Despite the many words, he kept his promise of secrecy. In several sentences, he quoted the Pope verbatim—using his astounding memory. "Smiling, the Pope said: 'How much misfortune could have been avoided had God led you to me earlier!'"

It seems strange for the highest authority in the Catholic church to have said that, since it implies a criticism of God for not bringing Karl Wolfffrom Darmstadt together with Eugenio Pacelli, the current Pope in Rome, in time. Pius XII cannot have viewed the situation so naively; he was a priest with a lot of experience of the world. From his many diplomatic missions, he was well aware of his own influence as well as that of an SS Obergruppenführer. When bidding farewell, he was also to have said, "You are doing something difficult, General Wolff!" Almost the identical words were supposedly said to Martin Luther in 1521 at the Reichstag in Worms as he began his mission. We cannot say whether the Pope or the SS general remembered that quote.

On the other hand, we do know that Wolff, getting ready to take his leave, stood at attention on the threshold and gave the Nazi salute with his right arm raised. The Pope viewed the gesture as a matter of habit, attaching no other significance to it. Wolff never mentioned that detail in recalling his audience with the Pope.

The many accounts that appeared over several decades may have led the Vatican to keep a detailed record of everything the SS general said about Pius XII. The Vatican is interested in sainthood for Pope Pacelli, and that strictly regulated procedure requires that everything known about the life and work of the subject must be carefully recorded. The consistory of the archbishopric of Munich and Freising heard the retired general as witness, recorded his statements and requested at the same time that these be kept confidential. The consistory wrote Wolff a letter dated March 28, 1972, thanking him. It also emerged from this letter that Wolff had provided a "record" for the files of his "conversations with Adolf Hitler from September through December 1943 regarding the instructions for the occupation of the Vatican and the abduction of the Pope." It may be assumed that in the course of the procedure of beatification this episode from the history of the Third Reich will be examined and possibly even cleared up.

The events are not as clear as Wolff described them. Following his report, no one besides Heinrich Himmler and himself were to be informed of Hitler's decisions. It was a State Secret. Documents, orders of any kind, or even a hint in some file cannot be found. In all probability they never existed. What does exist and in writing at the time were only Hitler's two statements, already mentioned in the *Table Talk*. One is confirmed by an annotation by Joseph Goebbels in his diary on July 27, 1943, two days after the fall of the Duce, where he mentions Hitlerintention to occupy the Vatican. Kidnapping the Pope, however, was not mentioned. The files also show that Martin Bormann, secretary to the Führer and unquestionably the most influential person within the permanent entourage, had a fanatical hatred of the Catholic church, the clergy, and most certainly the Pope. There is also no evidence showing that in those days he repeatedly mentioned that the undefended Vatican could be neutralized in one nonviolent sweep of the hand. On top of that, because Hitler was convinced that the Pope was involved in the fall of the Duce, it is certain that at the end of July 1943 and in the first weeks of August, acts of violence against the seat of the Catholic church were taken into consideration. It is therefore also logical that Hitler had discussed it with Wolff, the highest police officer in Italy. The "personal credit" that Wolff frequently mentions also makes it absolutely believable that the talkative Hitler did not carefully measure his words.

He no longer could remember on which day he was given the order, but he was able to write down a rather long dialogue verbatim about the project decades later. Obviously, he was given his mission before Mussolini had been returned to the political stage—meaning before September 14, 1943. Wolff had, as previously mentioned, two appointments with Hitler shortly before the arrival of the Duce at headquarters, one lasting ten minutes, the other twenty minutes. The shorter time span would have been just enough to speak of his first experiences and measures taken in Italy. During the second, Wolff introduced Professor Tassinari, his candidate for the position of prime minister of Italy, as already described.

During the following period, three times in October, twice in November, and once in December of 1943, Wolff had appointments with Hitler. According to his description, he reported on his preparations to occupy the Vatican, and at the same time, the information that he had come to a negative conclusion by trying to make it clear to Hitler how impractical it was to occupy the Vatican and kidnap the Pope. His reasoning was that the Church was the only authority that was recognized by all Italians, and whoever took action against it risked a popular rebellion. At some point in this time period, Wolff must have sent an oral message to the Pope through his colleague, Eugen Dollmann, who always maintained good relations with the Vatican. According to Dollmann the message was that the Pope had nothing to fear from the Germans as long as he, Karl Wolff, remained the Supreme SS and Police Führer in Italy. Were he to be replaced, it would be a sign that a harder policy had been decided.

Apparently all of this confirms the fact that Wolff was "completely credible," according to the Jesuit Dr. Burkhardt Schneider, professor of recent Church history, "in recording the instructions he received from Hitler for a 'liquidation' of the Vatican, and describing his efforts to block this order." However, Hitler's intentions, as Wolff described them, were soon no longer a State Secret. At the end of September 1943 everyone in Rome was talking openly about an action against the Vatican being imminent. Indeed the entire area of Vatican City was surrounded by police checkpoints, but this was mostly to prevent the German deserters and the opponents of the Italian regime from finding extraterritorial shelter there.

On October 7, an RSI (Italian Social Republic) radio broadcast announced that as a precaution quarters were being prepared for the Pope in Germany. That was a false report. Consul Eitel Friedrich Moellhausen, at the time the highest-ranking German diplomat at the German embassy in Rome under Mussolini's new regime, wrote that it was "not true that the Germans had decided to take the Holy Father away from Rome... All of these statements were exaggerations. Those responsible for German policy, including Hitler, had at most only occasionally considered those issues, but it never came down to a serious decision." "It is, however, possible" admitted Moellhausen, "that in the Party and in the SS there were men who would advocate such an atrocity."

No doubt the consul was mainly thinking of Goebbels, Himmler, and above all Bormann.

Hardly anyone considered Mussolini as having any importance. "Every German and every Italian...is convinced that the Duce and the Italian government have no further authority," said a report at the end of June written by the commanding general's staff. In the next report, already written under Wolff, it was determined at the beginning of August that "the development of the general situation," especially in the east and in Italy, as well as the strong increase of attacks and air raids . . . do not encourage . . . a positive attitude among the population toward the common prosecution of the war." The report concluded, "that it was not possible to handle the conscription of the age group as planned for work in Germany nor to get the terrible situation with the partisans under control . . . There is increasing fear on the part of officials of working with the Germans. "Seven Germans were killed by an attack on a restaurant in Genoa, seventy communists were shot and all restaurants and bars were closed for a week."

There were many signs indicating that Wolff, sooner or later, would no longer be involved in the war just sitting at his desk. Already in April 1944 his entire region was declared a "partisan war territory" and many protective measures became compulsory for all Germans. Secret instructions came from Himmler in June ordering "the construction of an SS fortification, to research a site for the reconnaissance of the Italian border defense installations." Also the Karst Caves in Krain and on the Adriatic coastal region—all of this being part of Wolff's territory—were to be explored as defensive positions. He now also had to clear out any areas that could fall into enemy hands during an unavoidable retreat in the near future. Everything that could be used by the Reich was to be removed; machines, vehicles, precious metal, resources, finished goods, food, even livestock and horses were taken north. From the area around Rome 35,000 heads of livestock were removed in this manner; it would have been twice as many had the enemy not advanced so quickly. Indeed, they did not leave only the "scorched earth" as it happened in the east, but the Allies would encounter enough difficulties in an emptied land since their soldiers were quite a mixed society: Americans, Britons, Canadians and other units from the Empire, French and North Africans, a Polish legion.

After the war Wolff prided himself a great deal in the fact that he saved many art and cultural treasures from being destroyed in the areas threatened by fighting by transporting them to safe locations. The initiative for this, however, came from Hitler, who ordered Wolff and Rahn to have cultural possessions moved by professionals from central Italy to Rome and Florence because there, under the status of the open city, they would be fairly well protected. In the second half of July there was fighting in the area around Florence and Wolff's representatives, with the help of soldiers, collected paintings from the houses and castles that were already in the line of enemy artillery fire.

Wolff reported one such rescue to Himmler by telegram. It involved two paintings by Lucas Cranach, entitled "Adam" and "Eve." Wolff remembered that "the Führer . . . during his visit to Florence" (on October 28, 1940) had "particularly appreciated" those pictures. Now they were brought to Bergamo and Wolff asked in his telegram whether they "should be taken to Führer headquarters so that the Führer could be in control of the famous pictures that we saved."

Until then Wolff had always opposed this method of collecting art. He soon discovered that Marshal Hermann Göring had many freight cars of such stolen property attached to the back of his special train by an art commission working for him. Wolff told Mussolini, who absolutely forbade the export of all artwork, thus forcing Göring to leave without his valuable loot. However, now there was an opportunity to please the Führer; for that Wolff was prepared to make an exception. But at headquarters, the offer was rejected, with a heavy heart. The Cranach paintings, as well as a number of other works of art, were to be stored in the South Tyrol, so that "for now the authority of the Italian state would not be offended." "However, it had to be made clear that the place where the paintings were located would, in any case, be under German protection."

A few days before the exchange of telegrams, Wolff was at Führer headquarters, together with the man he could not let travel unguarded and for whose security and presence he was totally responsible. The day of the visit with Hitler was July 20, 1944—a day that not only became memorable because the two dictators saw each other for the last time, before they both died almost simultaneously nine months later. It was also the day of the assassination attempt, when the conspirators—mainly army officers—wanted to save the German people and the Reich from complete catastrophe with a bomb attack to kill Hitler. There were no great state initiatives taken on that visit, as had always been customary, since the meeting took place incidentally. Mussolini wanted to check on the Italian nationals whom fate had brought to the Reich. This was not only four divisions of his future army; the more urgent cases were the so-called "civilian internees," the slave workers, who had refused to serve in the Italian army and were, therefore, confined to work camps. After various visits together with Wolff, Mussolini wanted to negotiate with Hitler about the fate of those Italians.

At the end of his trip to Germany, with his small entourage and Wolff, Mussolini was expected at the "Wolfsschanze" at 3:00 p.m. on the train platform. It was noticeable that the guards were inspecting the special train particularly carefully this time. As the guest and the host greeted each other, Hitler only offered his left hand to Mussolini, contrary to his habit. A black cape hid the fact that he could only move his right arm with difficulty. As the two walked into the third circle, with Wolff following them, Hitler recounted what had happened: approximately two and a half hours before, during the situation report in one of the cabins, a bomb exploded under a heavy oak table. Several people were killed and many others were injured.

The main foreign office interpreter, Dr. Paul Schmidt, accompanied the group to the scene. He saw "a picture of devastation," as if there had been a heavy air raid. "In shock," Mussolini's eyes "almost popped out of his head." After Hitler also showed the Duce his uniform that had been completely torn to shreds by the blast and the singed hairs on his neck, did the "superstitious southerner" rate Hitler's survival as "a sign from heaven" and a guarantee of victory.

It was agreed that the "war-internees would be transferred to the status of free workers or set to work as assistants within the framework of the German Wehrmacht." That was the communiqué. But Wolff was much more interested in the repercussions of the assassination attempt, what the investigation would reveal, who would have to be killed, and who would inherit the positions that now became free within the power apparatus of the Third Reich. It would lead us too far from our subject to describe the conspirators' plan, their connections, the course of action, and finally the reasons for their failure. It was the seriously wounded Colonel Claus Count Schenk von Stauffenberg who brought the bomb, equipped with a time detonator, in his brief case, placed it under the map table in the meeting room, and left headquarters immediately after the explosion. He returned to Berlin where he was to take over the leadership of the revolt. He was very quickly identified as the assassin and had already mistakenly alerted his co-conspirators with the news over the telephone that Hitler was dead.

Upon hearing this, they had begun taking over in the garrisons using the code word "Walküre." Due to a ridiculous coincidence, their plan failed in a decisive place, the capital of the Reich, where the occupation of the government quarter was to be handled by the guard regiment. An officer of that unit, who was told that the SS had murdered Hitler and that he must thwart their putsch, was able to speak with the "dead" Hitler on the telephone. Hitler ordered him to shoot anyone "who tries to disobey my orders." The rebellion fell apart.

From the point of view of the "Wolfsschanze" what mattered the most was to get the Wehrmacht units stationed in Germany under control. They reported to the Supreme Commander of the replacement army Senior General Friedrich Fromm. He was suspected of being a conspirator and was dismissed for that reason. Hitler considered Himmler, the most loyal of his loyal henchmen, as Reichsführer SS and Chief of the German police, Reich Minister of the Interior and holder of other positions as the least dangerous successor to Fromm. Wolff described, as "one of the few" who was present at this appointment, how Hitler asked the supreme commanders of the three sectors of the Wehrmacht for their opinion regarding this change. Göring's comment was, "My Führer, why, on this sad occasion, at which the only good thing is that you are still alive, don't you make Himmler Minister of War? Then we would finally have a clear set-up again." (As quoted by Wolff.)

According to Wolff, this was to be the "reform that was already long overdue." But Himmler, "true to his hesitant manner" thought about it and finally answered in a quiet, pathetic voice: "Mein Führer, I'll be able to manage the way I am." Then Hitler is supposed to have said to him: "Fly immediately to Berlin and take care of things at the source of the fire. You have every authority. Step in! Better too much and too harsh than too little." Together the Reichsführer SS and his Obergruppenführer, once again as close as they had ever been, drove to the airport. On the way, Wolff asked Himmler why he had turned down the Ministry of War. "Ah, Wölfchen," Himmler is supposed to have said, "the chubby one" (as General Field Marshal Wilhelm Keitel, Chief of the OKW, was called in the highest circles) "stood across from me, and he was always so decent. I would have taken his position away!"

Heinrich Himmler was used to stopping at nothing; stepping over dead bodies, even millions of them. But, according to Wolff, he was so sensitive that he could not manage to take the job away from a field marshal who was called a "Lackey" by his officers because he only said what

Hitler wanted to hear, and proved to be more obedient than competent. But before wondering about Himmler's soft heart, we should ponder the reasons why the Reichsführer SS happened to take the Highest SS and Police Führer in Italy, of all people, with him to the criminal court in Berlin. It would have been more fitting to take the Head of the Gestapo and a number of executioners. Did Hitler think that Wolff would be better acquainted with the circles of resistance than the Gestapo official who was responsible for them? Wolff and Himmler had withstood the critical Langbehn and Popitz affair together, coming out of it unscathed, although the Gestapo Chief and SS Obergruppenführer Heinrich Müller had set up the intrigue very cleverly against both of them. Dr. Langbehn was still in Gestapo custody because of his conspiracy with OSS in Switzerland, but he revealed nothing about his conversations with the SS leaders about replacing Hitler, knowing full well that he could sign his own death warrant with that information.

Popitz was still free, but it was a foregone conclusion that he would now be arrested. What would he testify? Perhaps that is the reason Himmler felt it was advisable to have his accomplice at his side and not near Hitler. Hadn't they both pleaded for limits to Hitler's omnipotent power? And hadn't they negotiated with people who were now to be persecuted? It is a fact that Himmler proceeded cautiously in chasing the enemies of the state; after landing in Berlin, he and Wolff certainly did not run directly to the source of the fire, the building of the Reich Ministry of War on Bendlerstrasse. At first, they waited to see which way the wind was blowing. They made sure their offices and the government quarter were secured by the Waffen SS units stationed in the Reich capital, and made telephone calls around the world. Himmler did not go to the Bendlerstrasse until two days after the assassination attempt. SS Obergruppenführer Ernst Kaltenbrunner, Chief of the Security Police and of the SD, the successor to Reinhard Heydrich, was in charge until then. Wolff was no longer with Himmler, but rather with Obergruppenführer Hans Jüttner, who as Chief of the Command Main Office had to provide recruits for the Waffen SS. He now became Himmler's representative in his function as Chief of the Replacement Army. Skorzeny asked himself: "Himmler was never in the military. How could he take on this task along with all his other duties?" At the same time, Wolff was given another appointment and became officially Plenipotentiary General of the German Wehrmacht in Italy.

He could now boast how his authority extended in every region between the Alps and the Apennines, between Carinthia and France. There were areas in which no German soldier and even less a Fascist militiaman could be in unless he wanted to desert to the partisans. Some of those units actually collected taxes that were made available to their leadership, and the orders of their leaders counted for more than those of police officers or officials who sympathized with the freedom fighters anyway. The partisan units were located mostly in difficult-to-reach mountain regions from where, during occasional advances, they supplied themselves with weapons, ammunition, and food. Many of the members of these units were highwaymen in the tradition of a land that one hundred years before still respected the brigand as an honest professional. However, most of them were patriots fighting for the freedom of their homeland. Almost all were revolutionaries who wanted to bring about a better order of society. However, they all wanted a different kind of order.

Their fighting power was different. It tended to diminish the more the number of brigands surpassed that of the patriots in the group. The strongest units operated on the French border in the west and on the Yugoslav border in the east. They received instructions and deliveries of material from the Allies. As Wolff planned a "week of fighting the partisans," for which he employed his forces in massive numbers, over eighty of his soldiers died, up to a third of them Italian militiamen, and there were over three hundred wounded and thirty missing. If one believes the victory report issued by his office, his soldiers killed more than 1,600 partisans, took almost as many prisoners, and rescued some 6,000 forced laborers from the "liberated" area. They captured a lot of artillery, including two salvo guns, six flame throwers, middle and light grenade throwers, tank defense weapons, many small arms, a large quantity of ammunition, hundreds of vehicles of every kind. They also blew up more than three hundred combat positions and shelters. So it was a small campaign against a significantly armed power and the Senior General Heinrich von Vietinghoff acknowledged Wolff's "very special contributions" to this success.

He had already been awarded two more decorations in May 1944, which he must have missed terribly until then: in addition to his Iron Cross First and Second Class from the First World War, he now received the bars that were added to them, for additional acts of war. Normally, every one of these decorations must be individually justified with the description of a war incident, but during the final year of the war, one was no longer that particular, especially for a general who was walking around without the insignia of bravery. The fact that Wolff had the bars of both classes pinned to his chest on the same day, namely May 29,1944, leads to the assumption that he was either being rewarded for an uncommon operation or that they were given to him late. After all, up to that point he had hardly had the opportunity to approach the enemy any closer than one thousand meters.

But the bars weren't enough. On November 11, 1944, the Supreme Commander Southwest filed the suggestions on the regulation forms to decorate "Wolff, Karl, born on May 13, 1900, in Darmstadt, with the German Gold Cross." The large, ostentatious medal was worn on the lower right breast and was named "German fried egg" by the soldiers. In the section "former employment in the war since 1939" that was typewritten, surely not without Wolff's help, two bits of information are worth noting. It states: "August 26, 1939–September 8, 1943, officer of the Reichsführer SS to the Führer." After the war, Wolff placed great value upon having been "Liaison officer of the Waffen SS to the Führer" because direct cooperation with Himmler could appear compromising. In the same column, it states after the list of Wolff's Italian posts: "also Chief of the Personal Staff of the Reichsführer SS since August 26, 1939." This may have still formally been the case at the time; he was not relieved from this post nor replaced by a successor. However, he was no longer involved in the activities from the time he was confined to the hospital at Hohenlychen. Himmler, his secretary, Dr. Rudolf Brandt, and the higher adjutants were all managing the "Main Office of the Personal Staff." On the other hand, there was a new "Officer of the Reichsführer SS to the Führer," SS Gruppenführer Hermann Fegelein, who married Gretl Braun, the sister of Hitler's lover, Eva Braun. Fegelein had thus become "the left hand" at his brother-in-law's side.

The OKH agreed to the suggestion for the decoration: on December 9, 1944, Wolff was decorated with the German Gold Cross. The award was justified, among other things, because "using predominantly Italian forces, with only weak secondary German units...was responsible for great undertakings in areas completely contaminated by partisans...leading to a sweeping success by completely destroying the partisans." Wolff "earned outstanding achievements for the military direction of the war as well as the maintenance of war production in the Italian territory." He was "worthy of the high decoration...with particularly high motivation." Such massive praise must have whetted his appetite for further decorations. The next step would be from the Knight's Cross to the Iron Cross. Wolff occasionally said that he had already been recommended for this medal, but the war was over before the award reached him. The snail's pace of the military bureaucracy cost him a necklace that, by the sixth year of the war, was almost a part of a general's uniform. The situation reports from the local positions sounded less glorious than the recommendations for medals, though. In these, it was stated, among other things: "For sustained fighting of the partisans, the current forces are not enough." And again, "Individual units are in control of their territories and have...taken over the administration. The organization can be counted on to continue to strengthen and separate groups are joining together so that in the future, planned operations with larger forces under united command can be expected."

On the other hand, the merging of the Highest SS and Police Führer and the plenipotentiary General of the Wehrmacht simplified the united operations of all available units in the war against the partisans. Wolff was therefore in command of an army of far more than one hundred thousand men, who represented a conglomeration of units having different morale and motivation, different nationalities, weapons, training, and capabilities as soldiers. "Only very few Italian units," it said in one situation report, "have proven to be reliable." In these forces, included units that spoke neither German nor Italian; they had been recruited from war prison camps in the East, and the men had joined in mostly because they didn't want to starve behind barbed wire. Next to Russian and Turkmen battalions, there was also one of Georgians; on one operation, it shrank by 120 men, who, together, deserted to the partisans. German soldiers stationed with the commanders of the Wehrmacht were certainly not top-quality fighters, otherwise they would have been sent to the front long before. The propaganda leaflets distributed by the Allied forces were successful even among them, not just with the Slav volunteers and the Italians; there were more and more deserters, and the population in the cities and towns willingly granted them help.

That pessimism and defeatism were to spread like an epidemic throughout Wolff's army was only to be expected. After the occupation of Rome on June 4, the Allies landed in Normandy. In the middle of August, there was another such landing on the French Mediterranean coast. In September, Allied soldiers had reached the German border near Trier. One after the other, the Romanians and Bulgarians declared war on Germany. In mid-October 1944, Hitler, in what was obviously his final attempt, called up the Volkssturm (German territorial army). In Italy, he was continually able to temporarily stop the advance of the enemy further north, but the population expected—as was written in the situation report—"the rapid extension of the fighting to northern Italy."

Mussolini's entourage had double the reasons to fear such a development. Not only was the enemy threatening them; the retaliation of their own countrymen would be even worse. The Italian people blamed the Fascists for the misfortune that had befallen Italy because of the war. The Fascist functionaries had experienced very little of this until then. In their idyllic location on Lake Garda, they saw streams of enemy bombers daily drawing lines of condensation in the sky, but they fell almost exclusively upon the German cities on the other side of the Alps. Occasionally a low-flying aircraft chased through the valley, and they had to seek cover because the enemy in the sky shot everything that moved, be it cars, boats, or persons. It was uncomfortable, but it was war. What could the people do about bombs falling on train stations, factories, and bridges in the cities and when their apartments were bombed out and people were killed? The bad news was easier to accept if one could always sleep peacefully, eat well and drink plenty on the banks of Lake Garda. In the restaurants, waiters quietly served their menus without requiring ration coupons—only it was more expensive than before. Everything came from the black market. But what was the big deal? Why should anyone save, in the face of an insecure future?

It was precisely this kind of uncertainty that caused such worries for Mussolini's entourage. "Victory or death" was still the official battle cry. Now, however, victory seemed more unlikely, and death a very real possibility—unless there was a way to avoid the noose; but there was very little time left. By mid-October, the enemy was already able to temporarily block important roads at the level of the Po River with its artillery fire. The Germans had successfully forced the Allies back a few kilometers, but it was easy to see that with one surprise advance, they could quickly reach the southern edge of the Alps. Rahn and Wolff addressed the issue at their residence on Lake Garda in passing at first but then officially that it could be advisable to begin sending away the women and children to safety; every man would fight with more energy and unconditionally knowing that nothing could happen to his family.

Up to a point Wolff was sensitive to these concerns. He knew that his two families were protected from the war in every way that was humanly possible. His wife Frieda lived with their four children in rural peace on the Tegernsee in Rottach-Egern. His wife Ingeborg, because of his transfer to Italy, had secured luxurious quarters in the Austrian

Salzkammergut with the three children in a castle on the Wolfgangsee near the famous guesthouse "Zum Weissen Rösl." The decision regarding quarters for the prominent Fascists, however, did not belong to either Wolff or Rahn. They had to ask Hitler. Some Italians, wishing to be deported to Switzerland, were easily rejected because the Swiss were expected to block such an influx. Also that kind of exodus would be viewed throughout the world as fleeing a sinking ship.

The Italians also argued as to who would probably be allowed in the last bastion, the Alpine fortress. Only prominent figures? Or also the armed forces? If at the beginning the talk was of tens of thousands, the Fascist party leadership reduced the number down to a few hundred chosen ones. Their shelter should be hard to reach, easy to guard and defend, but on the other hand not too far removed from civilized areas. If such a place existed on the southern edge of the Alps inside the Italian border, the partisans were already operating there.

Out of necessity, the top Fascists finally accepted the offer of a place to stay on the Arlberg. If they were in danger there, they could always retreat to southern Germany or over the mountain paths into Liechtenstein, and from there, trickle into Switzerland. The wives of the ministers, state secretaries and such moved with their children and servants to the plush winter sports hotel in Zürs, as guests of the Reich. To the majority of the Fascists in danger—meaning several tens of thousands—the mountain seclusion did not provide enough space. In the following weeks and months, they continued their escape north to the Frankenland between Würzburg and Nuremberg. But the beds there were to a great degree already filled by those fleeing the bombing of the large German cities, so the refugees looked for lodging in southern Bavaria and Austria.

Wolff wanted at least to keep the men in the south. Made up of Italians, South Tyroleans and other ethnic Germans he put together a unit that grew to no more than a battalion, but as the "24th Infantry Division of the SS, Kärst riflemen," it received a name and an emblem. From the same group, Wolff recruited volunteers for a "29th Infantry Division of the SS," which was given the ancient Roman symbol of the axe, showing their Italian-Fascist origin. That unit is also mentioned in the war diary of the OKW, where one can read, "A volunteer unit of the Waffen SS in the 14th army was given the name as Waffen SS Infantry Brigade (Ital) Nr. 1. It did not prove itself and therefore disappeared again." How could it be otherwise? since the Italians were justified in their opinion that they only fought for the Germans and, in doing so, they were shooting at their brothers and relatives. In the meantime, Italian divisions loyal to the monarchy were also fighting on the side of the Allies.

Wolff's volunteers obviously had a rather low turnout, otherwise he never would have thought of sending weapons and equipment for 1,500 soldiers to Himmler to help in a crisis. He could possibly have acquired some of this equipment from the partisans.

On January 31, 1945, he wrote the cover letter to this "small contribution to my position." Himmler had been the Supreme commander of the newly formed Army Group "Weichsel" for a week. With this group, he was to fill a huge hole that had been torn open by the Red Army, paving the way to Pomerania and Brandenburg. Regardless of this desperate situation, Wolff used the hackneyed National Socialist phrases: "It is with pride and confidence that we SS men look toward the gigantic task and responsibility the Führer, in his unlimited trust, has newly bestowed upon you."

It became already clear within just a few days that this trust in Himmler's commanding capabilities was completely misplaced. The Reichsführer SS was not able to build up a strong enough front. He decimated his divisions in one defeat after another. Before that he had already failed as military commander on the Upper Rhine. He had pushed for both assignments, hoping to win fame and respect with Hitler. One of his rivals for Hitler's favor, Reichsleiter Martin Bormann, had supported Himmler's plans and, at the same time, successfully speculated on his failure! Since then the Reichsführer SS avoided Führer headquarters as much as possible and, moved increasingly by fear, was seeking opportunities to appear as a peacemaker, thus hoping to unload the responsibility for all that had happened on Hitler.

In his name, SS Gruppenführer and General of the Police Dr. Wilhelm Harster, who was stationed in Verona, conspired behind Wolff's back with Italian industrial leaders. They were all in shock at Mussolini's plans to nationalize industry; and they therefore intensified the integration of their operations with other international companies. Himmler's suggestions amounted to ending the fighting in Italy and France and have the entire German army march against the anti-capitalist Bolsheviks. The Western Powers would be free to join the campaign against the atheist Marxists. This was not a new idea; many Nazis had toyed with it. Wolff claimed he had already presented it to the Pope.

Now that the German armed forces were clearly reaching a point of collapse, they could not come to any kind of mutual understanding. In

August, Himmler had announced in Posen that whoever doubted the victorious outcome of the war would be mercilessly persecuted. On the other hand, in the meantime, he had sent his SD Chief, Walter Schellenberg, to meet with the Swedish banker Jakob Wallenberg, seeking to benefit from his connections with western politicians. To use such contacts, he was prepared to work with the former mayor of Leipzig, Dr. Carl Goerdeler, who had been arrested by the Gestapo as a ringleader of the resistance movement against Hitler. In order to make contact with President Franklin D. Roosevelt, he was even ready to seek an agreement with the archenemy of the Aryans. Through SS Standartenführer Kurt Becher, he offered to stop the transport to the extermination camps of Hungarian and Swiss Jews, if there was a chance to negotiate. The unmentioned underpinning all his suggestions was that Hitler had to die.

Chapter 11

"When everyone betrays..."

By the end of 1944, only a handful of higher SS officers were still fully loyal to Hitler. Their idol had not lived up to their expectations and to his promises. As long as he seemed to guarantee victory, they accepted what was increasingly displeasing them now: total dictatorship within Germany, ruthlessness on the outside, increased personal danger, wartime shortages and the barbaric persecution of the Jews, assuming they secretly dissented with that policy. They were not allowed to protest; inside the Black Brotherhood only orders and obedience had any kind of value. To terminate one's membership was dangerous, if not impossible; after all, a brotherhood is not a club. The lower ranks could at least cause their own dismissal by neglecting their jobs. But even the upper ranks, especially the full-time officer and the soldiers of the Waffen SS, risked their freedom and more if they tried to shed the belt buckle bearing the inscription "Our honor is loyalty." Having no other ways of showing their displeasure, SS officers took some small liberties with the rules of the brotherhood. It was their way of showing that they no longer agreed with everything Heinrich Himmler ordered.

As the Reichsführer's right hand and especially as a favorite of Hitler, Wolff could allow himself a bit of heresy. He didn't do this out of serious opposition. He felt the need to prevent arbitrariness and injustice and, when they occurred, he simply enjoyed showing some element of insubordination so that one was compelled to notice what a "great guy" he was. One writer refers to him as the "happy boy" of the SS. He had previously rejected that description during the Third Reich as suspicious since it involved the schmaltzy pop singer in an American movie in which a white singer pretended to be a black man (wearing "black face"). The warrior from Darmstadt wanted to be a knight without fear or reproach, as in the idealized version popular among high school teenagers in imperial Germany.

Therefore the SS Obergruppenführer and General of the Police would inevitably one day reach the fork in the road that was to draw him away from his leaders Hitler and Himmler. At first it happened almost imperceptibly, but later so fully that Wolff felt compelled to go off on his own. Retrospectively, it is difficult to determine when and where their paths began to separate. Perhaps it was already the case in January 1943 when Wolff visited the Warsaw Ghetto with Himmler and could personally experience how Nazism degraded people. Perhaps the change began in the spring of 1943 when he was very ill in Hohenlychen in a private room, cut off from his comrades on Himmler's orders, in the stillness as he pondered whether the Reichsführer was attempting to cause his death inconspicuously by the violent massage of Felix Kersten. He felt, therefore, that his heretical impulses were amply justified as he and Himmler discussed a change of regime with Popitz and Langbehn. He often sang the SS tune, "When everyone betrays, we will remain true." Where were the loyal ones now? They were at the very least thinking of jumping off a ship that was about to sink.

If one leafs through the "denazification certificates" that Wolff presented as evidence of his "good deeds" after the war during the denazification process and at the Munich trial, those flamboyant incidents added up during his time in Italy. In his letter to his ex-wife Frieda he rejoiced in the independence he had finally achieved. For example, he was now able to save an army staff officer in Italy from a court martial and perhaps a death sentence. The officer in question, on the occasion of the July 20, 1944, assassination attempt at the "Wolfsschanze," had not spoken of Hitler with the necessary awe, and was thus reported by a lieutenant seeking to be a hero. However, Wolff, as plenipotentiary general and lord of the manor, looked at the file and summoned the accused to his office. In a long and conciliatory conversation that did not even remotely resemble an interrogation, he interpreted the officer's statements as harmless enough and terminated the inquiry.

Wolff received a note of thanks from the Bishop of Padua in March 1945 for saving the life of an Italian laborer working for the German army postal service. The Italian had stolen some small packages, thus harming German troops—a sacrilege that ex-lance corporal Hitler could only accept if it was punished by death. Wolff understood that this would be seen as incomprehensible harshness for the Italian mentality. He listened sympathetically to the bishop's request for a pardon. The patriarch from Venice, Cardinal Piazza, wrote a note of thanks because the SS Obergruppenführer saved a nun of the order (who was of Jewish heritage and had converted to Christianity), from being added to the transport meant for the Jews. Wolff also protected a German soldier from court-martial when the military bureaucracy threatened to destroy him because he repeatedly complained about being punished for "neglecting the Nazi salute." As plenipotentiary general, Wolff stopped all the accusations on the spot, helped the soldier take his leave to go home, which had been blocked as punishment, and even had the soldier accompany him in his car as far as the Brenner Pass. Wolff presented all of these "good deeds" (and many more) after the war as proof that, even within the awful group of the SS, he had remained a good person.

The suspicion that he had done all of this only to create an alibi for the future would seem groundless. Wolff was satisfied to appear in the role of the powerful man who fought injustice according to the principle used quite frequently at the time, that "unnecessary harshness should be avoided." American historian John Toland examined Wolff's account and interviewed him at length about his life. Toland described him as a "stately, energetic, and admittedly fairly naïve man who ardently believed in National Socialism." He could never have been so naïve that all the atrocities of the Nazi regime were hidden from him until the end. He soothed his conscience by countering them with his "good deeds." The better circles of Darmstadt had already taught him that one could earn "personal credit" that way and a reputation as a respectable human being. During his time as an advertising agent, he could increase his credit (sometimes even financially) with those kinds of favors, and once he began moving into positions of power, he improved his system. He was helpful wherever he could be, including for the little people, as every case enriched his account.

Wolff's historic participation in the negotiations leading to the surrender of the German and Italian armed forces in Italy on May 2, 1945, was of a different nature. The lives of hundreds of thousands of soldiers on both sides were spared five or six days of pointless killing and dying. He also risked his life many times because he was in danger as someone guilty of treason or high treason, and he was threatened with death from enemy planes or partisans. This episode must be discussed since Wolff constantly made sure that these achievements were not forgotten.

In this case, too, success has many fathers. Others also took credit for the capitulation. For example, the diplomat, Dr. Rudolf Rahn, the all-purpose intellectual of the SS Dr. Eugen Dollmann, army General Hans Röttinger, the Swiss citizens Dr. Max Husmann and Max Waibel, the Italian Baron Luigi Parilli, and the U.S. citizen and German emigrant Gero von Schulze-Gävernitz, and several other participants. Many books and articles were published but Wolff never went beyond copies of taped conversations and numerous manuscript pages, despite his desire for publicity.

The reason behind "Operation Sunrise"—the cover name "Sunrise" came from OSS chief in Bern, Allen Dulles—was not due to any of the men mentioned previously, but rather to a historical figure who was to find out about the betrayal shortly before his death, namely, Benito Mussolini. As the year 1944 drew to a close, he wanted to find out from Wolff how this war, given Hitler's promises, could possibly end in victory. The Obergruppenführer saw this question as a challenge, since the person who was to be most affected by this activity was the last one to know, and because Wolff was afraid that Mussolini would inform Hitler. In those days of insecurity, everyone played not only his own game, but also a double game at the same time. During the war, as it would be demonstrated later on, Mussolini remained in epistolary contact, albeit sporadically, with Prime Minister Winston Churchill. He was carrying the evidence of this correspondence with him among his private papers when he fled. Had Mussolini wished to use that connection, Wolff could have prevented him from doing so by quickly ending the war.

The relationship between the two at the end of the year 1944 was no longer as warm as it had been earlier. The advisor and protector had increasingly changed his role into that of a guard. He became even more annoying when the nominal ruler of a rump Italy sought to shed the German intrusion into all Italian affairs. Against Hitler's will, Mussolini named his state "Italian Social Republic"—the word "Socialist" would have been acceptable, but he announced his intention to nationalize major industries. It was a relapse of sorts: Mussolini began his political career on the far left, in the most extreme wing of the Socialist party. Now the capitalists in Italy feared that he could actually enter into agreements with the underground Reds. Furthermore, he was planning to fire Minister of the Interior Buffarini-Guidi. He rightfully assumed that this corrupt fascist functionary was keeping Wolff and Rahn constantly posted on the most recent news emanating from the fascist snake pit. He even decided to break out of the political greenhouse on Lake Garda and experience the raw air of Italian reality, directly with the people. Milan was the largest city among those remaining under fascist and German control; he wanted to create a new center of operations there. On December 16, 1944, he gave a speech at the Lirico theater in Milan where he was enthusiastically cheered as in his best dictatorial times. Mussolini subtly but clearly showed how he was standing up against Hitler by stressing Italy's achievements and its suffering for the alliance, and warned how the Germans would take horrible revenge if the Italians attacked them from the rear.

Aside from his attempt to win more ground with the workers, Mussolini also quietly courted the clergy. Through Archbishop Cardinal Ildefonso Schuster of Milan he sought a connection to the Vatican and, further, to the Allies and the partisans. At the same time Wolff was also his rival because SS Standartenführer Walther Rauff, the SD Chief of the region, was ordered to make efforts in the same direction. His SS past, however, was not such a good reference for a benevolent operation; in the East, he had been in charge of the operation using gas vehicles where prisoners of the extermination camps were killed by carbon monoxide engine exhaust. In Italy, however, Wolff considered that Rauff had performed well; a few weeks before the end of the war, he recommended him for the Gold Cross. By then relations between Wolff and the Italian head of state had sunk to a form of indifferent coolness. They lied to each other in silence and deceived one another through subterfuge. Then in February 1945, when Buffarini-Guidi was replaced, Wolff lost his source of information. This meant that Mussolini was being watched more closely than ever before. At the beginning of March, police detective Otto Kisnat reported to the Duce as his new bodyguard, a gift from Heinrich Himmler. He was experienced in guarding high-ranking officials, and since he had to guarantee the physical safety of those he was protecting, he had to be constantly at his side.

Before Wolff could begin his efforts to make contacts in the west, he wanted to know how far he could safely go and what he could offer. He therefore flew to Berlin, where Hitler had transferred his headquarters on January 16, 1945. Even though air-raid sirens could be heard at the time, the dictator was still receiving his guests in the huge undamaged office of the Reich Chancellery. Ribbentrop was also present while Wolff reported on the situation in Italy. On February 6, both visitors were eager to find out how Germany was going to continue waging war. In the west, the enemy was already on German soil—in the Ardennes. The failed offensive had eaten up the last reserves of manpower and supplies, East Prussia was cut off, and the Red Army had reached the Oder. Day and night enemy planes were bombing the cities and the V1 and V2 rocket weapons that had been used with such confidence had not delivered the expected results. Wolff had already given up any hope of a wonder weapon, although Hitler hinted at a weapon of extermination so appalling in its results that it would only be used in the worst emergencies. Together with Ribbentrop, Wolff pleaded that one must also try for a political solution parallel to military efforts. Perhaps the enemies were now ready to turn against each other.

Hitler did not reply to all this, remained friendly, and did not openly reject the suggestion. His two visitors therefore assumed that he agreed to let them engage in efforts to make contact. Ribbentrop was counting on the fact that Swedish diplomats could establish the necessary connections. After his return to Lake Garda on February 8, Wolff called his officers from the Wehrmacht and SS together and ordered that even the slightest sign of contact from the enemy be reported to him immediately. As a result SS Obersturmbannführer Guido Zimmer, working for the SD in Milan, reported that he had recently had many conversations about the situation with a representative of Italian industrialists, Baron Luigi Parilli, and that they had also discussed the destruction of the Italian industrial potential in the event of a German retreat. Also his Swiss friends were seriously worried, because their supplies from Genoa and other Mediterranean ports would stop. The Swiss water power stations in the Alps would stop providing supplies of electricity to Italy. International big business feared, along with the destruction of operations in Italy, losses in Switzerland in the billions. The Italian economy was, in addition, also threatened by nationalization—first by Mussolini's radical behavior, and in the long term by the future liberators who had no idea that a "red belt" would form right behind their backs, reaching from the south of France across northern Italy to Tito's partisans and the rest of the Balkans.

Since Wolff did not want any such developments either, and because he saw clues that could divide the enemy in these arguments, he gave Parilli permission to travel to Switzerland. On February 21, 1945, he met with

Dr. Max Husmann, who ran a well-known boarding school not far from Lucerne for the sons of wealthy families. The two knew each other so well that the Swiss provided a security guarantee of 10,000 francs that no undesired arrival would slip into the Swiss Confederation. Husmann, for his part, was friends with Max Waibel, professional soldier and a major in the Swiss Secret Service at the time. Waibel kept in contact with Allen W. Dulles, who was officially in charge of the Middle European Center of the OSS (Office of Strategic Services) in Bern. He was the brother of future Secretary of State John Foster Dulles and was regarded in Switzerland as President Roosevelt's envoy.

A man in such a position must do his best to appear unobtrusive. But the Gestapo and the SD knew that elements of the German resistance had already met with Dulles many times, Dr. Langbehn among them. Dulles knew, on the other hand, that the Chief of the SD, Walter Schellenberg, occasionally exchanged news with Captain Roger Masson of the Swiss Secret Service, and that they had begun an operation competing with Parilli's initiatives. However, up to that point, Schellenberg's suggestions had consistently been turned down as not being serious. This background caused Dulles at first to refuse to see Parilli, who was connected to the SS, although the Baron, Waibel, and Husmann all assured him that the SS in Italy were different from anywhere else.

At the same time, Dulles wanted his Swiss friends to continue the conversations and he sent one of his colleagues, a German émigré living in Switzerland and a U.S. citizen, Dr. Gero von Schulze-Gaevernitz. When Parilli mentioned to him that one of his SS contacts was the art historian Dr. Dollmann from Rome, the atmosphere of the conversation became much friendlier. Dollmann and Gaevernitz knew each other from years before. The latter was related to a Ruhr industrial family from Stinnes, who financed Hitler with large sums of money before 1933. Fritz Thyssen the head of the family then had a falling out with the German chancellor and published a book in the United States entitled *I Paid Hitler*. Parilli was asked to make it clear to the SS officer that, according to the resolutions at the Casablanca conference in January 1943, there could be no peace negotiations. Only unconditional surrender was possible. Parilli avoided reporting this specific point to his contacts, because they would then have decided to end the dialogue altogether.

Wolff and his team had no idea that yet another competitor wanted to bypass them. SS Gruppenführer Ernst Kaltenbrunner, the Chief of Police and of the SD sent one of his espionage specialists, Sturmbannführer Wilhelm Höttl, who was Austrian-born like Kaltenbrunner, to see Dulles and, through another middleman, offered the capitulation of German forces in Austria. He was requesting in return that those territories receive special status after the war and would not be thrown in with the Nazis in the vast criminal proceedings. In Bern Höttl naturally understood that he could not possibly carry out such a capitulation. His offer was not taken seriously. Wolff would later have to deal with this idea once more.

On February 27, Parilli returned to Milan and reported to Obersturmbannführer Zimmer, who informed SS Gruppenführer and General of the Police Dr. Wilhelm Harster, who was stationed in Verona. How quickly the next stages of the operation developed revealed that events were heating up too quickly for all the participants. Harster wanted to inform Wolff as fast as possible that it would be possible to have a conversation with Dulles, but when he called at Lake Garda, he found out that the Obergruppenführer was on his way back from a meeting with Marshal Kesselring at his headquarters. Wolff was traveling through Verona on his way. Harster was in such a hurry with his news that he positioned himself on one of the main roads leading out of the city and waited there for Wolff. Since Rahn came with him, the three could have a roadside war counsel. They decided to discuss the next steps the following day at Lake Garda. They met in the evening of February 28: Wolff, Harster, Rauff from Milan, and Zimmer, who commanded other SS units. Ambassador Rahn wished to remain in the background and would only provide advice since his participation could imply that the negotiations went beyond military resolutions. It was decided that Dollmann and Zimmer would travel to Switzerland with Parilli on March 3.

The day before their departure, Rahn told Kesselring, who was affected most by the plans, that two SS scouts were being sent to make contact with the enemy. The highest ranking soldier in Italy wanted nothing to do with the matter. He would not break the oath that he had personally sworn to Hitler, and he would never become a traitor. After many long discussions, Rahn obtained from Kesselring a promise not to take any action against the negotiations. When they parted the general, with a cold smile, wished Rahn every success.

As announced by Parilli, Dollmann and Zimmer drove to Switzerland on March 3. Husmann picked them up at the border and brought them to Lugano. Among others, Waibel met with a confidante of Dulles who was allowed to hear out the Germans' suggestions, but was in no way allowed to negotiate. Before he arrived in Lugano in the early afternoon,

Husmann and Parilli used the additional hours to prepare the SS officer for what was coming: a demand for unconditional surrender. Dollmann protested quite indignantly at first: he was not a traitor! But after hours of discussions, he gave in and agreed with Husmann that, yes, the war was definitely lost; yes, the Washington-London-Moscow alliance was indivisible; yes, he was aware that no one wanted to negotiate with Hitler or Himmler; yes, it now involved only Kesselring's units in the Army Group C; yes, the thrust of the statement could only be to spare the Germans from an even more gigantic catastrophe.

Limited to these five principles, the conversation with Dulles' representative, Paul Blum, lasted only twenty minutes. Parilli and his escorts were told that further discussions were only meaningful within this framework. Just in case it came to that, Blum gave Dollmann two pieces of paper. On each one there was a name: Ferrucio Parri, Antonio Usmiani. These were a resistance fighter and a U.S. agent who had recently fallen into German hands and were now sitting in Italian prisons. It was a wish, not a demand, on the part of Dulles, that they be set free. With that, Wolff could prove that he was serious in his intentions and that he did indeed have influence.

Dulles and Gaevernitz later admitted: "We both assumed that we would probably never hear from Dollmann again." They were completely mistaken. Three days later, on March 6, Parilli came and announced that the Highest SS and Police Führer in Italy, the plenipotentiary General of the Wehrmacht in Italy, the commander in the rear territory and head of the military administration, SS Obergruppenführer and General of the Waffen SS Karl Wolff (this information was on his business cards) would arrive in two days. Early in the morning on March 8, he came to the Swiss border, in civilian clothes, accompanied by Dollmann, Zimmer, Parilli, and Wolff's adjutant, Obersturmbannführer Eugen Wenner. They brought two other men with them; one was Ferruccio Parri, alias General Maurizio in partisan circles and later prime minister of Italy, and the other was Usmiani.

Waibel had prepared everything for their arrival at the border train station. By telephone he reported the sensational news to Gaevernitz that Parri and Usmiani were delivered "in good shape" to an officer of the Swiss Secret Service and were on Swiss soil. For the sake of expediency, they were hidden in a Zurich clinic—not for health reasons, but rather because their absence had prematurely betrayed the operation. In addition, Waibel had reserved two compartments on the Gotthard-Express traveling to Zurich for the group of Germans, so they could travel in a locked compartment with drawn curtains. Wolff's picture had appeared repeatedly in Swiss newspapers, and the political consequences were incalculable when the world found out that one of the highest SS leaders was in Switzerland to confer with the Americans. Because of his profession, Husmann was used to lecturing students, and since he felt that Wolff was not sufficiently prepared for a conversation with Dulles, he sat down with him alone in one of the compartments. He discussed in detail the list of crimes attributed to Hitler, the National Socialists, and particularly those of the SS. It was supposedly on that occasion that Wolff found out for the first time that the Jews had been murdered in extermination camps systematically and by the millions. It sounds improbable that one of the top officers of the SS, Himmler's longstanding right-hand man, and a member of the Führer's headquarters for years, and in particular a man with Wolff's innumerable connections inside the Third Reich, should have found out about the number one state secret in Germany just before the end of the war from a Swiss teacher. It appears, however, that Husmann was so impressed by Wolff's assurance and his word of honor, that he believed him. He was more mistrusting in another respect. Wolff repeatedly and insistently stated that neither Hitler nor Himmler had sent him to undertake the negotiations. He did, however, use a small mental reservation, in that he felt empowered by Hitler to make this contact. There was something Wolff did not know: even Himmler was pretty much in the picture because Police General Harster had reported to his immediate superior Kaltenbrunner that Wolff had sent Parilli to Switzerland.

Before Wolff left on his trip, he had consulted with Rahn. The diplomat had shown him a letter where Rahn's Swiss intermediary reported that Dulles was ready for negotiations with the Germans. Rahn recalled, "Wolff wanted to negotiate himself. I had no problem with that. Was it not highly symbolic that the first promising step to ending the war was taken by a high-ranking SS officer?" Did Rahn mean that the SS were ready to clear up the mess that they had played a significant role in creating? Rahn continued: "I eased my own concerns in letting someone with so little experience in political discussions lead such sensitive negotiations by giving him handwritten notes to use as a guide." They contained the suggestion that the Allies should temporarily defer their planned major offensive so that Rahn and Wolff could have time to win over Kesselring and his army group to a capitulation. In return the German divisions that were still holding out would slowly leave Italy without destroying anything. On the other side of the border, the soldiers of the army group would then surrender, but they were to be allowed to keep their weapons until the danger of violence and plundering in the homeland by the liberated masses of foreign forced laborers was over. After a short internment the soldiers were to be released from POW status back into civilian life. Wolff went to Dulles with this suggestion, but it was utter utopia. Whoever experienced the end of the war knows how much worse the fate of the soldiers of the Italian army was to be. Rahn, the confident negotiator, would certainly not have achieved anything more than Wolff, and even the little bit that was promised to him did not materialize. Whoever surrenders unconditionally must accept every decision of the enemy.

The harsh discussion with Husmann in the train compartment had taken its toll on Wolff, and as the locomotive became stuck in the snow, he grew increasingly nervous because this forced him to walk several hundred meters on the tracks to switch to another train. He must not be recognized lest all the participants get into trouble. Even Waibel was taking huge risks: he had neither informed his superior nor any government office of his private operation, which meant jeopardizing Swiss neutrality—an illegal misuse of secret service institutions and privileges. The four SS officers and the Italian baron breathed easily once they could disappear in Husmann's Zurich apartment to wait.

At this point in time, Dulles was not in any way disposed to speak with Wolff. He feared that this conversation could be used to drive a wedge between the Western Allies and the Soviet Union. Should nothing come from the meeting, but should it become known, U.S. Intelligence would be blamed for having fiddled with the Black Order of the SS, therefore giving them credibility. But Husmann felt that he was playing a role in shaping world history. He was so convinced of his mission that he managed to change Dulles' mind. Wolff had instructed him to give the American (according to Dulles) some "astounding documents in the German language, on which Wolff's business card with all of his titles was stapled." They were character references that later in Germany were called "Persilscheine" [detergent soap] that are mentioned often in this biography. Here they served as letters of credit. Among his "good deeds," Wolff referred to preventing the bombing of Rome when the Germans retreated, and when he saved many works of art from being destroyed, moving them to safety along with the coin collection belonging to the King of Italy. He referred to the fact that he ended the general strike without bloodshed; that he was responsible for an amnesty, which allowed the striking Italian workers and those who refused to report to the armed forces to return to civilian life. As a reference for information about himself he named "the former deputy of the Führer Rudolf Hess, now in Canada" first, and then the "current Pope: audience in May 1944," and after that a number of Catholic clerics and Italian aristocrats.

The OSS kept a safehouse in Zurich. Husmann drove Wolff there, but was not to be present during the discussion between Dulles, Gaevernitz, and the SS general. Gaevernitz was successful in starting off with a friendly note: a common acquaintance, the Countess Podewils had told him that ages ago, upon her request, Wolff had protected Catholic philosopher Romano Guardini from an investigation by the Gestapo. For Wolff, who had always been a collector of aristocratic acquaintances, the mention of this name meant that he was on somewhat more stable ground once again. He loosened up visibly—his host concluded—from the excited tension he was under. When he was offered a glass of whiskey, he no longer felt discriminated against because no one had offered to shake hands in greeting. Also he felt satisfied that they were negotiating in German since he did not speak English.

Once more he had to repeat that Germany was completely and inevitably defeated as far as he was concerned and that he was not speculating on any dissension among Allies. His main concern only regarded the SS and the police units under his command. Should the soldiers of the Army Group C, meaning the forces located in Italy, keep on fighting, he would have to convince Field Marshal Kesselring. However, he trusted that his influence as political advisor would be enough. His open break with Hitler, Himmler, and all National Socialist doctrine impressed Dulles that he was dealing with an honest soldier and not some kind of double-dealing politician. He became increasingly friendly and Gaevernitz felt the cease-fire could be reached within a few days. Euphorically Wolff assured them: "Gentlemen, if you can be patient, I will hand you Italy on a silver platter."

Dulles did not attend a second discussion the following day; he sent Gaevernitz alone. Wolff brought in Dollmann, who was very talkative and presented his plan. Together with Rahn and Kesselring, he could end the war very quickly. They would not only sign the cease-fire, but by retreating into southern Germany at the same time, the Germans could also prevent Hitler from attempting to take up his position in the much-discussed Alpine redoubt. By issuing appeals they would also win over other armies to join the surrender. Wolff agreed to release all the Jews still being held captive so they could cross into Switzerland. As soon as he reached the South Tyrol, he would get in touch with Kesselring at his headquarters. The general could possibly meet with Allied generals within a week.

It quickly became obvious that the chronically optimistic Wolff had promised too much. He crossed the border on March 9 and on the following day Rauff was waiting for him at the train station with a request from Kaltenbrunner that he come immediately to Innsbruck. Wolff felt this was not advisable; he excused himself by saying that because of his absence, he had too much work to catch up on. Even if Kaltenbrunner could not order him to do anything, the Chief of the Security Police was certainly authorized to have an SS comrade of similar rank arrested as soon as he was in German territory and, therefore, also within the reach of the Gestapo. Wolff also expected that Himmler would demand an explanation for the trip to Switzerland. His excuse was that he wanted to get a present for Hitler's 56th birthday on April 20. SS Obersturmmbannführer Max Wünsche, the Führer's favorite adjutant, was serving at the front for the single purpose of qualifying for a medal, when he ended up as a POW of the western Allies. Wolff supposedly was only seeking to have Wünsche freed as an exchange for Parri. To support this version, Parilli had to quickly travel to Zurich once more and at least suggest the idea of an exchange.

Even more serious was the fact that Kesselring had been called to Führer headquarters on March 8 and was ordered to take over the command of the western front. Kesselring's chief of staff, General Hans Röttinger, was temporarily representing him in Italy, and Wolff suspected that he would have the same mindset. It was, however, expected that a new commander-in-chief would soon arrive. There was also the suspicion that Mussolini was preparing to escape to Spain by plane. For Wolff, this meant dedicating more time and a higher level of surveillance to the Duce.

When Parilli took this news to Dulles, his trust in Wolff shrank quite a bit. The man from OSS found fault with all these unfavorable things that had caught Wolff unprepared. He said: "Now that word had leaked and he was or would be in trouble, he was hastily trying to devise a belated pretext for what he had done. He either considered himself even more powerful than he was or thought his stock with Himmler (or possibly Hitler) was so high that he could do no wrong. Or, worst of all, he simply didn't think ahead."*

On the other hand, Dulles wanted a lot more from Wolff. He therefore had a search made to locate Max Wünsche in Allied POW camps. He

---

* Allen Dulles, *The Secret Surrender* (New York: Harper & Row, 1966), p. 103.

was found, but had already been brought to Canada, and that made it difficult to get hold of him. Wolff then asked for a replacement, some prominent Party comrade, who had been decorated. His concerns, however, proved to be unnecessary. No one held it against him. In Berlin, they had other worries. Only Mussolini got upset when he heard that Parri was free.

In the following days, Parilli was traveling between Switzerland and Lake Garda almost without a break. He reported to Dulles that immediately after his arrival Wolff ordered all high-ranking SS officers within his territory to issue orders forbidding all violent operations. Even the partisans were to be spared, as long as they didn't attack. Dulles found out that Wolff was now waiting for Kesselring's successor: "If there is no other way," the SS general reportedly said, "then I'm prepared to deal with this alone." He had come to the conclusion that since he had dared move so far, there was no turning back. In this case, he wanted to have a plan for all those locations under his command, where he could facilitate the landings of naval and airborne troops. These by themselves would not immediately end the war, but the end would definitely come about much faster.

None of these discussions were committed to paper. According to the old espionage tradition the envoy Parilli had to memorize each of the texts. And so Wolff made a request that the Allied air force be ordered not to target any moving vehicles in the region of Lake Garda and Milan. Only through sheer luck Wolff was unharmed when his car was shot at from the air on a country road; his driver was wounded and the car destroyed. He let Dulles know that, without him, a surrender in Italy was impossible.

Dulles also had difficulties. After he had reported the result of his Zurich talks of March 8–9 to headquarters at Caserta, near Naples, everyone suddenly became very active. Dulles found out that the British Major General Terence S. Airy and the U.S. Major General Lyman L. Lemnitzer were on the way to Lyon in liberated France, and that he would be required to sneak them into Switzerland as negotiating partners with the Germans. This succeeded with Waibel's help. Dulles found out from the generals that Moscow had been told of the forthcoming negotiations. He thought he was free of all commitments once the Soviet Union sensed there was some kind of betrayal in his actions. He was very quickly to feel how much he was mistaken and immediately got a taste of the consequences. Stalin demanded that the Red Army take part in the surrender negotiations—something the Western Powers agreed to. He was requesting that three of his generals be present. It would be difficult and unreasonable for Waibel to get a disguised Soviet general across the border. And now three of them from a country with which Switzerland didn't even have diplomatic relations? With the British and American generals, this was easy: they presented themselves as non-commissioned officers from an American unit wanting to spend a vacation in Switzerland.

The two negotiators from Caserta made do with Wolff for a lack of something better, as he arrived in Ascona on March 19, with several escorts. The location on Lake Maggiore was chosen for the generals' meeting—the first between the top opponents in the war—because Gaevernitz's brother-in-law Edmund H. Stinnes owned two houses that were perfectly suited to accommodate both groups separately and keep them hidden. Wolff came with apparently good news: replacing Kesselring, Generaloberst Heinrich von Vietinghoff was taking over the Army Group C. Wolff had been fairly close friends with him for some time. However, he had never spoken with him about ending the war since Vietinghoff had been leading an army group in the Baltic countries during the last few months. It would not be easy to win him over to a surrender either, since he firmly believed in the iron Prussian military principles. It would probably be easier to convince him if Kesselring also agreed to the plan. Wolff therefore had to find the field marshal. He would need a week for that since allied air supremacy prevented him from flying. The warring parties were to delay their planned major offensive since it would be more difficult to implement a ceasefire in the midst of a battle.

But once again, things happened differently than what had been agreed upon. Back from Ascona, Wolff was to find out during an exploratory discussion with Vietinghoff that he would not discuss surrender. His chief of staff, General Hans Röttinger, proved to be more open-minded. From him, Wolff also found out that Vietinghoff advised his closest coworkers that they had to be careful in conversations with Wolff, because he could no longer be trusted.

Wolff therefore immediately went to Kesselring's headquarters in Bad Nauheim. The field marshal had no time for long conversations on March 23; the Americans had crossed the Rhine at Oppenheim and were threatening to divide north and south Germany. All the same, Kesselring agreed in principle that it was correct to hold talks with the Allies in the west. Wolff was so satisfied with this discussion that he passed on the results to Dulles through his office. Wolff liked those vague formulations because they were easy and gave him freedom of interpretation.

In three days, Kesselring had said, there would be more time for discussion. But it never came to that. When Himmler heard that Wolff was in German territory, he ordered him to come to Berlin immediately. On March 24, around midday, the general arrived there, somewhat shaken because low-flying aircraft along the way had once again shot at his plane. Together, Himmler and Kaltenbrunner gave him a going-over in the apartment of the SS Gruppenführer Hermann Fegelein, who was Wolff's successor as liaison officer of the Reichsführer SS at the Führer headquarters and now lived in the area of the Reich chancellery. Himmler condemned Wolff for meeting with Dulles without getting his permission beforehand, and without having reported to Schellenberg's office in the SD. From Kaltenbrunner's questions, Wolff concluded that he was only waiting for a reason to make an arrest. But since there were no further reproaches, Wolff knew that his much more incriminating meeting with the two Allied generals was not yet common knowledge in Berlin. He referred once again to the instructions he had received from Hitler on February 6. He had been successful, he said (as if it were a victory announcement), and had been able to establish a direct contact with the Western Powers. Peace, however, had never been discussed. The purpose of the discussion at first was to bring SS comrade Standartenführer Max Wünsche from a POW camp back to Führer headquarters.

Wolff indicated that on March 24, he had already spoken with Himmler and Kaltenbrunner about the possibility of an armistice in Italy. One can suppose that he only discussed this as one of many alternatives and that it should only come into play if the alliance between west and east could be either loosened or completely severed. The fact that on that occasion the forbidden word "capitulation" was even used by Wolff within Hitler's reach is even more improbable, since he suggested at the end that they continue the discussion with Hitler regarding his contacts and that they get his decision. Kaltenbrunner refused to take him to the Führer. He was so irritable at the time that the topic could not be discussed with him. In this respect, neither he nor Himmler had a clear conscience. Kaltenbrunner was planning a connection to Switzerland and the Reichsführer SS had cast a line to Swedish Count Folke Bernadotte.

As one can see, Wolff was playing poker in two games at the same time—which was admirable because he used his different negotiations as a joker in Berlin as well as in Bern. With Hitler and Himmler his suggestions sought to divide the Allies—the final objective being an alliance with half of the Allies forcing the other half to pay the high price for this war. This was not Wolff's idea; it had been making the rounds at Führer headquarters for some time, and even Hitler occasionally held monologues about it. Wolff had naturally opted for the west. As long as he took this direction to make his game believable to his Party comrades, he was in little danger of risking his neck. In Switzerland, he was playing his joker, namely, his readiness to negotiate, in a combination that was completely different, which according to requirements could be either an armistice or an unconditional surrender. He played as if he did not consider the deterioration of the Allied union as a possibility. In this case as well he believed he couldn't lose.

The danger, however, had not been completely averted with the interrogation in Berlin. On March 25, Kaltenbrunner took him by car to Burg Rudolfstein near Hof, where the SD had moved its headquarters because of an air raid. There he was confronted with Police General Wilhelm Harster and the statements he was making. Harster was brought in from Verona expressly for this interrogation session. Also, on the following day, Wolff was having conversations that sounded more akin to an interrogation. On the evening of March 26, the questioning ended with a warning to cease any further contacts with Dulles. Kaltenbrunner said that he could arrange for such connections at any time if they were required. Himmler, on the other hand, was looking for Wolff in Berlin and ordered him not to lose contact with the western Allies; however, he was not allowed to travel to Switzerland again without the specific authorization of the Reichsführer.

Chapter 12

Caught in the Middle

Upon returning south, Wolff stopped to visit his family on Lake Wolfgang and apparently decided they should move to South Tyrol. He arrived on Lake Garda again on March 29, exhausted from the strains of a dangerous trip, where he had very little sleep and was in fear both of low-flying aircraft and of being accused of treachery or high treason. He hid in his house in Fasano for almost forty-eight hours. He didn't do anything, and refused to receive anyone. Aside from that, Himmler called and said with cutting brevity that he had heard that Wolff was having his family come to South Tyrol. "That was a grave mistake. I took the liberty of correcting it. Your wife and your children are remaining at Lake Wolfgang. There, they are under my personal protection." The family had become hostages.

It had been arranged with Dulles that Wolff would visit him on April 2, Easter Monday. The general decided, however, that it was better not to go anywhere. He continued working on Generaloberst Vietinghoff with the stamina and conversational talents of a well-versed advertising agent. After three long conversations, with the participation of Röttinger and Parilli in the end, he got the Supreme Commander of the Army Group to the point where he agreed, in principal, to surrender. Vietinghoff also agreed that further bloodshed was pointless, but he had his own ideas about a surrender, demanding that weapons be handed over to the opponent with a military honors ceremony: the defeated were to stand at attention and receive the victors marching past. For a short time, in closed formations, the Germans would perform reconstruction work in Italy and, in the end, were allowed to carry their bayonets during an orderly return march home in a show of honorable defeat. Allied headquarters had no interest in such feudal traditions. Why such a fuss? Whoever surrendered unconditionally was not allowed to lay down any conditions. It was later possible for France to take large numbers of German soldiers from the Italian prison camps for forced labor in the mines. England also continued to need workers. In any case the Allies felt that it was too early to discuss these during negotiations.

They had other problems at that time: Stalin was thundering! The capitulation of the German Army Group in Italy did not fit into his concept of victory at all. He claimed that this allowed the Germans to transfer divisions from the south to the east, or, even worse, that anti-Communists in the western democracies could be holding the still intact German divisions in Italy to use in a united campaign against Bolshevism. What bothered him the most, however, he did not mention. Stalin had agreed with Yugoslav leader Tito (who was already in control of large parts of Yugoslavia) that the Red Army would move closer to him and then advance further west. Not only all of the Balkans, not only the Adriatic, but also all of Italy and the south of France would be bound together in a show of proletarian solidarity as soon as the Red Army overran the Po Valley in northern Italy establishing its rule. However, if the Germans opened the path to Venice and Trieste to the Western Powers without a fight, then the plan would fail. The Western Powers would not tolerate Communist partisans, but rather fight them, as had already happened in Greece once the Germans retreated.

The Vatican also had understandable reasons to voice its opposition to the expansion of heathens from the east. Whoever was betting on a western victory in those days, was actively seeking the participation of the Church. On March 1, Mussolini sent his son Vittorio to meet with Cardinal Schuster in Milan, who was in radio contact with the Vatican, now far removed from the front. Vittorio first returned with an oral response, followed by written suggestions, concerning the scope and the parties that should be involved in the negotiations. For weeks, the clever Dollmann had already been repeatedly visiting the palace of Cardinal Schuster with suggestions for a reconciliation. The Prince of the Church was to negotiate an armistice between Wolff and the partisans. The SS general's offer was, in effect, leave us alone and we will not harm you; we agree not to destroy Italian industry as we retreat. He had already promised the allied generals and Dulles the same, and in return was requesting that major offensives be delayed. Why should he not let a good deed be rewarded many times over?

Wolff didn't know it, but a storm was building up among the allied leadership. Hitler could not have wished for anything better. Washington informed Stalin that his generals could of course take part in the capitulation in Italy, but they would have no say in the matter. After all, the Western Powers had not been involved when German soldiers surrendered in the east. Participation by Soviet officers in the preliminary talks in Switzerland would not be necessary because the Germans would only be given instructions. In response, Foreign Minister Vyacheslav Molotov of the Soviet Union stated that the United States was refusing to honor its contractual rights to its allies and therefore the negotiations with the Germans must be terminated at once.

Since the Americans simply ignored this demand, Molotov sent identical notes to Washington and London in which the Western Powers were blamed for negotiating with the enemy "behind the Soviet government's back, which was carrying the entire burden of the war anyway." President Roosevelt wanted to placate the infuriated Stalin by declaring that the entire dispute was a simple misunderstanding, but he insisted that talks on a partial surrender did not violate any agreement. Stalin answered on April 3 with a letter replete with accusations. He claimed that the Germans would "open up the front" to the Western Powers "and let them advance towards the east, because the English and the Americans had promised to guarantee mild armistice conditions."

That was a blind shot; nothing anyone actually promised Wolff was to be fulfilled. Whether a German ended up in eastern or western captivity at the end of the war—he would be relieved of his possessions either way. Watches, rings and other personal items changed owners on many occasions. The fact that German soldiers preferred to surrender to the West originated in the reports about the atrocities committed by the Red Army. For example, they didn't believe that during the invasion of the open city of Stuttgart, the French generals would allow their North African soldiers to rape thousands of women and girls, but this did in fact happen.

The exchange of letters between heads of state dragged on with accusations and counter-accusations for a few more days. At one point it was thought that the German request for an armistice was only a trick to split the Alliance—Wolff denied this, but he certainly would have liked to have seen it happen. The real point in the argument, namely, the race between red and white for Belgrade, Milan, Genoa, and Marseille was never mentioned. Obviously, none of those involved in the dispute wanted to vent their innermost thoughts.

This was the reason why, since the end of March, the talks with Wolff made no further progress. Roosevelt wrote to Stalin on April 12: "I thank you for your frank expression of the Soviet point of view regarding the incident in Bern, which seems to have run aground without any meaningful results." Apparently, the cause of the conflict had dissolved into nothing.

This was one of Roosevelt's last letters. He died on the same day. Wolff learned of this exchange of letters many years later. Only then did he realize how much discord his actions had created among the Allies. The alliance itself, however, was not threatened. Wolff kept justifying his moves then and later—during the last thirty days of the war, he thought only of his surrender, that every hour, people were dying pointlessly and that it was high time for him to get his head out of the noose. He sent Dulles a telegram of sympathy for the death of President Roosevelt, and mourned the demise of a man whom his supreme commander-in-chief Hitler had always slandered as a criminal and the archenemy of the German people. Years later, Wolff used Roosevelt's death to enhance the value of his own participation in those momentous events. He asserted that the already sick and physically handicapped U.S. president became so upset about Stalin's suspicions that he had a stroke—just as he was writing his answer to Moscow. However, this could hardly be correct. On April 12, 1945, the argument between the Allies about the surrender was already as good as over.

Still recovering from the shock of his impressions of the trip, Wolff remained quiet during the first few days of April. He didn't want to endanger his family at any price. However, he would not give up his plan to end the war early, at least in the south. His emissary, Baron Parilli was commuting diligently between Lake Garda and Bern. On that occasion, a step was taken to improve communications between the deputies of the U.S. Secret Service and the Highest SS and Police Führer. Wolff and Dulles arranged for an Allied radio operator to be a guest of the SS. A twenty-six-year-old Czech, Vaceslav Hradecky, crossed the Swiss border, with

Waibel's help, and went straight into the lion's den. He was inconspicuous, as was fitting for a well-trained agent, spoke fluent German and in the worst case could be discovered because of the unbelievable amount of cigarettes he required. Wolff had accommodations set up for him in the attic of the Milan SD, where he could operate his transmitter and be assured that no one would unexpectedly intrude upon him. His existence was a life-and-death secret for Wolff and his accomplices; had Kaltenbrunner found out he would have seen to it that Wolff was sent to the gallows.

In the wild race among the Nazi bigwigs for future security and alibis for the unavoidable day of reckoning, they were all competing with one another. Wolff and his people were being watched from many sides, and anyone wanting to eliminate them needed only to report his suspicions to Himmler. There were increasing signs that Wolff's talks in Switzerland did not only deal with the liberation of a comrade held as a POW but were a contact to the West. On April 13, the Reichsführer SS called his general from Berlin and instructed him to come to the capital immediately to give a report. Since Wolff did not want to pick a date for the trip, on the following day Himmler, in two more telephone conversations, changed his request to an order.

Wolff at first could offer good reasons requiring his presence in Italy. Several days before, the long awaited enemy offensive had begun and was now increasingly successful. German troops were evacuating their positions, and it became clear that even Wolff's headquarters—as Highest SS and Police Führer and plenipotentiary General of the Wehrmacht—would have to be transferred to the north. Also, Mussolini had to be reined in once more. Through Cardinal Schuster in Milan and through the Vatican, he had secretly offered the Allies a separate peace. They had refused but he was now planning a heroic finale that would secure him a few lines in world history one way or another. With his three divisions, still part of the German defensive front at the time, and with the various units of the Fascist party militia, he wanted to create a redoubt in the Valtellina, an Alpine region near the Swiss border that was difficult to reach. There he wanted to set up resistance down to the last Italian. That could hardly have been Hitler's wish, nor was it Wolff's either, as he prepared for the surrender of all Axis armed forces in Italy.

Wolff could talk Mussolini out of this plan by offering him an alternative. The Head of the Italian Social Republic would give up his plans for nationalization—which bothered Hitler as well—and therefore secure the goodwill of the heads of Italian industries in London and on Wall Street. Mussolini apparently found this idea fantastic, but Wolff on the other hand was still under the impression, however, that the Duce was only waiting for an opportunity to attempt another escape from the German cage. Therefore, Wolff asked Mussolini for his word of honor that he would not move from Lake Garda without informing his guard and protector. He received that word of honor, but it would not be kept. The Duce, as a former soldier in the 11th Bersaglieri Regiment, had never learned the meaning of a word of honor to someone like General Wolff.

Wolff's objections to a trip to Berlin no longer convinced Himmler on April 15. On the phone, he curtly ordered his general to report to him the next day. Wolff could no longer delay the meeting. He had to decide. His situation resembled that of September 1931, although it was much more pressing, more dangerous with problems taking on a quite different dimension. Again, his own life and that of his family were in danger because of external circumstances, and again the only thing that could help him was if Germany was saved. Once again, he felt compelled to fight off what was troubling his homeland. That was the reason why he joined Hitler, Himmler, and the Party comrades back in 1931. Now, he had to abandon them. He had already taken the first steps and more were to follow if he survived the interrogation in Berlin. He would have to hide his cards once he got there. The oath of loyalty no longer forced him to be truthful. If Hitler and his Third Reich were caught in a vortex and were drowning in a worldwide catastrophe, that did not mean that the Obergruppenführer of the SS had to share their fate.

When he informed Dulles that he would have to answer questions in Berlin, the latter advised him to escape. Wolff, his family, and his co-conspirators could find asylum with the Allies. But this was useless advice; the families of all those involved were under Himmler's control, and the relatives of "traitors" were threatened with death because one of their members had "bad blood" running in his veins. And if everyone could successfully escape, the slaughter would continue. They all felt like patriots. All of a sudden, they were ready to give their lives for the Fatherland if it were absolutely necessary. However, at the talks in Switzerland, the point had been that Germany and the German people would not disappear with Hitler and National Socialism, but that a new order had to be established and that upstanding men would be needed. Men like Wolff, who could imagine himself as a future cabinet minister.

Whoever leaves to explore new shores can sink very easily. Therefore, before leaving, Wolff gave Parilli a letter to be delivered to Dulles, in which he promised to carry on the effort for the surrender until its conclusion, if he returned from Berlin in one piece, and without having lost his position. Should he, on the other hand, be arrested and executed, he then requested that Dulles defend his honor and announce that the SS Obergruppenführer Karl Wolff did not negotiate "in self-interest, nor as a traitor" but "only in the hope...of saving the German people." Aside from that, he asked Dulles that, in the event of such a conclusion, he protect both of Wolff's families—the one in the Salzburg area, and the other in Upper Bavaria. Before leaving for Berlin, he prepared himself with a letter drafted by Ambassador Rahn that Wolff was to hand over to Hitler. In this letter, he takes credit for the fact that his efforts to establish contact with the western Allies were successful, and that they were in the interest of Hitler's policies. He landed at an airport south of Berlin during the night of April 16–17. At several points the Red Army had almost reached the edge of the German capital, but the ring around it did not close until one week later. Wolff saw a favorable sign when SS doctor and Himmler's old friend, Professor Karl Gebhardt, picked him up at the airport: there was no threat of being arrested by the doctor. Wolff then thought of a letter that he had sent to Himmler a few days before in which he asked the Reichsführer SS that he come and inspect the SS units in Italy in the future. If that had happened he would have had Himmler arrested. Now he feared that a cell had been reserved for him. But Gebhardt brought him to the Hotel Adlon which still was functioning as the best in Berlin for illustrious guests.

Gebhardt picked him up there the next morning. Together they drove to Hohenlychen, some 120 kilometers north of Berlin, where Himmler temporarily had his field headquarters, protected by the red cross on the roofs of the sick bay buildings. The three of them ate lunch in friendly conversation, and during the course of the two hours Wolff once again managed to convince the Reichsführer SS that his general had not deviated by a single step from the path of loyalty. He admitted to having negotiated further with Dulles, but with Rahn's letter, he could show that a politically important chess move had succeeded. Hitler himself had even approved of that contact. This reassured Himmler, who was also making efforts to arrange for talks with the enemy. In the next few days, he wanted to meet Norbert Masur, an official representative from the Jewish World Congress, headquartered in New York.

Kaltenbrunner came after the meal. His massive face announced disaster. He wanted to speak to Himmler alone first. When Wolff was called back into the room, the atmosphere had become icy. Kaltenbrunner accused him of having negotiated with Cardinal Schuster in Milan regarding a comprehensive armistice on the entire Italian front; an agent had just reported this to him. Wolff was able to argue on this point in good conscience; he had personally never negotiated with Schuster. For the most part, he had used Dollmann because he had more experience in dealing with the higher clergy.

While the two SS Obergruppenführer were arguing, with increasingly bitter insults, Himmler avoided taking a position. He hesitated as to what he should believe. Both adversaries expected him to make a decision, but even hours later he could not decide. Kaltenbrunner wanted his opponent removed, if possible arrested and degraded because he knew that Wolff had blocked his own attempts to contact Dulles. Wolff, on the other hand, knew that he was fighting for survival. First he played at being misunderstood, then unjustly accused, outraged, and finally furious for having to defend himself against a conspiracy. This was all useless since, of course, he could not disprove the accusation, but also could not let it remain hanging. After hours of debate, Himmler was still incapable of exercising his authority. Then, Wolff unexpectedly pulled his biggest trump from his sleeve: let the Führer decide. The three of them, he suggested, should immediately drive to the Reich chancellery.

Himmler refused. For a very long time, he would shake when facing Hitler and did not like it. And for years, Wolff had been in better graces and Himmler was now deeply in "Reich shit." The two parties in this dispute should drive together, so that he would be free of that responsibility. And so, Wolff and Kaltenbrunner sat silently and resentfully next to each other in the back seat of the Mercedes, whose driver in front of them was straining, looking for the road during the night in the course of the two-hour drive, because the black covers over the headlights only let very little light seep through the narrow slits onto the pavement. They always had to be prepared for Soviet artillery to shell the road with rockets from a distance, or that the slow and low-flying Soviet airplanes would hit them with bombs.

At three o'clock in the morning on April 18, the vehicle reached the Reich Chancellery. While the two SS officers walked through the darkness to the entrance of the underground bunker system, Wolff warned his companion: he should be allowed to describe the thing with Dulles, because Himmler had always known of the talks and had even forbidden him to inform Hitler of them. Therefore it would not be advisable for Kaltenbrunner to pull out the most recent report from the files for Hitler. "If they hang me," threatened Wolff, "my place will be between yours and Himmler's." What he experienced during the early morning hours of April 18, 1945, at the Führer bunker, Wolff repeated dozens of times to his astonished listeners as an example of bravery in the course of his historical role. The mere fact that he returned unscathed to freedom was proof enough that he must have played his part as the hero very well. It must of course be mentioned that no one could dispute his account because he was the only survivor.

While he and Kaltenbrunner were waiting in the corridor of the Führer bunker, Hitler stepped out of his living quarters. On the way into the conference room, he greeted them in a friendly manner and was a bit surprised, "You are here, Wolff?" Did that rhetorical question imply that Wolff was not expected? Or that Hitler figured that the SS would slaughter its own black sheep? At least it was clear that the visitor was not announced. The two SS bigwigs were called into the conference room an hour later. Although Hitler had become a wreck, a prematurely sick and trembling old man, he asked with an energetic voice and inquisitive sternness where Wolff got the idea to openly disregard orders from the Führer. "Kaltenbrunner and Himmler have shed light on your negotiations with the enemy."

Wolff was prepared for that attack. He referred to their conversation of February 6 in the Reich Chancellery where he, in Ribbentrop's presence, suggested to Hitler that they seek contact with the Allies. There he had the impression that he had been given a free hand. Wasn't it because of him that the West and the East got into an argument? Triumphantly he announced, "I am happy to be able to report to my Führer that through Mr. Dulles, I have been successful in opening the gates of the White House in Washington and the door to the prime minister in London for talks. I request instructions for the future, my Führer!"

Clearly this was one of the great swindles on record! Wolff was the first to know that no one would negotiate with Hitler, and that the enemy would not even accept an unconditional surrender from him. Often enough, he had had to assure Dulles and the Allied generals that neither Hitler nor Himmler were behind Wolff's actions, and often enough he had been told that the talks would immediately end if this were found to be the case. Nevertheless, he bellowed out the sentences in his high tenor voice and strung them together fluidly, avoiding any kind of pause to think, appearing as convincing as the expression of his truly Germanic eyes. Kaltenbrunner stopped getting involved anymore. He felt that he, as the dark figure, no longer had a chance against the beaming blue-eyed boy and that, at that moment, his agent's report would be nothing more than a piece of paper.

Now Hitler in a milder mood, reproached his SS general only slightly. According to Wolff, he said: "Had your undertaking failed, then I would have had to let you fall like Hess." He was referring to his former deputy in the leadership of the Party, who, before the start of Barbarossa, flew to England to win over the British for a joint operation against the Soviet Union. The official version was that Hitler had known nothing of those intentions and only found out about them from a letter that Hess had left behind, before leaving, where he explained his actions. There had always been rumors, however, that Hitler had been part of the conspiracy. This was often being repeated, mostly among the higher ranks of the Party, but there was no evidence for this theory. If Wolff *was* quoting Hitler correctly, this could back up the assumption that the man sitting in Spandau, the then ninety-year-old Rudolf Hess, was following the Führer's orders when he took that flight. Once again the question remains: How credible was SS General Karl Wolff? He also stated that he told Hitler on that occasion that an unconditional surrender could no longer to be avoided—and that contrary to his usual reaction, the Führer reacted rather moderately, apparently only to say that he would consider it. That was not normally how he reacted when discussing that issue.

It was now past 4:00 a.m. and a tired Hitler wanted to go to bed. Wolff had to wait until the afternoon for his orders regarding his actions to come. He received them during a walk through the gardens of the Reich chancellery. Hitler wanted to take the opportunity to get some fresh air, as there were no enemy planes reported in the Berlin airspace. With great effort, he placed one foot in front of the other, supporting himself with a cane and stopping every few feet. During that walk, he explained his tactics for the upcoming weeks. Upon capturing the Reich, the Russians would not be satisfied with the regions that had been agreed upon, the West would protest, and it would end up in an argument. From an encircled Berlin, he could still choose which side offered him the best deal, and with the divisions still available—if no longer in the Reich territory, then in Italy, Bohemia, Austria, or Norway and Denmark—build up a balance of power. He would therefore set his price very high. It would be wrong to give up on any one of the fronts. And, for the same reason, it was right to keep the talks with Dulles going. Wolff should negotiate further and keep stalling his partner with attempts at obtaining better conditions for a surrender.

Soviet writer Lev Besymenski used Wolff's report as evidence that the capitalists in Washington and London had always been double-crossing the honest Joseph Stalin. Besymenski supported his claim that Wolff correctly depicted Hitler's plans, with texts that Hitler apparently dictated to his secretary Martin Bormann during February 1945, and by an annotation by the Minister of Propaganda Joseph Goebbels about a conversation with Hitler on February 24, 1945. According to those notes, Wolff becomes thoroughly believable as an eyewitness on this issue. On April 18, as Hitler explained his plans to him in the garden, he stood much higher in the Führer's good graces than his opponents Himmler and Kaltenbrunner.

What is astonishing is that Wolff managed to pull the wool over the eyes of both Hitler and his two far from stupid enemies so completely. Here he proved to be a true master of deceit. Perhaps it truly befits him—as mass murderer Eichmann once said—"the aristocrat as intriguer." On the other hand, he was very shocked later on when he thought back to the dangers he was able to avoid during those last few days. On his flight back to Italy, he was not at all sure anymore that he would see the conclusion of the surrender. His ambivalent feelings did not seem to fall in place until many years later when he admitted to reporter Erich Kuby from *Stern* magazine that at first he despised Hitler, then loved him, swore his loyalty to him and remained true to his oath. Such discrepancies in his memory never bothered Karl Wolff very much. Had Hitler not died and were he to attempt to return to power, Wolff could have been another Marshal Ney, who was sent to take the emperor (who had escaped from the island of Elba) to Paris as a prisoner, but who, during his first conversation with Napoleon, deserted the king to follow the emperor.

As Wolff's plane landed in Bergamo on April 19, he found out that his protégé Mussolini had left Lake Garda the night before to go to Milan. The Duce had assured the detective who was guarding him that he would only take a few escorts with him and would be back in a few days. These were lies. However, besides the Germans, he also deceived himself by his decisions. He was never to see Lake Garda again, since he only had nine more days to live. This deceit, the still-unclear situation of his two families, along with the terrors of the trip to Berlin, may have influenced Wolff to withdraw again for forty-eight hours from any outside contact. Risking achieving the best outcome, he was overextended to the point that he no longer could forecast what would happen next. Hitler had certainly cast his spell upon him once again, but the facts were clear that he must separate himself from the Führer once and for all.

Perhaps he would have worried less had he known that Dulles had been instructed in a telegram from Washington to break off all contacts with German negotiators because they were "not prepared at the current time" to "surrender under acceptable conditions… In view of complications arising with the Russians," Dulles was to "consider the entire matter as closed." The telegram was stamped "Top Secret!," and Dulles held to it so completely that he didn't even want to inform his German negotiating partner. He kept quiet also because he didn't know whether Wolff had returned safely from Berlin, and whether the Germans were even prepared to talk. He was also silent because he feared that the SS would take it out on his Czech radioman should he break off negotiations.

On April 21, Wolff was still uncertain as to his future standing when Rahn requested that he participate in a conference that, at Rahn's instigation, was to take place on the morning of April 22, at the headquarters of the Army Group in Recoardo. Wolff hesitated to accept. He said that there had to be one of Kaltenbrunner's spies among the conspirators. Before the spy was found, Wolff, who had just been absolved of all crimes, did not want to jeopardize his reacquired state of grace with the Führer. Rahn, however, pressured him; without the trappings of power or the participation of the Highest SS and Police Führer, the surrender could not take place. If Wolff didn't go along with it, the others would also pull out for personal security reasons. Finally, Wolff agreed to take part in the conference at the Army Group the next morning.

The commander began by describing how badly the front had been broken and how quickly the enemy was advancing. He had therefore requested to Führer headquarters by radio that they be allowed to undertake an orderly retreat, but as always, he had been instructed to defend every inch of ground, down to the last man. "Hundreds of thousands of German soldiers," said Vietinghoff, "are waiting for the words from me that will save their lives. Time is running out…" All those present agreed; General Hans Röttinger, Luftwaffe General Max von Pohl, the gauleiter of Tyrol Franz Hofer, and SS Obergruppenführer Karl Wolff and his staff. He reported that Hitler had ordered him to pursue the contacts with Dulles. This gave them all an alibi to take further trips to Switzerland. Wolff was requested to please bring the plan that he had started to a conclusion.

As they began discussing details, however, their show of unity began to crack. Vietinghoff once again requested an "honorable" surrender that, Wolff felt, would not be acceptable to the Allies; however he sensed that it would be a mistake to oppose the general. Hofer demanded that South Tyrol be separated from Italy and united to Northern Tyrol as part of a resurgent Austria. He wanted this to be guaranteed in the surrender documents. No one among the participants had yet understood that this time the defeated party would be unable to set conditions and that even the promises made by the victors could change later on. It wasn't until early morning that they agreed that Wolff would travel to Switzerland immediately, this time with two plenipotentiary negotiators. Vietinghoff appointed Lieutenant Colonel Hans-Lothar von Schweinitz. Obersturmbannführer Eugen Wenner, one of Wolff's adjutants, would act as the plenipotentiary for the SS and the Police. It was also decided that the headquarters of the Army Group would be transferred to Bozen because the enemy had already reached the outskirts of Milan. Lake Garda was also threatened at that point. Rahn and Wolff had to find new locations. Vietinghoff had to leave the move to his staff, while Wolff, Wenner and Schweinitz left for the Swiss border, during the early morning hours of April 23. Parilli once again was also part of the group.

Using a password they informed the Swiss border patrol that the Swiss Secret Service had authorized their entrance. Parilli called Waibel to inform him that the delegation was prepared to sign the surrender at Allied headquarters in Caserta, "That was, mildly stated, a hellish situation," Dulles remembered later. Now, he first told Waibel that he was no longer allowed to speak to the Germans, that he was convinced that his superiors would not have decided on this ban had they known "that the negotiators were already on their way." Waibel had to jump in and help out. He offered accommodations for the Germans in a secluded house above Lake Vierwaldstätter, near Lucerne, to wait for a decision from Washington. When it finally came, it was far from clear: Dulles should not negotiate, but let private Swiss citizens Waibel and Husmann do so, with Dulles passing along their reports to his superior's office. Roosevelt's successor, Harry S. Truman, still inexperienced in international affairs, was hoping in this manner to avoid accusations from Stalin.

Waibel and Husmann, as usual, took the Germans under their wing at the border. Wolff found out that Washington had first become suspicious since his trip to Berlin; he was to remain in Lucerne until the situation had become clear. Dulles was not allowed to meet with Wolff, but he did require first hand information and therefore sent his colleague Gero von Gaevernitz to the Hotel Schweizerhof in Lucerne. He let Wolff know that the Allies were suspicious that his visit with Hitler could mean that the German dictator was indeed behind the offer to surrender after all. All Wolff could do was wait.

On April 24, a radio signal from Himmler reached him in a roundabout way: "It matters now more than ever that the Italian front should hold… Not even the slightest hint of negotiations can be allowed at this time." As Wolff's escort read the text, he said to them, "What Himmler is saying now is meaningless!" On the other hand, Dulles made no moves. He didn't want to ruin his own career with this complicated matter. So the whole thing could have ended then and there had Waibel not been constantly keeping up the pressure. On the telephone, he told Dulles: "We will look ridiculous if we don't straighten this thing out. Here we have the German negotiators ready to offer an unconditional surrender, and the Allies don't even want to receive them. Do you want to end the war by having them kill everyone?"

The next day when the situation still appeared unchanged, Wolff lost his patience. He was required very urgently in Italy, he said. Schweinitz and Wenner had the authority to sign and it was not necessary for him to remain in Switzerland. The precarious situation at the front was his pretext, but he actually had to go to Milan. Dollmann had negotiated an armistice with the partisans through the mediation of Cardinal Schuster, agreeing that Wolff would appear at a final meeting during the next few days. But that was just a ruse by Wolff to keep the partisans quiet until he and the Allies had reached an agreement. Now time was running short. Once the rebellion broke out in all of northern Italy, it was not just the Wehrmacht that would be in great danger. It was feared that the communists would eventually take power from the Balkans to the Spanish border. And since the Duce threatened to return to his Socialist past, one no longer could even exclude that he had joined up with the left-wing partisans.

Cardinal Schuster summoned several leaders of the partisans to his office on April 25, leaving it open for both Wolff and Mussolini whether they agreed to negotiate with them or not. The SS general did not appear.

The partisans were demanding the unconditional capitulation of Mussolini's few divisions and of the Fascist party militia, which was far stronger in numbers, but whose units existed mostly on paper. Mussolini appeared ready to accept, if certain guarantees were offered. However, Marshal Graziani objected that this could not happen without the Germans' agreement. He and Mussolini were then told that the SS had no such scruples, because they had been negotiating an armistice with the partisans for days.

Mussolini screamed in outrage, "The Germans did this behind my back. This time, we will be able to say that Germany betrayed Italy!" He compared the situation to the First World War alliance. At the beginning Italy was allied with Germany and Austria-Hungary in the *Triple Alliance*, but the kingdom of Italy at first remained neutral at the outbreak of the war and then joined the English, French, and Russians. In this respect, coming from Mussolini, betrayal was a harsh word to use against an ally who only appeared to be doing something (as a ploy) that Mussolini was about to do himself. At any rate, this was how he managed a melodramatic exit from the palace. He no longer felt that he could switch sides. Since Milan was now practically controlled by the partisans, he and his entourage got into their cars. They drove to Como. There, they spent the night, only a few short kilometers from Wolff.

On April 25, Wolff returned to Italy shortly before midnight by train through the Swiss border station at Chiasso. Very close to the border at Cernobbio, a few kilometers before Como on the western bank of Lake Como, the SS had an office at Villa Locatelli, the home of a millionaire cheese manufacturer. Wolff decided to sleep there. But early that morning another guest came to the same house: Marshal Rodolfo Graziani, who had separated himself from Mussolini in Como and was now seeking the protection of the SS. The plenipotentiary who was to go to Caserta was also supposed to sign the surrender of the Italian divisions, which had not yet been authorized. Wolff first attempted to quiet the Marshal, who was furious because of the unauthorized decision to negotiate, but then succeeded in having him sign a paper giving Wolff authority to negotiate for the Italians.

He could have sent the document to Gaevernitz, but since he wanted to continue his trip, a strong and well-equipped partisan unit was blocking him. It had taken positions around the entire estate. An attempt to escape would have been suicide. The telephone, however, was working.

Standartenführer Rauff* was asked for support over the phone, but he could only send a few men. They arrived in two armored scout cars and an 8/8 gun. During the attempt to break the encirclement, the artillery and the vehicles were damaged.

Again, it was Waibel who handled the situation. He was moved not only by the disadvantages that would come to Switzerland because of the continued fighting in Italy, but also by the responsibility he felt towards the Germans, since he was instrumental in starting the negotiations. He told Gaevernitz, that if Wolff became a victim of the partisans, the surrender would fail. They decided to use a man who resided in Lugano, working as a U.S. agent, by the name of Scotti, who occasionally supplied the partisans with dollars to acquire weapons on the black market.

From Lugano, Waibel called the Villa Locatelli. The line was still operating. He told Wolff that the U.S. agent would try to get through with two cars that night. The undertaking was successful; the partisans were persuaded by their "friend Scott" to lift the siege. At about 2:00 a.m. on April 27, Wolff reached the train station restaurant in Chiasso. There Gaevernitz and Waibel were waiting for him. Wolff said, "I will never forget what you have done for me." In the afternoon, he began the journey to headquarters, which, in the meantime, had moved to Bozen. The partisans blocked the fastest way; Waibel had to smuggle him through towards the north of Switzerland to the border station at Arth-Goldau. Near Feldkirch he could cross to Vorarlberg. After a long detour across the Arlberg and Reschen Passes, he reached Bozen at midnight on April 27. He knew by then that the two negotiators were flying to Allied headquarters in Caserta to sign the surrender. Stalin had no further objections; he sent several of his own military as observers.

Wolff immediately called a conference at the offices of the Gauleiter in Bozen. Those present were Vietinghoff, Röttinger, Rahn, and Hofer, among others. The building was on a steep cliff, where Hofer had carved out air raid tunnels. Since he felt that he was hosting the conference he demanded to sit at the head of the negotiating table. When Wolff reported that the German negotiators had signed unconditionally in Caserta, Hofer

---

* Walther Rauff, SD Chief in Milan, died in 1984 in Chile. After the end of the war, he found support through the Catholic church, apparently lived illegally for two years in a convent, and then was smuggled out to South America. Rauff's "claim to fame" was being the inventor of the gas vans, used first to kill the mentally ill and later the Jews.

interrupted him to ask whether his political demands had been negotiated. Wolff replied that in view of the desperate military situation, anything of that nature was no longer possible. The gauleiter then demanded that he be regarded as the highest authority for all decisions in South Tyrol, whether political or military. Vietinghoff, Rahn, and Wolff disagreed. After many hours of debate, they separated, completely at odds with one another.

Because he did not have the power to enforce his claim, Hofer called Field Marshal Kesselring, the Commander-in-Chief in the West. His headquarters were already far to the east—the Americans having pushed him back to Pullach near Munich. Kesselring knew that Wolff had negotiated with Dulles, when the SS general had visited him a month ago. Dollmann had in the meantime also traveled to Bavaria to inform him expressly. During these talks, however, an unconditional surrender had not yet been mentioned. As former liaison officer between Kesselring and Wolff, Dollmann knew what he could expect of the Commander-in-Chief. He was, Kesselring wrote later, at that point, still opposed to it because he wanted to gain more time for German troops in the east to save themselves from being taken prisoner by the Soviets.

When Hofer called Kesselring for help, they both knew that Hitler would very shortly give the general the supreme command of all German units in the southern Germany. This would also place Vietinghoff's army group under his command. He already took advantage of these rights to get involved in what was going on in Italy. He went to see Hofer in Innsbruck. As General Röttinger was being summoned there, he used the pretext of urgent military business and sent Oberst Josef Moll as his representative. Kesselring interrogated him and threatened him with a court-martial for treason—in other words, a death sentence. Moll, however, was not intimidated that easily. If such a procedure were necessary, he said in Hofer's presence, then the gauleiter must be condemned as well. At the beginning of April at a meeting of the Army Group, Hofer had said that Hitler had gone mad, and that he would not blindly go to his death by following the orders of the Führer headquarters. Moll was sent back to Bozen after midnight.

Between the Brenner Pass and Innsbruck he encountered the car of his supreme commander. Vietinghoff was also summoned for an interrogation. Moll warned him, but the senior general would not stay behind. He was held in Innsbruck from the early morning of April 29 until midday the following day. He returned to Bozen on the afternoon of April

30, in the company of General Friedrich Schulz and Lieutenant General Fritz Wentzell; respectively, the new Supreme Commander of the Army and his Chief of Staff. The dismissed Generals Vietinghoff and Röttinger were ordered to make their way to Lake Karer where a court-martial would issue a sentence. Röttinger was allowed to remain in office in Bozen for twenty-four hours so he could give instructions to his successor.

Kesselring could do nothing against Wolff; the SS general did not report to him. So Kesselring left it to the discretion of SS Obergruppenführer and Chief of the Security Police Ernst Kaltenbrunner, who had gone to Innsbruck to avoid the issue, to arrange that his orders would be carried out. The SS special units of Skorzeny and Begus were safely in South Tyrol, and they would accept any assignment that would keep them as far away from the war as possible; Kaltenbrunner could therefore use them in a coup against his archenemy Wolff.

That was the reason why Wolff had arranged for protecting his office in the palace of the Counts of Pistoia in Bozen against attacks with an SS unit. Czech radio operator Hradecky had a transmission room where he slept on the third floor. On his door, there was a sign that read: "Entry only with the Obergruppenführer's permission." Now Wolff could send messages to Switzerland through that radio antenna: the negotiators Schweinitz and Wenner had to avoid Tyrol on their return to headquarters if possible, but most importantly they should stay away from Innsbruck. Kaltenbrunner and Hofer were there, waiting to have them arrested.

The two negotiators had already signed the armistice at 2:00 p.m. on April 29. According to Article I the capitulation would take place unconditionally. The ceasefire was to begin on May 2 at 12:00 p.m. English time. Now the two negotiators had to return to their headquarters to report and deliver the document. Waibel brought them through Switzerland, and told them about the dangers of their trip home; but first there was a problem at the border crossing at Bludenz, because one of Waibel's rivals in the Swiss Intelligence Service wanted to disrupt the operation. Schweinitz and Wenner were stopped for six hours. Wolff sent a car to the border to pick them up. They reached the Reschen Pass by way of Landeck and arrived without a hitch in Bozen in the early hours of May 1.

Since their departure a week before, many momentous events had taken place. The dictatorial system run by Hitler and Mussolini now melted away as quickly as the snow in the Alps. As they arrived in Switzerland on April 23, Mussolini was just beginning his failed attempt to extract himself from the whole mess through an understanding with the Milan partisans. After leaving Milan, he spent the night of April 26 in Como, only a few kilometers away from his former advisor and guard, Wolff, who was spending the night at the Villa Locatelli. However, neither of the two men knew how close they were. When they left in the early morning, Mussolini wanted to get rid of his SS escort as well, but SS Untersturmführer Fritz Birzer asserted himself, threatened to use his weapons, and insisted that his men and their vehicles be part of the convoy. The convoy took the western bank of the long lakeside drive north, always barely a few kilometers from the Swiss border. On the afternoon of April 26, the cars turned west on a road leading to Lake Lugano that also reached into Switzerland. They stopped in the town of Grandola. Two of Mussolini's ministers attempted to slip into Switzerland on a scouting mission. When this failed, the convoy turned back toward the banks of the lake. Mussolini spent the night in Menaggio. He announced that he wanted to drive as far as Merano the next day—a road where the distance to the border was constantly changing, but at the same time could lead to his bastion in the Alps, the Valtellina, and to Wolff's headquarters as well.

They started at 5:30 a.m., but did not get very far. Already after the next town, just before Dongo, a tree trunk and a few boulders blocked the road. Partisans had set a trap; the road had a very steep drop to the lake on the right-hand side and to the left a cliff climbing straight up from the edge of the road. In front of the obstacle, there was a line of vehicles continuing for a few kilometers because Mussolini's column had been joined by a Luftwaffe intelligence unit that was not very experienced when it came to fighting. An armored scout car made up the lead of the convoy. Behind them, there were regular cars and trucks of all kinds, and among them some motorcycle riders.

When the head of the convoy was shot at, the armored scout car became immobilized because its tires got hit. Intimidated by this, no one thought of clearing away the obstacles. The built-in machine guns in the armored scout car provided some cover. However, the SS, the Luftwaffe company, and the Italians were so demoralized by the defeat that each of them was only thinking of saving his own skin.

From the front, two young Italians approached the head of the column with a white flag. They demanded that the weapons be handed over to them. No one from Mussolini's people could be seen. The commander of the Luftwaffe company took charge of talking with the partisans because he spoke fluent Italian. He went to Dongo with them and returned after six hours—after the partisans had called in reinforcements from the entire region. Proud of what they had achieved, he announced that the Germans were allowed to continue driving on to Switzerland without weapons, of course. Only the Italians would be held back. The fact that the resistance movement had used the radio to call for the immediate execution of all Fascist leaders was known to most of the Germans in the convoy. But in a situation like this, every man looked after himself.

At the marketplace in Dongo, the vehicles were searched and personal effects were inspected. Hidden on a truck between two gasoline containers, the partisans discovered the former Duce and current Head of State of the Italian Social Republic. He was disguised in a German military coat and a Wehrmacht steel helmet and pretended to be a sleeping drunk. He was led away, followed by the screams of hatred from the crowd that had gathered. His ministers and Party functionaries were arrested along with Clara Petacci, who insisted on sharing his fate.

On the afternoon of April 27, the Germans in the convoys were allowed to drive on north, across Chiavenna to the Maloja Pass. At the Swiss border they had to wait for a long time before they were allowed through, but they were not stopped or opposed at any time. They were taken to the road leading to the Reschen Pass into Austrian territory via St. Moritz and through the Engadin. They were the only German soldiers allowed into Swiss territory as a unit. The question will remain unanswered whether or not it was their duty to protect the Italians, Mussolini included, from the blind rage of popular justice. It would have allowed for proper court proceedings to deal with their actions and the atrocities they had committed.

When journalist Erich Kuby was assigned to write a story on Claretta Petacci for a German magazine, he traveled with the then almost eighty-year-old former General Karl Wolff around Italy and Germany in search of facts and witnesses. Fritz Birzer, who headed the SS escort commandos, said that handing over Mussolini was the only way to control the situation. Otherwise more than two hundred people would have died because of one man. Wolff then completed that statement: "If he had kept his word of honor"—and he was referring to the instance when Mussolini had acted against the instructions of the SS Obergruppenführer—"he would have been well cared for." No one was to blame for what had happened.

During the night of September 27 following a short stay at a customs house, Mussolini, together with Claretta Petacci, was taken to a farmhouse by the partisans. She insisted on accompanying him. The farmer's wife prepared her children's bedroom for the couple, not knowing who they were because the partisans had wrapped the man's head in bandages to keep him from being recognized. A guard stood in front of the door. At approximately 11:00 a.m. the next morning the couple was served breakfast in their room. A Communist partisan leader picked up the prisoners and drove aimlessly around with them in a car in search of a suitable place for the "execution." Finally he stopped in front of the driveway of a country home. The property was separated from the street by a high wall. Mussolini and Clara Petacci were told to get out, go through the gate and stand on the inner side of the wall. The partisan then announced that a liberation committee had sentenced them both to death and shot them with his submachine gun.

In the meantime, sixteen Fascist party and government leaders were executed in Dongo, along with Clara Petacci's brother, Marcello. The corpses were loaded onto a truck. The two dead bodies from behind the garden wall were also added to the load. The dead were displayed in Milan on the pavement of the Piazzale Loreto. And once the people had vented their rage on Mussolini's corpse, his body and that of his lover were hanged by the feet at a gas station.

When Hitler heard of this, in the bunker of the Reich Chancellery, he ordered that his body be burned immediately after his suicide—which actually took place two days later. He no longer intended to engage in the fighting in the south, although Kaltenbrunner in the Tyrol challenged him to do so by reporting that "after the breakthrough by the Americans, a disorderly flight to the north had begun." After the "outbreak of planned rebellions in all the large cities" he had "reason to fear that the demands of the regional liberation committees would be accepted by the top leaders...and according to Hofer, these included Wolff and Vietinghof." Kaltenbrunner suggested blocking all the roads in the South Tyrol leading north by "immediately setting up strong demolition squads," and therefore preventing a breakthrough of enemy tanks to the Brenner Pass.

Chapter 13

Cooperation Has Its Price

In the chaos of Berlin during the last days of April no one followed Kaltenbrunner's suggestion. At the same time in South Tyrol, his plan to either hold a number of the most prominent concentration camp prisoners of the Third Reich as hostages or execute them as witnesses for the prosecution if negotiations broke down also failed. Since the beginning of April those prisoners had been gathered from various concentration camps and were then transported south of Dachau by bus. They were closely guarded by the SS, but were always treated reasonably well. Among them was former French prime minister Léon Blum and his wife, a nephew of Soviet foreign minister Molotov and two English secret service officers whom Hitler suspected of having organized the assassination attempt on his life with a bomb in the Munich Bürgerbräukeller during the evening of November 8, 1939. These also included Pastor Martin Niemöller and several other protestant clergymen who had taken a stand against National Socialism in the German Confessional Church, the former minister and Reichsbank president Hjalmar Schacht, who had helped finance Hitler's armaments, but had refused to cooperate in the war plans, generals and other officers of the Wehrmacht—some two hundred people in all.

The transport finally stopped on April 29 at Niederndorf in Pustertal, not far from Toblach, because the SS guards did not know what else to do. While they tried to get further instructions, Captain Bogislaw von Bonin called the headquarters of the army group in Bozen from a Wehrmacht office. He asked General Röttinger for help, since they had occasionally worked together in the past. Röttinger immediately sent the officer in charge of his headquarters, Captain Wichard von Alvensleben, with a commando of eight well-armed NCOs with experience at the front. When Alvensleben asked the commanding officer of the SS guards about the destination and purpose of the transport, the man replied that his mission would not be completed "until the prisoners are dead." Because the SS men were in the process of enjoying a few hours of relaxation in town, they had only left a few men behind to guard the prisoners. Alvensleben had them individually arrested and locked up in the Town Hall, some eighty-six men in all. Once they figured out that they were stronger than their guards, they threatened to turn things around but relented when Alvensleben called in a motorized Wehrmacht company from Toblach.

Wolff was involved in the operation since he had spoken to Bonin on the telephone and had agreed to help. He also instructed the guards to withdraw from Niederndorf, and ordered that the prisoners be set up with accommodations in a luxurious hotel on the Pragueser Wild Lake, an idyllic valley parallel to the Pustertal. There, they could wait in freedom for the arrival of the allied troops. However, they were not sent back home that quickly, and were first taken to the island of Capri where they were questioned by the OSS. In later years when Wolff was repeatedly on trial, he made it a habit of using the liberation of those prisoners to his advantage as one of his "good deeds." However, Captain Bonin, when questioned as a witness, stated that he did not know former Obergruppenführer Karl Wolff, and was not aware of owing this man anything. Another witness, however, did confirm Wolff's statement to a degree, but here (as it so often happened) Wolff presumably told the truth in a way that enhanced his image much better than the facts themselves.

It was also news to the negotiators who had returned from Caserta that their most important client, General Heinrich von Vietinghoff, who provided their legal cover, had been removed. As ordered, he waited for his sentencing by a court-martial in a hotel on Lake Darer, high up in the Dolomites. Only his Chief of Staff, General Röttinger would still be active, until May 1. When he heard from the new arrivals that none of the requested concessions would be honored by the victors, that the surrender would literally be unconditional, Wolff had to give him moral support. The two generals, one from the SS and the other from the Wehrmacht, came to the conclusion that now they absolutely must cross the Rubicon of legality. They ordered that all information channels going north to Kesselring and to Berlin be blocked. Röttinger had the newly named commander of the Army Group General Schulz, and his Chief of Staff Lieutenant General Wentzell, informed that a fundamental change in the situation made it impossible for him to relinquish his position. Röttinger had the two locked up in their rooms in the gauleiter bunker and the doors guarded by officers with submachine guns. It was actually a small mutiny. It was obvious which side Wolff was on. He had been busy for weeks trying to end the war, and was prepared to pay almost any price. His conscience did not bother him too much; the oaths he had sworn to Hitler and Himmler were *one* thing, the war and defeat were *another*. He convinced himself that he had always told his Führer the truth (even though some things were kept silent) and that he had even been authorized by Hitler to negotiate the way he did. He secretly saw himself as the executor of the Führer's will. He was part of the group that was to implement the surrender signed by Schweinitz and Wenner— this had to take place immediately because the ceasefire was to begin on the following day.

And so, on May 1 at about 10 a.m., at the headquarters of the Army Group, the contortions regarding the "oath of allegiance" began. For those involved, it was an exciting and, at times even a tragic, spectacle; but for the others it included some grotesque and even comic scenes. First, the Supreme Commander of the German Navy (a very small force) and the Supreme Commander of the Luftwaffe in Italy (which due to a lack of fuel and airplanes existed only on the ground) were informed of the situation. They were careful in their reactions. Before commenting on the events taking place, they wanted to consult their chiefs of staff. Röttinger then informed the members of his staff. Many young officers were demanding that the war go on; they did not want to turn their backs on the Führer, especially at a time like this. General Joachim Lemelsen, Commander of the 14th Army (which was holding the western flank) refused over the telephone; even if his soldiers' situation seemed hopeless, he would only agree to an order to surrender from the legitimate supreme commander of the Army Group. This was General Schulz, who was by then confined to his quarters. Even General Traugott Herr, the supreme commander the 10th Army, which occupied the western segment of the front, voiced his concerns against the surrender, but seemed prepared to negotiate.

The officers' code of conduct called for committing suicide by shooting oneself in the head as the only solution in such cases. General Röttinger felt that he had failed and decided to take his leave of the world by blowing his brains out. Wolff found out about this and decided to stand by his comrade in word and deed. Once again, he saw a possible compromise where others could find no way out. He recommended that the generals who had been locked up be returned to their offices and that they be persuaded to change their mind. He was convinced that in the end, under current conditions, the new broom would not sweep better than the old one—and he turned out to be right.

General Schulz, who was now in command, was unable to report to his immediate superior, Field Marshal Kesselring, anything different from his predecessor, namely, the situation was hopeless and further fighting was pointless. Kesselring, however, insisted on his order to keep fighting, come what may. When Schulz informed the generals assembled at the gauleiter bunker at 6:00 p.m., all of them agreed with his analysis of the situation, but no one was prepared to stop the fighting as long as he had not been ordered to do so by Schulz himself. Even though he wanted to he felt incapable of issuing those orders unless he received instructions from Kesselring. But even the Army Commander was still waiting patiently for a word from his commander in chief. Hitler, however, had been silent for over twenty-four hours now, and would never again issue orders of any kind. In Bozen, no one knew this yet, and possibly not even the Supreme Commander of the West, who was now compelled to withdraw his headquarters back into Austria.

The generals who were conferring in the gauleiter bunker had reached a dead end. However, Wolff, always eloquent, called Kesselring once more. Since he didn't reach him, he suggested to his chief of staff that the field marshal name another general as supreme commander in Italy, to replace Schulz, someone prepared to surrender without Kesselring's consent. This was a bizarre suggestion and he never did get an answer.

While those gentlemen were brooding silently over the apparently insoluble conflict, the Commanding General got up at around 10:00 p.m. He had reached a decision and ordered his staff officer that on the following day at 2:00 p.m., midday English time, the 10th Army would cease fire, as stipulated in the agreement. Also, General Lemelsen of the 14th Army and Luftwaffe General Pohl agreed to endorse the order. Wolff was therefore able to report to allied Field Marshal Sir Harold Alexander, through the Czech wireless operator, that the agreement would be honored, even without the approval of the Supreme Commander of the Army Group.

At about 11:00 p.m. the head intelligence officer came into the conference room with momentous news. He simply said: "The Führer is dead!" With those four words, all oaths of allegiance became null and void. News of Hitler's death lightened up the worried faces of the men around the table. It was clear that they had no longer had any reason to argue. The new supreme commander would not oppose the surrender. He was only waiting for Kesselring's decision.

It reached them by telegram two hours later—but it was different than expected. Kesselring was ordering the arrest of Generals Vietinghoff, Röttinger, and three other officers; a court-martial would be convened to sentence them. Young officers, upon reading that telegram, got together and suddenly took positions at the conference room door with submachine guns ready to carry out the order. Wolff led the threatened group to safety through another exit out of the bunker system he knew so well. Those still loyal to Hitler wanted to force Wolff out of his headquarters by using tanks, but they decided against it when the SS general had seven Waffen SS tanks drive out around the Pistoia Palace for his own protection. Through the Czech radio operator, he signaled Marshal Alexander to request help from Allied paratroopers who would probably land in Bozen immediately. He was not only worried about himself and the capitulation in general; his wife Ingeborg was now living with the children inside SS headquarters.

At 2:00 a.m. on May 2, ten hours before the start of the ceasefire, Kesselring called Wolff one more time. He accused him of driving those soldiers facing the Red Army into Soviet captivity in Siberia because of the surrender. They would not have enough time to make their way to the British or American lines. Besides, he was endangering the retreat of German troops from Greece and Yugoslavia. As a countermove, Wolff could prove to the Army Commander that only an immediate surrender would guarantee that western troops rather than the Communists would occupy the key position at Trieste. And indeed, British motorized units immediately reached the city on a fast march and occupied it before Tito's partisans could take over.

The conversation between Kesselring and Wolff, including technical interruptions, continued for two full hours, and it seemed as if the field marshal was refusing to yield. However, a half-hour later over the phone, he gave General Schulz his approval to surrender, and rescinded his orders to arrest the officers. At dawn, the headquarters of the Army group clearly broadcast the order to all Wehrmacht units that all firing was to cease at 2:00 p.m. local time and that weapons were to be handed over to the enemy.

The war continued for several more days in the west and the east. However, on May 3, even Kesselring was ready to bring an end to the fighting and the dying. He called Wolff in the morning and asked him to also arrange for an armistice for the armies of the Supreme Command in the West. The Czech radioman, who was still in Bozen in Wolff's headquarters that were still operational, sent Marshal Alexander the following text: "Wolff, under instructions from Kesselring, to Alexander: request information, which Allied headquarters is responsible for negotiations for the surrender of Commander in Chief in the West." Wolff's radioman received the answer that Eisenhower was the man responsible, and that the inquiry had been immediately sent on to him. Through the same channel on the following day, instructions were received as to where Kesselring's negotiators were to appear at the American lines.

General Dwight D. Eisenhower, Supreme Allied Commander, later wrote in his memoirs that the surrender in Italy sped up the unavoidable complete capitulation, thereby shortening the war by many days. Retrospectively in the 1960s, Allen Dulles wrote about Wolff's role: "He made his great contribution to the success of the Sunrise operation."*

That sentence could obscure the achievements of several other men in the Wehrmacht and on Wolff's staff. What they had done was less striking whereas he happened to possess the voice, the bearing, and the stature that easily eclipsed others around him. He did take great risks but only Himmler and Hitler could call him to account for anything—and everything had always gone smoothly with both, perhaps because in their relationship to Wolff they were victims of their own insanely grotesque views on race whereby such a specimen of the aristocratic German and the knight in shining armor could only be completely loyal. Besides, they were always far removed from action during all these operations. The generals of the Wehrmacht in northern Italy were in a much worse position. They were under scrutiny from every direction, even by their commander in chief Adolf Hitler himself, who during the final phase of the war wanted to be informed of the movements of every single company. They could

* Allen W. Dulles, *The Secret Surrender* (New York: Harper & Row, 1966).

therefore only attempt to end the war underhandedly. For all these reasons, many South Tyroleans consider Wolff as the one man responsible for saving their homeland from the fury of war. When he visited the wine country at Eppan near Bozen many years later, he was celebrated as an honored guest and showered with applause at a local festival. All of this moved him to tears.

His final days in the South Tyrol in May 1945 were full of short-lived joy and sunshine. Wolff had somehow managed to avoid problems once again; everything that appeared so threatening before—the war and court-martial, Hitler and Himmler, the Gestapo and the enemy—all had vanished like ghosts. The victors were not being harsh; they had moved past Bozen toward the Brenner Pass, leaving behind a relatively weak unit to occupy the city. The local commander left it up to the Germans to worry about peace, order and discipline among themselves. As long as they were acting as deputy policemen, they were even allowed to carry weapons. Almost everyone in the region had reason to celebrate, the South Tyroleans, the Allies and the defeated German troops. Even the Germans were not lacking in food and drink. The warehouses of the Wehrmacht quartermaster were still full, and whoever wanted more could obtain it by exchanging army goods on the black market.

In the first few days following the surrender, Wolff had invited by radio his American partners from Bern to come to Bozen. The lawyer Dulles could not endanger his OSS career because of a friendship with one of the highest ranking officers in the SS, but Gaevernitz landed at the Bozen airport on May 9. He was surprised by the almost peaceful atmosphere in the streets, and most of all by the SS troops standing guard in front of Wolff's palace presenting arms whenever an officer went through the gate. During the afternoon coffee, Wolff introduced his family to the guest. He showed him to Vaclav Hradecky in his radio cabin, and the basement where he kept the coin collection belonging to King Victor Emmanuel III that he had taken from the Quirinal Palace for safekeeping when the Germans retreated. Finally, he traveled with Gaevernitz to St. Leonhard in the Passeier Valley north of Meran. This was not because one and a half centuries before the Tyrolean national hero Andreas Hofer had served wine and bacon there as an innkeeper, but rather because in this town at the bottom of the valley Tuscan art treasures were stored and Wolff had supervised their transportation out of Tuscany. Gaevernitz found paintings and sculptures of incalculable value in the town hall and in a shed near a sawmill that were kept unwrapped and not very well stored. He felt that it was urgent for American art experts to take care of the preservation of these works.

On May 12, Gaevernitz left Bozen. He knew for sure what would happen on the following day, and had no desire to watch. Wolff celebrated his 45th birthday that day with champagne and a cold buffet in the palace gardens, in the tradition befitting a general. However, that afternoon, soldiers from the 38th U.S. Army division burst into the festival loudly requesting that everyone quickly get into their trucks. Whoever wore a German uniform in Bozen was taken to a prisoners' camp in the south. Rank and honor were barely respected, and upon entering the camps watches and rings, the little man's spoils of war, were more important. In this respect, the GIs were no different than the soldiers of the Red Army. If anyone had told General Karl Wolff that he would spend the next four years behind barbed wire, bars, and locked doors, he would certainly not have believed it.

By the evening of May 13, 1945, as he sat in his cell at the prison in Bozen, did SS Obergruppenführer Karl Wolff, General of the Waffen SS and Plenipotentiary General of the German Wehrmacht realize that after his fat years, he was on the threshold of the long lean ones? The American GIs handled him somewhat roughly, disregarding his rank. They had also arranged for accommodations for his wife, his three children, and his mother-in-law at the camp. He kept his outrage to himself, however, when he remembered what his guest Gaevernitz, even though an OSS agent, had told him two days before—the victors must first lock up the Highest SS and Police Führer in Italy, whether he liked it or not, because the entire world expected it; then after a few days or weeks at the most, they would return him to freedom in Germany so he could start whatever job he wished as had already been discussed during the surrender negotiations.

The Allied generals had agreed with the German negotiators in Caserta that they would treat prisoners of war with honor, even chivalrously. The *Stars and Stripes* newspaper had gone so far as publish that stipulation. It could only be a verbal promise, since a written commitment would violate the agreements among the Allies because the surrender could only be unconditional. Based on that, Wolff and his friends were already planning on when they would be with their families, which could take two or three months, as the railroad tracks over the Brenner Pass had to be repaired and returned to working order. Transporting the prisoners could then take some two months; generals and staff officers would be the last to go and could be home in time for Christmas.

Several of Wolff's acquaintances in Italy, however, did not share his optimism and were not counting on being back home that soon. One of these was the ambassador to the Vatican, Baron Ernst von Weiszäcker. Protected by his diplomatic status and the extraterritoriality of the Vatican State, he had been overrun by the Allied armed forces in Rome. He thought that, as the former State Secretary under Foreign Minister von Ribbentrop, he would have to stand trial. He was indeed sentenced to seven years in prison at the "Wilhelmstrasse Trial" at Nuremberg, although he made every effort in the foreign office to prevent Hitler's war and had not participated in any atrocities.

In every war, as the saying goes, if you went along with it, you can be hanged for it. Major General Kendall, in command of the 88th U.S. Army Division was not at all impressed that Wolff had been responsible for the surrender in Italy. He did nothing to prevent his soldiers from stealing from the SS general and his family. Wolff's cash—several thousand reich marks, a thick bundle of Italian lire and several hundred Swiss francs—disappeared into their pockets. Wolff's wife Inge, her mother and their children, the youngest being eight, were placed in a miserable displaced persons camp in Verona, home to a motley assortment of the flotsam of the war. Wolff was taken to Modena and handed over to British Intelligence. From May 16 on, he was kept at a large interrogation camp set up in the Cinecittà film studios in Rome.

On the third day after his arrival, things seemed to be changing. In the evening, one of Marshal Alexander's adjutants called him to the office of the camp commander and told him that in a few days he and his family would be moved to a house with a garden. That property, however, and his family still had to be located. In order not to upset the Italians, Wolff had to temporarily use a different name. He decided to become Count Bernstorff—he always had a weakness for the aristocracy, and besides his wife was still using her old passport.

But this never did get too far and just five days later a fiesty first lieutenant of His Britannic Majesty curtly told Wolff that he was to remain as a POW at the camp, no reasons given. Three weeks later, the general almost got the opportunity to complain at the highest level. The Commander in Chief, Field Marshal Harold Alexander, visited the camp, but avoided speaking to an SS general. From a distance, Wolff had to watch as the British field marshal, General von Vietinghoff, and General Lemelsen shook hands together.

On August 21, the Americans took the prisoners back to Germany. The plane landed in Nuremberg, the city of the Nazi party rallies. In a wing of the prison for prominent figures, in the same hallway as Göring, Wolff was assigned a cell as a war criminal. It was a narrow room with a barred window high up in the wall, a small table, a stool, a fold-up bed, and a gray woolen blanket. Everyone in that wing was living just as comfortably. The electric lamp on the ceiling had been removed. When it was dark, light would seep through the observation flap, which was always to remain open so that at all times the guards in the hall could watch what every prisoner was doing. The noise made by the guards and the employees, along with a cold draft, filtered through that hole.

At the beginning the Allies were planning to place Karl Wolff as Himmler's former chief of personal staff on the dock during the first trial, along with Göring, Hitler's former ministers, military officers and SS Obergruppenführer Kaltenbrunner. (Himmler had poisoned himself when he was arrested.) However, even though Allen Dulles had issued a veto from the OSS, he remained unreachable to his former negotiating partner in the surrender. When Wolff wrote a number of outraged appeals for help, Dulles pretended not to hear but still wanted to spare him a seat at the dock knowing how that would end. When Husmann again returned from Bern to speak on Wolff's behalf, Dulles said: "Let time pass by this man. Perhaps we can help him later."

Patience and reserve had never been among Wolff's strengths, and in this situation he was certainly not able to take things in stride. His natural ambition and strong self-confidence were unbroken. During the negotiations in Switzerland, his partners commented that a man like him appeared destined to take over a leading role in a democratic Germany. It was even mentioned that Field Marshal Kesselring could become president of Germany and Wolff could become the first chancellor of the new German State. Blushing with joy, he had refused such an honor, but declared himself prepared to take part in the re-education of the German people to become democratic.

In the Nuremberg prison, there was no such talk. Wolff, therefore, saw himself forced to bring it to his jailers' attention that they were constantly violating the rules of human fairness. One week after his arrival, he wrote a long letter of protest "to the Colonel and the Prison Commandant." He began by complaining about a young U.S. lieutenant who repeatedly searched his cell and took Wolff's personal army boots, a pair of gold cufflinks with green gems, and the stars from his general's epaulettes.

His insignia of rank, the lieutenant had announced, would be taken from him very soon anyway.

Wolff saw this as "human and military degradation," which he did not deserve in the least due to the list of his achievements in the surrender and the risks he took to secure an early peace. In Rome a commission had flown in from London just to interrogate him thoroughly; a radio signal to General Lemnitzer in Casarta would confirm that Wolff was not a war criminal. Also General Airy and Allen Dulles would not approve of the treatment that he was receiving. Against this assault on his "human and soldierly honor" he protested with a hunger strike. "Come what may," he proclaimed, "MY HONOR has always stood much higher than my life and will continue that way in the future." He wrote this word in capital letters, as the word GOD was sometimes written in Christian writings.

The letter was typed in English; someone must have translated it for Wolff. It was directed to U.S. Commander Burton C. Andrus, a tough jailer with a clear aversion to the Germans. Already at Mondorf in the Eifel, he had jailed and harassed the Nazi leadership imprisoned there. Once he had handed them over in Nuremberg, the prison that was filling up allowed him to fully vent his feelings. The prisoners defended themselves by disregarding his orders and cursing him. When he took the press to visit the rooms where the main defendants were having lunch during the trials, former economic minister and Reich Bank president Schacht defended himself against a photographer who held the camera right in his face by pouring a cup of coffee over his head. Andrus took this as an excuse and ordered that Schacht be denied his walk in the prison courtyard and no breakfast coffee for four weeks.

Wolff could do without the prison food without difficulty. It was bad and there was not enough of it. Andrus wanted his prisoners to be no less hungry than ordinary Germans who were still using grocery and ration cards. Wolff would not starve for very long. Already after a few days he was assured that he would keep his epaulettes and be allowed to continue wearing them. His stars were also returned to him. As he repeated with pride, he was the only German general in Nuremberg to wear his shoulder decoration; all the others had been removed. He viewed this as proof that because of his achievements, he could request special privileges. Since Andrus always found reasons to punish him, he got back at him by whistling the melody of the SS loyalty song whenever the commandant appeared. If the commander objected, Wolff could always say that he was only whistling the national hymn of the Netherlands, one of the allies of the United States.

Twenty-five years later, in November 1961, he had one of his fellow prisoners swear how valiantly he had behaved at the Nuremberg prison. Since a preliminary examination was already taking place for the Munich trials, this declaration was to be used as evidence for the defense against a future accusation. It said: "Despite the fact that it was strictly forbidden to speak with one another" during the walks in the courtyard, "Wolff did not obey that rule. He used every opportunity ... to encourage ... his fellow prisoners. In that situation, Wolff was similar to Göring and a few others who, by their dignified behavior, gave their comrades strength and courage to get through this difficult time in a respectable manner."

Before the main trial began in November, where, aside from the surviving leadership of the Third Reich, the Party and its ancillary organizations were being charged, Wolff felt compelled to save the honor of the SS. In letters to each of the supreme allied judges, he offered to stand accused in replacement of the dead Reichsführer SS and assume responsibility for the Black Guard of the Nazi party, "as a soldier who must jump in to fill the breach when a superior falls." He believed he could thus prevent the SS from being branded as a criminal organization and that he could avoid each member being incriminated until there was proof of his innocence. His reasoning was presented in such mystical terms that it only made the lawyers shake their heads in complete disbelief. Although he repeated his request many times, they never gave him an answer because they neither had the time nor the desire to deal with his arguments.

Two years later, when Wolff was asked during a Nuremberg interrogation whether he had seriously intended to take responsibility for Himmler's crimes, it became obvious how absurd those statements were. He would have clearly been sent to the gallows in that case. That was not at all what he had wanted, he said. They had misunderstood him; he was guilt-free and could prove that most of the SS did not take part in the crimes and only very few had even known of them. Two decades later when he was accused of having been involved in the mass murders, when the state attorney demanded that the jury of the Munich court condemn Wolff with a life sentence, the accused announced once again in his reply that he had only heard of "the mass killings in gas chambers for the first time from an American interrogation officer at Nuremberg."

Most of the accused at the main War Crimes Tribunal in Nuremberg, even Hermann Göring, whom Hitler had employed as the highest official responsible "for the solution to the Jewish question," provided similar declarations of innocence. The judges would therefore have reacted to such assertions by Wolff with derision and scorn. It was his luck that he had no opportunity to issue such a statement early on. In the middle of May 1946 Wolff disappeared. The regular companion on his daily walks asked the guard where he had gone, and found out that he had been taken to an insane asylum. His mental condition was under observation and improved at the St. Getreu clinic in Bamberg. He had a bed in a room of the closed ward where sixteen other men were also living day and night. Several were constantly bedridden and incapable of controlling their bladders or bowels; others were argumentative to the point of being violent, and from morning til night the room was filled with an infernal noise of screaming, unpleasant singing and other wild rumblings. Wolff had to live in that environment. He spent another month in the lunatic ward in a sick bay in Augsburg. There are no files of medical examinations from that time. There is only the final report issued when he was released to the generals' camp at Neu-Ulm on August 7; it stated that the patient was of sound mind.

The Nuremberg military court explained Wolff's stay at the asylum stating that he suffered from a "delusion of self-sacrifice" with occasional fits of rage. The diagnosis, however, was only supported by isolated moments of excitement and by the written statements where he demanded to be allowed to represent the SS in Himmler's place before the court. He was certainly not keen on being hanged or gaining fame as a martyr. He only wanted to give an example of courage and heroism. Up to that point, his name was known only in higher Party circles, but after such a trial and his acquittal, he would be known throughout the world. He considered a verdict of guilty as impossible, even though he repeated his assurances that he was prepared to give his life for his Fatherland and his comrades.

Wolff also repeatedly asserted later that they made him disappear so that he would stop fighting for the truth. His suspicions became even more believable because the psychiatrist who sent him to the lunatic ward was U.S. Major Leon Goldensohn, who as a Jew must have naturally hated everyone in the SS. He could even prove his theory with dates: he was of sound mind in August, once the evidence for the main Nuremberg war crimes trials was completed, and the opportunity for statements from witnesses had passed for the Malmedy trial, held against soldiers of the Waffen SS for crimes during Hitler's final offensive at the Battle of the Bulge.

During his first months of incarceration at Nuremberg, Wolff was occasionally interrogated, but without any specific direction and in a fairly lax manner. He was not yet being confronted with documents. The Allies had not yet examined the mountains of papers that the Nazis had left behind. While Wolff was at the psychiatric hospital, a U.S. prosecution officer determined in a file memo that from his point of view there was no further interest in him. In another entry written very shortly after that he commented that Wolff should be released.

In the meantime, the British had developed an interest in him. In August 1946, he was flown to London where he was held for two months and interrogated often, primarily about events in Italy, the hostage murders in Rome, Kesselring's role and that of other Wehrmacht generals who were later placed on trial. Wolff expected to be tortured during those interrogations, because among the prisoners, in what was known as the "London District POW Cage" the rumor was that statements were obtained by torture. He was certainly spared such experiences; otherwise he would have mentioned them. He quickly became of little interest to the British. They returned him to the Americans, who at first placed him, due to his rank, under automatic arrest in a huge internment camp in Ludwigsburg, and then kept him in a camp for generals in Garmisch.

But already at the beginning of 1947, the Nuremberg courts were calling for him again. He was required as a witness many times. One of his comrades from the "Fighter Days," meaning before 1933, had to answer to the First American Military Court for crimes against humanity. He was Viktor Brack, who came from a good Munich family, who happened to be the last senior administrator at the "Chancellery of the Führer" and an SS Oberführer. Fifteen years before, they had both marched together as Hitler's propagandists through Bavaria's cities and towns carrying the swastika flag. Now Brack was on trial because, on orders from Hitler, not only was he responsible for murdering the mentally ill in a clinic in a "euthanasia" operation, but his experienced team and their equipment participated in the Holocaust.

Wolff could not help his friend Viktor. Despite a statement that Brack was "an extremely respectable, extraordinarily helpful person, whom any thought of committing an inhumane act was …farthest from his mind," he still could not save him from the gallows. Even Brack's statement that he had wanted to save the Jews from extermination by suggesting to Hitler in a conversation with Himmler that they could sterilize all the Jews so that the hated "Jewish blood" would die out without creating any ripples, did nothing to lower the sentence imposed by the American judges. One passage in Brack's statement should have served as a warning for Wolff; the friend admitted that it was "an open secret in 1941 in the higher Party circles" that "those in power intended to eradicate the entire Jewish population in Germany and the occupied territories." Did SS Oberführer Brack include his Munich mate, SS Obergruppenführer Karl Wolff in those higher Party circles?

Wolff was just as unsuccessful as a witness in saving his friend Oswald Pohl, SS Obergruppenführer and Chief of the Economic and Administrative Main Office in the Reich Leadership of the SS, from the gallows. The former navy paymaster reached that position because Wolff sponsored him. When Wolff became ill and was placed in the sick bay in Hohenlychen following his kidney operation, Pohl did not let Himmler's displeasure prevent him from remaining friendly, as opposed to most high-ranking SS officers. Since Pohl supervised all workers in the SS operations and, therefore in all the concentration camps, he was now accused at Nuremberg of having killed, or at least having impaired the health of millions of slave laborers—opponents of the National Socialist regime, Jews, prisoners of war, and civilians who had been taken by force from the eastern regions—in a brutal system of ruthless exploitation and starvation.

Wolff's assurances that Pohl had always been an honest man, who had been forced by Himmler to act against his own conviction, didn't help at all. Pohl had even tried to save Jews from "evacuation" (one of the many code words for murder) by stating that he could not do without their work if his operations were to fulfill their deliveries for the military. Wolff's praise for Pohl as an excellent business manager turned to his disadvantage. The death sentence characterized Pohl's set-up as "an efficient enterprise" but that was in reality managing "a criminal undertaking." Wolff's well-intentioned help would wind up haunting him. At his interrogation at the trial on June 4, 1947, the judges took from the flood of papers of the Third Reich, for the first time, the exchange of letters with State Secretary Ganzenmüller, dealing with transporting the Jews from the Warsaw ghettos to an extermination camp, which later provided the motive given by the court in Munich to sentence Wolff to prison.

Chapter 14

Prisoner at Nuremberg

As in the proceedings against Pohl and Brack, Wolff was also a witness called by the defense in the case of one of the most powerful men in the German economy on trial, the big business man, Friedrich Flick. Among other things, as one of the members of the "Circle of Friends of the Reichsführer SS" he was accused of having supported a criminal organization with large donations. As Himmler's chief adjutant and then as chief of the personal staff, Wolff had managed the donation funds. He testified that the money was used "only for social, cultural and representative purposes," therefore not at all for criminal purposes.

Besides that, he testified that Flick had been an opponent of Hitler's policies of war and conquest. In September 1938, during the crisis in the Sudetenland, this rich man was very much concerned about peace because the Führer's demands could lead to a terrible disaster for Germany and the world. At that time, Flick had asked Wolff to make this clear to Himmler so that he could support the idea of a peaceful solution with Hitler. Wolff responded vehemently that Hitler did not want war, and that he was so sure of this that he would put his money on any kind of wager. Although Wolff, as it later emerged, had completely misjudged Hitler's intentions, he won the bet, at least for the year 1938. Flick sent the

Obergruppenführer a valuable hunting weapon, a triple-barreled shotgun, as his prize. It was simply a habit of his of maintaining friendships with small gifts. How helpful Wolff was to him with his testimony in Nuremberg is an open question; the big-business man received a prison sentence, like most others on trial, of which he only served a small part.

Wolff's testimony also failed to protect Field Marshal Erhard Milch, who had risen from a fighter pilot in Göring's fighter squadron in the First World War to master aircraft general in the Second World War, from being sentenced to life-imprisonment by the Nuremberg court-martial. However, Wolff's testimony may have exonerated him of one charge, for which Milch could have been hanged. It dealt with the experiments by the physician Dr. Sigmund Rascher, also an SS Hauptsturmführer and later staff doctor of the Luftwaffe reserve, who locked concentration camp prisoners in pressurized chambers below atmospheric pressure, to simulate conditions at higher levels of the atmosphere. With another series of experiments he was searching for a way to save personnel from death from hypothermia in freezing seawater. Again, concentration camp prisoners were the guinea pigs. Many died or had severe damage to their health for the rest of their lives. He therefore turned to Himmler and managed to continue his experiments in the name of and with the money from the SS organization "Ahnenerbe." In the bureaucracy, the "Ahnenerbe" reported to the Chief of the Personal Staff, and in this capacity Wolff had to deal with Rascher's experiments. He even witnessed tests in the low-pressure chambers, and when he was later questioned about it, said he would have made himself available for such plans without a second thought. But many prisoners in the concentration camps volunteered because they had been promised shorter prison terms. Others, who had already been sentenced to death, were told that the sentence would not be carried through if they survived the experiments.

In Nuremberg, Milch was blamed for testing on humans as a crime against humanity. An exchange of letters between the master aircraft general and Wolff apparently incriminated him. Wolff testified that the Luftwaffe was no longer involved during the most hideous of the sadist Rascher's experiments, where he enjoyed watching people die in the freezing water of a pool and in the air pressure chambers. Milch was also convinced that the victims had volunteered for the experiments.

During these interrogations, held mostly in 1947, Wolff was persistent and industrious in fighting for his own freedom. In letters to the American justices, to Dulles, Gaevernitz, to Waibel and Husmann, he reminded them of the promises made at the surrender: whoever had not committed any crimes should be allowed to return home after a short time as a POW. Dulles was to have told him at some point: "Even if you had made no personal requests, I certainly hope to have your help for later employment in Germany." At the end of February 1947 Wolff wrote to President Truman, listed his accomplishments in some detail without any kind of false humility, requesting he be released from prison, citing the promises made in Switzerland. He was already known as a complainer for some time in Nuremberg, but in some ways he felt betrayed—and rightfully so. Gaevernitz and Husmann even recognized this. Because the latter was named by Wolff as one of his "guarantors" regarding the arrangements made at that time, he managed to obtain permission to visit Wolff in prison. Wolff's behavior in custody did not exactly put the victors in a good mood. In February 1947 he complained furiously to one interrogator: "A Jew is killed in the gas chamber in a few seconds, without having an idea or even knowing it. My comrades and I have been allowed to die once every night for twenty-one months. This is much more inhumane than the extermination used on the Jews. Too much has been grossly exaggerated." It was not surprising that the Americans could not trust him with the planned reeducation and retraining of the German people to embrace democratic principles.

Dr. Eugen Dollmann former SS Standartenführer, and Eugen Wenner former SS Obersturmbannführer, Wolff's partners in Italy were much more clever than the general. Wenner had been Wolff's adjutant and this made him interesting for the Allies' investigations, but on the other hand, he had signed the surrender agreement and had to be rewarded. Dollmann was in greater danger. The Italians were saying that he had temporarily been SS police chief in Rome and that he had worked with a violent Fascist police officer, a torturing sadist named Pietro Koch. However, Cardinal Schuster, the archbishop of Milan, made sure at first that nothing happened to Dollmann. In the summer of 1946 he and Wenner were no longer willing to deal with the semi-illegality that was tolerated by the Allies, and the uncertain conditions it created. They requested that Baron Luigi Parilli, who was once again an influential manager in Milan, make sure that the promises by Allen Dulles, Gaevernitz, and the ominous Mister Blum were kept.

At the beginning of July they met in Parilli's office. He already had a solution. As the Vatican chamberlain, he had recently met the U.S. Lieutenant General W. D. Morgan, Chief of Staff at Allied headquarters in

Caserta, who was now just outside the office of the Holy Father. Because Parilli had also privately been helpful to this American, he could be useful for his German friends. Together with Husmann, Parilli managed to get Dollmann and Wenner safe conduct passes to the offices of the OSS in Rome to negotiate their reward. Parilli already knew what the Americans would suggest to the former SS officers—they would each be offered a new existence abroad and all losses that they incurred during their imprisonment would be replaced. SS officers could always be useful, in the view of the Americans in OSS.

A U.S. Army vehicle drove them to Rome. They were provided with an apartment, U.S. rations and plenty of cigarettes, which in those days was the only valuable currency. It must have made them suspicious, however, that only people from the OSS were living in that house. A U.S. captain, who simply called himself Jim, made more specific offers to both of them that clearly implied espionage activities. They refused. In conversations lasting far into September, it was urgently suggested that they immigrate to Brazil. In case they refused that offer, the Americans then brought up the accusations that the Italians were leveling against Dollmann. The two Germans agreed that they could be dealt with quite differently.

The situation eased somewhat when they were given personal identification cards with assumed names and money was made available. They could now move about the streets of Rome. Dollmann was, of course, arrested by the Italian police on December 8, 1946, and Wenner shortly thereafter. The OSS intervened, but not strenously. The two were left to stew for a while. When they were finally released, they were offered passage to South America. But then suddenly they were required once again in Germany. In May 1947, they were taken to Oberursel, to the OSS center in the Taunus. At first they were placed in individual cells, but shortly after they were moved to better quarters, received good care, additional cigarette rations, and were allowed to take longer walks outside.

After a few more weeks, the OSS officers finally agreed that there wasn't much to be gained from these SS officers. They were allowed a short vacation to visit their families and advised not to return to Oberursel. It was preferable that the SS officers escape to Italy because they could avoid what could become awkward for the occupying forces and the SS officers, namely interrogations by German de-nazification commissions. To start, they each received one thousand Swiss franks, four cartons of Chesterfield cigarettes and two bottles of whisky, which in those days was something of a small fortune on the black market. In addition, they each received 3,400 reich marks in back pay. Furthermore, they found out that Italian officials and the Catholic church had been informed that the United States wanted no further complications where they were concerned. They were driven to Lake Tegern. The purpose according to their vacation permit was for relaxation. A man working to assist SS fugitives, who was sponsored by the Vatican and directed by Bishop Alois Hudal, the rector of a theological college in Rome, took the two men from Upper Bavaria through Austria and into Italy. Wenner agreed to be smuggled to Brazil. The Church could use the services of art historian Dr. Dollmann, and they agreed to hide him until he was no longer threatened by accusations.

Wolff had also requested leave on vacation privileges, but his request was denied at first. It was only on October 12, 1947, that he would be free for seven days. He also went to Lake Tegern where he visited both his families. Later he said that the Americans suggested that he not return to custody. However, this does not appear to be correct, because two days after starting his vacation, American officials protested; Wolff was a prisoner of the British, and they had not been consulted.

They were probably happy to be rid of Wolff so they could avoid fulfilling the promises that Allen Dulles had made in Switzerland.

At that point, the U.S. judges could not do without Wolff's presence for long periods. In the course of twelve months, he was interrogated seventeen times and eleven of the examiners attempted to get useful testimony from him and sometimes they heard fantastic and odd stories. As he described his relationship to Himmler, he said that of course Hitler exerted the greatest influence on the Reichsführer SS. Reinhard Heydrich as Chief of the RSHA always egged Himmler into being more extreme, while he, Wolff, influenced him "in a balanced and soothing" manner, until the beginning of the war when he was called to the Führer headquarters. Himmler's demise, his "purported" suicide, remains a mystery. It seems improbable that the man would seek death in such a strange way by marching into British headquarters to give himself up, immediately state his name, and poison himself. There are "many old SS veterans who are still absolutely convinced that Himmler was tortured to death." In a memorandum, written for the Americans in April 1947, Wolff developed the theory that Himmler, "based on conversations the Führer had in general with the Reichsführer," had decided "to relieve the burdens...from the shoulders of the new messiah Adolf Hitler. The Führer was to remain free of sin." Himmler therefore wanted to perform the dirty work in silence." By this he meant making the "newly acquired *lebensraum* in the east germ free" through the mass murders. Was he implying that the Holocaust was therefore a misunderstanding between Hitler and Himmler?

Wolff remained convinced until his death that Hitler did not know what happened in the extermination camps. He admitted under questioning by the American interrogator Dobbs on April 24, 1947, that he was being dishonest with himself at that time. He gave assurances that he had never heard about the Einsatzgruppen before the end of the war. Could he truly not remember that he, together with Himmler in Minsk, had watched as Einsatzgruppen 8 pushed over one hundred people into a ditch and murdered them there?

Journalist Gitta Sereny tried to explain how someone can shut himself off from such atrocities after a nine-day visit with Hitler's armaments minister, Albert Speer (published in the ZEIT magazine in 1978). After serving his sentence at Spandau prison, following his conviction by the Nuremberg tribunal, Speer was living in Heidelberg writing his memoirs. He also stated that he knew nothing of the mass murders, which may appear believable since he had relatively little to do with Himmler and the SS. The Nuremberg Tribunal accepted that he was not informed of the mass murders. However, with Gitta Sereny, Speer did admit, "I can say that I had an idea... that something horrible was happening to the Jews." Anyone able to observe the happenings in Hitler's Reich from the lofty standpoint of a minister or as an SS Obergruppenführer, had to at least have an *idea* of something dreadful was taking place. Wolff, however, would never admit that.

After April 1947 Wolff was no longer considered a prisoner under investigation in Nuremberg. Perhaps his numerous protests had some effect, or perhaps the decision not to prosecute him made the difference since he had been transferred to POW status. In addition, he was a "senior" prisoner of war, and therefore the POW representative with the U.S. authorities and had to guarantee everyone's good behavior and well-being. If the food was bad, he had to file a complaint. When the Americans dismissed the German cleaning women who up to that point had been cleaning the hallways, stairs and toilets, he wrote to the "prison director," a U.S. Army lieutenant colonel, that he please "have the regular cleaning of the common rooms continued."

However, Wolff could not handle his concerns about his family. Frau Frieda (neé von Römheld) pulled through bravely with her four children in difficult times with help from her relatives and wrote comforting letters to her ex-husband. Frau Inge (the divorced Countess Bernstorff), with her three children from three different husbands, had to face mounting difficulties. In the summer, Wolff asked for help in a letter to his interrogator Rapp, with whom he obviously got along well. The cash that had been taken from him during his captivity in Bozen—Swiss francs, lire, reich marks—had still not been sent to his wife. Some soldier had simply let it disappear into his own pocket. His wife was without income now for two and a half years and had been forced to sell her last valuables at giveaway prices. Recently, they had even impounded the furniture, which was a normal reprisal against high-ranking leaders of the Nazi party.

Many months later, Wolff sent Husmann a request. He said that his wife Inge, who was ill, complained to him: "Both doctors prescribe rest, inner peace" and medication that "can only be found abroad." "More recent emotional burdens could lead to the slow end of a human life." Wolff "begged" Husmann to "obtain a corresponding dose of the medication as quickly as possible. I will repay your expenses, of course, as soon as I can. Should anything serious happen to my wife as a result of the continued inconsideration" (the still unfulfilled promises to protect him and his family from persecution) "it would mean the public bankruptcy of your guarantees and obligations."

Husmann did not take this stern reminder of his role as negotiator during the surrender too badly. He continued to help Wolff whenever he could. He understood that Wolff turned to him and Waibel as "guarantors" of the rather vague promises made by the Allied negotiators. The two Swiss private citizens, the director of a boarding school and an officer without official support, could at best obtain something through their persistent appeals. Allen Dulles would have responded to Wolff's complaints. However, he did have reasons to play deaf; as a politician, he was on his way to becoming director of the CIA, and his brother John Foster Dulles was attempting to be appointed U.S. Secretary of State. During a speech in New York, Allen Dulles could indeed afford to recommend economic aid for the starving Germans so soon after the end of the war, but had he openly pleaded for an SS Obergruppenführer, it would not have helped his career.

The interrogating officer Rapp told Wolff that Allen Dulles' station had been closed "at the end of the war"; the attorney had "due to his contacts, at most an indirect influence...but no power to issue orders." Robert Murphy, the political advisor to General Lucius Clay, the U.S. High Commissioner for the American Sector, was a more likely official to be able to help. Murphy would be in a favorable mood if Wolff could clear up several facts that remained unclear during the last weeks of the war. This was how Rapp established a statement made by Wolff that there had been a "traitor" during the negotiations for capitulation, someone who had continually informed Kaltenbrunner and Himmler of the treachery of the Highest SS and Police Führer in Italy.

"It was," said Wolff, "the Chief of the Swiss Defense, Colonel Masson." SS Gruppenführer Walter Schellenberg, chief of German espionage in the last phase of the war, told him this during a chance meeting in the Nuremberg prison. Indeed the role of Roger Masson was discussed among Swiss citizens; he handled the exchange of information with Schellenberg, when the latter was still Chief of the Foreign Department of the SD. Masson played both ends in establishing a central exchange of secrets between the Axis powers and the Western Allies. From his subordinate, Major Waibel, he found out the general outline of what was happening between Wolff and Dulles. Schellenberg did not like the situation, as he wanted to control contacts to the OSS in order to save himself at the right time, and also because Himmler and Kaltenbrunner were both demanding that he be in contact with the Western Allies. Both were hoping to somehow manage to cheat their way out of the Nazi *Götterdämmerung*.

The question as to why the Americans never tried Wolff in Nuremberg was asked many times. Wolff answered it himself the same way on every occasion; despite thorough and lengthy examinations, nothing criminal could be discovered. Telford Taylor was chief prosecutor during the second phase of the Nuremberg trials, a New York lawyer by profession. During the investigations of the Munich court against Wolff, Taylor testified before a Bavarian examining judge and said, among other things, "Mr. Wolff was at first in the group of people who could have been prosecuted... After he became a British prisoner, he was no longer under American jurisdiction." As Taylor was asked if the accusations against Wolff that were presented in Munich would also have been sufficient for a condemnation in Nuremberg, he said, "It would have been the proper place." In the indictment of the Munich prosecution, Taylor's sworn testimony, "with several perjured statements," according to Wolff, led to the conclusion that "the American criminal prosecutors" who did not have to proceed according to German legal procedures, "made a free choice among the many possible defendants at that time." Wolff "belonged to the suspects in Nuremberg who were spared final examination and prosecution." Why did this happen? Allen Dulles, whom Wolff called disloyal, could probably have cleared this up.

In January 1948 Wolff was finally handed over to the British, and was received very badly. They stuck him in a detention institution called "Tomato" in Minden in a cell that was constantly locked, without a windowpane, heating, a table or a chair. They took almost everything he had brought, including his files, and, what hurt him the most, all of his medals. In a letter "To the Prison Commandant Tomato" under the heading "urgent" and the short formulation "Sir," he protested; he was "neither a war criminal nor released from the Wehrmacht," and therefore was entitled to the "status of a prisoner of war with the rank of a full general." He threatened to complain through Ambassador Murphy (whose name he knew only through the interrogator Rapp), and Field Marshal Alexander, and he would take this "scandalous case to the English and the American public." This did not impress the commandant, who let the SS general freeze in the cold cell for twelve days. Wolff became ill and was transferred to the former concentration camp at Neuengamme near Hamburg. There he was informed he could no longer claim rights as a prisoner of war, however few those may have been; he was now a civilian prisoner awaiting trial because he had belonged to an organization that was declared to be criminal in Nuremberg.

In a list of his "imprisonment data" Wolff names the camp at Neuengamme an "Eng. internment concentration camp." He obviously did not want to remember that it had been a place of SS terror for many years, and that the British, as liberators of the prisoners, stood in disgust in front of piles of corpses—those who had died of starvation, epidemics, and being worked to death.

Wolff was informed that denazification proceedings against him would now be carried out. Every German was subjected to it during the first years following the end of the Nazi regime. The courts, specifically created for this purpose, were handling the procedure. Simple membership in the Nazi party or one of its organizations was reason enough for an investigation. This was even more of a certainty in cases of affiliation to something like the SS, which had been declared a criminal organization in Nuremberg. Anyone who had reached the rank of an Obergruppenführer was regarded automatically as "incriminated in principle." According to rank, position, and personal incrimination, a defendant could be sentenced to prison for many years, or be condemned to pay fines, have his assets confiscated, be banned from any profession, and other lesser punishments.

Formal incrimination could be lightened by providing proof that, although one paid dues and had occasionally given the Hitler salute when singing the national anthem, he had done nothing to strengthen violent Nazi rule. Any deviations from the National Socialist laws were virtually worth gold, especially if confirmed by sworn oaths by persons racially or politically persecuted, such as Jews, Christians, Marxists, or even state enemies actively opposed to the former regime. Since the majority of Germans had belonged to one National Socialist organization or another in some capacity, most of them were more or less seriously affected by denazification. For that reason, in those days many people created files of documents where friendly persons confirmed that they only wore the swastika under duress, out of gullibility, to cover their secret opposition, or out of misled idealism (anything not applicable was to be deleted).

Wolff already had an impressive collection of such "Persil certificates" at Nuremberg. He now used the three months in Neuengamme to increase the stack. Gaevernitz sent in a reference. The pastor of his former Lutheran congregation in Munich confirmed that, even in his SS uniform, he had visited the church, before leaving the Church altogether. A millionaire German banker certified that Wolff had been involved in the liberation of Baron Rothschild, his Viennese colleague. However, this was interrupted, because the British believed they still had to take him to court for murders in Italy, similar to the case of Field Marshal Kesselring. Therefore Wolff had to sit in the war criminal camp in Braunschweig for three more months.

In the summer of 1948, the British stopped trying to issue any criminal indictment against Wolff. They sent him to the internment camp at Fallingbostel, north of Hannover. In the meantime he had hired a lawyer from Hamburg, but could not pay his fees. He could merely transfer the 40 Deutsche marks "head money" that every German received after the currency reform of the summer of 1948. However, he made the lawyer aware of other sources of funds. There was, for example, Max Waibel, who had in the meantime been promoted to lieutenant colonel in the Swiss Army and was now the military attaché in Washington. He was wealthy enough to help out, but, even more importantly, he could persuade Dulles and Gaevernitz ("both supposedly very wealthy") to also make a contribution.

Chapter 15

The "General" Representative

The Cold War had become a reality and was a confirmation for Wolff that in Italy he had already found the path to a new German future. "My surrender," he wrote to a friend, "was the Tauroggen of the 20th century… and still contained all the related opportunities for Germany." He saw himself in the historic hero's role of General York von Wartenburg of Prussia, who retreated from Russia with his army in 1812, and then on his own, broke the alliance with Napoleon to sign a pact with the former enemy. "My case," Wolff wrote, "is neither criminal nor a case for the courts, but rather a specifically political issue related to the honor and the broken assurances of President Truman, Churchill, and Field Marshal Alexander. That is my luck and my tragedy at the same time."

The public prosecutor from the court at Hamburg-Bergedorf was ready with the indictment at the end of August 1948. These were ordinary criminal proceedings in the British zone of occupation, and preceded the actual judgment chamber's sentence. Wolff's case was heard from November 3 to 6, and the injustice done to him was announced to the entire world. During the summer he had written to Husmann that it would "lead to an outrageous scandal and loss of prestige for the Anglo-Americans if they" decided not to "keep their promises, that were already three years overdue" by letting this come to a criminal prosecution. "If the vast crimes against humanity and justice which have been committed not only against us, but also against the thousands of innocent women and children, become public, then the world will hold its breath as horrified as when they learn of the Nazi atrocities." His comparison proves once more that the perspective changes radically as soon as the oppressor becomes the oppressed.

Husmann attended the hearing as a witness. He was allowed to testify thoroughly about Wolff's part in the surrender in Italy. The chairman of the court, a district court director, and two Hamburg citizens as assessors were impressed by the respectful recognition that a Swiss neutral participant of that operation was giving to a German. Husmann emphatically refuted the suspicion that Wolff "only acted out of selfish motives." He referred in this case to his knowledge of human nature that he had acquired in the teaching profession. He pointed out to the court that the Allies had decided not to "press charges against Wolff because they were so convinced by him. I ask the Germans," he continued, "to show the same understanding to Wolff that we Swiss, the Americans and the English have shown the defendant."

As much as he impressed the court with this, it must be remembered that the enthusiastic witness had only known the accused during his last eight weeks as an SS officer. The court could not forget that this man had worn the SS uniform for years and the awful deeds carried out in the name of the SS ideology.

As Wolff recounted his achievements to the court, he occasionally contradicted himself; on one hand he wanted to show how effective he was during his rise in Hitler's set up, but on the other hand he avoided responsibility whenever possible. Chief of the Personal Staff, according to his description, was a misleading title; in truth, he was only Himmler's chief of protocol. When he was told that based on the Nazi organization chart, his role must have been much more important, he replied that the chart had been written by Dr. Robert Ley, the Reich Leader of Party Organizations, and that one could "not take that man very seriously." He most certainly "did not find the concentration camps pleasant," but because "of social situations before the war" he was often told "jokes and tales of atrocities," while he had "asked individual prisoners about their treatment during every visit, with the promise of my protection. None of them had ever complained." He openly admitted having witnessed the medical altitude experiments when Luftwaffe Dr. Rascher used concentration camp prisoners as guinea pigs since there was already a lot of this information in the Nuremberg court files. However, Wolff stated once again that he would volunteer anytime for those experiments because of their important purpose.

At the Bergedorf hearing he described his relationship to the Vatican in guarded terms, compared to his later declarations on the subject. He never discussed Hitler's orders to kidnap the Pope and remove him from Rome; only an evacuation of the Head of the Catholic Church from the approaching Allies had been considered, and he had also opposed it. At that time he received "an invitation to the Vatican from a person of high standing," and only vaguely mentioned his audience with Pius XII. In that conversation on May 10, 1944, he was risking both "his neck and position" because he wanted to enlist the Pope as a peace negotiator. Unfortunately nothing came of this, because the next planned meeting never took place. He had fallen ill and the Allies had occupied Rome in the meantime.

He had never taken anti-Semitism seriously at first as an element of the Party program. He found it "unfortunate and unpleasant" that all Jews be forced to wear a yellow star. Himmler explained to him why the mark of identification was necessary; it was because the world leader of the Jews, Chaim Weizmann, had called all the Jews on earth to wage an active fight against National Socialism—that they had to mark them all as enemies of the regime. The Germans ran the danger, otherwise, of unknowingly passing on information to them during simple conversations. "I had the impression," Wolff said about the yellow star, "that for the racially conscious Jews, it was an honor." The absurdity of such a remark makes one wonder.

When he telephoned State Secretary Ganzenmüller at the Ministry of Transportation to order the railroad cars for the trains from Warsaw to Treblinka, he believed he was only fixing a temporary delay in transportation. "It is possible," he said, "that I knew this was a transport of Jews." Not until Ganzenmüller's "letter did I find out about the large transports... I was not aware of anything criminal happening." The hearing lasted from Wednesday to Saturday, more than four days. That was rather long for a hearing before the court. Attempts to prove the personal guilt of the defendant were somewhat weak and always wound up in general discussions about Nazi crimes. The Ganzenmüller incident, which led to Wolff's sentencing sixteen years later as an accomplice to mass murder, was used only to prove that he *knew* that Jews were being persecuted. He was sentenced at Bergedorf, according to the indictment, as "a member of a criminal organization after September 1, 1939," and "with the knowledge that it was related to acts that, according to Article 6 of the statute of the International Military Tribunal, were declared criminal." He was sentenced to five years in prison; the two years he spent in prison while awaiting trial were counted as served.

Wolff's sentence was meaningless since it was never enacted because the court had bungled the appointment of the assessors, apparently out of laziness, making an appeal inevitable whether the sentence was faulty or perfect. The appeal, of course, changed nothing for Wolff, who remained in custody. Immediately after the hearing, he was taken to the Esterwegen "Internment concentration camp" (as he called it) in Emsland, where "the mud soldiers" hostile to the state were shoveling snow. Wolff had been there once, as Himmler's escort.

On March 8, 1949, the sentence of the court was reversed and Wolff returned to the district court prison at Bergedorf. This was, he hoped, the final battle with the justice system, so he collected more material with a zeal that he never showed before. In court he immediately requested a typewriter in his cell, as his defense attorney said, "to refute the mistakes of the first judgment." In the weeks that followed, Wolff collected more "Persil certificates." Among others, former minister Dr. Hans-Heinrich Lammers confirmed from prison in Nuremberg what little influence Wolff had with Field Marshal Albert Kesselring, Field Marshal Milch, former secretary of state and ambassador Ernst von Weiszäcker, from Baron Parilli in Italy, Allen Dulles in the USA and SS Obergruppenführer August Heissmayer. The Stinnes son-in-law, Gero von Gaevernitz, promised to travel from the United States to the hearing in order to testify on Wolff's behalf.

The second hearing also took four days, from May 31 to June 3, 1949. A different district court was chairman, whom Wolff quickly charmed, according to the press report, by answering "the questions of the court in the most obliging manner." Among others, retired envoy Rudolf Rahn and former secretary of state in the ministry of propaganda Gutterer, both prominent figures from the upper crust of the Third Reich who had survived and had been released, now spoke well of the defendant under oath.

The highpoint of the hearing was the arrival of Gaevernitz, whom a Hamburg daily newspaper falsely called a U.S. diplomat. It was not easy for him, he said, "to testify on behalf of an SS general," because he had "fought against him and the ideas he represented since the beginning of

National Socialism." However, justice demanded "that I testify about what I know in connection with the surrender in Italy." It was thanks to Wolff that it happened at all, and that during the German retreat, the large Italian hydroelectric power station at the foot of the Alps and the docks in Genoa and Trieste were not blown up, as Hitler and Himmler had ordered. In addition, Wolff had the most valuable pieces of art saved from destruction during the fighting, and prevented the killing of a large number of political prisoners by the Gestapo during the Allied advance. Although Wolff had ended up in life-threatening situations many times during the surrender negotiations, he never "demanded any special treatment after the war."

At the hearing, he asked that Husmann certify in writing that Allied representatives had promised him that he would be given an important position for the establishment of democracy in Germany. But he then decided that it would be better not to taint his nobly described portrait with such untimely requests. The court was clearly becoming increasingly sympathetic toward him. The district court counsel regretted that "the defendant had been treated harshly and detained for a long time."

At the time of the hearing, Wolff was already released on a 4,000 new Deutsche marks bail bond, a small fortune at the time; friends had lent the money. They were convinced that things would start to improve for him, so his "personal credit" was not cancelled. He could be satisfied with the second sentence: four years in prison, but because the four years of detention while awaiting trial were counted, from this moment on, he was no longer threatened with imprisonment. The court could hardly have let him off with less if they wanted to see an SS Obergruppenführer have rights to the democratic state's benefits, because they had held him in prison too long. "In the court's opinion, the only fault was the restrictive language and many qualifying clauses, by which the defendant admitted his knowledge of Nazi atrocities." On the other hand, the court regretted "imposing a prison sentence that was fairly proportionate to the sentences of lower SS ranks." Wolff was indeed "an outcast in the SS" and could leave "the courtroom with a clean slate."

Wolff's defense attorney was not satisfied with that. As he left the courtroom, he protested within earshot, "Acquittal! Acquittal!" Then the state treasury would be required to pay his fees, and not his near-broke client. Wolff, however, from then on wore his belated freedom as if it were another medal. He was once again someone, and on top of that he had received the democratic seal of approval. Since his release from prison, he was living in Hamburg once again, in a respectable neighborhood near the oceanfront. Now he was getting into new territory. The chief of police in Lüneburg still had a personal file on Wolff following his stay at the Fallingbostel camp, and because of the sentence he was required to approve any change of residence. Wolff requested that he be allowed to move to Lake Tegern, to the house of Professor Padua. His life-sized oil painting of Wolff dressed in white still existed, and soon decorated one of the walls of his house.

At the start of his new life he possessed, besides a certificate from the men's' prison at Hamburg-Bergedorf that entitled him to grocery coupons until June 18, 1949, a notice from the court that he had been classified as a minor criminal (category III). According to his rank, he should have been classified as a serious criminal (category I) or at least as a criminal (category II). While many SS members of lower ranks were only allowed to work as unskilled workers with an hourly wage of approximately one DM, the only job closed to him was anything in the public service.

He was not interested in that kind of career anyway; the public sector was quite stingy during the lean years of reconstruction. In November 1949, he was informed that he had been switched to category IV as a casual participant; it was addressed to the "former General of the Waffen SS," but he already had a different title and now called himself a "general representative." He was working in the advertising department of a weekly magazine, the kind of publication seeking to conquer a broad readership among the West German public. Wolff had his office in Cologne, in the economically strong region of the Federal Republic. He made good wages, and after a short time brought his second family to Starnberg to an apartment with a wonderful view of the lake and the mountains. He was living in a four-room apartment in Cologne. His self-confidence was unscathed and he told his acquaintances that he was living once again in a little castle, as once before on Lake Wolfgang. The Starnberg home however had only three rooms on the first floor. Wolff's rise proved to be unstoppable. With the acquaintances he still had among industrial giants and bankers from Himmler's circle of friends, he had no problem contacting the advertising departments of large companies. His knowledge of the material since his days in the Munich advertising company and his talent for making rather common issues seem more important through long presentations made him a representative equal in rank to a general. It was his luck that in those days many companies did so well that they placed their additional profits into advertising rather than pay extra taxes. In view of the increased business of the Cologne office, the publisher in Munich—who was actually an active anti-Fascist—had no reservations about making a former SS Obergruppenführer a rich man. His income was dependent on the business; it rose every year until his retirement and reached, according to Wolff's own statement, more than 120,000 D-Marks a month (over US$40,000 in the 1950s). He didn't find it difficult to buy the small manor by in 1953. It had 7,000 square meters on the waterfront, a dock, a bathhouse, and landing pier. Frau Inge and her three children were once again living in the lifestyle they were used to. Since Frau Frieda, who now had two grown daughters and two younger sons, also lived in Bavaria, family connections were not difficult to maintain. The father of both families now had the opportunity, as a private citizen, to lead a secure and affluent life; his dark past only to be discussed among a circle of trusted individuals.

However, he did not want to let that heroic past sink silently into oblivion. In so far as he had any free time, aside from earning money and taking care of relationships and friendships, he began to write his memoirs. He never got past some loose fragments, and even though he said that he wanted to tell what really happened during the Third Reich, those snippets of memoirs contain only very little that is unknown and a lot of unimportant information. Since he quickly understood that he would not succeed in carving out his place in history he looked for connections to professional writers and discovered that his publishing company wanted to turn the past into an economically fruitful enterprise.

In those days Germans were hungry for information about the reasons behind the National Socialist regime. They were working industriously at blotting out the consequences of the catastrophe, but also wanted to know how and why it all happened. As long as Allied occupation rules were in force, any publication dealing with the Nazi past ran the risk of official censorship for suspected support of the outlawed Nazi regime. Then when the young democracy announced freedom of the press, the emerging yellow journalism offered German readers fantastic discoveries, such as the cleverly forged diary of Hitler's girlfriend, Eva Braun. Wolff's employer, the illustrated magazine *Revue*, located in Munich, wanted to offer their readers something better. Their author Heinrich Benedikt wrote a series of reports under the title "The Unsolved Cases," and as early as May 1950 Wolff himself was presented to the readers in words and pictures in three issues as a general of the Waffen SS.

The story mainly dealt with what happened during Wolff's glorious time in Italy, garnished with anecdotes of internal SS operations. The crimes of the SS, however, were not mentioned. Since Wolff, in the glory of his office, had been photographed often and never missed an opportunity to make prints for himself, the *Revue* readers got to know his best side, at least visually as a smart-looking man and soldier with engaging features, who stood with Himmler and every now and then with Hitler or Mussolini. Without a doubt, he had been an important man.

Wolff was no longer the protagonist after the third issue; someone else was used in the series. The response to the publication was minimal. Even among the former SS officers few paid any attention, because from their viewpoint Wolff was trying to sit on too many SS stools at once. The former members of the Waffen SS wanted to be considered as the real soldiers and fighters for Germany or even for a Germanic Europe. The others, the so-called "Black SS," included all those who wore the uniform, from functionary to secretary, from the lowly militant to the industrial giants and business leaders. The majority did not relish being reminded of their membership. Finally, there were the dubious characters from the Gestapo, the SD and the concentration camp guards that the other two groups and Wolff wanted nothing to do with. The soldiers rejected him because after his service as a lieutenant during the First World War, he had hardly heard the rifle bullet whiz past. He was not popular with the majority of the SS veterans because he apparently had been too much of an intriguer as Himmler's right-hand man, and now through his public appearances, he was seen as drawing attention back to the SS. All were saying that he had learned nothing from his experiences during the years after the war.

In 1952, when he wanted to donate his papers to the Munich "Institute for Contemporary History," he said—as he later mentioned to this author—that Hitler had not ordered the extermination of the Jews, and only found out about it at the end of 1944. Heinrich Heim, an official who at times took stenographic notes of Hitler's table talk at Führer headquarters, reported a similar absence of orders in a letter. He and Wolff knew each other from the "Wolfsschanze." Heim obviously included the former general among the community of true believers in sending him the letter. When a long text came from the still anti-Semitic Heim years later, where he was apparently attempting to prove that the gas chambers had not existed in the concentration camps, Wolff did not even attempt to correct that falsehood, but instead saved all of his correspondence as material for the Institute of Contemporary History. In 1950 he was informed that along with the legal end of his denazification in Hamburg, restrictions to his professional activities were also removed—not only did he acquire the untainted quality that the courts certified, but he also had faultless personal papers once again. In 1953 he was allowed entry into Switzerland (with his wife Inge) without difficulty to visit his former negotiating partners.

Wolff and his wife were guests for two days in August at the home of Max Waibel, who in the meantime had risen to colonel. The residence was located in Dorenbach near Lucerne. There, eight years before, the decisive negotiations with Dulles had taken place. "Now a circle has closed happily once again," Wolff wrote in the guest book. He had already won the sympathies of Frau Waibel during his first visit. She had found him to be a "well-groomed and cultured guest" and she was concerned that she should, "for God's sake, find a bed for this giant." At that time, she deeply regretted "that he was in the SS." Now she read in her guest book, "Hopefully we will see you again soon in Germany."

In 1956 Wolff's oldest daughter married the son of a well-known and wealthy athlete whom Karl Wolff had grown to like during the preparations for the Olympic games in 1936 in Berlin. Now he produced the revelation that he had kept modestly hidden through the years, namely that, on April 20, 1945, ten days before his suicide in the bunker under the Reich Chancellery, Hitler had promoted him to the rank of senior general of the Waffen SS. The promotion was never recorded in the official archives. However, it was mentioned in the "German Book of Genealogy," volume 175, the Gotha for commoners.

A "Central Office" was established in Stuttgart during the postwar years where all the material regarding Nazi crimes was collected and archived. This was necessary, because the events could often only be recorded in bits and pieces by the justice administration in the different states. The records of both victims and criminals were usually spread throughout Germany. This state of affairs, often doubling the work required during the investigations, was unavoidable and some connections only came to light when all the documents were brought together in one place. With some delay, increasing numbers of those guilty were being found and indicted.

The state attorney's office in Munich was investigating former SS Hauptsturmführer Dr. Otto Bradfisch because as commander of Einsatzgruppen 8 during the invasion of the Soviet Union behind the front lines, he had ordered the mass murder of Jews and Communists. On June 9, 1958, as he was questioned about shootings in Minsk that had taken place in the middle of August 1941, he stated that those executions were legal and that he had been ordered to them carry out. This could easily be verified simply because of the presence of the Reichsführer SS and Karl Wolff. Everything took place following instructions from higher up, and if he had refused, he would have placed himself in a dangerous position.

Still no one in the department of justice even thought of accusing Wolff, simply because he was present when those murders took place. Exactly one month later, the state attorney questioned him whether Bradfisch was correct in referring to an emergency situation where he was following orders. Wolff confirmed that statement. Bradfisch's civilian position as a minor senior civil servant in the Gestapo hardly allowed him to not follow orders or even to counter Himmler. As an Obergruppenführer, Wolff was allowed a bit more leeway—"for example, in starting the negotiations for surrender in Italy... because I had rank and position so that they could not just make me disappear without a trace."

At that point the whole matter appeared to be settled. Bradfisch was sentenced by the District Court in Munich in 1961 to ten years in prison. At the hearing, he said that he asked Himmler in Minsk whether the executions were covered by law. Himmler dismissed those scruples offhand; an order from the Führer was the law and Hitler had given them the order to wipe out the entire Jewish population in the East.

Chapter 16

Eichmann's Accomplice

An alarming signal from a very different source affected Wolff with the publication in 1960 of a book entitled *Eichmann and His Accomplices*. The author, Dr. Robert Kempner, was a top senior civil servant in the Prussian government service until 1933, when he emigrated as a hated political opponent persecuted by the Nazis. After the war, he was part of the American prosecution team at the International Military Tribunal at Nuremberg. He was the most knowledgeable member of the prosecution and very familiar with the procedures and connections in Germany during the Third Reich, and was determined to hunt down all the Nazi criminals. As a lawyer, the American legal system became as familiar to him as the German, and he mastered both languages which turned out to be extremely useful.

Karl Wolff was held responsible during the Nuremberg trial against the chief of the administrative and economic main office of the SS for his exchange of letters with State Secretary Ganzenmüller (the purpose being to obtain railroad cars to transport the Warsaw Jews to the extermination camp at Treblinka). Kempner was determined to put Wolff on trial at Nuremberg. Chief Prosecutor Telford Taylor, who was his boss at the time, would not have stopped Kempner had he not been clearly instructed by Robert Murphy, political advisor to General Lucius Clay, American High Commissioner for the U.S. Zone, to spare Wolff. But Kempner refused either to forgive or forget. After the founding of the Federal Republic, he remained in Germany, working as a lawyer in Frankfurt. In his book, the exchange of letters with Ganzenmüller was introduced as evidence concerning a man living in West Germany and who had taken part in the extermination of the Jews. When Taylor was later questioned as a witness at the Wolff trial and asked why the SS Obergruppenführer had not been indicted back then for his involvement in the transport of the Jews, he said that "other ways...seemed to be more favorable" to "take care of" this case, either through the denazification process or within the German system of justice. Kempner wanted to remind the Germans of this unfinished business; the time seemed to be ripe because of the kidnapping of the former SS Obersturmbannführer and Jewish expert for the Gestapo, Adolf Eichmann, from Argentina and his trial in Jerusalem. Eichmann had also mentioned Wolff as the type of SS officer who usually took care of his business with "white gloves" to avoid getting his hands dirty.

According to the Cologne newspaper *Neue Illustrierte*, the Eichmann trial was a good occasion to inform the German people about "what a true believer among Hitler's followers had said about the dreadful deeds of the Third Reich." Under banner HEADLINES EICHMANN'S BOSS: HEINRICH HIMMLER in the spring of 1961, it published "a portrait" of the Reichsführer SS, written "by Karl Wolff, General of the Waffen SS." The introductory paragraph said: "For the first time since the collapse of the thousand year Reich, a man who belonged to the innermost vicious circle around Himmler for ten years speaks ... Wolff reports the facts, and gives his personal opinion, which is not that of the editors..." He saw himself as the leading witness and the readers were to be the judges and issue a verdict.

Himmler had already been damned for eternity by the whole world. What about Wolff? He had never felt guilty; even his punishment under denazification had been erased from his character reference. He expected that the readers would be more vocal in their approval of the basic attitude and actions of a general who, unfortunately, was still not well known. The opening issue therefore began with a sympathetic account about the near fistfight in August 1943 when Wolff supposedly chased Himmler from behind his desk. After that scene, he reported on the mass murder in Minsk, or rather (as it is called in the report) the "execution of one hundred Jewish spies and saboteurs." Then, Himmler's curriculum vitae followed, beginning with his early years in the Nazi party, which Wolff had no first-hand knowledge of.

Even though he did not write a single line of that article, the text begins this way: "I, Karl Wolff, SS Obergruppenführer and General of the Waffen SS, request to speak. My conscience forces me to do so." A journalist from the *Neue Illustrierte* did the ghostwriting. Once again Wolff thought he had found an eloquent spokesman for his deeds. The writer had been in the Waffen SS. But by the second issue it became obvious that one could not rely even on such comrades any more. The former SS soldier made an editorial decision, and after the third issue Wolff was no longer the main topic. He announced in the introduction: "Since the end of the war, I have kept silent, full of shame for having served Heinrich Himmler for so long." Now, once again he returned to silence: the magazine told him that his story wouldn't sell.

But it did sell in a way he had not anticipated. The readers protested. Wolff had once again stated that neither Hitler nor he knew anything of the mass murders in the extermination camps. Someone attacked him for spreading "monstrous assertions," as he had already done as a witness at a criminal hearing in 1952. And a doctor from Innsbruck said that either Wolff was lying, or that he had been such an incompetent adjutant to Himmler that one had to wonder how he could have kept his position for ten years. Even the author Axel Eggebrecht spoke up; in his letter, he simply called Wolff an "accomplice."

Robert Kempner shared the same opinion. In his letter, he placed under his name the title "private deputy to the U.S. main prosecutor at Nuremberg." He was often asked, he wrote, "in connection with people like Wolff," why this high-ranking SS officer had not been charged at Nuremberg, where only a total of 199 of the main war criminals were brought to justice. The German, French, Dutch, and other courts sentenced many more guilty parties. Numerous pieces of evidence relating to the crimes committed were "not found until years after the end of the Nuremberg trials." "For this reason no one can refer back and say that the Allies had not found anything against him at Nuremberg. The comment often used—'even Dr. Kempner had tested my case and let me go'—legally meant nothing. In that sense, whoever was only a witness in Nuremberg was in no way protected from German courts." For the German prosecuting attorneys, this was an obvious hint.

Even from his SS comrades, Wolff received no applause. There was a club of former soldiers of the Waffen SS, the HIAG. Their legal status was often in doubt, but as a club they were never banned. This club sent a newsletter, called *The Volunteer*, to its members seeking to make it clear to the public that the SS had not always been the same everywhere. The "field troops named the Waffen SS" had "constantly distanced itself from the main SS in its mission and had nothing more to do with it in that sense." Himmler had indeed made the Higher SS and Police leaders Generals of the Waffen SS, but they only had the rank and never a military command. This explained by a committee of "the federal association of soldiers of the former Waffen SS."

In one of the following newsletters under the title "The Devil's Adjutant," an interview appeared with "Comrade Wolff…in order to find through questions and answers an explanation for the articles" in the Cologne paper. The Baden Württemberg State association of the club had already sent a letter to its members and informed them of "Wolff's shame for hire." In the interview, Wolff admitted that he had not written the report himself and had only provided the journalist with "hints, documents and pictures." What was his motive? It certainly could not have been large royalties. "In the course of the Eichmann Trial" he said, "I feared a new wave of collective blame against the Waffen SS," and he wanted to ensure a truthful account. Did he cooperate one more time to cover up even worse things, or did he want to call attention to his own laurels?

The unavoidable questions came from his interviewer as to whether or not he had even been a General of the Waffen SS. He countered that he was, "The first to be named a general of the Waffen SS." Did he ever lead a unit in war? He referred to his rank and position as lieutenant and company leader in the Infantry Bodyguard Regiment 115, and to his service description as "plenipotentiary General of the German Armed Forces in Italy," who "kept the supply routes open" for Kesselring's southern front, "and had to fight the partisans in the rear, at times with up to 300,000 men." (Others reported hardly half that strength.) For that he was decorated with the German Cross of Gold and then in February 1945 was recommended for the Knight's Cross. This decoration never reached him, however, as the enemy was faster than German military bureaucracy. When he was asked about his negotiations with Allen Dulles, he said: "After a very critical examination of my motives and my conduct in acting without authority," Hitler "completely approved" his behavior—this was a lie, because he had hidden the already agreed-to surrender from the Führer, and because it had been expressly forbidden.

Wolff's assertion that he first heard of the murders of the Jews in March 1945 cost him credibility, his interlocutor said. "One must," countered Wolff, "understand the dictatorship and its power and task distribution to comprehend this ignorance. Even the slightest violation of the regulations of secrecy was threatened with death and all family members were liable for the crimes of one. According to Eichmann's statements, the order to murder had only been given verbally. Himmler "never spoke to me personally or in confidence about these things." For that reason, he could "not have had even the slightest knowledge of those procedures."

Ironically, his SS opponents answered in the next issue of *The Volunteer:* "He was the liaison officer between the most powerful and the second most powerful two men in the Reich. How could he not know what privates found out?" He apparently forgot during his interview "that he had told *Neue Illustrierte* the story of how, during a mass execution, the brains of a victim were splattered in Himmler's face... In view of such incidents, did he feel like a simple-minded Parsifal? Did Wolff enjoy Himmler's trust? That was a key question. We never heard of top leaders appointing adjutants whom they did not trust."

Certainly General Karl Wolff was not as ingenious a strategist as the famous Count Moltke back in 1870, but he would have been better off had he at least learned from him to keep quiet. His employer at the magazine felt compelled to fire such a simple-minded employee because of the articles; however, it was agreed that Wolff's stepson (from the marriage to Inge), who lived in Cologne and was in the advertising business, would take the position. In another irony, whether the arrest warrant issued by the district court of Weilheim (which was presented to him on January 18, 1962, at his "little castle" in Kempfenhausen, thus preventing the newly unemployed executive from indulging in his favorite pastime, the writing of his memoirs), stemmed largely from his efforts to secure a pedestal for himself in the German halls of glory.

The arrest warrant came, as he said, out of nowhere. It assumed that Wolff knew the dreadful secret of the Third Reich when he ordered the railway cars for the Jewish transport at the Reich Ministry of Transport. On the last of the eight type-written pages, the warrant states: "The organized mass murder of the Jews in the extermination camps occurred as the result of base motivations and were carried out in a cruel manner"—which, according to the Criminal Code, the facts of the case were sufficient for a murder indictment. "The accused is therefore suspected of abetting the murder of hundreds of thousands of Jews. The arrest is ordered because the crime gives the grounds for examination, and counters the risk of escape, and aside from that, in consideration of the extent of further necessary investigations, there appears to be the danger of suppression of evidence."

He was taken into custody at the Weilheim jail for several weeks before he was transferred to the prison at Munich-Stadelheim, and handed over to the district court in Munich. As legal advisor he chose the Munich lawyer Dr. Alfred Seidl, who had experience in the defense of Nazis before the International Military tribunal in Nuremberg. Wolff hoped for help from someone who really could not say much about the charges—his American friend Gero von Gaevernitz, who had already testified at the prosecution in Munich at the beginning of February. This had not been very effective, but the call for assistance implied, however, that Wolff expected in exchange for his part in the surrender activities, a sort of general amnesty for all the sins of his Nazi past.

Attempts by the defense attorney to spare his client being held in custody while awaiting trial also failed. He offered to post one hundred thousand marks bail, and also mentioned that the deputy camp commandant at Auschwitz was temporarily freed from prison for half the amount. The court decided that the danger of an escape attempt always existed in such a case, because "this precise circle of people, strongly suspected of having had a part in such crimes, would typically attempt to escape from their punishment by fleeing to another country."

The defense already in the early stages of the proceedings, in mid-February 1962, argued to subvert the trial just as it was beginning, and to which Wolff would refer repeatedly in the time that followed. In a legal document Dr. Seidl pointed out that the American counsel for the prosecution at Nuremberg "presented" the accused "with the exchange of letters with Dr. Ganzenmüller during cross-examination" and that they "naturally also checked the question as to whether the accused in this case had been guilty of punishable behavior." At no time had charges been brought against him.

The next legal document contained additional remarks that such an accusation was reasonable at that time in preparation of a trial in Nuremberg against several SS officers. In that trial Obergruppenführer Gottlob Berger and Brigadeführer Walter Schellenberg, among others, were sentenced to long prison terms, but were pardoned in 1950.

From Dr. Seidl's perspective, the Americans had done their protégé a disservice by preventing his criminal prosecution. Namely, had he been sentenced for the Ganzenmüller matter, he would have been free anyway, and no court could have prosecuted him.

The prisoner's situation got worse, when on July 31, 1962, a second arrest warrant was issued accusing him "in his capacity as SS Obergruppenführer and SS Chief of a Main Office" he had "at least provided psychological assistance" during the massacre in Minsk in August 1941. The reason for that visit by Himmler and the "highest SS officer" had been to ease the consciences of the men in the Einsatzgruppen. "He provided equally strong support to the men, of which he was well aware."

It may have still been possible to keep him out of prison had they been successful in getting one of the two charges against him dismissed. Dr. Seidl had defended SS Obergruppenführer Oswald Pohl at Nuremberg and Wolff had testified as a witness in that trial—to stand by Pohl, as he asserted. However, after being sentenced to death, Pohl blamed Karl Wolff of having transferred his own responsibility to other heads of the main offices by providing a misleading description of the organizational structure of the SS. In that trial on June 4, 1947, Wolff once again stated that he did not know what was happening to the Jews. The prosecutor had, however, shown him the exchange of letters with Ganzenmüller and asked: "Does this refresh your memory, Herr General?" To deny it would have been pointless. Wolff's answer was, "I do not in any way deny, after this refreshing of my memory, that I came in contact with these matters... but I can actually not find anything criminal in transporting Jews." The prosecution then tried to prove through other questions that Wolff had been informed by way of Himmler' speeches or written notes. On the next day, once the topic returned to the exchange of letters, Seidl jumped in, and with his questions gave Wolff the opportunity to report his version of the exchange of letters. After his description, only a chain of unlucky circumstances made him appear as an accomplice.

"The Honorable Judge Phillips," he had added to his statements, "placed doubt on the credibility of my statement yesterday." Now the judge should please state "whether his doubt remains unchanged. I may comment that to continue in this doubt would have the same unfavorable consequences practically speaking, which resulted from my being placed in an insane asylum last year."

This example of Wolff's aggressive rhetoric shows how he can impress people in critical situations. Judge Phillips was softened back then and only said: "I will accept your explanation." Was that the equivalent of an acquittal? Wolff now told the Munich examining judge that he should understand that his efforts would be fruitless. If an Allied court had indeed already heard of Wolff's activities about the railroad cars, then on the basis of the agreement between the Allies and the Federal Republic, he could not be accused of the same crime again.

This objection was taken seriously in Munich. Judge D. Donald Phillips, now back in North Carolina, was asked under oath how far his statement about Wolff as a witness was to be considered as an acquittal. The judge remembered that "General Wolff had been subjected to an extremely pressing cross-examination by counsel for the prosecution Robbins, by Judge Musmanno, and from those testifying." He also remembered that he had said: "I accept your explanation." At the end, according to Phillips, a confidential judge's consultation took place as to whether the War Crimes court should recommend bringing charges against Wolff. Since this had been denied, the Second Tribunal of the International Military Tribunal had closed the case. Former U.S. Prosecuting Attorney Telford Taylor was also heard. He explained, "a person who was not charged" and was let go, can not draw the conclusion "that he will not later be prosecuted by some other court." It was thus noted in the indictment that Wolff was among the suspects in Nuremberg "who were spared continued prosecution."

With that, the hope of avoiding the German justice system disappeared. The defense did not use this argument. Wolff would have liked to have used Phillip's statement in another way, however. In his handwritten conclusion, which he wrote in prison, Wolff filled many pages after his sentencing, blaming the German judges for not listening to the opinions of their American colleagues. He ignored, however, that from newly discovered documents and additional statements, the German court could infer that he did in fact know about the Final Solution.

The prisoner awaiting trial brooded for hours over the ingratitude of the Fatherland. He had served for many years—as a true believer, a man who was both conscientious and without a conscience at the same time. He had not been rewarded with money, but with power and honors instead. When he claimed to have shortened the war by months, he calculated that Hitler could still have continued to resist in the "Alpine redoubt" for a long time—and an honest Wolff would have to admit to himself that this fortress had actually only been a bluff on Hitler's part. No one knew better than he that in the Alps there were no prepared positions, no supplies stored or the industrial capacity to continue to fight. And didn't he, Obergruppenführer Wolff, spare the Germans the atom bomb at the end, by prematurely ending the war? In his written conclusion, he presented all of this for the consideration of the court, and must have examined all of it before the hearing.

The charges now descended upon him with the relentlessness of the bureaucratic justice system. In December 1963, it was reported to the examining judge that the accused was suffering from depression and speech impairment. He was taken to a unit of the University Clinic in Munich.

On July 13, 1964, the first day of the trial began in an uproar. Even before the accused was taken into the courtroom, a man from the visitors' seats yelled that he would not tolerate a second Eichmann trial. "I am," he announced far too loudly, "a pure-blooded SS soldier." He was led out.

That initial display made the elegant gentleman, escorted by two guards to the dock, appear even more serious. The dark blue tailored suit, the silver-gray tie, the decorative white hair and dignified behavior were not necessary to establish that there were not only rowdies among the Nazi Black Guard. The presiding judge of the district court let him recite his spotless curriculum in detail and also dress up his "good deeds" with many asides. "I claim," said Wolff, "to have been an idealist." He presented himself—something that was up to date during the cold war—as an anti-Bolshevik, who joined the SS in 1931 for that reason and, with the same basic convictions, agreed to the surrender to the Western Powers in 1945.

The listeners were surprised that instead of seeing a hard-line violent person, the man in front of them was obviously a conciliatory and educated gentleman who, with a soft, high voice, was almost sentimentally complaining that the Nazis had used and deceived him. As he all too readily described his achievements for the Fatherland, the chairman interrupted him, "The court is not here to carry out historical research. We can assume that you, even though at a late date, did achieve certain merits. But how does this reconcile with what you are accused of? Were you at that time a different Wolff?" He used the opportunity to say that all the terrible things of the Nazi period took place behind his back.

As long as the trial lasted, the press coverage was not favorable. The major daily newspapers had sent experienced journalists to the proceedings and even dedicated more than one hundred lines of print to him in one issue. The journalists involved were mostly critical intellectuals, who could hardly approve of the motives of the SS Obergruppenführer. The reporter from the Munich daily *Süddeutschen Zeitung* described him as "a tall, corpulent man who, full of vanity, effectively projecting his sharp profile to his advantage, who was bursting with a need for admiration." He was "the accomplished kind of staff officer, who could easily be sent anywhere in the Third Reich; a decorative type behind whom the reality of terror could be hidden." And: "One hears a man of pathetic garrulousness, who drowns out the gloom of the Third Reich with the conventional hogwash about knighthood, tradition, and higher idealism."

A psychiatrist, testifying as an expert, concluded that the Zeitgeist of the Nazi era "found a kindred spirit" in Wolff, who had an exaggerated need for admiration and persisted in playing the role of the general. "The accused tends to betray himself. People like him feel they have no accountability." As Wolff was asked what qualified him to be a general, since he had only been a lieutenant in the First World War, he answered confidently that he had continued to educate himself. As general, he had "fulfilled all the tasks assigned to him satisfactorily." The prosecution claimed that his achievements were so wretched that a real soldier, like SS General Felix Steiner (who came from the army), "could only muster a weary smile in this courtroom."

Wolff's claim that, at the Führer headquarters, he had been the representative of the Waffen SS was also refuted. Among more than sixty witnesses, there were SS officers who actually filled that same position and were now reporting that Wolff almost never concerned himself with issues regarding the troops, and was almost never allowed to attend the situation reports. Therefore, he was not a vital participant at headquarters during the crisis in Stalingrad in January 1943, as he asserted, but was traveling through Poland with Himmler at the time, to begin dismantling the Warsaw ghettos and organize the transportation of the Jews. A number of witnesses testified that he helped people who, because of their "non-Aryan" heritage, were in desperate straits, but those good deeds were not considered in his favor this time. The court asked why he provided such help if he was so convinced that nothing terrible was happening to the Jews?

Wolff called anyone who could testify to his good deeds. Gero von Gaevernitz appeared once again insisting that Wolff spared innumerable people from death because of the surrender. However the judge discounted such speculation. After all, the trial was not about how many lives Wolff saved, but rather how many lost their lives due to his share of the blame. And his complicity became clear when the court came to the conclusion that he knew that the purpose of the transports was the "Final Solution."

Witness Ganzenmüller, who had provided the railway cars, didn't dare admit that he had even an inkling of the destination the Jews were headed for back then. However, one of his officials, the director of the Federal Railroad Administration, admitted that he knew. "Not officially," he said, "but from below. It was known among the railway employees." Ganzenmüller even pretended that he had not even read Wolff's thank-you letter, written by a secretary and signed by him, because the expressions used in the National Socialist code would have made him suspicious. The entire procedure, according to Ganzenmüller, simply passed through him. This was the formula Wolff also used whenever something in writing placed any kind of blame on his shoulders.

In the course of the hearings it was often the case, but the more this defense argument was heard, the harder it was to believe. Even Rudolf Rahn, Wolff's diplomatic aid during the surrender, testified that "Wolff could not have missed the execution of the Jews by shooting." And the friend with whom he had a "Du" personal relationship, SS Obergruppenführer Erich von dem Bach-Zelewski, who had already been sentenced to life imprisonment as a mass murderer, said in court, "It is simply unbelievable that today someone who had such a high position can say that he knew nothing."

The difficult task of proving not a deed but rather the knowledge of deeds forced the court to go well beyond the dates they themselves had set. Three hundred kilos of files had to be examined, as well as medical and contemporary expert reports presented in court. Wolff's defense was also known for practices that took a lot of time. Dr. Rudolf Aschenauer, who also had experience at the Nuremberg trials, replaced Dr. Seidl. He had a difficult task with a defendant who smugly admitted when someone called him an influential man in the Third Reich, but who, on the other hand, only wanted to have the responsibility of being Himmler's chief recordkeeper. The lawyer was also restricted from being effective by another situation in which he was also defending former SS officer Robert Mulka before the Frankfurt court. Mulka had been the adjutant of Auschwitz Camp Director Rudolf Höss, who had in the meantime been executed. Because of that Aschenauer was forced to constantly commute between the Bavarian and the Hessian capitals. The hideousness being discussed in Frankfurt unavoidably made its way to Munich as well. It raised the fear that once again, the small sinner in Frankfurt would hang and the greater one in Munich would go free.

On September 15, the prosecution had its turn; two prosecutors had divided the material in the trial. The indictment requested that the accused be sentenced to life imprisonment for complicity in the murder of at least 300,000 people. This was the estimated number of Jews who were sent to the gas chambers in Wolff's railroad cars. The indictment regarding the shootings in Minsk was dropped; that crime no longer mattered, and perhaps it could only be useful to prove that in 1941 the defendant already knew what would happen to the Jews. The prosecution did not want to have the so-called good deeds considered. Even Hitler, Göring, and Himmler had protected individual Jews, and it would be absurd to reach a verdict of not guilty for that reason.

Attorney Aschenauer pleaded for his client's innocence for four hours without a break. He portrayed him as a convinced National Socialist who was not motivated, however, by political ideas. He was therefore a completely different kind of person from the sadistic Nazi criminals who often committed the worst crimes. In Italy Wolff finally found the opportunity to show his true nature. It is impossible to prove that he knew of the atrocities before 1945; his character by itself would have prevented him from serving a system that he had viewed as being criminal, and it would have been impossible for him to participate in those crimes. Anschauer therefore requested a verdict of not guilty. Wolff made a short closing statement. A longer written statement was issued after sentencing. He was certain, he said in the courtroom, "that the judges would know how to honor his life's purpose, which was to serve the Fatherland in a fair way."

Things turned out differently. On September 30, he was taken to the courtroom in handcuffs for the reading of the sentence, and the police stood guard at the courthouse which was unusual. There had been a threatening phone call of physical violence should Wolff be set free. That was a crank call, however, because nothing of the sort happened and the presiding judge read the sentence and gave the explanation—15 years in prison as an accessory to the murder of 300,000 Jews. The maximum sentence would have been life imprisonment; but as an accessory to the actual crime a lesser sentence would apply. As Wolff received his written version of the sentence in his Stadelheim cell, he began immediately to plough through the 354 pages. He and his lawyer were set to fight this "judicial murder," because, in his opinion, that was what it was when a man of outstanding merit, at 64 years of age, respectable and innocent in this case, was to live behind bars for more than a decade, and most likely die there.

He vented his outrage by making notes in the margin of the massive sentence. Wherever it stated his knowing about the annihilation of the Jews, he noted with a thick pencil the word "Proof!" At one point there was a description of how he watched a woman receiving corporal punishment in a concentration camp. There one can read in his handwriting "5 blows!"—a note that not only shows his good memory but also means that such a small matter was not worth mentioning.

The reasons for the sentence confirmed to a certain degree that the indictment for the massacre at Minsk constituted proof. Regarding the incident it states, "Because of this the Court is convinced that by the middle of August 1941, at the latest, the accused was aware of Hitler's and Himmler's orders to exterminate the Jews...because of what had happened at Minsk. The sentence, however, must "take into consideration that the accused gradually came to the conclusion during his activities in Italy that he could no longer follow Hitler, Himmler, and the other leading men of the Third Reich in their inhuman politics of violence."

One newspaper wrote that this was a surprising sentence. On the one hand, "even for experienced and legally knowledgeable trial observers it was in no way" clear that the evidence would "be sufficient for sentencing." On the other hand, the court "had fully used punishment time in prison as provided, and only avoided life imprisonment due to extenuating circumstances." That was why neither the defendant nor the prosecution was satisfied with such a split sentence. Both demanded an appeal. Wolff's defense pointed out a number of factual contradictions. The prosecution wanted the defendant sentenced not only as an accessory, but also as an accomplice. The sentence would then have had to have been life imprisonment.

But what did this difference mean to a prisoner of his age? Would he even survive all those years? With a sentence limited in time, the chance was actually greater that with a pardon he could be free once again with a reduced sentence. Wolff was very disappointed that the Federal Supreme Court refused his request for an appeal at the end of October 1965, but he at least had the ray of hope that the request from the prosecution had also been denied. The defendant awaiting trial became a prisoner. He was moved from Stadelheim to the prison at Straubing.

He was not satisfied by the sentence "with injustice screaming to the high heavens." A fellow prisoner said that Wolff had counted the months in prison from his time as prisoner of war. Since he was not required to work due to his age, he at first used the time and quiet of his cell to write letters to everyone in the world. His German friends, the Swiss and American friends, politicians of the Federal Republic, the higher echelons of the Catholic clergy, and influential men in the business world all received his calls for help. But who could do anything against a legal sentence, as long as no new evidence made it necessary to re-open the proceedings? As this was not to be expected, a pardon was the only remaining hope. However, one could not expect it that soon from Bavaria's district government; it would have caused a political scandal. All those approached for help only responded to continue to have patience.

Once the prisoner realized that he could not change the situation at the moment, he wrote fewer letters and applied for work. With the traditional prison work of gluing bags he thus began his fourth career. Because he was obedient and always remained distinguished as a prisoner, he was well liked by the staff, from the guards all the way up to the director. Soon he rose to better paid tasks, and in the end he even received an office job outside the jail at the Straubinger branch of the machine factory at Augsburg-Nuremberg. His wages were ridiculously small, but came very welcome nonetheless. Because once again he was in trouble financially.

The wealth he had acquired so quickly as an advertising salesman was almost completely used up by attorney's fees for his defense. Frau Inge and her children wanted to live in style. She had long reverted back to her more attractive family name, calling herself Countess Bernstorff-Wolff. The court costs were to be paid by the defendant, and because of the length of the trial and the many witnesses, they were shockingly high. As long as Wolff still had anything to his name, the state grabbed it. Frau Inge therefore asked her husband to give her a general power of attorney for all family financial matters. She and her sons took whatever could be salvaged. The house on Lake Starnberg was sold. Later Wolff complained that his family took the rest of his money for themselves. Besides that, Frau Inge was tired of being married to a man who had to spend his life in prison. She requested a divorce and went to court, but in the end the couple agreed to remain formally married. The woman moved to Switzerland, where her son by Wolff took residence. Later, when the father was free again, he wanted to visit her there, but some Swiss citizens who were opposed to the former general refused him entry. Whoever was the driving factor behind that decision remained unknown.

In the end, some help did come from the outside. The most dependable friend once again proved to be Gero von Gaevernitz. He wrote to the Bavarian justice minister, asking him to finally pardon Wolff; he had earned it long before. The Munich government, as Wolff told his biographers, also got the agreement of the bishop and the CIA. The justice minister refused all petitions, because the situation was still too controversial. However, there was another way that was less noticeable. Once again, the general went to see the doctors. He complained constantly about his ailments and an internist and a urologist both certified that he was unfit to remain in prison because his suffering would only get worse inside his cell. At the end of August 1969, because of an "incapacity to remain in prison due to illness" he was released from the prison for a year—to begin with.

Chapter 17

An Enigmatic Personality

Where was Wolff to go? Back to his first wife or to one of their children, who with one exception were all married in the meantime? To his second wife or one of their children? He was not really welcome anywhere for very long. So to start the homeless man, who had rendered outstanding services to the Pope and the clergy in Italy, found shelter in the Benedictine cloisters in Bavaria. They guaranteed him some respect as God's reward, because he was nearly penniless, apart from his little retirement money. For two years he lived moving around as a guest of friends, acquaintances and people who enjoyed sheltering a former general.

More insistently than before, he now promoted himself to the German public as the Pope's savior, claiming to have protected him from being dragged into Nazi imprisonment. Pius XII had died in the meantime; he could no longer confirm or deny anything. The archives of the Vatican remained characteristically silent, according to tradition. Wolff gave lectures to gatherings of Catholic groups. Reports about this activity appeared in the daily newspapers. He caused some sensation with a report several pages long in *Stern*; and from then on he was assured of getting the journalists' attention. What he told them was self-serving but put him far too much in the limelight. Nazi chaser and concentration camp survivor Simon Wiesenthal, who lived in Vienna, sounded the alarm. The Bavarian justice minister reacted and had a high clergyman tell the glorious SS general that if he was healthy enough to appear in public and carry on with long speeches, then he could once again go back to serve his sentence.

On the other hand, his stories were taken seriously here and there. In the Vatican, information about the dead Pope's life was being collected, according to tradition, in order to have Pius XII beatified and later canonized. The Vatican magazine *La civiltà cattolica* addressed the purported plans for a kidnapping. However, Wolff was only incidentally mentioned. Despite that he was called to the bishop's office in the spring of 1972 to make a statement regarding everything he knew about the Holy Father. The statements were recorded. Whether they matched his preferred version, the one published description in *Stern*, shall remain unanswered. Religious institutions do not like to provide information if it deals with the Vatican or especially regarding the Pope himself.

Even if Wolff was successful in conveying his importance as a person to the German public, he was even more concerned that his freedom was only seen as temporary. He had to have a physical every year, and each time he was only considered to be sick for twelve months. In the summer of 1973, the results were shockingly positive; perhaps he was ready to live in a prison cell again soon, since his letter of temporary release was only for half a year. He had to report to the examination location repeatedly in the first weeks of 1974, and an order from the State's attorney even sent him to the psychiatric clinic at the University of Munich for a whole week to a unit for forensic medical psychiatry.

He had more to lose besides his freedom. In the last two years, he was settled once again, had rented an apartment in Munich, and a small apartment in the house of a school friend was available to him in Darmstadt. He had not yet managed to write his memoirs, but now it was going to take place. He did not want his connections to old comrades to fall apart; perhaps they could help him search for evidence of his innocence. At events or in smaller circles, he especially impressed women with descriptions of his experiences at the Führer headquarters and in Italy. During the war, they had been in the women's service or were enrolled in the female Hitler youth. Since his days as a lieutenant, he had enjoyed his effect on women, and even now it was not difficult to find some who wanted to help the older man.

To the doctors, however, he complained of heart palpitations, head congestion, moments of dizziness, shortness of breath when climbing stairs, disrupted sleep, the frequent need to urinate, depressing dreams and depression to the point of having crying fits.

On the other hand, one professor determined that Wolff had "an upright posture, was dressed neatly and showed polite, elegant manners." His "present mood is depressed." "Walking with a lively and elastic gait" was only possible "for short stretches." He was plagued by the fear of having to return to a prison cell. The professor did not consider it impossible that a resumption of his sentence could cause a suicide attempt. For psychiatric reasons, Wolff was not capable of being in prison; a "return to prison was not to be expected again" in the future.

This sealed his freedom for all time. Now he no longer had to fear being interrupted in fulfilling his most important projects. But first, the shame of the prison sentence had to be erased. For that, he was to get help from glass worker Norbert Kellnberger from Wartenberg, not far from Munich. Kellnberger had been a juror when defendant Wolff had to answer to the court. The master craftsman who had his own business had called Wolff shortly before and told him a story that he thought could reverse the sentence of the court. Wolff had therefore referred Kellnberger to his present lawyer. On May 10, 1973, the master craftsman stated that in September 1964, matters had not been properly handled in the jury room.

After the summation by the prosecution and Dr. Aschenauer, as reported by Kellnberger, the three presiding judges and the six lay judges were not unanimous on the verdict of guilty for several days. At least three of the jurors had called for not guilty due to a lack of evidence. The most zealous advocate of a guilty sentence was Judge Jörka of the district court administration. He argued that the public demanded that Wolff be sentenced and, after a very long deliberation, he had convinced the required majority for that sentence by impressing upon the lay judges that this was a political process that had to end with Wolff's sentencing, but that the defendant would be let out of prison after one year anyway. When Kellnberger found out later on that Wolff was still subject to judicial proceedings, he went to Bishop Neuhäusler in Munich and asked that the Church do something for a man he thought was being unjustly condemned.

Since nothing happened, Kellnberger informed Wolff's lawyer in May 1973. His report triggered an investigation of Judge Jörka by the Munich prosecution for suspicion of undue influence in court. It didn't move ahead quickly, although Kellnberger repeated his report before a state's attorney and also mentioned that two other jurors were led to change their vote because of Jörka's misleading reasoning. In the spring of 1974 Wolff believed he could force this process with help from the Catholic church. He secured the good will of the *Neuen Bildpost*, which according to its own numbers was a "35-Pfenning weekly newspaper," the "largest Christian weekly newspaper in Europe" with 350,000 copies per issue.

This tabloid for believers, with its sensational headlines and the wild graphics was a poor take off of the *Bild*, published by Axel-Springer in Hamburg. It published a report about an event of the "Catholic educational works in Berchtesgaden province" to help the lecturer, namely General Karl Wolff. Eight issues of some length were published. Including Kellnberger's statement. The paper described the speaker as "a mature man with silver gray hair, who thirty years before had been one of the most powerful men in Europe." Now "along with Rudolf Hess" he was the "most important leader of the National Socialist period still alive." This was of course not a commendation, but rather an attempt to create sensation. Therefore in the introduction it was stated that Wolff "was a highly controversial man that historians would be analyzing for quite some time." On the other hand he was introduced as the "only SS officer who was received by Pius XII in a private audience." The first issue included a quote of the supposed words uttered by the Pope, according to which a great deal of misery could have been avoided had God brought Karl Wolff and the Pope together sooner.

All eight issues ran with the title "The Man Who Was to Kidnap the Pope." Since every reader knew that Wolff did not follow the supposed order from the Führer, the subscribers had their hero right from the start despite all the attempts by the editors to caution the readers. The *Bildpost* never questioned whether or not Hitler ever really issued that order for the kidnapping. Because the readers would hardly subscribe to a newsletter by former Waffen SS soldiers, they never found out that his old comrades greeted this part of Wolff's story with disbelief.

To this day the Vatican never made a statement regarding the entire matter. No one on the Nazi side besides Wolff could confirm such an order from Hitler, since the Führer had only given the orders to him and the Reichsführer SS alone. Any other person could only repeat what he had heard from one of these two men. Typically enough, no one had referred to a confirmation from Himmler. On the other hand, former SS Hauptsturmführer Richard Schulze-Kossens spoke up in reference to the

Bildpost publication in the *Freiwilligen* ("Volunteers"). In 1943–1944 he had been Hitler's adjutant at headquarters, and had also regularly participated in the situation reports as the actual representative of the Waffen SS. He wrote in the SS publication that when Wolff claimed to be "the savior...for having thwarted Hitler's plan...it was better that he remain silent because there never was a serious order from Hitler to kidnap the Pope. Men from Hitler's entourage would confirm that."

Whom can one believe? It is up to the reader to ask as objectively as possible: Who could benefit from that much debated story—Who has something to gain from it? Wolff had certainly benefited a great deal from the matter. On the other hand, he and his adversaries were not always on good terms. In earlier years, Obergruppenführer Wolff had occasionally let Hauptsturmführer Schulze-Kossens feel the difference in rank, because he viewed him as a rival, no matter how small, vying for Hitler's favor. Now they were also divided by the breach between the Waffen SS and Nazi party units during and, even more, after the war. Schulze-Kossens belonged to those SS officers who were saying that Wolff only received his rank and title for decorative reasons. However, it gave him no advantage once he turned his back on his former comrades.

The breach between the two was made public when Schulze-Kossens informed his comrades in the *Freiwilligen* early in the summer of 1974 that a reputable auction house had announced a military auction of "three uniform pieces once owned by Oberstgruppenführer and Generaloberst of the Waffen SS, Karl Wolff." It was simply the fact that the increase in rank had not been recognized in SS circles and created some displeasure with the readers. Schulze-Kossens was incensed and he added up the offerings: a general's cap, size 58; the personal field-gray jacket...specially tailored in the manner of the field shirt used during the Second World War...as it was only worn by General Wolff, Göring and Udet in the rest of the Wehrmacht"; and further the "personal white jacket...with buttoned-on gala shoulder ribbons in braided aluminum...probably unique." Every piece came with a free "original personal certificate from General Wolff," and for each item the starting price was set at one thousand marks.

The owner was parting with these articles of noble memories only because he was always short of money. His pension was too small to cover his needs; to improve the situation he went to court against the Office of Federal Employees. He expected future monies from his memoirs. Supposedly, several years before his trial, a major American literary agency had offered him two million marks. Now he would have done it for less, but there still were no memoirs. In his search for a ghostwriter, he spoke of several hundred thousand marks that he was expecting, but as long as no partner could be found he could not approach a publisher about an advance. And so as a source of money, aside from lectures and publications, all he could do was to take things out of mothballs where he kept his memorabilia.

It is difficult to grasp why discarded articles of clothing of a former historical figure should be worth collecting—unless they have a historical meaning. That indeed a limited number of dim-witted collectors of such old material even existed was made public during the trial that took place in Hamburg in the late summer of 1984. One of the two defendants, the 53-year old former *Stern* reporter Gerd Heidemann, had already been friendly with Wolff for some time. He owned many such pieces of memorabilia, including the pistol with which Hitler was said to have shot himself or the motor yacht with which Reich Marshal Hermann Göring sailed the seas in his years of glory. Also accused in that trial was a 46-year-old Stuttgart man, Konrad Kujau, who never had a specific job, but was a dealer in discarded parts of uniforms, weapons, medals, and other items from Hitler's Reich.

The reasons why newsman Heidemann became interested in Hitler and his group was a case study for psychologists. He was fourteen years old when the Führer and Reich Chancellor shot himself beneath the Berlin Chancellery. Along with that, he had been in the war briefly as a Hitler Youth in the ruins in Hamburg, but probably had never even witnessed the seamy side of Nazism, nor suffered due to its legacy. Heidemann knew how to use a camera and started working at *Stern* as a freelance photographer. Since he took good pictures, the chief editor sent him in the late fall of 1955 to Camp Friedland when the last German POWs returned from the Soviet Union. Having no scruples or consideration for the feelings of those involved, he captured the faces of those returning and their families, in moments of great pain and joy, his photographs became true documents of contemporary history. He was given more work and a permanent job. Not only did he take great photos, he was also good at investigating as well. His tactic was to ask the people very few questions, but he had a knack of getting them to talk, and listened with a tape recorder as they often revealed more than they actually intended.

When he turned to contemporary history, he only had a sketchy kind of knowledge. However, with great tenacity he filled the gaps, and since he was looking for expert informants for a topic where the SS was mentioned, a colleague from the editorial staff referred him to one SS general who always talked exhaustively about himself, Karl Wolff.

Wolff and Heidemann liked each other immediately. The younger man showed the older man the respect he demanded because of his rank and, conversely, the general did not let his partner sense the social distance that divided them due to their backgrounds. They had interests that complemented each other: Heidemann wanted to expand his knowledge of the Third Reich and find sensational stories from any period, Wolff could serve a purpose in opening doors to big wigs from Hitler's Reich who were still alive. The general, on the other hand, was hoping to have found the writer for his biography. The biography actually did get started and Wolff was able to record the stories he had told repeatedly on a tape recorder. He always used the same word sequence in recounting those anecdotes, as if at some point he had memorized the entire text. They sounded like the memoirs of an upper-middle-class man dictated in the ornate language of Wilhelmine Germany. During the years they were acquainted Heidemann never wrote the epic that Wolff so desperately desired for two important reasons. First, he could only use known facts that would remain unproven. Second, while he could investigate well, he was unable to write well. Despite this, they went on working together. Heidemann managed to secure some advantages for Wolff for his information, and took him on trips using large expense accounts; Wolff felt that he was correcting the history of the Third Reich.

The first travel opportunity for a nice trip came with Erich Kuby, a journalist with *Stern*, who of all people had been sent to a concentration camp by the SS as a young man, and because of his horrible experience viscerally hated anyone who had worn the Nazi uniform. Kuby was a fairly leftist intellectual who saw himself more as a writer than a reporter. The chief editor and later publisher, Henri Nannan, gave him the assignment to write about the life and death of Clara Petacci in a long report. Some years before *Stern* had already published a rather touching account about her, but Nannen felt that they had not done justice to Mussolini's lover and that the fascination surrounding her fate would certainly grip the readers. As a war journalist in Italy, Kuby had observed, from a distance, her final years with the Duce with a great deal of sympathy, and he empathized with the tragedy of her life. Kuby traveled to Italy in 1977, and Heidemann was assigned to him as an investigator. He also took along the former Highest SS and Police Führer and SS General Karl Wolff as an informant. The anti-Fascist Kuby was able to overcome his feelings and got on with his work.

He did not write the Petacci story. His book, *The German Betrayal*, was published instead. The article did not appear in *Stern*, even though it had financed the trip with salaries, advances and expense accounts, and the book was even published by another company. Kuby and Nannen had a falling out and their enmity went so far that the journalist called his former employer a pig in a pamphlet he wrote. In his book Kuby writes that the Italians did not betray Germany by changing sides in 1943, breaking away from the Axis and switching to the Allies, but rather that Hitler had permanently betrayed and deceived his friend Mussolini and the Italians. In the end, according to Kuby, Wolff also betrayed the Duce and his people by negotiating the surrender with the enemy without consulting the Italians and without their agreement. Even if Kuby did not say it explicitly in his description of those events, he additionally blamed the general as responsible for the execution of the Duce and Clara Petacci in a cloak-and-dagger operation. Wolff did nothing to protect either one because the Duce was now in his way.

In some respects, Kuby was right—in politics and war, basic morality always plays a role. But if the topic is morality, did the SS general by any chance find out during the trip to Italy what he had gotten himself into with Kuby?

Without Wolff's information, the author would not have written his book that way. At one point he also called his traveling companion a "charming old man" who had "made himself available for those investigations with his candid recollections." Blinded by his vanity, Wolff told the *Stern* journalist about all the various stages of important and intimate events. Wolff was in high spirits due to the local memories, and recounted his proconsular splendor; of big and small intrigues while unwittingly being, at the same time, the object of critical observation by the author. "We hear," Kuby writes, "utterances from him that lead one to think of a sovereign authority." Or, "We could also be speaking to Napoleon at St. Helena." He often uses the corporate "we" and writes how "Wolff's friendly courtesy" was not dampened by any bad memories because of his return to the same locations. The journalist sees the former general "as typical of our entire people, in a way"; that he developed the ability to "shake off an era of crime like a raindrop sliding down oilskin."

Kuby had seen through Wolff's attempts to avoid blame, so that his descriptions of his work become "belated embellishments, after-the-fact inventions" and patently false recollections. He views the account about kidnapping the Pope in a dubious light, as he is generally of the opinion that Wolff's "good deeds" in Italy, including the surrender, were basically an alibi to forget earlier and more disgraceful deeds. In Italy "the elegant Wolff became the Wolff who knew all the tricks." Was he not like that long before? Apparently Kuby had not thoroughly investigated the background of his traveling companion.

The book was published in 1982, and Wolff appears in the index with the most page numbers; he couldn't have found much joy in that, however, despite the strong attention. He therefore did not like to remember that his and Kuby's names appear next to each other with a meaningful text in the guest book aboard Heidemann's yacht. Heidemann captured that contemplative moment with his very odd friends in a snapshot. They are together at a table on deck, sitting and talking in front of glasses, with the riverbank, buildings and trees in the background. When the militant anti-Fascist was questioned about this text many years later, he said, "That is a dig at Herr Wolff; I find it very nice."

The yacht was Heidemann's favorite toy, but at the same time it worried him the most. He bought it in the mid-1970s in a dilapidated condition. The price, the renovation and maintenance went far beyond his own resources. He named the ship "Karin II" just as its first owner, Göring, had named it after his dead wife, who was Swedish. The new owner's ambition was to put the ship back in the same condition as when it belonged to the Reich marshal. He hoped to get his money back in two ways, and make a good profit. Some mogul would buy the ship as a historical relic, laden with tradition, for a fantastic price. Until then, it would serve as a meeting place of former prominent Nazis who wanted to talk about the past in a confidential setting aboard those historical planks "to allow the glorious Third Reich to rise again." He would eavesdrop with a microphone and tape recorder, and their conversations would then be published under the title "Conversations on Board" in *Stern*, and as a book. Before he even got started, he was already cashing in on the advances.

His friend Karl Wolff, whom he already addressed with "Du" for a long time, served as bait. Who from the old comrades could resist the temptation of meeting with Himmler's right-hand man and Hitler's special favorite? Several of the old guard had already met—for example, Wilhelm Mohnke from Hamburg, Brigadeführer of the Waffen SS (Major General) and the last commander of the Führer bunker beneath the Reich Chancellery until the bitter end on May 1, 1945. When Heidemann married for the fourth time on December 1, 1978, he got the two old warriors from the SS involved as best men. As usual, Wolff was asked about his profession for the record by the Hamburg registrar. He proudly answered, "Retired General." Mohnke, on the other hand, answered the same question with a simple, "senior citizen." With that, the scene was no longer befitting his rank. Loudly and as a reprimand, Wolff cried out, "Wilhelm! You were also a general!"

The honeymoon took the newlyweds to South America, and was partially paid for by *Stern* because it also served as a business trip for Heidemann to pick up the trail of the Nazis hiding there. He was looking for Klaus Barbie, former SS officer and Gestapo official in France, known as the "butcher of Lyon"; the other SS and concentration camp doctor, Joseph Mengele; Eichmann's Dutch friend Wim Sassen; and, strangely enough, Martin Bormann, Reichsleiter of the NSDAP, the secretary to the Führer and according to official certificates, already dead since May 1, 1945, as a result of suicide in Berlin.* Wolff was allowed to accompany the happy couple and *Stern* also paid for this. His task was to give lectures about his "glorious time" in war and peace for the members of the German Clubs in the South American capitals. Heidemann counted on the fact that Party comrades and the SS would appear out of curiosity. He wasn't mistaken. Several dark figures showed up who avoided Germany because they would be called to account for their crimes. Barbie was among them. They needed several trips, however, and Wolff was therefore able to see a lot of the new world as an older man.

Until 1981, the Wolff-Heidemann team was out and about in Latin America. On August 22 of that year, the reporter wrote a letter to Klaus Barbie, in which he apologized because he had caused the addressee some difficulties in Bolivia with his articles. "I truly regret losing a friendship because of this stupid situation." He was successful in "acquiring the majority of Hitler's possessions—highly interesting sketches, watercolors and oil paintings, the pistol with which the Führer took his life in the bunker (a handwritten letter from Bormann guarantees its authenticity), cases of files from the Reich Chancellery, and most importantly the "Blood Flag." Hitler used to consecrate the flags of new units with that swastika cloth at Party conventions by touching them with the old banner. The Blood Flag had supposedly been present on the day of the putsch on November 9, 1923, in Munich, when many National Socialist marchers were shot as revolutionaries during their demonstration in front of the Feldherrnhalle.

---

* Jochen von Lang, *The Secretary.*

In that summer of 1981, Heidemann and Wolff were already busy with a project that would make the journalist well known throughout the world, and be more spectacular than all their other successes and investigations. They also hoped for profits in the millions, to avoid the bankruptcy Heidemann got himself into with the ship and the purchases of the National Socialist memorabilia. His speculations were only partially correct in that he did come into a large sum of money, which took him to prison.

The whole thing began when, through Mohnke, he met a wealthy businessman from the Stuttgart area who had bought up an unbelievable amount of National Socialist memorabilia—handwritten documents, sketches, watercolors, all by Hitler, but unfortunately, as it was later ascertained, all forgeries. Further this collector owned such dubious utensils as the supposed first flag of the National Socialist Party, the medals, watch and camera belonging to Adolf Hitler, as well as his tuxedo and top hat.

The Stuttgart military dealer Konrad Kujau had acquired these Nazi relics and many more. A purported diary kept by the Führer was also in his possession. It was a handwritten notebook, in the A4 size of regular writing paper; the book cover made of black material was decorated with a red cord and a red seal. Heidemann introduced himself to the owner of these splendid items as a collector who wanted to buy or trade, and also because he thought that this obviously rich man could arrange some interested parties for his yacht. However, when he saw the diary, he sensed it was a journalistic sensation.

The whole grotesque affair need not be told here—how Heidemann, after much talk back and forth, bought sixty such notebooks from Konrad Kujau in the course of time; how *Stern* announced its discovery in May 1983 with great fanfare, published the first report; and how one of the chief editors, Peter Koch, loudly announced that according to the newly discovered diaries, the entire history of the Third Reich had to be rewritten. German readers were spared this entire work because all sixty notebooks plus several addendums, for which the publishing company of *Stern* paid more than nine million marks (over five million U.S. dollars) to Heidemann, who passed it on to an alleged unknown supplier, proved to be forgeries when tested by experts. In May 1983 Konrad Kujau and Heidemann were taken into custody while awaiting trial on the suspicion of fraud, and the former confessed to being the forger.

Due to the investigations of the Hamburg prosecution, it became known how Heidemann wanted to use the coming to terms with the

German past to overcome a mountain of debt from his own past. Even more than that, he wanted this coup to ensure that he would be taken care of for the rest of his life. His publisher paid as a premium another 1.5 million marks for his difficult (and, according to his description, dangerous) acquisition of the diaries, was just icing on the cake. He had actually given a small portion of the nine million to the forger Kujau and had started other businesses with his easily earned working capital.

He had rented rooms for a "Gallery" in the chic Hamburg section, not far from the Outer Alster, where he wanted to present and sell his National Socialist junk. To expand his stock, he bought, for more than a quarter of a million marks, more old material from the Nazi period from Munich military dealers Wolff usually sold his clothing to. He then bragged about rarities, like a blue double-breasted suit from Hitler's closet, a Göring uniform and objects allegedly dug from the rubble of a plane that crashed in the Erz mountains; and the diaries in Hitler's possession, for example sketches he made and a wandering stick belonging to Friedrich the Great. He also bragged about a pistol that he had supposedly come across in Berlin during his own dogged research, with a piece of paper and a handwritten note: "30.4.45—Our Führer shot himself with this pistol. The situation is hopeless. Heil Hitler. Martin Bormann." The paper was not removed. An old acquaintance of Wolff's, SS Sturmbannführer Otto Günsche, Hitler's valet at that time, visited Heidemann and determined that it was indeed the wrong weapon, since he was the first person to pick up the suicide pistol from the floor of the Führer bunker; it was different, made by a German manufacturer. (How could such a lapse get passed Heidemann? After all, a German Führer would also remain true to his Fatherland in death, and would prefer a weapon made of German steel.)

Wolff also benefited from Heidemann's windfall. He received cash, bundled in 500-mark bills, as the publisher delivered them for the purchase of more diaries; 30,000 marks for the honorary rapier, which Himmler usually bestowed upon deserving SS officers. It could only be worn at his side on celebrations. The piece of steel was certainly not worth that much, according to the market price; unquestionably there were also premiums included for services rendered. Wolff had, after all, also participated in Heidemann's other speculative businesses.

The two had also looked for South Tyrolean hotel owner Franz Spögler during their trips to Italy working with Kuby. Despite his Italian citizenship, he was admitted to the SS under Wolff's regency. As SS Untersturmbannführer and member of the SD, he had to protect and guard Clara Petacci at Lake Garda. Aside from that he supervised a phone tapping operation in the basement of Mussolini's office, which stenographically wrote down every telephone conversation of the Italian Head of State. Wolff and Heidemann had also spoken with him about the last days of the Fascist regime and about the fabulous treasure of Dongo. Discovered in the baggage of the Duce and his last loyal followers, the horde was thought to have ended up at the bottom of Lake Como. As a result of this conversation with Spögler, in August 1983 two of Heidemann's diver friends tried to find the treasure. The unsuccessful venture cost almost a half a million marks.

The trial against Heidemann and Kujau began in the District Court of Hamburg at the end of August 1984. More than sixty witnesses were subpoenaed, among them Henri Nannan, the past publisher of *Stern*, who had since retired; journalist Erich Kuby; former SS Brigadeführer Wilhelm Mohnke; and, as number 35, "Karl Wolff, Kirchenweg 9, Prien am Chiemsee." He once again had finally managed to have a suitable address. However, the witness could no longer testify; he had died on July 15, 1984, at Rosenheim Hospital.

Karl Wolff reveled at being the center of attention his entire life. He was successful now in this last act because in some form or other he still played a role. Also the obituary afforded him one more appearance to the German public. The German Press Agency distributed it with a CV. There was hardly a newspaper or broadcaster that did not announce his death. "The man who uncovered Hitler's plans" died

Retired Senior General
Karl Wolff
born May 5, 1900 died July 15, 1984
In silent memory:

Frieda von Röhmheld	Irene Halt, born Wolff and family
Dora Maass, born Wolff	Helga Heeren, born Wolff and family
Edeltraud Ziegmann	Thorisman Wolff and family

Widukind Wolff and family
Hartmut Wolff and family

8210 Prien am Chiemsee, Kirchenweg 9, Tel. 0 80 51- 26 38
Funeral Saturday, July 21, 1984, at 11:30 a.m. Cemetery in Prien

announced a German newspaper with one of the highest circulations in a prominent headline. It referred to the Pope legend. The newspaper named him "one of the most enigmatic figures of the Nazi regime"—and he lived up to that reputation once again in Heidemann's company.

What would have happened if he had testified as a witness under oath about how much he knew about the forgery caper? Did he once again know nothing? The evidence speaks against him. When asked by a reporter from an English newspaper, *Sunday People*, about Hitler's diaries, he said: "What my friends and I have been saying for years has now been confirmed: Hitler had never ordered the extermination of the Jews. Hitler's image had always been blackened by that accusation and the reputation of the German people had been damaged. The diaries cleanse his reputation and also my own. We are national-thinking people and idealists, not criminals."

Wolff did as much as he could to prove the validity of the diaries by supporting the legend of their origin. Heidemann stated that the notebooks had been loaded on an airplane in Berlin on April 21, 1945, to be flown to Innsbruck. Wolff admitted to having heard of this plan at Führer headquarters. He had taken his leave of Hitler forever on the afternoon of April 18, but allegedly it was discussed in the bunker that the Führer's most important sketches were to be flown out by the pilot who died in the plane crash three days later.

Although almost all those who lived at Hitler's side never saw any diaries and almost all doubted that Hitler would have found the time and the opportunity to write them in secret, Wolff considered them authentic. He had always stated that Hitler not only agreed to Rudolf Hess's flight to England in 1941, but actually wanted it so that a peace agreement with England would free his back for the attack against the Soviet Union. And that was written in so many words by the author of the diaries. In their writings, the Reichsführer SS was blamed for lacking military experience in the First World War, and for being a small animal breeder possessed by a paranoia about race.

It is highly unlikely that Wolff helped write the texts of the diaries. Clearly, however, they place the Führer in the same light Wolff had always described him. Several installments came at just the right time for Wolff in his personal matters; he wanted to use them to once again appeal the sentence of the Munich court, after the legal proceedings against Judge Jörka. Wolff's argument was that if Hitler wanted to let the Jews live and wanted to create a territory for them, something Obergruppenführer Karl Wolff allegedly had always believed, then he could rightfully assume that the transport of the Jews from Warsaw was part of this goal. So rather than being an accomplice to murder, he had performed a "good deed."

One can speculate that Wolff's thinking affected the Nazi-oriented and historically simple-minded Heidemann to buy into Kujau's forgery. It is also conceivable that these views are commonly held in the circles of Nazi junk enthusiasts. Whoever delighted in Hitler's remnants must also be sympathetic to his system.

That Wolff always ends up in the first row of those deceived and abused is neither coincidence nor bad luck. Overestimation of one's own abilities, ambition, and vanity had always pushed him forward where he would be seen, heard, and honored. His appearance, his origins, upbringing and tactical skills helped him along the way. He was even successful in holding on to the tip of the dress of the goddess of fate for a brief moment in 1945. At any rate, a public obituary called him "one of the most enigmatic of figures." He ended up with a superlative after all.

APPENDIX I

Karl Wolff as Negotiator with the Soviets

The issue of a separate peace between Nazi Germany and Soviet Russia remains among the more persistent mysteries of the Second World War. There are many indications of such attempts and at least three high level contacts have been identified. The Second negotiations mentioned below involve Karl Wolff who never hinted during his lifetime that he participated in any such talks. Wolff was however a logical choice as Himmler's representative at Hitler's headquarters known for his diplomatic ability as a polished upper class negotiator—a trait that was clearly out of character within the rough SS milieu—and for his absolute trustworthiness. Wolff was the number two man in the SS and with Heydrich until the latter's assassination in 1942, Himmler's heir apparent. Wolff also enjoyed the confidence of Hitler himself. As is customary with documents coming from the Russian archives no facsimile is available and the accompanying maps mentioned in the documents were not present in the file.

First negotiations: October 1941

According to *The Sunday Times* of May 28, 1989, former Bulgarian diplomat Dimitar Peyev who was posted in Moscow in 1941 remembers that Lavrenti Beria acting on orders from Stalin approached Bulgarian ambassador N. Stamenov to transmit a message to Hitler. Stalin in the face of the German offensive that had reached deep into the Russian heartland, was ready to concede much more than the Treaty of Brest Litovsk of 1918 when the USSR surrendered large portions of Baltic, Polish and Ukrainian territories to imperial Germany. According to the recollections of military historian General N. Pavlenko in a conversation Marshal G. Zhukov told of instructions from Stalin to Beria to send a peace offer to Nazi Germany through a third party. A very pessimistic Stalin mentioned the idea of "another Brest Litovsk" to Zhukov on October 7, 1941 to create "breathing space" in order to rebuild the Soviet armed forces. Pavlenko also mentioned but did not name the Bulgarian go-between. There appears to have been no face-to-face meeting, however at that time between German and Soviet negotiators.

Second negotiations: February 20–27, 1942

Former GRU (Soviet military intelligence) officer Vladimir Karpov (See: Vladimir Karpov, *Generalissimus*, 2 volumes (Moscow: Alta, 2002) second volume pp.4–21) reproduces the instructions provided to the Soviet negotiator and a report detailing the results of the secret meeting between German and Soviet negotiators at Mtsensk in Belarus behind German lines on February 20 to 27, 1942. The text is of particular interest because the German side was represented by SS Gruppenführer Karl Wolff as reported to Stalin by V. Merkulov the NKVD negotiator. There is obviously no trace of such a meeting in this Wolff biography or in any of his interviews, nor did Wolff make any mention of the meeting to any of his acquaintances. It should be pointed out that in an interview with *Komsolmolskaya Pravda* author Vladimir Karpov comes across as a rabid anti-Semite and unreconstructed Stalinist. Specialists in Soviet wartime intelligence operations and historians have vouched for the authenticity of the following documents. The maps and drawings mentioned were not included in the file.

> "Stalin felt that the Soviet offensive was demoralizing the German leadership, which could therefore agree to his peace offer.
>
> Stalin did not consult his military leaders, and not even with the members of the Politburo, which is why none of them mentions the event in their oral reminiscences or published memoirs.
>
> Stalin ordered the NKVD to carry an offer of a ceasefire to the Germans in his, Stalin's, name and set the stage for more far-reaching plans for a radical change in the war. NKVD agents contacted their German "colleagues" (possibly through the SD); the meeting took place in Mtsensk on February 20, 1942. Mtsensk at that time was in occupied German territory. Apparently, Stalin decided to hold these negotiations at the very start of the counteroffensive, and NKVD agents had begun the search for contacts immediately. There is no information as to how the initial contacts took place.
>
> Stalin personally wrote the following "Proposals to the German Command." Only two copies were made, one held by Stalin, the other for the person conducting the talks. This document, evidently, was not intended to be handed over to the Germans; it was an abstract, a list of questions to be used as a guide for the Soviet representative.

That the "Proposals" were drawn up by Stalin is confirmed by his signature. The fact that this was only an abstract is indicated by the short "Stalinist" phrases printed not on a regular state or party form, but on a simple piece of white paper without any indication of the executor and the number of distributed copies, which was required in such official documents.

These documents are published here in English for the first time and are considered to be authentic by major historians and researchers.

Proposals to the German Command

1) Cease military actions beginning 5 May 1942 at 6:00 along the entire line of the front. Declare a ceasefire until 18:00 of 1 August 1942.

2) Beginning on 1 August 1942 and up to 22 December 1942 German troops must pull back to the boundaries designated in diagram No. 1. It is proposed to establish a border between Germany and the USSR along the length of the line designated in drawing No. 1.

3) Following the redistribution of the armies, the armed forces of the USSR by the end of 1943 will be ready to begin military actions with German armed forces against England and the USA.

4) The USSR will be ready to examine the conditions to declare peace between our countries and to accuse international Jewry represented by England and the USA of instigating war, and to conduct a joint offensive during the course of the subsequent years of 1943-1944 with the goal of creating a new world order (diagram No. 2).

OBSERVATION: In the event of refusal to carry out the aforementioned demands in points 1 and 2, the German armies will be destroyed, and the German leadership as such will cease to exist on the political map.

Warn the German command of its responsibility.

Supreme Commander in Chief of the Union of the SSR
(I. STALIN)

Moscow, Kremlin, 19 February 1942

FIRST DEPUTY
OF THE PEOPLE'S COMMISSAR OF INTERNAL AFFAIRS
OF THE USSR
No. 1/2428 27 February 1942
To Comrade S T A L I N

REPORT

In the course of negotiations at Mtsensk from 20-27 February 1942 with a representative of the German command and the chief of the personal staff of the Reichsführer SS, Gruppenführer SS Wolff, the German command did not consider it possible to satisfy our demands.

The Germans proposed that we leave the boundaries along the line of the front as they are until the end of 1942, after having ceased all military action.

The government of the USSR must immediately put an end to Jewry. It was therefore initially suggested to move all Jews into the far northern regions, isolate and then completely annihilate them. In so doing, Soviet authorities will guard the external perimeter and impose a severe martial regime over the territory of a group of camps. The actual killing and utilization of the corpses of the Jewish population will be handled by Jews themselves.

The German command does not exclude the possibility of creating a united front against England and the USA.

Following consultations with Berlin, Wolff announced that under a new world order, if the leadership of the USSR accepts German demands it is possible that Germany will draw its eastern boundaries to benefit the USSR.

The German command as a sign of such changes will be prepared to change the color of the swastika on the state banner from black to red.

In discussing positions according to diagram no. 2 there were the following differences of opinion:

1) Latin America. Must belong to Germany

2) A difficult point is the meaning of "Chinese civilization." According to the opinion of the German command, China must become an occupied territory and a protectorate of the Japanese empire.

3) The Arab world must be a German protectorate in North Africa.

Thus, it must be noted that the negotiations resulted in a total divergence of opinions and positions. As representative of the German command Wolff categorically rejects to consider the possibility of the destruction of German armed forces and defeat in the war. In his opinion, the war with Russia will last for several more years and end with Germany's complete victory. The basic calculation is based on the fact that, in their opinion, Russia, having lost forces and resources in the war, will be compelled to return to the talks concerning a ceasefire, but under much more severe conditions, two to three years from now.

First Deputy of the People's Commissar
Of the Internal Affairs of the USSR

(MERKULOV)

Third negotiations: June 23, 1943

As reported by the *Los Angeles Times* and the *New York Journal American*, on May 18, 1947, "Secret Nazi Files Disclose Plan for Sneak Red Truce." The article mentions a conference between Hitler and his naval commanders held on July 17 and 18 where the Führer stated

> "...a threat by Japan that she will enter the war against Russia will help to make the latter accept the German offer of an unannounced armistice on the eastern front to be kept secret from the Anglo-Saxons. Russia would continue to accept lend-lease materials. This political goal is worth every sacrifice."

A secret meeting between Molotov and von Ribbentrop was held in June 1943 at Kirovograd some 200 kilometers behind the German lines according to B. H. Liddell Hart in *History of the Second Word War* (New York: Putnam, 1970) p. 488. At that point the Germans were strongly encouraged by the Japanese who had always been averse to a war with Russia and by the Italians who wanted a Mediterranean strategy directed against the Anglo-American forces then threatening the mainland from Sicily.

The talks were possibly mentioned by Hitler to Mussolini during their secret conversations at the conference at Feltre, near Venice on July 19, 1943. The meetings between the two dictators were to be held originally over a three day period however those initial plans were shelved when Hitler announced at the last minute that he would need to fly back to Germany that same afternoon. The diaries of fascist minister of education and close Mussolini confidant Carlo Alberto Biggini contain the mention of a possible participation of Molotov at the Feltre conference. (See the diaries of C.A. Biggini: Luciano Garibaldi *Mussolini e il Professore. Vita e diari di Carlo Alberto Biggini* (Milan: Mursia, 1983) page 299.)

APPENDIX II

Comparative Waffen-SS Officers' ranks

Reichsführer SS (RFSS)	Heinrich Himmler
SS- Obergruppenführer	Army Commanding General
SS- Gruppenführer	Divisional Commanding General
SS- Brigadeführer	Major General
SS- Oberführer	General
SS- Standartenführer	Colonel
SS- Obersturmbannführer	Lieutenant Colonel
SS- Sturmbannführer	Major
SS- Hauptsturmführer	Captain
SS- Obersturmführer	Lieutenant
SS- Untersturmführer	Second Lieutenant

APPENDIX III

Archives

Document Center, Berlin
Bundesarchiv Koblenz and Kornelmünster
National Archives, Washington D.C.
Ministry of War, London
Imperial War Museum, London
Public Record Office, London

Documents

Karl Wolff, Munich
Denazification Office, Hamburg-Bergedorf
International Military Tribunal, Nuremberg

Interviews Conducted by the Author

Axmann, Artur—Hitler Youth Leader
Bormann, Albert—Adjutant and brother of Martin Bormann
Dietrich, Sepp—General Waffen-SS
Dönitz, Karl—Admiral
Halder, Franz—General
Hoffmann, Heinrich, Jr.—Son of Hitler's photographer
Kempner, Robert M. W.—US Attorney
Linge, Heinz—SS
Mohnke, Wilhelm—SS
Naumann, Werner—State Secretary
Puttkamer, Karl Jesko von—Admiral
Schirach, Baldur von—Hitler Youth Leader
Schulze-Kossens, Richard—Adjutant
Schwerin von Krosigk, Lutz Graf—Minister
Skorzeny, Otto—SS
Speer, Albert—Minister
Steiner, Felix—General Waffen-SS
Strechenbach, Bruno—SS
Wenck, Walther—General
Wolff, Karl—General Waffen-SS
Zander, Wilhelm—SS

APPENDIX IV

Documents

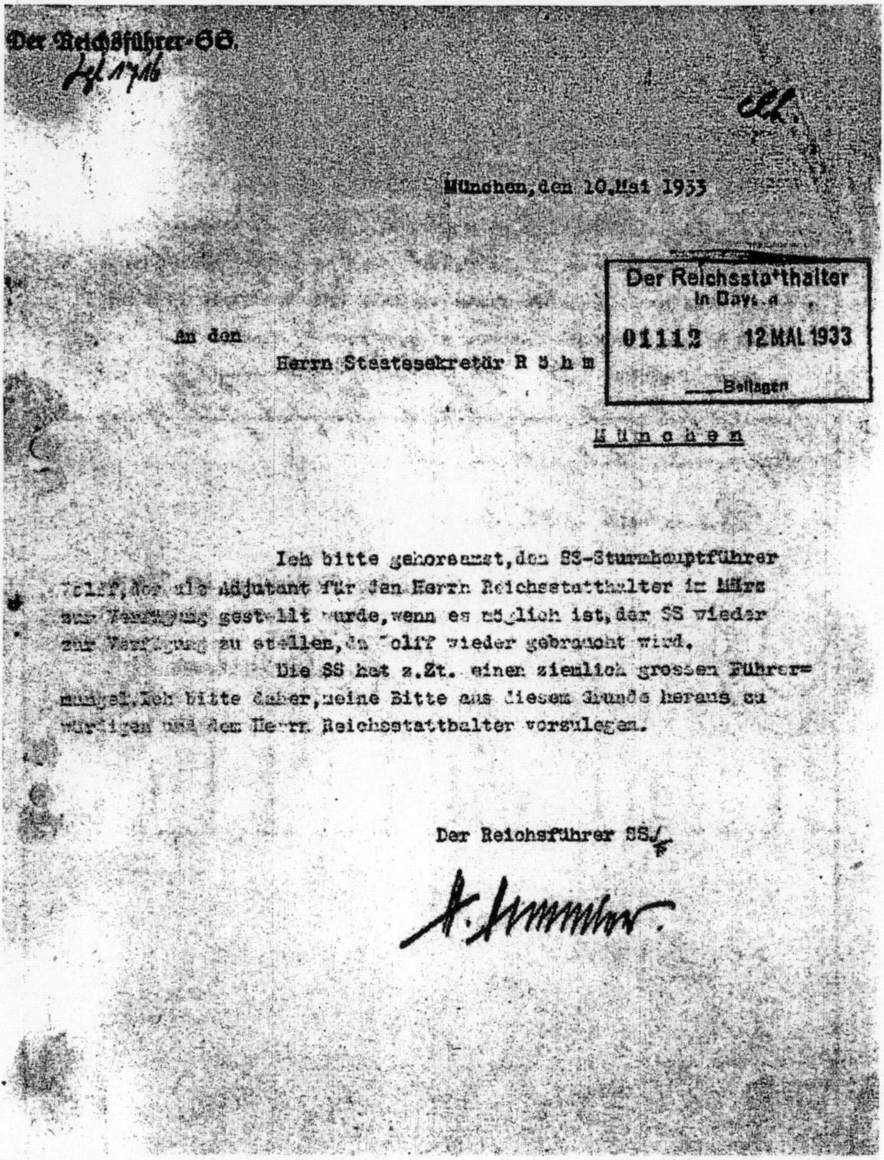

Der Reichsführer-SS.

München, den 10.Mai 1933

Der Reichsstatthalter
in Bayern

01112 12 MAI 1933

____Beilagen

An den

Herrn Staatssekretär R ö h m

M ü n c h e n

Ich bitte gehorsamst, den SS-Sturmhauptführer Wolff, der als Adjutant für den Herrn Reichsstatthalter im März zur Verfügung gestellt wurde, wenn es möglich ist, der SS wieder zur Verfügung zu stellen, da Wolff wieder gebraucht wird.

Die SS hat z.Zt. einen ziemlich grossen Führermangel. Ich bitte daher, meine Bitte aus diesem Grunde heraus zu würdigen und dem Herrn Reichsstatthalter vorzulegen.

Der Reichsführer SS.

H. Himmler.

1. Himmler asking that Karl Wolff be excused as adjutant of the governor of Bavaria because of an SS leadership issue. It is addressed to Ernst Röhm, the chief of staff of the SA, still nominally Himmler's direct superior. After the takeover Röhm was also undersecretary in the Bavarian government.

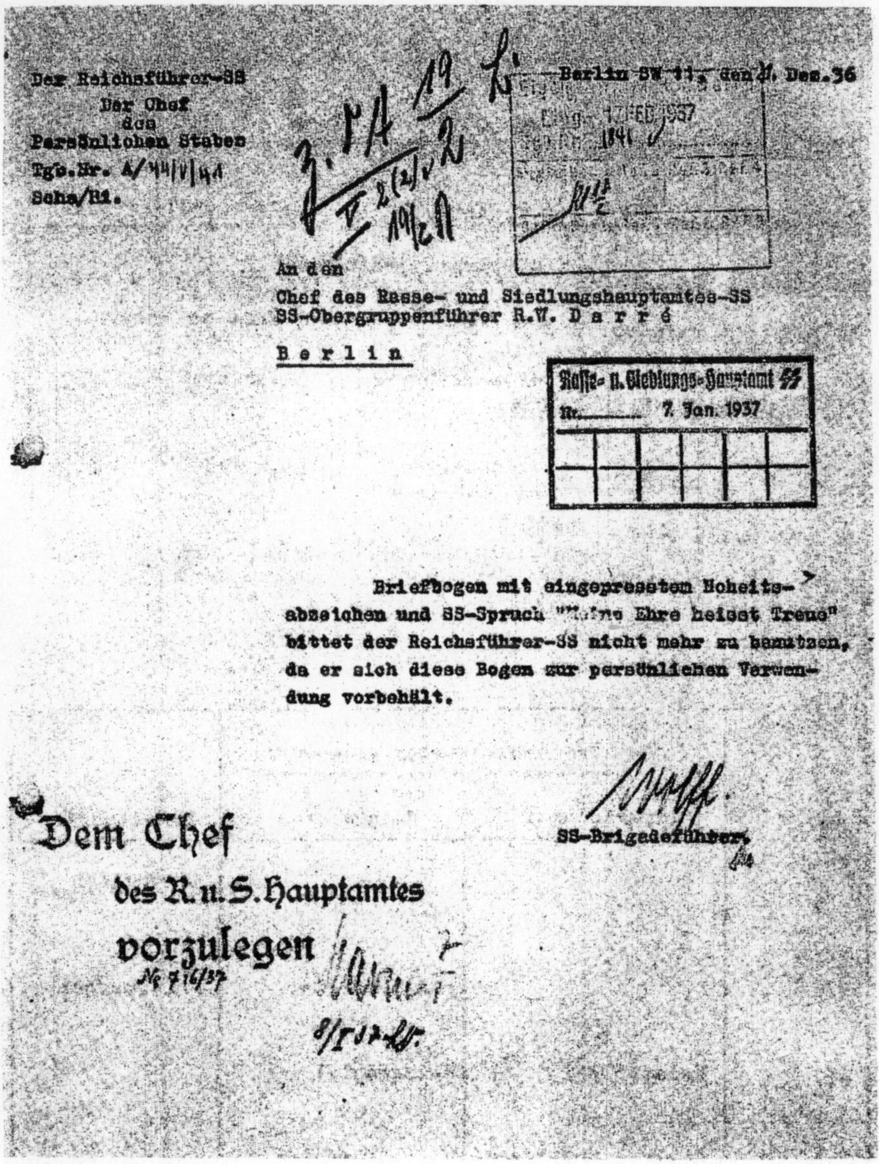

Der Reichsführer-SS
Der Chef
des
Persönlichen Stabes
Tgb.Nr. A/44/V/41
Scha/Bi.

Berlin SW 11, den 31. Dez. 36

Eing. 17 FEB 1937

An den
Chef des Rasse- und Siedlungshauptamtes-SS
SS-Obergruppenführer R.W. D a r r é

B e r l i n

Rasse- u. Siedlungs-Hauptamt SS
Nr. ...... 7. Jan. 1937

Briefbogen mit eingepresstem Hoheitsabzeichen und SS-Spruch "Meine Ehre heisst Treue" bittet der Reichsführer-SS nicht mehr zu benutzen, da er sich diese Bogen zur persönlichen Verwendung vorbehält.

Wolff
SS-Brigadeführer.

Dem Chef
des R.u.S. Hauptamtes
vorzulegen
Nr 716/37

8/I 37

2. Wolff's appointment as chief of the personal staff of the Reichsführer SS H. Himmler.

117

z. Zt. Führerhauptquartier

Der Reichsführer-SS
Der Chef des Pers. Stabes
Tgb.Nr. 17
Schn/RA

Berlin, den 13.9. 1939

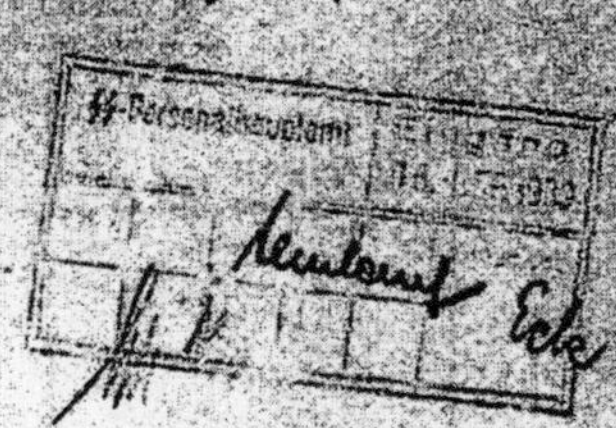

An das
SS-Personalhauptamt

Berlin

Zur Beiheftung zu meiner Personalakte melde ich, daß mir durch die Präsidialkanzlei des Führers verliehen wurden:

1) die Erinnerungsmedaille anläßlich Wiedervereinigung Österreichs mit Deutschland;

2) die Erinnerungsmedaille anläßlich Wiedervereinigung des Sudetengaues mit Deutschland.

Des weiteren wurde mir am 18.X. 1938 das Groß~~offiziers~~kreuz mit Band des Ordens der Krone von Italien und anläßlich des Staatsbesuches des Prinzregenten Paul von Jugoslawien das Groß~~offiziers~~kreuz des Ordens vom heiligen Saba verliehen.

Wolff

SS-Gruppenführer

3. Award of a medal to Karl Wolff. The letter carries the rubber stamp imprint for the first time: "at present at Führer headquarters."

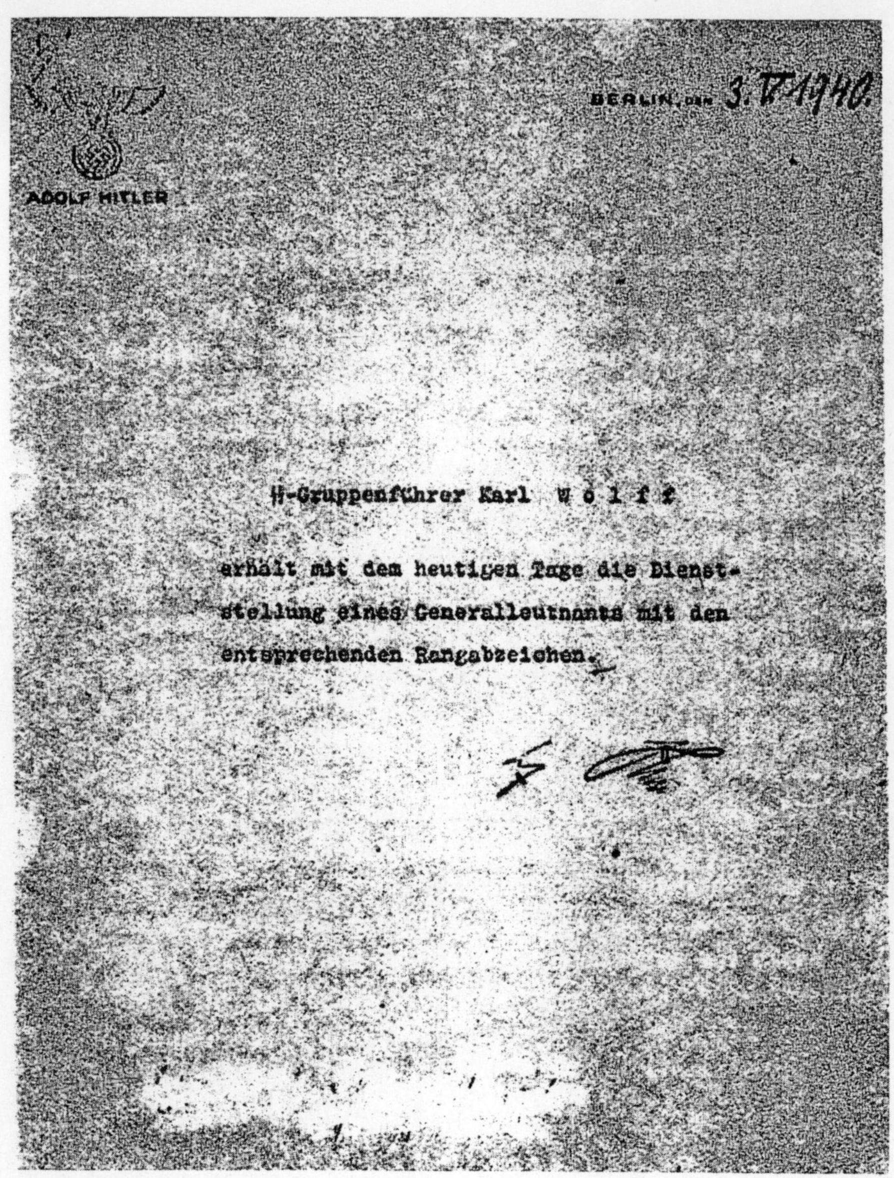
ADOLF HITLER

BERLIN, DEN 3. V 1940.

SS-Gruppenführer Karl W o l f f

erhält mit dem heutigen Tage die Dienststellung eines Generalleutnants mit den entsprechenden Rangabzeichen.

4. Hitler promotes Wolff to the rank of lieutenant general in May 1940 and makes the Nazi party officer the equivalent of the Wehrmacht generals.

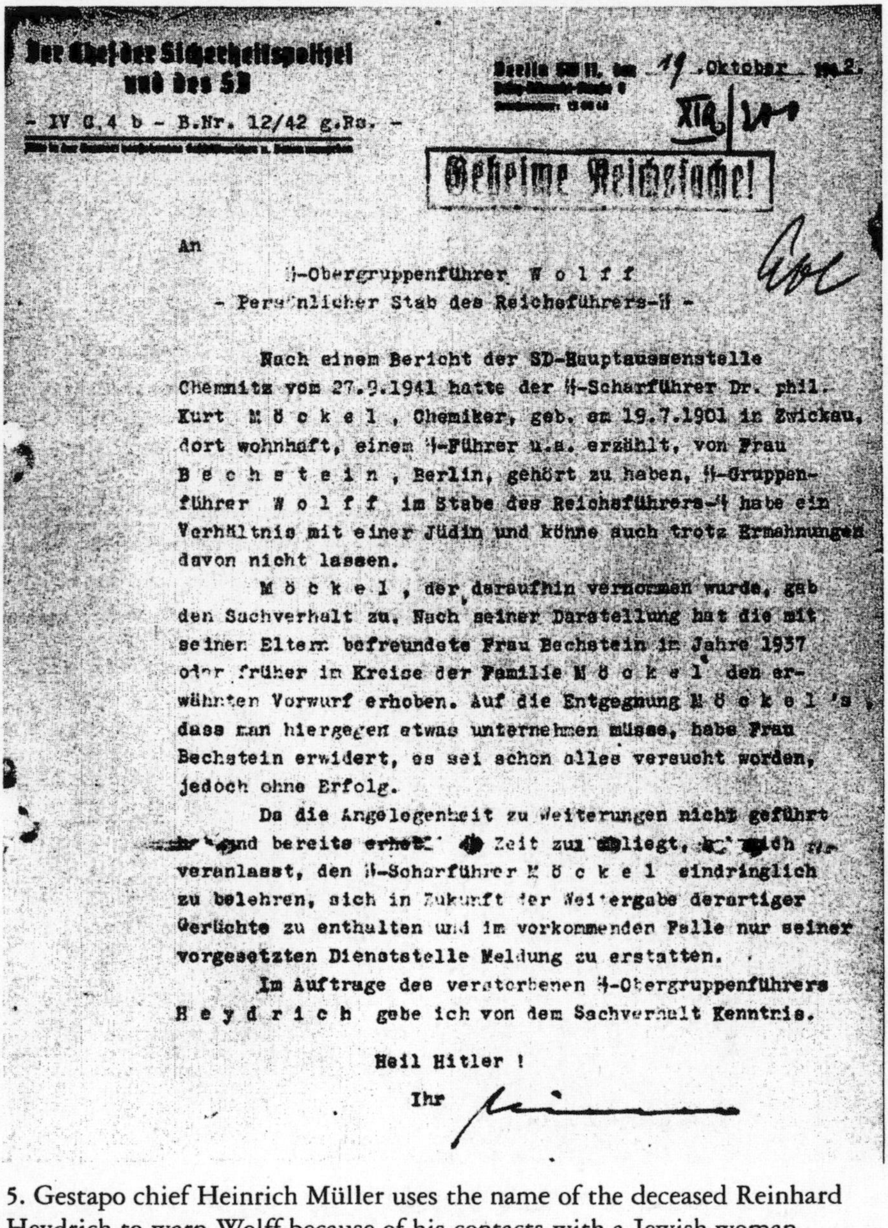

Der Chef der Sicherheitspolizei
und des SD

- IV C 4 b - B.Nr. 12/42 g.Rs. -

Berlin SW 11, den 19. Oktober 1942.

XIA/200

Geheime Reichssache!

An

SS-Obergruppenführer W o l f f
- Persönlicher Stab des Reichsführers-SS -

Nach einem Bericht der SD-Hauptaussenstelle Chemnitz vom 27.9.1941 hatte der SS-Scharführer Dr. phil. Kurt M ö c k e l , Chemiker, geb. am 19.7.1901 in Zwickau, dort wohnhaft, einem SS-Führer u.a. erzählt, von Frau B e c h s t e i n , Berlin, gehört zu haben, SS-Gruppenführer W o l f f im Stabe des Reichsführers-SS habe ein Verhältnis mit einer Jüdin und könne auch trotz Ermahnungen davon nicht lassen.

M ö c k e l , der daraufhin vernommen wurde, gab den Sachverhalt zu. Nach seiner Darstellung hat die mit seinen Eltern befreundete Frau Bechstein im Jahre 1937 oder früher im Kreise der Familie M ö c k e l den erwähnten Vorwurf erhoben. Auf die Entgegnung M ö c k e l 's, dass man hiergegen etwas unternehmen müsse, habe Frau Bechstein erwidert, es sei schon alles versucht worden, jedoch ohne Erfolg.

Da die Angelegenheit zu Weiterungen nicht geführt [illegible] und bereits erhe[illegible] Zeit zu[illegible]liegt, [illegible] ich veranlasst, den SS-Scharführer M ö c k e l eindringlich zu belehren, sich in Zukunft der Weitergabe derartiger Gerüchte zu enthalten und im vorkommenden Falle nur seiner vorgesetzten Dienststelle Meldung zu erstatten.

Im Auftrage des verstorbenen SS-Obergruppenführers H e y d r i c h gebe ich von dem Sachverhalt Kenntnis.

Heil Hitler !

Ihr

5. Gestapo chief Heinrich Müller uses the name of the deceased Reinhard Heydrich to warn Wolff because of his contacts with a Jewish woman.

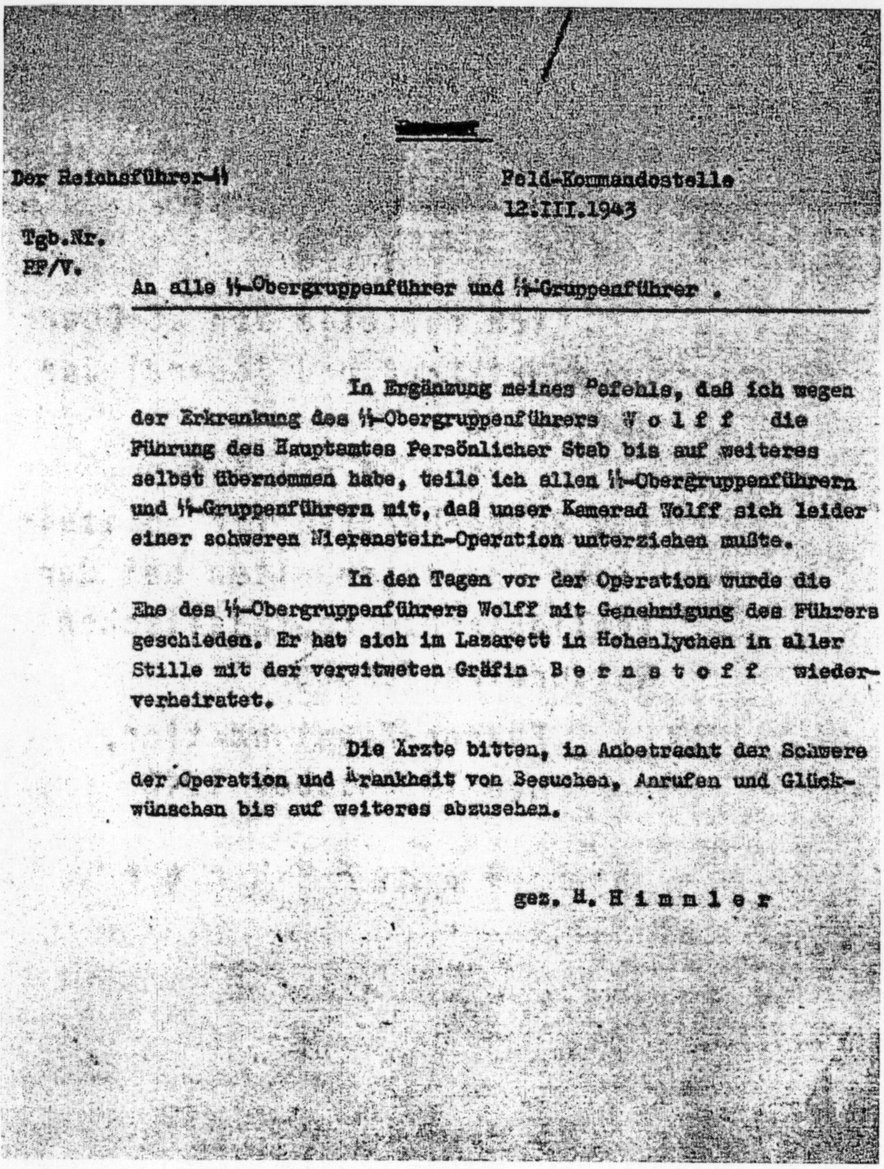

Der Reichsführer-SS

Feld-Kommandostelle
12.III.1943

Tgb.Nr.
RF/V.

An alle SS-Obergruppenführer und SS-Gruppenführer.

In Ergänzung meines Befehls, daß ich wegen der Erkrankung des SS-Obergruppenführers W o l f f die Führung des Hauptamtes Persönlicher Stab bis auf weiteres selbst übernommen habe, teile ich allen SS-Obergruppenführern und SS-Gruppenführern mit, daß unser Kamerad Wolff sich leider einer schweren Nierenstein-Operation unterziehen mußte.

In den Tagen vor der Operation wurde die Ehe des SS-Obergruppenführers Wolff mit Genehmigung des Führers geschieden. Er hat sich im Lazarett in Hohenlychen in aller Stille mit der verwitweten Gräfin B e r n s t o f f wiederverheiratet.

Die Ärzte bitten, in Anbetracht der Schwere der Operation und Krankheit von Besuchen, Anrufen und Glückwünschen bis auf weiteres abzusehen.

gez. H. H i m m l e r

6. Wolff falls out of grace with the Reichsführer SS. Himmler forbids higher SS leaders to visit the sickbed of the chief of his personal staff.

Ich bestelle den SS-Ober-
gruppenführer und General der
Waffen-SS

Karl W o l f f

zum Sonderberater für polizei-
liche Angelegenheiten bei der
Italienischen Faschistischen
Nationalregierung.

Führer-Hauptquartier,
den 11.Oktober 1943

D e r F ü h r e r

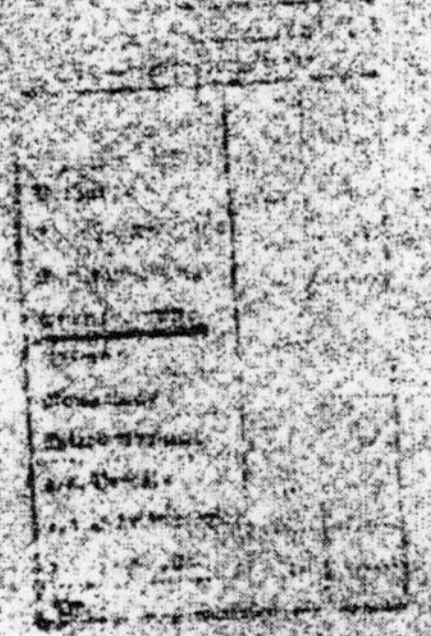

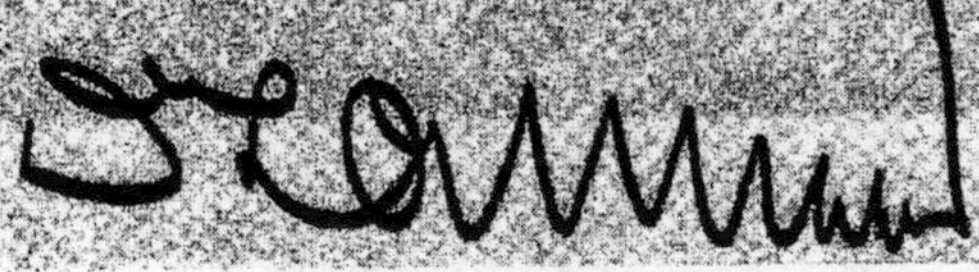

7. Wolff's appointment as ambassador extraordinary to the fascist government of Italy by Hitler on October 11, 1943. The head of the Reich Chancellery, secretary Hans Lammers, records the appointment.

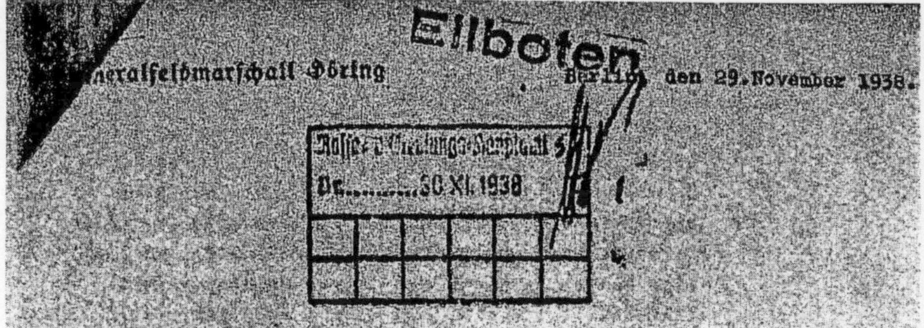

Elboten

[Ge]neralfeldmarschall Göring Berlin, den 29. November 1938.

Rasse- u. Siedlungs-Hauptamt SS

Nr. .... 30 XI 1938

Oberst a.D. v. T h a d d e n , Weimar, hat sich an mich gewandt mit der Bitte, ~~ihm~~ Ihnen bezüglich der Abstammung seines Sohnes, Assessor Dr. Eberhard v. Thadden, SS-Untersturmführer, Aufschluss zu geben. Sie haben festgestellt, dass der Ururgroßvater Ludwig Epenstein, geb. 1776, im Alter von 32 Jahren von der mosaischen zur evangelischen Religion übergetreten ist. Nun steht fest, dass der Thadden von diesem Ludwig Epenstein jedoch nicht abstammt, sein Urgroßvater, der angebliche Sohn des Ludwig Epenstein, ist vielmehr, wie urkundlich zweifelsfrei feststeht, von einer Julie Riedel (arisch) unehelich geboren worden. Wie allgemein in der Familie bekannt ist, stammt das Kind von einer hochgestellten Persönlichkeit, wahrscheinlich von dem russischen Fürsten Balaschoff, von welchem sich noch einige wertvolle Geschenke in der Familie erhalten haben. Ludwig Epenstein (Jude) hat später die Julie Riedel geheiratet und sich, um den Makel zu verschleiern, als Vater nachträglich in das Kirchenbuch eintragen lassen. Dass das Kind nicht von diesem stammt, ist wiederholt von der Familie glaubwürdig versichert worden. Der Großonkel des

An

[d]as Rasse- und Siedlungsamt,

B e r l i n SW,

Hedemannstr. 24.

8. Letter from Hermann Göring wherein he states that before the World War "a Jewish question did not exist at all" within his circles. In the summer of 1941, as a chairman of Hitler's ministerial committee for the defense of Germany, Göring passed on to the SS the order for the "Final Solution of the Jewish question."

Thadden, Dr. Ritter Hermann von Epenstein, hat lange bevor es eine Judenfrage gab, d.h. schon vor dem Weltkriege, mir selbst sowie auch meiner Familie wiederholt darüber Mitteilung gemacht. Diesen Dr. Hermann von Epenstein kenne ich persönlich sehr genau. Er ist vor 2 Jahren (86 Jahre alt) gestorben. Er verkehrte sehr viel in unserer Familie. Es lag also keinerlei Grund vor, in der damaligen Zeit irgendwie von dieser jüdischen Abstammung, falls sie gegeben gewesen wäre, Notiz zu nehmen, da vor dem Weltkriege in unseren Kreisen eine jüdische Frage garnicht existierte. Es war in der ganzen Familie Epenstein nicht der geringste Zweifel vorhanden, dass die Angelegenheit sich so verhielt.

Ich bin also in der Lage zu versichern, dass ich unbedingt von der Wahrheit überzeugt bin, zumal es urkundlich feststeht, dass die Julie Riedel ihren Sohn zunächst unehelich geboren hat und dass die Vaterschaft erst nach der Ehe von dem Epenstein anerkannt wurde, ein Vorgang, wie er sehr häufig ist. Ich werde noch selbst mit dem Reichsführer SS über die Angelegenheit sprechen. Somit kann nach meiner festen Überzeugung an der arischen Abstammung der Mutter des Thadden, der geb. Epenstein, und von ihm selbst kein Zweifel sein.

Heil Hitler !

Continued from previous page.

Der Regierungspräsident
Tgb. Nr. 0.
Fernruf 1411

Minden (Westf.), den 20. November 1940.

Lieber Herr Wolff !

Von Nachfolgendem bitte ich dem Reichsführer SS in geeigneter Weise Kenntnis geben zu wollen ;

Jn die Angelegenheit, die sich mit den vegetierenden Geisteskranken befaßt, bin ich einbezogen worden dadurch, daß die Anstalt Bethel in meinem Bezirk liegt. Gemeinsam mit dem vom Gauleiter Dr. Meyer beauftragten Gaupersonalamtsleiter Beyer bin ich vom Reichsleiter Bouhler empfangen worden. Dieser hat mich zusammen mit Dr. Brandt am 27. September in der Reichskanzlei unterrichtet und mir seine und Dr. Brandt's Auffassung dahin auseinandergesetzt, daß es sich um die Obengenannten handeln solle. Von dem ~~[illegible]~~ Führer gewordenen Auftrage bin ich durch Einsichtnahme ebenfalls unterrichtet. Dadurch, daß die Ausführungen weiterhin betrauter Organe mit der eindeutigen Erklärung des Reichsleiters vielfach sich nicht in Einklang bringen lassen, erwachsen mancherlei Schwierigkeiten. Jnsbesondere wird die Angelegenheit vielfach schon in der Öffentlichkeit diskutiert; sie ist sogar von amerikanischen und schwedischen Journalisten aufgegriffen, was im Widerspruch zu den ursprünglichen Jntentionen zu stehen scheint.

Meine Stellung ist erschwert dadurch, daß ich im Auftrage des Reichsleiters Bouhler, ~~daß ich~~ einigen Stellen, die sich an mich als Regierungspräsident gewandt hatten, die mir in Berlin als bindend erklärte Auffassung bekanntgegeben habe, und daß im Gegensatz hierzu nachgeordnete Stellen den gleichen Fragestellern wesentlich andere,

nun

9. Wolff is informed by a Westphalian district president from Minden about the euthanasia actions ordered by the Chancellery of the Reich.

Der Regierungspräsident

zum Teil gänzlich widerstreitende Mitteilungen machen und von diesen Handlungen verlangen.

Es liegt mir daran, daß der Reichsführer SS über meine Einspannung in die Angelegenheit unterrichtet ist. Falls er es für nötig hält, würde ich mündlich berichten.

Der Reichsminister Frick hat die Ober- und Regierungspräsidenten etc. zum 3. Dezember nach Berlin in das Haus der Flieger zu einer Tagung in Kriegsverwaltungsangelegenheiten eingeladen. Ich werde am Montag, den 2. Dezember zwischen 2 und 3 Uhr in Berlin eintreffen (Hotel Fürstenhof) und stehe am Nachmittag, bzw. am nächsten Nachmittag zur Verfügung.

Mit freundlichen Grüßen von Haus zu Haus und mit

Heil Hitler!

Ihr

Continued from previous page.

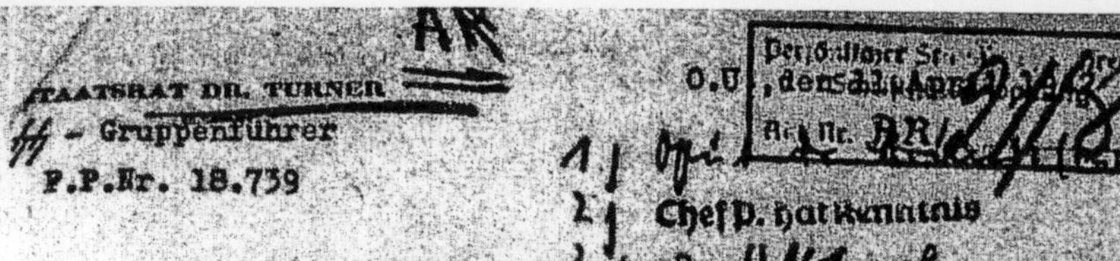

STAATSRAT DR. TURNER
SS - Gruppenführer
F.P.Nr. 18.739

O.U., den

Lieber Kamerad Wolff !

Nachdem nunmehr die Entscheidung zu meinen Gunsten ergangen ist, möchte ich nicht verfehlen - da ich überzeugt bin, dass das ganz einzig und allein Ihrem Einfluß und Ihrer unermüdlichen Tätigkeit zu verdanken ist - Ihnen meinen kameradschaftlichsten und herzlichsten Dank auf diesem Wege zu übermitteln.

Ich kann auch heute wieder, zumal Sie mich ja gut genug kennen, nur noch einmal wiederholen, es hat sich nicht um meine Person bei der Sache gehandelt- der Betreffende hätte ebenso gut einen anderen Namen haben können - sondern um einen notwendig durchzufechtenden Kampf gegen einseitige Wehrmachtsinteressen, bei denen unausgesprochen letzten Endes der SS-Führer ,damit auch die SS und im weiteren auch die Beamtenschaft getroffen werden sollte.

Der beste Beweis hierfür ist einmal in einem offiziellen Schreiben von WB Südost die hineingewobene Bemerkung " die Einsetzung des Höheren SS-und Polizeiführers,die nicht auf hiesigen Antrag erfolgt ist" oder so ähnlich im Wortlaut, zum anderen die Bemerkung des Chefs des Generalstabes WB Südost nach dem Eingang der für mich günstigen Entscheidung " damit hätte die Wehrmacht eine Schlacht verloren".

Jedenfalls herrscht hier in allen Kreisen selbst der Wehrmacht,die diesen Kampf irgendwie verfolgt haben eitel Freude über diesen Sieg und diese Freude haben Sie al -

10. Wolff is informed about anti-Jewish actions by the Higher SS and Police Leader in Serbia, state councilor Dr. Turner.

lein ,wie ich glaube,allen diesen Menschen bereitet .
Dafür meinen Dank !

Darf ich diese Gelegenheit benutzen, um Ihnen anliegend die Abschrift eines Briefes von mir an den Reichsführer vom 15.Januar 1942 zu übersenden, auf den ich bis heute ohne Antwort geblieben bin.Ich möchte nicht erinnern, weil solche Dinge wie ich weiss Zeit brauchen und ich mich nicht für berechtigt halte, den Reichsführer an die Erledigung einer Sache zu erinnern. Immerhin weiss ich,dass Sie für diese Dinge Interesse haben und warum ich Sie jetzt darauf aufmerksam mache, hat einfach seinen Grund darin, dass demnächst diese Frage mehr als akut wird . Schon vor Monaten habe ich alles an Juden im hiesigen Lande greifbare erschissen und sämtliche Judenfrauen und-Kinder in einem Lager konzentrieren lassen und zugleich mit Hilfe des SD einen " Entlausungswagen " angeschafft,der nun in etwa 14 Tagen bis 4 Wochen auch die Räumung des Lagers endgültig durchgeführt haben wird,was allerdings seit Eintreffen von Meyssner und Übergabe dieser Lagerdinge an ihn, von ihm weitergeführt worden ist. Dann ist der Augenblick gekommen, in dem die unter der Genfer Konvention im Kriegsgefangenenlager befindlichen jüdischen Offiziere nolens volens hinter die nicht mehr vorhandenen Angehörigen kommen und das dürfte immerhin leicht zu Komplikationen führen .

Continued from previous page.

Werden nun die Betreffenden entlassen, so werden sie im Augenblick der Ankunft ihre endgültige Freiheit haben, aber wie ihre Rassegenossen nicht allzulange und damit dürfte dann diese ganze Frage endgültig erledigt sein . Das einzigste Bedenken könnten Rückwirkungen auf unsere Gefangenen in Canada sein, falls herauskommt, dass die Freigelassenen hier nicht frei herumlaufen... ich persönlich teile diese Bedenken nicht.

Mit den besten Wünschen für Ihr persönliches Wohlergehen, besten Grüssen und

Heil Hitler!

bin ich wie stets

Ihr getreuer

Continued from previous page.

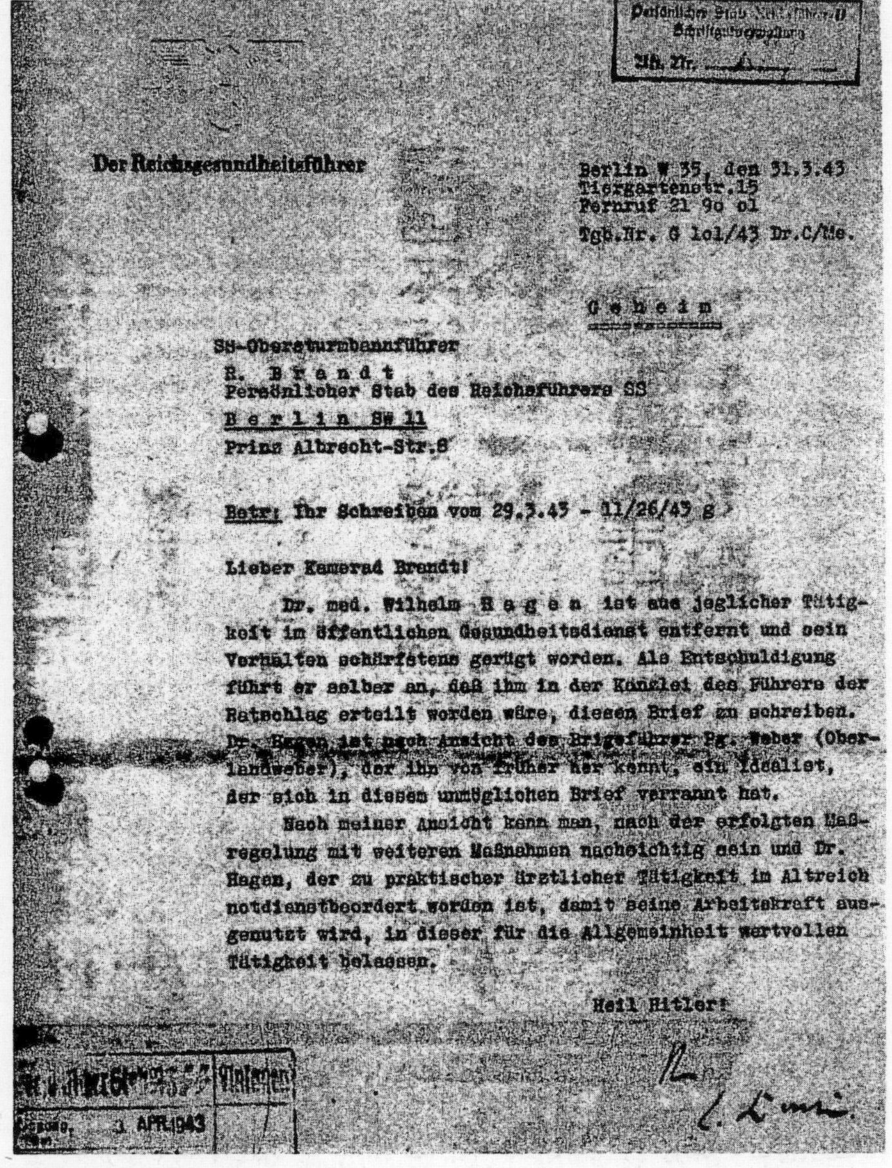

Der Reichsgesundheitsführer

Berlin W 35, den 31.3.43
Tiergartenstr.15
Fernruf 21 90 01

Tgb.Nr. G 101/43 Dr.C/Me.

G e h e i m

SS-Obersturmbannführer
R. B r a n d t
Persönlicher Stab des Reichsführers SS
B e r l i n SW 11
Prinz Albrecht-Str.8

Betr: Ihr Schreiben vom 29.3.43 - 11/26/43 g

Lieber Kamerad Brandt!

Dr. med. Wilhelm H a g e n ist aus jeglicher Tätigkeit im öffentlichen Gesundheitsdienst entfernt und sein Verhalten schärfstens gerügt worden. Als Entschuldigung führt er selber an, daß ihm in der Kanzlei des Führers der Ratschlag erteilt worden wäre, diesen Brief zu schreiben. Dr. Hagen ist nach Ansicht des Brigaführer Pg. Weber (Oberlandweber), der ihn von früher her kennt, ein Idealist, der sich in diesem unmöglichen Brief verrannt hat.

Nach meiner Ansicht kann man, nach der erfolgten Maßregelung mit weiteren Maßnahmen nachsichtig sein und Dr. Hagen, der zu praktischer ärztlicher Tätigkeit im Altreich notdienstbeordert worden ist, damit seine Arbeitskraft ausgenutzt wird, in dieser für die Allgemeinheit wertvollen Tätigkeit belassen.

Heil Hitler!

L. Conti

3. APR. 1943

11. German health leader Dr. Leonardo Conti protects Dr. Hagen from severe punishment by Hitler.

XIX/67

Der Chef der Sicherheitspolizei
und des SD

IV B 4 1474/42 g

Berlin SW 11, den 17 September 194[illegible]
Prinz-Albrecht-Straße 8

Geheim

An den

Chef des Persönlichen Stabes RF-ℌ
ℌ-Obergruppenführer General der Waffen-ℌ Wolff

B e r l i n.

Betrifft: Lösung der Judenfrage im
Generalgouvernement.

Im Anschluß an Ihre fernmündliche Mitteilung bezüglich der Evakuierung von Juden, die s.Zt. als Arbeiter bei der Beskiden-Erdölgesellschaft tätig sind, habe ich den Befehlshaber der Sicherheitspolizei und des SD in Krakau anweisen lassen, die Evakuierung dieser Juden nur in solchem Ausmaß vorzunehmen, als Ersatzkräfte eingesetzt werden können.

In Vertretung:

12. Gestapo chief Heinrich Müller delays Wolff, who had demanded a rapid evacuation of the Jews working for the Beskiden petroleum company in the General Government.

Der Reichsführer-SS   Feld-Kommandostelle, 1.1943

Tgb.Nr.38/22/43 g

RF/V.

Betr.: Bericht über die Rohstofflage auf dem Spinnstoff- und Ledergebiet.

Bezug: Dort v. 9.1.1943 Geh.Tgb.Nr.44/43

1.)

Mein lieber Pohl !

Ich habe Ihren Bericht über die Rohstofflage auf dem Spinnstoff- und Ledergebiet voll und ganz, aber ohne jedes Erstaunen gelesen.

Ich bin sehr einverstanden, wenn Sie mir einen solchen Befehl, der gut ausgearbeitet sein muß und nicht zu kurz sein darf, um den Einheitsführern die Dinge tatsächlich klarzulegen, zur Unterschrift übersenden.

Wieviel an Textilien haben wir eigentlich durch die Judenumsiedlung dem Reichswirtschaftsminister geliefert ?

Heil Hitler !

Ihr

2.) SS-Obergruppenführer Wolff

durchschriftlich mit der Bitte um Kenntnisnahme übersandt.

I.A.

W.v. 31.1.43 bei SS-Ostubaf.Dr.Brandt

SS-Obersturmführer.

13. Wolff is copied in on a letter from Himmler to Administrative Chief Oswald Pohl, who was responsible for the concentration camps, and makes sure that clothing taken from murdered Jews is brought to the Ministry of Trade and Commerce.

Fernschreiben

Persönlicher Stab Reichsführer-SS
Schriftgutverwaltung
Akt. Nr. Geh. /–

An den

Höchsten SS- und Polizeiführer Italien

SS-Obergruppenführer Wolff

Ich bitte Sie, dem Professor Marcello P e t a c c i , Schildhof Meran, den Eingang seines Briefes an den Führer zu bestätigen. Der Führer selbst ist verständlicherweise bei der heutigen zeitlichen Beanspruchung nicht in der Lage, Herrn Petacci zu empfangen.

Ich bitte jedoch Sie, liebes Wölffchen, mir Nachricht zu geben, um was es sich handelt bei der Arbeit des Ingenierus G r o s s i . Petacci schreibt, er soll ein grosser Erfinder sein.

Wenn es wichtig ist, bin ich bereit, ihn zu empfangen oder durch einen guten Fachmann empfangen zu lassen.

Heil Hitler!
Ihr
gez.: H. Himmler

15.9.44 RF/M.

14. Telex from Himmler dated September 15, 1944, showing the resumption of the friendly tone with Wolff. Himmler again calls him "dear Wölffchen" (underlined).

BIBLIOGRAPHY

(When possible the publisher has added the English-language edition of the titles in German and updated the list with relevant new titles.)

Ackermann, Josef. *Himmler als Ideologe* (Göttingen: Musterschmidt, 1970)

Anders, Karl. *Im Nürmberger Irrgarten* (Nuremberg: Nest-Verlag, 1948)

Armstrong, Anne. *Bedingunglose Kapituation* (Wein: Molden, 1961)

Aronsen, Schlomo. *Reinhard Heydrich und die Frügeschichte von Gestapo und SD* (Stuttgart: dva, 1971)

Auerbach, Hellmuth. *Hitlers politische Lehrjahre und die Münchener Gesellschaft* (dva, Vierteljahreschefte für Zeitgeschichte 1/1972)

Bayern, Konstantin Prinz von. *Der Papst* (Bad Wörishofen: Kindler und Schiermeyer, 1952)

Below, Nicholaus von. *Als Hitlers Adjuntant* (Mainz: Hase & Koehler, 1980)

Bertoldi, Silvio. *Salò. Vita e morte della Repubblica Sociale Italiana* (Milan: Rizzoli, 1973)

Besymenski, Lew. *Die letzen Notizen von Martin Bormann* (Stuttgart: dva, 1974)

Biss, Andreas. *Der Stop der Endlösung* (Stuttgart: Seewald, 1966)

Boberach, Heinz. *Meldungen aus dem Reich* (Luchterland, 1965)

Breitman, Richard. *The Architect of Genocide: Himmler and the Final Solution* (New York: Alfred A. Knopf, 1991)

Browning, Christopher R. *The Origins of the Final Solution. The Evolution of Nazi Jewish Policy, September 1939–March 1942* (Lincoln: U. of Nebraska Press and Jerusalem: Yad Vashem, 2004)

Buchheim, Karl. *Die Weimarer Republik* (Munich: Kösel, 1977)

Buchheim, Hans *Die höheren SS-und Polizeiführer.* (dva Vierteljahrshefte für Zeitgeschichte, dva 4/1963)

Buchheim, Hans, Martin Broszat, Hans Adolf Jacobsen, Helmut Krausnick. *Anatomie des SS-Staates* (Olten: Walter-Verlag, 1965)

Bundeszentrale für politische Bildung Bonn 1964: *20. Juli 1944*

Burckhardt, Carl J. *Meine Danziger Mission* (Munich: Vallwey, 1960)

Churchill, Winston S. *Memorien* (Bern: Scherz, 1954) U.S. edition: *The Second World War,* 6 Volumes (Boston: Houghton Mifflin, 1948–1953)

Cospito, Nicola and Neulen, Hans Werner. *Salò-Berlino: L'Alleanza Difficile* (Milan: Mursia, 1992)

Darré, R. Walther. *Um Blut und Boden* (Munich: Eher Verlag, 1940)

Deakin, F. W. *The Brutal Friendship: Mussolini, Hitler and the Fall of Italian Fascism* (New York: Harper & Row, 1962)

De Felice, Renzo. *Mussolini. L'Alleato Vol. I Part 2. Crisi e agonia del regime Mussolini. La Guerra civile* (Turin: Einaudi, 1996-1998)

Deschner, Gunther. *Reinhard Heydrich* (Esslingen: Bechtle, 1977)

Diels, Rudolf. *Luzifer ante portas* (Stuttgart: dva, 1950)

Dietrich, Otto. *Auf den Strassen des Sieges* (Munich: Eher Verlag, 1939)

——. *Zwölf Jahre mit Hitler* (Munich: Isar Verlag, 1955)

Doerries, Reinhard R. *Hitler's Last Chief of Foreign Intelligence* (London: Frank Cass, 2003)

Dollmann, Eugen. *The Interpreter. Memoirs of Doktor Eugen Dollmann* (London: Hutchinson, 1967)

Domarus, Max. *Hitler* (Munich: Süddeutscher Verlag, 1965)

Dulles, Allen W. *Verschwörung in Deutschland* (Zurich: EuropaVerlag)

Dulles, Allen W. and Gero von Gaevernitz *Unternehmen Sunrise* (Düssdeldorf: Econ, 1967)

Engel, Gerhard. *Aufzeichnungen des Majors E.* (Stuttgart: dva, 1974)

Fest, J. C. *Das Gesicht des Dritten Reiches* (Munich: Piper & Co., 1964)

Fleming, Gerald. *Hitler und die Endlösung* (Weisbaden: Limes, 1982)

Fraenkel-Manvell. *Himmler* (Berlin: Ullstein, 1965)

Friedlander, Henry. *The Origins of Nazi Genocide: From Euthanasia to the Final Solution* (Chapel Hill: U. of North Carolina Press, 1995)

Gaevernitz, Gero von, Fabian von Schlabrendorff. *Offiziere gegen Hitler* (Zurich: EuropaVerlag, 1946)

Gilbert, G. M. *Nürnberger Tagebuch* (Frankfurt: Fischer, 1962)

Gilbert, Martin. *The Holocaust: A History of the Jews of Europe During the Second World War* (New York: Henry Holt, 1985)

Goebbels, Joseph. *Tagebücher 1945* (Hamburg: Hoffmann & Campe, 1977)

Goldhagen, Daniel J. *Hitler's Willing Executioners. Ordinary Germans and the Holocaust* (New York: Alfred A. Knopf, 1996)

Graber, G.S. *The Life and Times of Reinhard Heydrich* (New York: McKay, 1980)

Halder, Franz. *Kriegstagebuch* (Stuttgart: Kohlhammer, 1962)

Haffner, Sebastian. *Anmerkungen zu Hitler* (Munich: Kindler, 1978)

Hausser, Paul. *Waffen-SS im Einsatz* (Göttingen: Plesse-Schütz, 1953)

Heiber, Helmut. *Die Republik von Weimar* (Munich: dtv, 1966)

——. *Reichsführer, Briefe* (Stuttgart: dva, 1968)

——. *Lagepesrchungen im Führerhauptquartier* (Stuttgart: dva, 1962)

Heydrich, Lina. *Leben mit einem Kriegsverbrecher* (Pfaffenhofen: Verlag W. Ludwig, 1976)

Hill, Leonidas. *Die Weiszäcker-Papiere*, 2 vols. (Berlin: Propyläen, 1974, 1982)

Hillel, Marc. *Lebensborn* (Wien: V. Zolnay, 1975)

Himmler, Heinrich. *Geheimreden* (Berlin: Propyläen-Ullstein, 1974)

Höhne, Heinz. *Der Orden unter dem Totenkopf* (Hamburg: Verlag Der Spiegel, 1966)

Hofer, Walther. *Der Nationalsozialismus. Dokumente* (Frankfurt: Fischer, 1957)

Hüser, Karl. *Wewelsburg 1933–1945* (Paderborn: Bonifatius-Druckerei, 1982)

Hüttenberger, Peter. *Die Gauleiter* (Stuttgart: dva, 1969)

Irving, David. *Hitlers Weg zum Krieg* (Munich: Herbig, 1979)

——. *Hitler und seine Feldherren* (Frankfurt: Ullstein, 1975)

——. *Rommel* (Hamburg: Hoffmann & Campe, 1978)

——. *Wie krank war Hitler wirklich?* (Munich: Heyne, 1980)

Kater, Michael H. *Das Ahnenerbe der SS* (Stuttgart: dva, 1974)

Keegan, John. *Die Waffen-SS* (Munich: Moevig, 1981)

Kempner, Robert. *Der SS-Staat* (Munich: Kindler, 1950)

——. *Eichmann und Komplizen* (Zurich: Europa-Verlag, 1961)

Kesselring, Albert. *Soldat bis zum letzen Tag* (Bonn: Athenäum, 1953)

Kielmansegg, Graf. *Der Fritschprozess* (Hamburg: Hoffmann & Campe, 1949)

Kimche, Jon. *General Guisans Zweifrontenkrieg* (Berlin: Ullstein, 1961)

Klinkhammer, Lutz. *L'Occupazione Tedesca in Italia 1943-1945* (Turin: Bollati Boringhieri, 1993)

Kordt, Erich. *Wahn und Wirklichkeit* (Stuttgart: dva, 1947)

Kuby, Erich. *Verrat auf deutsch* (Hamburg: Hoffmann & Campe, 1982)

——. *Der Fall* ("Stern" konkret Literatur, 1983)

Kurzman, Dan. *Fällt Rom?* (Munich: Bertelsmann, 1978) U.S. edition *The Race for Rome* (New York: Doubleday, 1975)

Lang, Jochen von. *Hitlers Tischgespräche im Bild* (Munich: Herbig, no date)

——. *Adolf Hitler. Gesichte eines Diktators* (Munich: Herbig, no date)

——. *Der Sekretär, Martin Bormann: Der Mann der Hitler beherrschte* (Stuttgart: dva, 1977) U.S. edition: *The Secretary. Martin Bormann: The Man Who Manipulated Hitler* (New York: Random House, 1979)

——. *Das Eichmann –Protokoll* (Berlin: Severin & Siedler, 1982)

Lazzero, Ricciotti. *Il Sacco d'Italia. Razzie e Stragi Tedesche nella Repubblica di Salò* (Milan: Mondadori, 1994)

Leber, Annedore. *Das Gewissen stecht auf* (Berlin: Mosaik-Verlag, 1954)

Liddell Hart B. H. *History of the Second Word War* (New York: Putnam, 1970)

Ludendorff, Erich. *Meine Kriegserinnerungen* (Berlin: Mittler & Sohn, 1919)

Maier, Hedwig. *Die SS und der 20. Juli 1944* (Stuttgart: dva, 1966)

Martin, Bernd. *Friedeninitiativen und Machtpolitik* (Düsseldorf: Droste, 1974)

Maser, Werner. *Adolf Hitler* (Esslingen: Bechtle, 1971)

——. *Nürnberg* (Düsseldorf: Econ, no date)

Meier-Beneckenstein. *Das Dritten Reich im Aufbau* (Berlin: Junker & Dünnhaupt, 1939)

Mitscherlich-Mielke. *Medizin ohne Menschlichkeit* (Frankfurt: Fischer, 1949)

Moellhausen, Eitel Friedrich. *Die gebrochene Achse* (Alpha-Verlag)

Mollo, Andrew. *A Pictorial History of the* SS (London: MacDonald and Jane's, 1976)

Monelli, Paolo. *Roma 1943* (Milan: Longanesi & C., 1963)

Mosley, Leonard. *Dulles* (New York: Dial, 1978)

Mussolini, Rachele. *Mussolini ohne Maske* (Stuttgart: dva, 1974)

Papen, Franz von. *Der Wahrheit eine Gasse* (Munich: List, 1952)

Pendorf, Robert. *Mörder und Emordete* (Hamburg: Rütten & Loening, 1961)

Picker, Henry. *Hitlers Tischgespräche* (Stuttgart: Seewald, 1963)

Rahn, Rudolf. *Ruheloses Leben* (Stuttgart-Zurich: Europäischer Buchklub, no date)

Rohdes, Richard. *Masters of Death. The SS Einsatzgruppen and the Invention of the Holocaust* (New York: Alfred A. Knopf, 2002)

Rosen, Edgar R. *Viktor Emanuel III und die Innenpolitik des ersten Kabinetts Badoglio* (Stuttgart: dva, 1964)

Rothfels, Hans. *Die deutsche Opposition gegen Hitler* (Frankfurt: Fischer, 1958)

Schellenberg, Walter. *Memoiren* (Köln: Verlag für Politik und Wirtschaft, 1956). U.S. edition: *The Labyrinth. Memoirs* (New York: Harper Bros., 1956)

Schmidt, Paul. *Statist auf diplomatischer Bühne* (Bonn: Athenäum, 1949)

Schwarz, Urs. *Vom Sturm umbrandet* (Frauenfeld: Verlag Huber, 1981)

Skorzeny, Otto. *Wir kämpften, wir verloren* (Siegburg: Ring-Verlag, 1962)

Smith, Arthur. *Churchills deutsche Armee* (Bastei Lübbe, 1978)

Speer, Albert. *Der Sklavenstaat* (Stuttgart: dva, 1981)

——. *Erinnerungen* (Berlin: Ullstein, 1969) U.S. edition: *Inside the Third Reich* (New York: Macmillan, 1973)

Tippleskirch, Kurt von. *Geschichte des II. Weltkriegs* (Bonn: Athenäum, 1959)

Toland, John. *Das Finale* (Munich: Droemer, 1968) U.S. edition: *The Last 100 Days* (New York: Random House, 1965)

——. *Adolf Hitler* (Bastei Lübbe, 1977) U.S. edition: *Adolf Hitler* (New York: Doubleday, 1976)

Thiel, Edmund. *Kampf um Italien* (Wein: Langen-Müller, 1983)

Vogelsang, Reinhard. *Der Freundeskreis Himmler* (Göttingen: Musterschmidt, 1972)

Wegner, Bernd. *Hitlers politische Soldaten* (Paderborn, 1982)

Weinberg, Gerhard L. *A World at Arms* (New York: Cambridge U.P., 1995)

Weiszäcker, Ernst von. *Erinnerungen* (Munich: List, 1950)

INDEX